Chronicles of the
Worcestershire Home Guard

The author dedicates this book to ex-Home Guards and GHQ Auxiliaries everywhere, who gave up so much of their time and energy to keep the Home Front safe, and prepare for the battle that did not occur.

Chronicles of the Worcestershire Home Guard

by
Mick Wilks

Logaston Press

LOGASTON PRESS
Little Logaston Woonton Almeley
Herefordshire HR3 6QH
logastonpress.co.uk

First published by Logaston Press 2014
Copyright © text Mick Wilks 2014
Copyright © illustrations as individually acknowledged 2014

ISBN 978 1 906663 87 2

Typeset by Logaston Press
and printed and bound in Malta
by Gutenberg Press

Contents

Acknowledgements

This study of the Home Guard of Worcestershire has arisen out of my retirement hobby and work as a volunteer researcher with the County Council's Historic Environment and Archaeological Service (WHEAS), now part of the County Archive and Archaeology Service, where I have been investigating and recording civil and military defence sites for the last 19 years, firstly for the national Defence of Britain Project and latterly for the successor local initiative, the Defence of Worcestershire Project. Much credit is therefore due to Malcolm Atkin, the former County Archaeology Officer, and his colleagues in WHEAS, for giving me the opportunity to do the work as well as provide practical support to me and other volunteers working on these projects. Unlike many other archaeologists, Malcolm has a great interest in modern defences and specifically the Home Guard. In fact he never ceases to amaze me with his knowledge of the most obscure facts about the force. The County Archive and Archaeology Service, now led by Victoria Bryant, continues to support this work.

Over the last eighteen or so years, I have made many friends in the world of modern defence study and recording, who have provided support and advice about defences in general, and the Home Guard in particular. Of these, special thanks are due to Bernard Lowry, one time West Midlands Regional Coordinator for the Defence of Britain Project and prolific author of books on defence matters, and to the late Colin Jones who was a fellow researcher for a period of over sixteen years, as well as being the County Coordinator for the Defence of Worcestershire Project. Other former stalwarts of the Defence of Britain Project who have helped me with advice over the years are Major Jim Earle and William Foot, the successive coordinators for the national project, John Hellis, Dr Mike Osborne, Dr Will Ward and Austin Ruddy.

Many local people have helped me in researching the Home Guard of Worcestershire, most notably: Elizabeth Atkins, John Badger, Roy Bates, Sandy Clarke, John Collett, Bob Cross, Pat Dunn, Sheila Edmonds, Gill Edwards, Graham Evans, Stuart Hadaway, John Hancox, Helen, Paul and Mark Harding, Ken Hobson, Alan Johnson, Bill Kings, John Kyte, Dr Tom Locke, Paul Meekins, Howard Miller, Tim Norton, Tom Padgett, Bernard and Olive Poultney, Vernon Pratt, Angela and Charles Purcell, Sue Roberts (of the Three Kings, Hanley Castle), Jo Roche, John V. Sanders, Roy and Janice Slim,

Steve Taylor, Don Tomlin, Peter Trevett, Neil Turley, Mike Webster, Simon Wilkinson, and Dr Dennis Williams. Mike Johnson has been especially helpful to me following his extensive research of the Redditch Battalion Home Guard.

I should also like to thank the staffs of the County Record Office, Bewdley Museum, Malvern Museum, Pershore Heritage Centre, Tenbury Museum, Worcester City Museums Service, as well as the various branches of the County Library in Worcestershire for their help and guidance in tracking down local Home Guard information. In addition, the local history groups and societies of Alvechurch, Bewdley, Cookley and Wolverley, Crowle, Feckenham, Hagley, Vale of Evesham and Wollaston, together with the Black Country Society and the Kidderminster and Stourport Civic Societies, have also given much assistance. The successive Regimental Secretaries and their staff, both full time and voluntary, of the former Worcestershire and Sherwood Foresters Regimental Headquarters (and latterly until its closure, the Mercian Regiment Outstation) at Norton Barracks, together with Trustees and Curator of the Regimental Museum, have been particularly welcoming and helpful over a long period of time. Before its closure, the staff at the former Army Medal Office at Droitwich, were most helpful in allowing me to analyse original Home Guard enrolment forms and Part 1 and 2 Orders then held by them. More recently, the staff at the new Army Reserve Centre in Lowesmoor, have also contributed to the study.

Further afield, I must also acknowledge the help given to me by the staff at the Imperial War Museum, Lambeth, the staff at the National Archive, and the Dudley Records Centre. John Warwicker MBE, formerly of the Museum of British Resistance, at Parham, in Suffolk has, through his friendship and his publications about the GHQ Auxiliary Units, provided much help over the years.

The local media notably BBC Hereford and Worcester Radio, BBC Midlands TV, *The Black Country Bugle*, *Evesham Journal*, *Malvern Gazette*, *Redditch Advertiser*, *Upton News*, *Wolverhampton Express and Star*, and the *Worcester News*, have from time to time given publicity for the projects referred to above which, in turn, led to contact with Home Guards or their families.

The following Home Guardsmen and women, and members of the British resistance, or relatives of such men and women, have all shared with me their memories of wartime Worcestershire and I hope more will come forward with information while there is time. Sadly, many of the people listed have passed away since I met them, and so I am very glad to have recorded at least a part of their life experiences for posterity. They are: Bill Alliband, Bill Allington, Jack Ankers, John Annis, Don Archer, Mary Ashfield, Ivor Atkinson, John Badger, Major John Bailey, William Bainbridge, Eric Barber, John Barker, Dr Tony Barling, Michael Barnard, David Barton, Chris Bayliss, Sam Beard, Gordon Bennett, John Bennett, Len and Jack Bennett, Michael Bingham, John Bone, Mr J.M. Bowden, Harold Bramwell, George Briney, Robert Brown, John

Boaz, Chris Bullock, Dennis Burrows, Edwina Burton, Peter Byrd, Dennis Chance, John Chater, Jack Clements, Jim Colebrook, Frank Cox, Colin Curnock, Roger Curtiss, Dr Terry Daniels, Bert Davies, Norman Davies, Dave Devereux, Geoff Devereux, Eric Doughty, Sheila Edmunds, Norman Fairfax, John Fernihough, Harry Fisher, Wilf Gamble, Egbert Ganderton, Paul Gibbons, Peter Grace, Mrs Andrew Green, Jim Griffin, Mike Guilding, Geoff Gurney, Doug Harries, Vera Hale, Bill Harper, Keith Hartwell, Gwen Harvey, Tom Harwood, Bill Hay, Les Haynes, Tom Healey, June Hebden, Ron and Jan Henshall, Stuart Hill, Vic Holloway, Jim Holt, Horace Hooper, Geoff Hutchinson, Joe Hurley, Llyn James, Desmond Jasper, Bill Jauncey, Harry Jones, Lavender and Michael Jones, Joe Kennedy, Joe King, Sir Reginald Lechmere, Jack Leighton and his son John, Clifford Lord, Lt Colonel Pat Love, Richard Mills, Shirley Marler (née van Moppes), George Marshman, Margaret Mathews, Fred Mayo, Ted McGee, Mrs Angus McGregor (née Ashton, via Jo Roche), Jack Miles, Richard Mills, Arthur Minett, Les Moore, Pamela Van Moppes, Robin Morom, Mrs C. Morris, Roland Morris, Wilf Mound, Geoff Neil, Jack Oliver, Tom Padgett, Derrick Pearson, Dick Philips, Horace Phillips, Keith Porter, George Pitman, Bill Preece, Toby Preston, Jack Pritchard, Dr Ernest Putley, Stan Ratcliffe, Maurice Reynolds, John Rowberry, John Sanders, Ron Seymour, Leyland Shawe, John Smith, Harvey Southall, Charles Stallard, John Stephens, Pam Stubbs, Marion Szczesniak, Basil and Ruth Tadman, Jim Terry, John Thornton, Albert Tolley, Albert Toon, Gerry Tysoe, George Vater, Mr Waldron, Joan Warren, David Westley-Smith, Albert Wharrad (via Mike Johnson), Tim White, Joseph Whitehead, Robin Whittaker, Wilfred Widdows, Harold Wilkins, the family of Reg Wilkinson, David Williams, Reg Wiltshire, Tim and Mrs Wood, Peter Wright, J. Wyle, and John Wythes.

Andy and Karen Johnson of Logaston Press have been their usual helpful and efficient selves in bringing this publication to fruition.

Last, but by no means least, I must acknowledge the help and support of my family and close friends, and apologise for the long periods of silence and absence while I studied and researched the Home Guard. Of my family, I must specifically thank my late uncle, Howard Inight, who as a member of MI9 operating in north-west Europe after D-Day, was able to 'liberate' a number of enemy documents, some of which have been used to illustrate this account.

If I have missed anyone, I'm sorry, my memory is not what it was, but I would say that your contribution has been just as important as those listed.

Foreword

The recording of defence sites for the Defence of Britain Project and Defence of Worcestershire Project, has brought me into contact with a significant number of former Home Guardsmen in the county. It has been a privilege to have spoken to this dwindling group of men, and the women who supported them. They, and their colleagues, had given up so much of their spare time to train and ready themselves, from May 1940 onwards, for an expected German invasion, and the growing number of defence tasks the government and the Home Guard leaders expected them to carry out over the lifetime of the force. Their role, and the training for it, was fulfilled, in many cases, by men and women who were already employed for long hours in armament industries or in agriculture. The majority of these former volunteer soldiers took their role very seriously; after all a significant number of the men were experienced veterans of the First World War.

Inevitably there were humorous moments in the training and activities of the Home Guard, but it was not the perpetual shambles portrayed by the television comedy series 'Dad's Army'. Entertaining though this comedy programme is, and it seems as popular now as it was when first made in the late 1960s, it is not a true reflection of the times. Despite this criticism, it has to be acknowledged that the programme has kept the Home Guard in the public eye although, perhaps, many of the post-war generations may, as a result, now have a distorted impression of the force.

Sadly, and partly for the reasons above, it has become fashionable to denigrate the efforts of the Home Guard, so this account provides the opportunity to put the record straight, to properly reflect the time and effort the men put into their preparations for battle, as well as describe their place in the defence of Britain, and Worcestershire in particular. I hope to demonstrate that the Home Guard, and the resistance organisation which was formed largely from its ranks, were a key element of the defence arrangements to deal with a Nazi invasion or the expected sabotage attacks on Britain during the period from 1940 until 1944, when the force was stood down. This publication seeks to set out, for the first time, a comprehensive account of the Home Guard in the historic county of Worcestershire, which, it should be remembered, included a significant part of the Black Country in the 1940s. In order to avoid recent, and I fear distorted, opinion, and to approach the subject as objectively as possible, I have quoted extensively from contemporary documents throughout the account.

In the course of researching the organisation and role of the Worcestershire Home Guard, I have become aware that there is now only a limited number of the official and accessible contemporary documents relating to the force still surviving. In the Worcestershire area particularly, there seems to have been a wholesale destruction of military orders and defence schemes at the end of the war which has made the task of researching the Home Guard and their defences more challenging. What remains, therefore, is far from comprehensive and, to fill in some of the gaps in the story, I have had to rely to a degree both on hearsay evidence, and draw on accounts of Home Guard affairs and experiences outside Worcestershire. There is still the possibility of undiscovered documentary resources held by former Home Guards or their families coming to light. These documents may include photographs, notebooks, papers on the organisation of the Home Guard and perhaps the defence plans for specific localities. These are now precious and irreplaceable – sadly many have already been destroyed as being thought to be of little interest or importance, or because they are marked 'secret'. They are no longer secret, but they are of great interest and value to researchers and I would urge anyone with such documents to deposit them with the County Archive at The Hive, Sawmill Walk, The Butts, Worcester, WR1 3DT.

At the end of the Second World War, Home Guard battalion commanders throughout Britain were encouraged by higher command to write a history of their particular unit's activities during the period 1940 to 1944. Sadly, the majority of officers did not complete the task, and so only a limited number of unit histories were published. In Worcestershire, histories were written for the Evesham, Halesowen and Warley battalions and the companies based at Abberley and in Upton upon Severn. These have been used as sources of information for this more general account.

To properly describe the evolution and changing role of the Worcestershire LDV/Home Guard over its lifetime, as well as the influences on it from national and local perspectives, Part I provides a general history of the force in broadly chronological order, while Part II deals with the GHQ Auxiliary Units, women in the Home Guard, the training of the force, armaments, uniform, badges and so on. Appendices cover the more detailed aspects of the wartime force, including a list of known fatalities in Worcestershire and awards made for meritorious service.

What you will read on the subsequent pages will not be the whole story of the Worcestershire Home Guard; it would need a giant publication to set out every 'jot and tittle' that I have discovered about the force. For the same reason, it has not been possible to mention every man, women or boy of Worcestershire who served in the force at different times – possibly 40,000 people – although some of the main characters are referred to, and quotes are used from some of those former Home Guards and women I have interviewed. If this account encourages more people to come forward with their memories of the Home Guard and teases out a bit more of the story, or result in corrections of inaccuracies and additions to the appendices, then I shall be pleased. Such contributors are encouraged to contact the publisher, Logaston Press, or the Defence of Worcestershire Project at the County Archive and Archaeology Service, The Hive, Sawmill Walk, The Butts, Worcester, WR1 3DT. Telephone 01905 765560.

Introduction

'The shock of our peril after Dunkirk galvanised us into an intensity of effort which has never been surpassed by any nation at any period … In this spirit the Home Guard was born, and it is this spirit which has shaped its course and all its activities during the long years of the war.'

Major General W. Robb CBE DSO MC,
Commander, Mid-West District of Britain, August 1944.[1]

From the declaration of war by Britain on Germany on 3rd September 1939, following the German attack on Poland, until the attack by the Germans on Norway on 9th April 1940 – the so-called 'Phoney War' period – the majority of the British people and their government do not appear to have been greatly troubled by the thought of an enemy invasion. With most of the Regular Army field force and Territorial forces forming the British Expeditionary Force (BEF) then preparing defences in northern France, Winston Churchill had foreseen, as early as 8th October 1939, while serving as First Sea Lord and a member of the War Cabinet, the need for an additional home defence force and had written to Sir Samuel Hoare, the Lord Privy Seal:

Why do we not form a Home Guard of half a million men over forty (if they like to volunteer) and put all our elder stars at the head and in the structure of these new formations. Let these five hundred thousand men come along and push the young and active out of all their home billets. If uniforms are lacking, a brassard would suffice, and I am assured there are plenty of rifles at any rate … I hear continual complaints of the lack of organisation from every quarter on the Home Front, can't we get at it![2]

Tom Wintringham, one-time commander of the British Battalion of the International Brigade during the Spanish Civil War, and former member of the Communist Party, had similar ideas and in the same year proposed a home defence force of 100,000 men in a booklet called *How to Reform the Army*. The War Office expressed interest, but took no action.

Predicting the likelihood of parachute troops being used against Britain, and clearly frustrated by the apparent lack of action by the government, Lady Helena Gleichen of Hellens in Herefordshire, in March 1940, organised her staff, estate workers and tenants to watch for such an attack from the high land on the Marcle Ridge. This irregular force of about 80 men was supplied with brassards stencilled with 'Much Marcle Watchers' and armed with shotguns as well as antique rifles and bayonets from Lady Helena's own collection of weapons.[3]

Another concerned Midlander, Mr J.B.L. Stevenson of Cradley in the Black Country, wrote, on 8th May 1940, to Neville Chamberlain to propose the employment of ex-servicemen as a 'Town Guard' to withstand or at least hinder the activities of invaders. Such men were organised in the Cradley area (which straddles the northern boundary of Halesowen) by a Major Eric Holloway as early as the 11th May for the 'protection of vulnerable bridges, etc … against parachutists and saboteurs'.[4] These local examples of the desire by civilians to help with defence of the homeland were not by any means unique, and the government was badgered with offers to help from all corners of Britain.

Parachutists, Blitzkrieg and the 'Fifth Column'

The apparent invincibility of the Germans with their then new form of all-arms warfare, combining fast-moving armoured columns with motorised infantry and preceded by air attacks, which had been used in their invasion of Poland in 1939, was an early warning of what was to come. The use of a Fifth Column under Vidkun Quisling, widespread subterfuge, together with parachute and airborne troops in the German occupation of Denmark and Norway in April 1940; and then the use of the whole panoply of these techniques in their simultaneous and ultimately successful attacks on the Dutch, Belgians and French on 10th May that year, brought the threat of an invasion of Britain into sharp focus. The earlier lessons of the Polish and Scandinavian campaigns by the Germans appear to have gone largely unheeded by the Neutral countries and the Allies on the Continent, who still had the defensive mentality which had been such a feature of the early years of the First World War. They were consequently largely out-manoeuvred by the Germans, leading to the capitulation of the Dutch on 14th May and the Belgians on 28th May, but it was the evacuation of a large proportion of the BEF, together with some French and Belgian troops, which had been surrounded at Dunkirk during late May and early June, that really destroyed French morale. Although the fighting would continue to the south of the River Somme for another three weeks, and more of the BEF would be evacuated from western France, the French signed an armistice on 21st June.

The speed at which the Germans had subjugated a large part of Europe had been impressive and with their troops and aircraft massing on the channel coast in late June, a mere 22 miles away from Kent, an invasion of Britain must have seemed

Dutch Foreign Minister van Kleffens said 'German parachutists landed like rain.' In fact there are just 36 parachutes falling from these three Junkers JU 52 aircraft and some of those will be carrying weapons containers. Prompt action by the Local Defence Volunteers was intended to counter this form of attack. (Courtesy of the late Howard Inight)

inevitable. It must also have seemed inconceivable to the British people, given the efficient way in which the Germans had overcome the continental armies and our own BEF, that they would not have already made preparations for an invasion of Britain soon afterwards. It is difficult now, nearly 70 years later, to imagine the fear that must have gripped the nation at that time, or the desire of able-bodied men, and many women, to do something to defend the country. The reports coming in from the continent must have given the impression that nowhere in Britain was safe from saboteurs and Fifth Columnists, that every stranger was a potential spy, and that untold numbers of enemy parachutists, probably disguised, could be expected to land almost anywhere in the country.

The years of appeasement of Germany by the British government and its allies in the late 1930s, together with the poor response of the British land forces to the German invasion of Norway in particular, had already brought about the fall of the Prime Minister, Neville Chamberlain. His replacement by Winston Churchill and the formation of a coalition government came on 10th May. The result was a complete change of pace, an outwardly more belligerent approach in the prosecution of the war, and support for the establishment of a Home Guard.

After just three days' discussion at the War Office, the action that set in motion the establishment of this volunteer defence force, initially to be called the Local Defence Volunteers (LDV), was a radio broadcast appeal by Anthony Eden, the newly appointed Secretary of State for War, on the evening of Tuesday, 14th May 1940, just after the 9 o'clock news. On that very day Holland had capitulated after parachute and air-landed troops, some dressed in Allied uniforms, allegedly coupled with a Fifth Column, had been used extensively by the Germans. Eden explained that the function of enemy parachutists was to seize important points, such as aerodromes, power stations, villages, railway junctions and telephone exchanges, either for the purpose of destroying them at once, or holding them until the arrival of reinforcements. The success of their attack depended on speed and consequently the measures to defeat such an attack must also be prompt and rapid. Eden acknowledged that since the war began, the government had received countless enquiries from men of all ages who wished to do something for the defence of the country. Now the government wanted large numbers of men who were British subjects between the ages of 17 and 65 to come forward and offer their services. He said that the name of the force, Local Defence Volunteers, described their duties and he emphasised that it was a spare-time job; there would be no need for any volunteer to abandon his present occupation. The period of service was to be for the duration of the war and although volunteers would not be paid, they would receive a uniform and be armed. Reasonable fitness and knowledge of firearms were necessary, but the duties would not require men to live away from their homes. In order to volunteer, they were asked to give their names to the local police station.[5]

The LDV is formed

The impact of the broadcast was immediate, widespread, and far exceeded the government's expectations, with men, and later women, responding enthusiastically. The government was expecting about 150,000 men to volunteer nationally, but within 24 hours over ¼ million had come forward, and in six weeks 1½ million. At its peak in late 1942, the Home Guard (the name of the force was changed in July 1940) was to reach a membership of 1,850,757 men.[6] This size for the force was more or less maintained throughout the rest of the war, although compulsory service from 1942 was necessary to keep the levels of manpower up and fulfil the Home Guard's expanding role in defence.

The German reaction to the broadcast by Anthony Eden was immediate and threatening:

> The British Government is committing the worst crime of all. Evidently it permits open preparation for the formation of murder bands. The preparations which are being made all over England to arm the civilian population for guerrilla warfare are contrary to the rules of international law. German official quarters warn the misled British public and remind them of the fate of the Polish franc-tireur and gangs of murderers. Civilians who take up arms against German soldiers are, under international law, no better than murderers, whether they be priests or bank clerks. British people, you will do well to heed our warning![7]

The British government moved quickly to legalise the formation of the new defence force by passing, on 17th May, The Defence (Local Defence Volunteers)

Regulations, 1940, under the provisions of the Emergency Powers (Defence) Act of 1939. The regulations made it clear that the Local Defence Volunteers were members of the armed forces of the Crown and subject to military law as soldiers.[8] How much this legal status would have influenced any invading Germans, when faced by men dressed initially in civilian clothing with only an arm band declaring that they were the LDV, is debatable.

Plans for the defence of Britain
On 25th June, General Ironside, who had been appointed by Winston Churchill to take command of Home Forces less than a month before, reported to the Joint Chiefs of Staff on his plans for the defence of Britain. He considered that the Germans were likely to use the shortest sea and air route for the main effort of their invasion, but that the possibility of diversionary attacks against other parts of Britain and Ireland should not be discounted. The possibility of a German attack on Eire was taken very seriously and influenced the subsequent Worcestershire defences. Ironside thought a sea-borne invasion would cross the English Channel in the hours of darkness, landing in the area between the Wash and Newhaven, and that the Germans' tactics, once landed, would not differ materially from those used in France, with widely spaced columns being pushed on without support or protection of their flanks. Simultaneous attacks at numerous widely scattered points were also expected, using parachutists and air-landed troops to capture landing grounds and disorganise communications. To defeat Britain, Ironside considered that the Germans would attempt to capture the centre of government and centres of production and supply, including those in the Midlands. To counter these threats he planned for a defence in strength on the potential landing beaches, a second line of defence parallel to and about 50 miles inland of the south and east coasts (the GHQ Line), and a strategic reserve of the Field Army held inland which would counter-attack when the direction of the main thrust of the German attack had been recognised (see Fig. 1). Separately, plans for the evacuation of the Government and Royal Family to Worcestershire had already been made and suitable properties requisitioned in readiness to accommodate ministers, their staffs and the royalty should London become untenable.

In addition to these main elements of Ironside's plan, there would be other subsidiary stop-lines both in front and behind the GHQ Line, together with defended nodal points or 'Anti-Tank Islands' to obstruct or delay enemy armoured columns probing inland. Road and rail blocks, pillboxes, gun emplacements, barbed wire and minefields would make up the majority of these defences. With these static defences manned largely, but not exclusively by the LDV, he expected to delay enemy forces and allow time for mobile columns of the Field Army and other regular forces to form-up, manoeuvre and counter-attack. The method of dealing with enemy

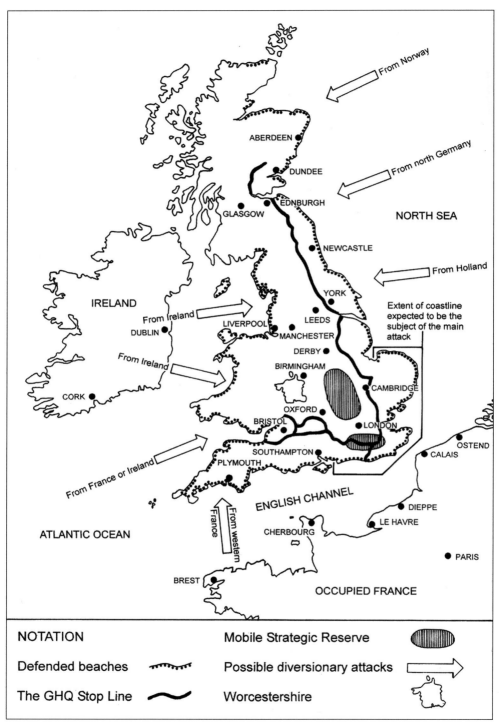

NOTATION

Defended beaches

The GHQ Stop Line

Mobile Strategic Reserve

Possible diversionary attacks

Worcestershire

Fig.1 General Ironside's Plan

parachutists and troops landed from aircraft was to be immediate offensive action to prevent assembly and execution of their plans. The use of gliders that could land in small spaces and floatplanes landing on stretches of water was also to be taken into account.[9]

Ironside's plan for the defence of Britain was accepted by the Chiefs of Staff and Winston Churchill, and set in motion the largest defence construction project Britain has ever seen. Throughout the summer and autumn of 1940, while the Royal Air Force fought the air Battle of Britain, Field Companies of Royal Engineers would design and supervise the work of constructing the defences, utilising men of the Army's Pioneer Corps, local authority direct labour and civil engineering companies, as well as the LDV and other volunteers, to do the work. History tells us that the Royal Air Force were able to deny the Germans the air superiority over south-east England required for a successful invasion but, in 1940, men were not to know this and were working feverishly to complete the defences required to resist an invasion that could come at any time. This construction work would continue into the following year and beyond.[10]

The purpose of stop-lines was to counteract an attack by an enemy armoured column that had broken through the beach defences and made its way inland. The photograph shows a German column held up at a border crossing during the continental campaign. (Courtesy of the late Howard Inight)

Covert defence forces

It was apparent to Churchill's War Cabinet that if the British were to mount an effective resistance to German forces, and match them for ruthlessness, the country would have to forget about gentlemanly warfare and learn how to 'play dirty'. The Secret Intelligence Service (MI6) had a number of ideas for achieving this, and as early as 1938 had organised an intelligence and sabotage force, known as D/Y or Home Defence Organisation. This organisation was activated in June 1940, at about the same time as the War Cabinet approved the establishment of Commando Units from the Regular Forces to take the fight to Europe and Scandinavia and the Special Operations Executive 'to set Europe ablaze', as Churchill had decreed. The Home Defence Organisation can be seen as a precursor to the GHQ Auxiliary Units, but it may well have continued to exist after the Auxiliers were recruited and could be an explanation for the existence of other resistance units in Worcestershire which appear to be entirely separate from them. The Auxiliary Units recruited in Worcestershire from the Home Guard are described in Chapter 8.

A separate wing of the Auxiliary Units, but also having their origins in SIS and D/Y, was the Special Duties Section, a network of civilian spies, message carriers and radio operators whose role was to gather intelligence on any invading troops and via a radio network feed this information back to military intelligence. They also provided security reports on local people and later on any security leaks regarding the mobilisation for the D-Day landings in 1944. The greater cloak of secrecy surrounding this organisation has made it difficult to get to the bottom of their story. What has been found so far is explained in both *The Mercian Maquis* and *The Defence of Worcestershire*, but because the participants, both men and women, were not so closely connected with the Home Guard it is not intended to examine them further in this account.

What about the women?

Anthony Eden's radio broadcast made it quite clear that the government wanted only men to volunteer for the LDV, yet Lady Helena Gleichen was not the only women to see the need for armed resistance to invaders. In a campaign led primarily by the MP Dame Edith Summerskill, and starting in December 1940, women demanded to be part of the force and to bear arms. The War Office and successive Directors of the Home Guard resisted this demand almost to the end, and then only reluctantly agreed to women being associated with the force in non-combatant roles. Nevertheless, women were involved from the outset, usually as casual volunteers, or as members of the Women's Voluntary Service. Some did train for combatant roles, very often with the connivance of local Home Guard commanders (see Chapter 9).[11]

PART I

A general history of the
Home Guard in Worcestershire

1   Worcestershire in the summer of 1940

'Arm yourselves and be ye men of valour and be in readiness for the conflict, for it is better to perish in battle than to look upon the outrage of our nation and our altar.'
From Winston Churchill's first broadcast as Prime Minister on 19th May 1940

May 1940 – The LDV Companies Form

On the evening of Tuesday, 14th May, the reaction to Anthony Eden's call in Worcestershire was immediate and reports in local newspapers indicated the high level of response, the *Worcester Evening News and Times* being typical in its reporting of the scenes in the city. It observed that a number of volunteers had turned up at the Worcester City police station shortly after the broadcast, the first to enrol being the Town Clerk, Mr Digby Seymour, just beating Colonel F.M. Buck, the former Commanding Officer of the 8th Territorial Battalion, The Worcestershire Regiment. By noon the next day, 50 men had registered, including one who had been in the Cambridge University Rifles in 1899, claiming he was still fit at 64½ and 'could not stand being out of things at such times as these'. A one-legged veteran of the Great War was heard to say, as he signed on, that he 'had a good packet at them last time and I'm ready for another'. The newspaper also reported that the Worcester Royal Grammar School had requested 20 forms for boys over the age of 17 who, because of their OTC training, should make valuable members of the new force. Many of the city factories had also made requests for forms.

Not everyone called in person and it was reported by the press that the City Chief Constable, Mr E.W. Tinkler was concerned that people were making heavy demands on the telephone system for particulars. He explained that the role of the police was that of registration and not administration and was at pains to say that it did not follow that all who registered would be called upon.[1] LDV/Home Guard enrolment forms indicate that it could take anything up to a month from registration before the men were formally enrolled in the force, giving time for the police to investigate each man's background and so avoid the enrolment of Fifth Columnists, enemy agents, or at this stage of the war, communists. A number of the Worcestershire candidates had distinctly Germanic names, two in the Stourport area even declaring themselves to be former members of the Austro-Hungarian royal family. This must have caused a bit of head scratching at the local police station, but nevertheless they were enrolled. Each enrolment form was endorsed and signed by a local police officer that the man was 'Approved by the Police' and returned to the appropriate LDV or, later, Home Guard leader.[2] At this stage of the war, the local police station would sometimes also provide temporary accommodation for the headquarters of the LDV as well as a secure weapons and ammunition store.

At Kidderminster the first man had registered almost before Anthony Eden had finished his broadcast and three others before 10pm that night. By Friday, 350 had volunteered, but the figure was expected to rise considerably higher. Over 100 signed on at a meeting in the Town Hall on the weekend following. By the following Tuesday, the total was 600.[3] Redditch also had a splendid response, the first volunteer appearing within minutes of the broadcast, and by Friday there were 431 volunteers. Nearby Astwood Bank had 48 enrol, while at Wythall the figure was 180.[4]

The Black Country had always been a good recruiting area for the Worcestershire Regiment, and so it was no surprise that the northern boroughs of Dudley, Halesowen, Oldbury and Stourbridge also reported an excellent response to the invitation to join the LDV. At Dudley, over 500 men, described by the local newspaper as 'parashooters', were on duty by the end of the first week, more than half being ex-servicemen who were claimed to need little training either in discipline or in handling a rifle.[5] In the Oldbury/Halesowen area the response was beyond all expectations and in a short time the unit became too unwieldy for one command. It was to be divided into three separate commands by July.[6]

In the smaller towns of Worcestershire, the reaction was much the same. At Malvern, men were apparently not slow to realise that the district, with its scattered settlements and stretches of common land, was just the type of countryside that Anthony Eden had in mind as vulnerable to parachute attack. Major W.C. Kendall, a Malvern councillor and magistrate, and Mr F.W. Romney, a local solicitor, telephoned Malvern police station to set the ball rolling as volunteers for the new force. They were followed by a steady stream of volunteers, including one youth of 17, Stuart Hill, who on returning home from the Royal Grammar School in Worcester, and still wearing his OTC uniform, was whisked off to the police station by his father to sign on. Police Sergeant Mound remarked that he was the first volunteer to turn up in uniform! Because of his apparent experience of up-to-date infantry training and weapons, the young cadet was quickly made an NCO in charge of the local squad of the LDV. The squad included his father, who had served as a sergeant in the First World War and had vastly more experience of soldiering. By noon on the 15th, over 50 had been enrolled, increasing to 100 at the end of the day. Two days later the total was 250 registered. A considerable number of the applicants claimed to have had experience of firearms and were former members of school cadet corps, or had served in the previous war. Some of their applications revealed records of service in all parts of the world.[7]

At Evesham the reports were similar, with 400 enrolling in the district in four days, including two clergymen from country parishes outside the town who were amongst the first to arrive at the police station. At Pershore, men were pouring into the police station, with 50 registrations by the end of the following day.[8] Major Maurice Jewell, who was to lead the Upton upon Severn unit, noted that within a few hours every eligible man in that town seemed to have volunteered, some shedding ten of their years to make themselves eligible.[9] Bewdley saw the first volunteer, who lived next door, enter the police station at Wribbenhall just after Eden's broadcast, and just as the desk sergeant was placing a sheet of paper in his typewriter to begin the list of names.[10]

Old soldiers come to the fore

On 15th May, telegrams were sent out by Anthony Eden to the Lords Lieutenant of each county seeking their cooperation in the establishment of the LDV. Since every Lord Lieutenant was automatically the President of the County Territorial Army Association (TAA), Eden was sure that he could count on their cooperation and help in connection with organising the new force. Consequently, in Worcestershire, Lord Cobham, the then Lord Lieutenant, called a meeting at the County Police Headquarters in Castle Street, Worcester, in the evening of Saturday, 18th May,

Arguably the birthplace of the Worcestershire Local Defence Volunteers in May 1940. The former County Police Headquarters in Castle Street, Worcester, was the venue for a meeting called by Lord Cobham to appoint the LDV 'local organisers'.

attended by the Chief Constable, Captain Lloyd Williams MC, all of the Police Superintendents in the county, and a number of retired army officers who were seen as having potential as local leaders of the LDV. A significant number of the LDV volunteers in Worcestershire were retired officers from the Regular or Territorial Army, many with experience of battle in the Great War, only 22 years or so before, and were now stalwarts of the TAA or British Legion. By the time of the meeting in Castle Street, Colonel W.H. 'Bill' Wiggin, then of St Cloud, Callow End, had already been appointed by the Lord Lieutenant as the County LDV Organiser, with Colonel Mallett as his assistant, and Major H. Heath as Acting Adjutant. Colonel Gilbert Mallett was the then manager of the Worcester Branch of the Westminster Bank and President of the Worcester Chamber of Commerce, while Major Heath had had a long association with the 8th Battalion of the Worcestershire Regiment in which he had served as Adjutant.[11]

Colonel Wiggin clearly had the right credentials to organise the new force, and would know well many of the retired officers in the county. At the meeting in Castle Street he explained the purpose of the LDV and that it was decided to raise a company of LDVs in each of the county's police divisions. During the meeting, the following retired officers were appointed as local leaders responsible for organising the volunteers in each division: for the Worcester City division, Colonel E.M. Buck, succeeded soon afterwards by Colonel W.E.L. Cotton OBE MC TD; for the Bromsgrove division, Colonel E.F. De Sautoy TD; for Dudley, Captain A.R. Tanfield; for Evesham, Major W.H. Taylor; for Oldbury

> ## Biographical note on Colonel W.H. Wiggin CB DSO TD
>
> Son of Alfred H. Wiggin JP, of Bordesley Hall, Alvechurch, W.H. 'Bill' Wiggin was born in 1888 and educated at Eton and Trinity College, Cambridge. He was first commissioned into the Worcestershire Yeomanry (The Queen's Own Worcestershire Hussars) on 25th June 1907, and was serving as a senior subaltern when the First World War broke out. He fought on several fronts and took part in the notable cavalry charge at Huj in Palestine in November 1917 and was fortunate not to lose his life. He was mentioned in despatches six times in 1916, and was awarded the DSO. He was later awarded a bar to the DSO. He was twice wounded, first at Katia, where many Worcestershire men fell or were taken prisoner, and again at Huj. Later, he was appointed to the command of the Sherwood Rangers Yeomanry, and between the wars commanded the Brigade of Worcestershire and Warwickshire Field Artillery. Colonel Wiggin served as a military member of the Worcestershire Territorial Association from 1919, and at the start of the Second World War he commanded an anti-tank regiment, but because he had for many years been connected with local Territorial units he had practical experience of organising units similar to the Home Guard. Colonel Wiggin was later to be appointed Home Guard Zone Commander for Worcestershire, and in March 1944, became the Home Guard adviser for the West Midlands District.[12]

(including the Warley, Quinton, Blackheath and Halesowen districts), Captain T.S. Lancaster MC; for Kidderminster, Major R.W. Painter MC; for Malvern, Colonel F. St J. Tyrwhitt DSO; for Redditch, Mr E.A. Grace, succeeded later by Lt Colonel A.E. Scothern CMG DSO; for Stourbridge, Major Laughton Goodwin; and for Stourport, Captain H.B. Long, but after a week or so he was replaced by Lt Colonel F.W. Robinson, with Captain Long staying on in the Stourport unit as its adjutant.[13]

These leaders, initially referred to by their former service ranks, then organised meetings in their own areas and appointed their local organisers, who in turn organised their men into sections, until a hierarchy of experienced officers to lead and administer the LDV in Worcestershire had been formed. As an example, Major W.H. Taylor, of Birlingham, was asked to form his company and man observation posts by 4pm the next afternoon. He called a meeting at Evesham at 10am on the Sunday, with another at Pershore at 12. These meetings were attended by many of those who were subsequently to become officers of the Evesham Home Guard Battalion. Major Taylor, together with Superintendent Price of the Evesham police division and his staff, then worked 72 hours non-stop to create a workable force. Parties of men were sent out armed with a few rifles and shotguns issued by the police, and other weapons apparently acquired by devious means.[14]

This pattern of appointments was repeated elsewhere, and to take an example at the next level down in the hierarchy: at a meeting called by the police and military authorities in the Malvern police division, Major M.F.S. Jewell was appointed to

The Upton upon Severn officers and NCOs in 1944, outside the town police station. Seated in the centre of the second row is Major M.F.S. Jewell (U Company Commander), with, it is thought, Mrs Phillips, the wife of the local police inspector, to the right of him. Of the original leaders of the Upton Company in May 1940, Captain D.P. Morgan MC is fifth from the left in the second row, Captain Sir Ronald Lechmere Bt DL is seventh from the left, next to Major Jewell, and Colonel C.B. Grice-Hutchinson is sitting next to Mrs Phillips. (Courtesy of the late Bob Cross)

lead the volunteers in the Upton upon Severn police area and form a section. He, in turn, appointed the following sub-section leaders: Captain Sir Ronald Lechmere Bt DL for the Upton upon Severn Sub-Section, comprising the volunteers in Upton itself and Hanley Castle; Colonel C.B. Grice-Hutchinson DSO for the Welland and Hanley Swan Sub-Section; Colonel V.N. Johnson DSO to lead the men from Severn Stoke, Earl's Croome, Strensham and Ripple; Captain D.P. Morgan MC to lead Bushley, including men from Longdon and Queenhill; and Mr A.M. Allen to take Berrow and Eldersfield. A Section Headquarters was established in the police station at Upton, courtesy of Inspector Phillips, while the inspector's wife volunteered for, and was appointed, to carry out clerical work. She did so until the stand down of the force in 1944.[15]

It is interesting to consider just how many of the volunteers had had previous military experience. Official estimates for the country as a whole in the early months of the force put the figure at 40%,[16] although John Brophy thought that the figure might be as high as 75% or more.[17] However, some of the older volunteers would be first to leave the force as the winter approached and the long hours of duty in the cold weather, or the heavy demands of their employment as well as military duty proved to be too much for them. Graves suggested that by 1943 only 7% of Home Guards were ex-servicemen.[18] An analysis of LDV/Home Guard enrolment forms for the period 1940 to 1944 indicated that in Worcestershire approaching 20% of the

The Heenan and Froude factory in Worcester raised a Company of two platoons of Home Guard. This picture, taken in 1944, of No 10 Platoon, shows the Company Commander, Major Richard Wareham, seated in the centre of the second row, with his Second in Command, Captain Edmund Wedgebury DSO MC DCM MM, to his left. (Courtesy of the late Ted McGee, who is third from the left in the front row)

volunteers had been members of the armed forces during or before the First World War, the Bromsgrove area showing a higher figure of 28%. One man was noted as having served in the Sudan, like Corporal Jones of 'Dad's Army'. Many of the volunteers had served in South Africa during the Boer War, but a higher proportion were First World War veterans and had already been 'shot over' as one retired officer put it. Many were well decorated for bravery in battle, none more so than Captain Wedgebury, who was to become firstly a platoon commander, then company second in command, with the Heenan and Froude Home Guard in Worcester. Add in an average of 10% having served between the wars, before being released from service, together with about 5% of former OTC cadets, and it can be seen that a large proportion of the new force in the county had already had military experience, some having fought the Germans as recently as the Battle of France in early May 1940. The latter men were largely from the Territorial battalions which had been mobilised in September 1939 and formed part of the British Expeditionary Force. These men had returned to England from Dunkirk, but had then been quickly released from service to return to their civilian occupations where they had the special skills now required in the armaments industries which were working 24 hours a day to replace the vast quantities of armaments left in France. About 5% of the ex-servicemen had previously served in the various battalions of the Worcestershire Regiment, while former members of the Royal Navy, Merchant Navy, Royal Flying Corps and Royal Air Force were also represented.[19]

> ## Biographical note on Captain Edmund Wedgebury DSO MC DCM MM
>
> Edmund Wedgebury joined the 8th Territorial Battalion, The Worcestershire Regiment, in 1911 and served with the 1/8th Battalion throughout the First World War. His MM and DCM awards were made while he was still a Sergeant. He was then commissioned into the Gloucestershire Regiment in June 1917, but continued to be attached to the 1/8th Battalion after this date and finished the war as a Lieutenant. His MC came as a result of leading his platoon in the capture of machine guns at the Battle of Beaurevoir in the Ypres Salient in October 1918, while the DSO was awarded as a result of leading a company in the capture of three German howitzers and killing or capturing their crews. He was subsequently wounded at the Battle of the Sambre and was mentioned in a despatch of Sir Douglas Haig in March 1919. His combination of gallantry awards is unique. While employed as an accountant at the Heenan and Froude Company, in Worcester, he joined the factory LDV in June 1940, becoming the commander of one of two platoons raised by the Company. He was again commissioned as Lieutenant in the Home Guard in February 1941 and promoted to Captain in 1944. He died in 1956.[20]

A large number of fit and enthusiastic teenagers also joined but, of course, they would need training. An indication of how many youngsters is given by an analysis of the age profile of the 23 men that made up the Kemerton unit in south Worcestershire (later to become No 7 Section of 21 Platoon of the

Evesham Battalion Home Guard) for which records have survived. This shows that on enrolment six men were aged between 17 and 19; three between 20 and 25; four between 26 and 30; two between 31 and 35; three between 36 and 40; two between 41 and 45; one between 46 and 50; and two between 51 and 55.[21]

Newspaper notices by the Ministry of Agriculture, Fisheries and Food expressed the view that, to deal with a possible invasion by parachutists, some farmers might be able to cooperate by joining the LDV. However it was thought more likely that the majority of farmers and their employees would be so fully engaged in the work of food production that they would be unable to spare the time for additional duties. On the other hand farmers and farmworkers were the very people who were about the countryside at dawn and dusk – the time when invasions by parachutists might be anticipated. They were accordingly asked to report at once either to the nearest military establishment or to the nearest police station any suspicious circumstances that came to their notice in the course of their normal work.[22]

The LDV Section at Kemerton, which lies in the shadow of Bredon Hill, was dominated by men employed in agriculture: ten were labourers, two were farmers, two were tractor drivers, and two were market gardeners. There were also two carpenters, a chauffeur, an electrician, a gardener, a roadman, a motor mechanic, a butcher and a storekeeper. While the age profile of the LDV units in the urban areas of the county would be similar, the occupations would be entirely different to those of Kemerton, particularly in the northern

Biographical note on Tom Wintringham

Thomas Henry Wintringham was born into a middle class family of Grimsby solicitors, in May 1898. He was educated at Gresham's, a public school which produced a number of intellectuals, and became the Alma Mater of some of the better known British communists. It was while still at school that he developed an interest in military history and the concept of a People's Army. He served in the Balloon Corps as a despatch rider during the First World War, seeing action at Vimy Ridge. After discharge from the RAF in early 1919, he studied Modern History at Balliol College, Oxford. The 1920s and '30s saw him heavily involved in communist activities, leading to a spell in prison in 1925 for sedition. Wintringham went to Spain in 1936 as a reporter for the Communist Party Great Britain, to help the Republican cause, and was instrumental in forming the International Brigade. He was to rise to the rank of Captain and command of the British Battalion of the Brigade until the Battle of Jarama, where he was wounded in the thigh. After recovery, he ran a Republican officers training school, where he would develop his ideas for guerrilla tactics. He was later to rejoin the International Brigade as a staff officer, before being wounded again at the Battle of the Ebro. He returned to Britain in 1937 where, through the medium of newspapers and magazines, he would expound his views on the formation of a People's Army as the antidote to Fascism and the practical lessons learned in the Spanish Civil War.[24]

boroughs. In Oldbury, for instance, there was a preponderance of men employed in factories, although the wholesale and retail trades and the professions were also represented.

On the same day as the meeting had been held at the County Police Headquarters in Worcester, the War Office sent out a letter to the County Organisers explaining that the LDV would form part of the armed forces of the Crown and be subject to military law. It also explained that the intention of the Army Council was that the outstanding features of the administration would be simplicity, elasticity, and decentralised control, plus a minimum of regulations and formalities; there was to be no establishment, no officers or NCOs in the normal military sense; no pay or emoluments; and engagement would be for a period not exceeding the present emergency, although it could be terminated at any time by giving 14 days notice on either side. An individual could consequently resign if he found the task of defending his country too much for him, or he could be dismissed if he was found to be not up to the task by his leader. Any casualties (meaning those leaving the force for any reason) and appointments were to be reported to Company Commanders and the details entered on the back of the individual's enrolment form, which was to become their record of service.[23]

It really was the epitome of a 'People's Army' in those early days, but that would quickly change as the Army Council and the War Office sought to gain control over what, initially, had become a series of small private armies. There were even fears that, under the influence of publicity generated by *The Daily Mirror* and *Picture Post* magazine, popularising the views of Tom Wintringham and promoting the slogan, 'Arm the People', it might develop into a 'Red Army'. George Orwell wrote that there would be red flags flying from the Savoy Hotel by Christmas!

The LDV goes on duty in Worcestershire
The minutes of the TAA meeting in October, 1940, noted that so great was the enthusiasm throughout Worcestershire that, in some parts, armed patrols were indeed on duty in the evening following the meeting at the County Police Headquarters, rifles having been collected from OTC units as far away as Bath. In those very early days of the LDV, many men were doing two or even three nights of duty each week, in addition to the evening and Sunday training which had soon begun. For the training, the services of the ex-soldiers in the force became invaluable, at a time when only the briefest of instructions had been issued by the War Office. The serious approach to duty with which these formerly retired officers and experienced men treated their LDV service, and their standard of soldiering, is at very much at odds with the impression given by the 'Dad's Army' series. Much of this early instruction would later be seen as out-of-date, although it did develop a sense of discipline and comradeship. In the absence of training manuals, despite

Local Defence Volunteers digging defence positions alongside the Guarlford Road, almost opposite Chance Lane, and to the west of Guarlford village. In the early days of the force, when there were insufficient firearms to go around, Malvern volunteers were expected to form working parties for constructing defences. (Courtesy of Sheila Edmonds)

the concern about former communists the War Office circulated 100,000 copies of Wintringham's article from *Picture Post*, 'Against Invasion – Lessons from Spain'.

On Sunday, 19th May, a claim was made in the national press by the Chatham LDV that they had been on patrol as early as Tuesday evening (the 14th). This was immediately followed by a declaration in *The Daily Mail* that the Cradley (West Midlands) LDV had been on patrol the day before Eden had made his broadcast! Lady Gleichen could have made a claim for the Marcle Watchers being on duty much earlier than this. Clearly an element of competition had crept into LDV affairs, but for most volunteers in Worcestershire their first active duties began at dusk on 19th May.

The newspapers were restricted in what they could report of the activities of the new force, now popularly described as 'parashots' or 'parashooters', and the public were asked not to show any curiosity about the men's duties which were being performed between dusk and dawn. Despite the reporting restrictions of those days, *The Worcester Evening News and Times* described those duties as being 'to keep watch and ward, to give police information of any attempt at parachute landing, and to interrupt any such landing by armed force to the utmost of their ability, pending the arrival of a properly organised military force'.[25]

The local newspapers reported that the Kidderminster men on that first Sunday patrolled the outskirts of the borough, armed with rifles and ammunition, and that patrols had been out every following day. As no official armlets were available by Monday, the Women's Voluntary Service, Women's Hospital Supplies and pupils of Kidderminster High School had made 40 armlets for temporary use until official armlets became available. Under the guidance of Major Roland Painter MC, who initially set up his headquarters in the police station, an administrative staff was quickly established utilising experienced officers, including an adjutant's department, a quartermaster's department, musketry instructors and other headquarters staff. The list of appointees rapidly expanded as Major Painter organised his men into 16 sections of about ten men each. All 160 men selected for operational service up to that time were described as ex-servicemen and trained riflemen, although Major Painter said that he had not dealt with all the applications and expected that another 100 men would be enrolled in the next ten days. An auxiliary squad of 35 men had been enrolled in connection with the Staffordshire, Worcestershire and Shropshire Electric Power Depot and substations in the district, as well as vital points in the borough.[26]

The *Malvern Gazette* was also able to report that a day and night watch was being conducted on the Malvern Hills by the 'parashots'. It was explained that the men on patrol up to that time were accustomed to firearms and equipment had already been issued, and that, until uniforms arrived, the men were wearing buff identification arm bands.[28] In fact, in this initial period at Malvern there were only ten rifles and a hundred rounds of ammunition together with shotguns, to arm patrols responsible for 250 square miles. Such was the enthusiasm amongst the men, that Major Kendall, who had been appointed as local organiser, found it necessary to issue an order that: 'In case of any misunderstanding, it should be made clear that volunteers assembling without arms will not be expected to offer any resistance to any invader. Their duties will be confined to observation and report, and they would be available as working parties.' The working parties would help with the construction of defence posts, digging trenches and erecting barbed wire barriers.[28]

The public's role in defence
The Malvern Gazette of 25th May, and other local newspapers, posed the question: 'What would you do if you saw a German parachutist landing?' and suggested that 'every member of the public should know the answer'. Essentially, the public were asked to immediately inform their nearest police station or military headquarters by the quickest means. The public were also asked to cooperate with the LDVs.

That issue of *The Malvern Gazette* also announced the appointment of the local organisers for the Malvern area, which included for the Powick area, General Sir George Weir.

Observation posts established

Since the key function of the new force was to observe and report any suspicious activity, observation posts (OPs) were quickly established throughout the county. Usually sited on high land or buildings, a number have been identified by the Defence of Worcestershire Project, and perhaps the most effective OP was that located on the balcony around the top of Abberley Clock Tower. The room just below the parapet of the Clock Tower was also the base from which the local roads were patrolled. The duty roster

Biographical note on Major General Sir George Weir KCB CMG DSO
Son of Dr Archibald Weir, of Malvern, Sir George began his military career as a trooper in the Worcestershire Yeomanry in the Boer War and rose to command the Worcestershire Squadron within his first year of service. He was honoured for his services in that campaign and commissioned as a Captain in the 3rd Dragoon Guards in 1902. He received further honours in the First World War, including the DSO, when he was serving on the staff of the 2nd Cavalry Division. He later commanded an infantry brigade in France, Salonika and Palestine, for which service he was made a CMG. After the First World War, he held a number of military posts in India, Egypt and at home. He was awarded the CB in 1923 and KCB (Military Division) in 1934, when he was General Officer Commanding British troops in Egypt. He held that post until April 1938. He was living in Kings End Lane, Powick, when he joined the LDV in May 1940 and was appointed to lead the Powick Platoon. Shortly afterwards he was appointed to the command of the Worcestershire Zone Home Guard. He retired from that position in February 1942, having reached the upper age limit of 65.[29]

Abberley Clock Tower was one of the better LDV observation posts, with a view of six counties from the balcony above the clock faces. Accommodation for resting LDVs was provided in the room below the clock, although many steps would have to be climbed between patrols to reach it or the balcony. (Author's photo) showed that each man had four hours on duty and four hours off through the night. Beds were provided for resting. Albert Tolley, a local farmer, recalled that this duty would be repeated about four times in a week for each man, although this would be reduced later in the year. It was usual for Albert to go straight to milking the cows from duty at the tower.[30]

Other OPs with extensive views across Worcestershire were those on Bredon Hill, the Worcestershire Beacon, and on the reservoir at the top of Ankerdine Hill, from any of which pretty well the whole of the county could be observed on a moonlit night. In the flatter and lower parts of the county, the local church tower would often provide a suitable OP, good examples being the cathedral in Worcester and that of Powick Church, overlooking the lower Teme valley. In both of these cases a garden shed was erected on the roof of the tower to provide some shelter for those on duty in these exposed positions. Where a suitable high point was not available, LDVs would patrol in pairs along the roads, lanes and alleyways in their area of responsibility.[31]

OP procedure was normally to have one man observing or listening, a cyclist or runner to take information back to the nearest communication point, one man resting or feeding and another asleep, although some would find it impossible to sleep and would spend their off-duty hours playing cards! The night patrols necessary to establish the location of the enemy were to be trained in moving quietly, with the men wearing gym shoes; carrying no money in their pockets; not wearing steel helmets; rifle slings removed and swivels tied back to their rifles; bayonets, if fitted, tied firmly to the bayonet boss and, on moonlit nights, the bayonet covered; wearing no luminous watches, but wearing gloves and covering their faces with a sandbag, or using face and hand blackening made from burnt cork for example. The men patrolling were expected to halt at intervals and listen for unusual sounds.[32]

During 1940, a system of wireless communications, codenamed 'BEETLE', was developed between all branches of the services to overcome the weakness in intelligence gathering and dissemination that had been displayed by the French Army earlier in the year. The LDV were to have contributed to BEETLE by gathering intelligence on the whereabouts of enemy forces during an invasion of Britain and, by a system of runners and despatch riders, taken the information to the nearest point of contact with the Beetle system. This might be a telephone operated by the Observer Corps, or a wireless set operated by the local searchlight site.[33]

Initial instructions, equipment and countering parachutists

In an effort to gain some control over the activities of the LDV and coordinate their efforts, the War Office issued its first instructions in late May. These set out the reasons for having road blocks, the siting and design of road blocks, and the defences required around the blocks. The second part of the instructions dealt

One of the earliest observation posts established by the LDV was on the side of the Worcestershire Beacon. This photograph was taken some time after May 1941, when 'Home Guard' shoulder flashes had been introduced, but before battalion codes and numbers. These men of the Malvern Company are showing a degree of pride in their shelter against the weather. The location can be recognised as being on the footpath to the Beacon from the Wyche Cutting. (Courtesy of Sheila Edmonds)

with the defence of villages, including a description of the purpose and tactical layout of the defences. Other sections dealt with the use of buildings for defence, communications and maps.[34]

As an additional means of imposing some order on the LDV, and providing the force with a voice at the Army Council, Lt General Sir Henry Pownall, formerly Chief of Staff to Lord Gort, commander of the BEF in France and Flanders, was appointed Inspector General of the LDV on 18th June 1940. However, Pownall was to be replaced in turn by Lt General Eastwood in September 1940, and by Viscount Bridgeman CB DSO MC in 1941. By this time the title had changed to Director General of the Home Guard and he was to serve in this capacity until 1944.

General Ironside, GOC Home Forces, noted in his diary that the LDV were mad keen but in need of coordination, and consequently met LDV leaders in York on 6th June. The meeting was almost certainly a reaction to a series of articles in *The Daily Mirror* by Tom Wintringham, calling for mass arming of the LDV and a more active role in the war. Ironside's speech was subsequently printed and sent out as an LDV instruction. He reiterated that the main duties of the LDV were static defence and providing information – in that order. He explained that there had been no organisation in France to stop the Germans, once they had pushed their way through the front line, from rushing about the country unhindered, and a static defence was needed to prevent that happening here. The prime aim was to hold up the enemy so that counter-attack columns could come and deal with him.

He informed the meeting that he thought that 80,000 rifles had been issued, with more coming, but he did not want his audience to misjudge the shotgun. Over a million rounds of solid shotgun ammunition was being issued, which would kill a leopard at 200 yards. In a city, he did not want a high velocity rifle being used, but at dusk or in the woods the shotgun was about as useful a weapon they could possibly want. He also wanted to develop the Molotov Cocktail, a bottle filled with resin, petrol and tar which, if thrown on top of a tank would ignite, saying that 'if you throw half-a-dozen you will have them cooked'. He wanted the LDVs to meet brutality with brutality.

When the LDV discovered parachutists he advised them to 'shoot them, shoot them, shoot them', suggesting that here the shotgun was possibly the best weapon. He wanted the LDV to prevent the enemy from seizing buildings such as telephone offices from which they could start sending messages, or important buildings like electricity works. He also thought that parachutists would aim to capture places where troop carrying planes would then arrive, and that the LDVs should aim to isolate them and get back information by liaising with searchlight units and the observer corps who had telephones. He explained that German tanks in France had filled up at wayside filling stations and so immobilisation of petrol pumps must be carried out.[35] Appeals were subsequently made to the public to hand in their shotguns to the police for use by the LDV in a broadcast by Sir Edward Griggs, the Under Secretary of State for War, and locally by Colonel Wiggin through local newspaper articles.

Despite all the promises and statements made by the military leaders about the supply of proper equipment, improvisation was still very much a feature of the LDV's activities. Shortage of ammunition for their service rifles in the Evesham area was remedied by local villagers, who, having had numbers of troops billeted on them after the Dunkirk evacuation, would charge five rounds of ammunition for a hot bath![36] Over at Upton, Jack Leighton remembered the guard on the road bridge over the river being supplied with an elephant gun from the armoury at Croome Court, together with three rounds of ammunition. They felt that they should at least have a test firing of this fearsome weapon, but the first round proved a dud and the kick from the second was so terrific that the gun was almost dropped into the river. The guard was now down to one round of indeterminate quality with which to face the invaders![37] Arming the LDV/Home Guard is the subject of more detailed attention in Chapter 11.

The Junkers Ju 52 aircraft was used in great numbers in the assault on Holland on 10th May 1940 for dropping paratroops, and for air-landed follow-up troops on captured airfields, open spaces and roads. Three-view drawings of this and other German aircraft were widely published in local newspapers to alert the LDV and the population at large to the possible appearance of such aircraft over Britain and the need to report their presence to the military authorities. (Courtesy of the late Howard Inight)

Probably influenced by what Ironside had said at York, a number of local newspapers carried articles by their 'Military Correspondent' describing the methods adopted by German parachutists during an attack, the apparent aim being to drop a company of men in an area, 200 by 400 yards, where they could be assembled in a quarter of an hour. The height at which they were dropped could be as low as 150 feet. Details of the uniform and the light equipment carried by each man were included, and it was explained that ammunition, as well as heavier weapons and equipment, was dropped separately in containers. The objectives of the enemy parachutists were listed as: organising members of the Fifth Column and arming them; creating panic amongst the civilian population; harassing lines of communication (road and rail); damaging bridges, power stations, wireless stations and telephone exchanges, stores and dumps; signalling information to aircraft; and doing as much damage as possible. They expected to be reinforced by air transport or ground troops. It was reported that the Germans had made successful use of their parachute troops in Poland, Norway and in the Low Countries, but particularly in Holland. Numerous cases had been reported of parachute troops giving the appearance of offering to surrender, but holding grenades in each hand and throwing them at persons preparing to apprehend them.[38]

The Territorial Army Associations take over the running of the show

The desire to have the minimum of paperwork proved a pious hope, the administrative effort, and indeed many of the associated costs, largely falling onto the shoulders of the retired officers who were now the local organisers. It was clear that this was unfair, and so it was agreed that the Territorial Associations should take over the administration of the LDV, although it would be 24th June before an Army Council Instruction[39] would formally place that responsibility with the county TAAs.

In Worcestershire, the County Association was already helping the police and local organisers with the administration of the new force, and consequently the offices of the TAA in Worcester, then located in the Drill Hall at 16 Silver Street, had already become the focus of much of this work and the *de facto* county headquarters for the LDV. General Sir George Weir, the Powick LDV platoon leader, took on the role of Worcester Zone Commander with effect from 28th June, while Colonel Wiggin continued with the advisory role and the extra administrative duties which had been thrown onto the County Association. The Army Council Instruction also set out proposals to reorganise the LDV so that the previously designated LDV companies became battalions; platoons became companies; and sections became platoons, creating an organisation and command hierarchy more akin to the Regular Army. To cope with the increasing administrative demands of the LDV, the employment of an administrative assistant by each battalion was also authorised. By this date, the total number of LDVs enrolled in Worcestershire was 6,172.[40]

No 16 Silver Street, Worcester, the former Territorial Army Drill Hall, became the headquarters of the County Organiser of the LDV, and subsequently the Worcestershire Home Guard Zone Headquarters. As such the building was a focus for LDV/Home Guard administration from May 1940 until 1945.
(Courtesy of the Army Reserve Centre, Worcester)

The hurried way in which the initial LDV officers had been appointed was by now resulting in some problems. A meeting of LDVs called by Major Kendall, the then Malvern LDV Platoon (later Company) Commander, was held in the Winter Gardens, Malvern in late June, to explain the work of the force. One of the points he raised was that there had been criticism of the appointment of some of the officers. He suggested to the men that it

had been done in a rush and that mistakes may have been made, but he emphasised that 'feelings of jealousy or resentment had no place in the world at this time'.[41]

The problem was not unique to the Malvern LDV. Bill Allington recalls that Major Kay, Bill's section leader, had the equivalent rank of a sergeant, but insisted on being referred to by his former rank of Major. Well liked by his men, he had paid out of his own pocket for some of their equipment, training and even for some of the defence works to be dug by labourers in the Wychbold/Stoke Works area. He also organised drill training by a former Guards NCO from an OCTU then billeted in Droitwich. However, his insistence on maintaining his rank and wearing a tailored uniform with his former insignia caused difficulties with other section leaders in the platoon. He was consequently asked to leave the force, but his men went on strike and refused to do their duty unless he was reinstated. Realising the difficulties being caused by his attitude towards maintaining his rank, Major Kay resigned his position anyway. Such problems must have been quite commonplace in the early days of the LDV when so many retired officers of substantial rank were, in their eyes, demoted.[43]

The Battle of Bewdley

In the late afternoon of Sunday, 30th June, an event occurred which has become the stuff of legend and tested the mettle of the LDV in a way that no exercises were likely to achieve. A number of people in Bewdley were convinced that they had seen parachutes dropping in the vicinity of Ribbesford Woods, just after some aircraft had passed over. The Bewdley LDV, which had been conducting a Sunday exercise near the Folly Point Aqueduct over the River Severn, to the north of the town, were gathered together by Captain Goodwin, and drew arms from Wribbenhall police station. The bells of St Anne's Church in Bewdley were rung to sound the alarm and to call other LDVs to assemble in the Black Boy Hotel car park, opposite the police station. There the LDV were given a number of tasks: man the road blocks and traffic control points in the town to stop the enemy crossing Bewdley Bridge and to hinder the movement of enemy agents and saboteurs; man the observation posts on the high land to the west of Bewdley; and throw a cordon around Ribbesford Woods where it was thought that the parachutists were hiding.[44]

Once people heard the Bewdley church bells, further bells were rung elsewhere and LDVs called out over a wide area, stretching from Stourport and Kidderminster to Abberley, Rock, Clows Top and Mamble, with road blocks erected and observation posts manned, and a number of suspicious people apprehended.[45] Regular troops from Norton Barracks were called out and, forming both a mobile and a marching column, made their way to Bewdley.[46]

Bewdley, then as now, was a popular destination for tourists and, being a Sunday, the town was crowded with day trippers. The call for civilians to 'stay put' when an invasion occurred had little effect and the crowds thronged the roads in the area, hoping to catch a glimpse of the action. Clearly, dealing with enemy parachutists in Britain had all the elements of a spectator sport!

The Black Boy Hotel, Wribbenhall, was the headquarters of the Bewdley LDV in June 1940, and a focus for activity during the 'Battle of Bewdley'. St George's Hall in the centre of Bewdley replaced it as the Company Headquarters of the Home Guard for most of the Second World War. However, the Black Boy once again became a Home Guard headquarters for the Bewdley Company in the 1950s. (Author's photo)

The search for parachutists carried on into the darkness, but nothing was found, and it was finally concluded that the whole affair was a false alarm. A number of theories were subsequently put forward for the false alarm, the best explanation being that hay cocks, which had been drying in the Long Bank area of Bewdley, had been drawn up into the sky by the hot rising air, possibly disturbed by a low flying British aircraft that had passed by a few minutes before.[47] Nevertheless many useful lessons were learnt by the LDV and their leaders, not the least that members of the force, despite their limited training and armaments, had showed great courage in wishing to get to grips with the supposed enemy. Kidderminster LDVs had been called out on this occasion and their local organiser, Major Painter, recalled later in the war that the problem of selecting the first officers and NCOs had been solved by the Battle of Bewdley. They were subsequently chosen by him as a result of their behaviour on that day when for all they knew they were on active duty.[48]

Newspapers had publicised the fact that the signal for an enemy attack was to be the ringing of church bells, but later instructions made it clear that this would occur only when enemy parachutists had actually been seen. The purpose was to call the LDV to their posts at once and be in a position to deal with the parachutists as quickly as possible. How much this later instruction was influenced by the Bewdley experience is not known, but much of the unnecessary effort made by LDVs for miles around had been caused by bells being rung simply because bells from elsewhere had been heard!

Western Command sets out its defence proposals for the Midlands and the West
On 5th July 1940, Western Command, whose area of responsibility included the Midlands and Wales, and reached up to the Scottish borders, issued instructions to the local commands setting out their policy for defence. In general terms it was to prevent hostile attempts at invasion by airborne or seaborne troops by defending all west coast beaches suitable for landing; by defence of aerodromes and by the siting of obstacles on other areas suitable for airborne landings; and by creating a number of stop lines in which the enemy, advancing with or without tanks, from east and west, would find no gaps or weak places, and where he would be held up until mobile troops could attack and destroy him. Defensive posts, road blocks and anti-tank obstacles, to be manned by the local LDV, were to be constructed throughout the vulnerable parts of the command. Affecting Worcestershire, stop lines were based on the River Severn, from Tewkesbury to Shrewsbury; the River Avon, from Tewkesbury to Coventry; and the River Teme, from the Severn to Ludlow, which thereby formed part of an almost complete defensive circle around the important munitions producing areas of Birmingham, Coventry, Wolverhampton and the Black Country. Certain of the towns were designated as Anti-Tank Islands and were to be prepared for all-round defence. In Worcestershire these were Worcester, Kidderminster and Redditch (see Fig.2).[49]

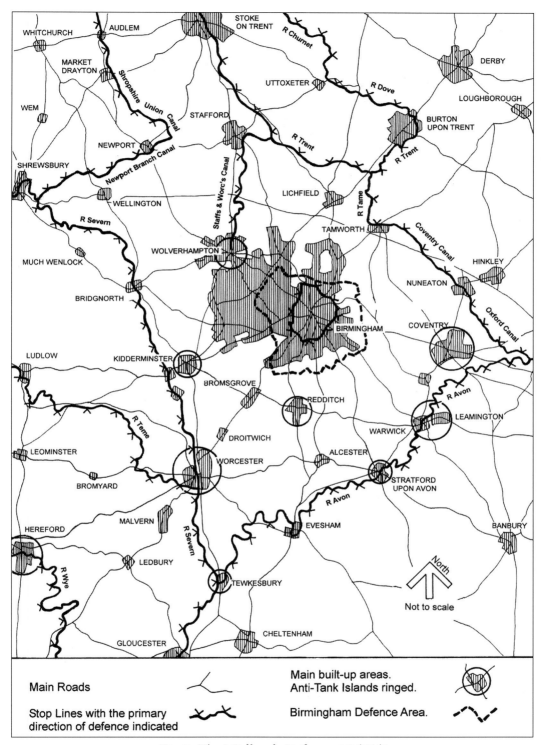

Fig.2 The Midlands Defences 1940/41

Despite the early enthusiasm for joining the LDV, the range of defence tasks allotted to the force, even at this early stage of its existence, were becoming extensive – and exhausting for the part-time recruits. Efforts were therefore made to increase the number of recruits. For example, more recruits were enrolled at a meeting in Bewdley Town Hall, called by the Mayor, on 28th May. Another meeting at Far Forest School was also well attended and Captain A. Betts was appointed as Section Leader.[50]

Protecting the VPs

Folly Point Aqueduct, mentioned in the account of the Battle of Bewdley, was one of a number of vulnerable points (VPs) in Worcestershire which were considered to be of national importance. At Folly Point, the bridge-like structure carried the main water supply from the Elan Valley in Wales to Birmingham over the River Severn, and its destruction would have interrupted the water supply to a large population and numerous munitions factories. Protecting VPs of national and local importance, in Worcestershire and elsewhere, was one of the early, and enduring, tasks of the LDV, and later the Home Guard.[51] To illustrate what this entailed, an example is given of one small part of the county. At a conference between representatives of Southern Command Headquarters and Malvern Urban District Council at the Council House in Malvern on 2nd July, regarding assistance with defence measures, it was concluded that the vital points to be guarded were: the British Camp Reservoir, the Gas Works, the Electricity Works and Bromsberrow Pumping Station. A guard had already been placed at the reservoir, and it was considered that the Electricity Works was more important than the Gas Works. General Weir was to communicate with Gloucester about the guarding of the pumping station, which also stored spare parts, valves and pipes for the repair of any damage to the water pipeline between Bromsberrow and Malvern. An assurance was given by the military authority that they would pay all reasonable expenses incurred in the defence measures, and the District Council was to be asked to supply labour and materials, and to allow its surveyor to supervise the erection of the defence posts and any road blocks.[52]

Guerrilla Warfare

To put his experience in Spain to good use, Wintringham established a training school for LDVs at Osterley Park sponsored by Edward Hulton, the proprietor of the *Picture Post* magazine, where Wintringham and his fellow tutors, who were mostly Spanish Civil War veterans, were to teach a total of 5,000 officers and men the essential elements of guerrilla warfare and street fighting. The focus on guerrilla warfare was not welcomed by 'the establishment', and soon after the Osterley school was opened, Brigadier Whitehead, Commanding Officer of the London District LDV, requested that Hulton and Wintringham close the school down, because the

The BBC transmitting station at Wychbold was designated as a Priority 1 Vulnerable Point of national importance, and had two Home Guard Platoons, as well as regular troops to protect it from enemy attack. By May 1942, it was necessary to release some of the engineers from its own, No 13 Platoon Home Guard, from duties. (Author's photo)

sort of training they were giving was not needed – all the men had to do was to sit in a pillbox and shoot straight! His request was ignored and the subsequent storm of protest from Wintringham and Hulton led directly to the creation of a War Office department for Home Guard training. Every effort was then made to sideline Wintringham and in September the school was taken over by the War Office and then closed down.

The topic of guerrilla warfare was raised again in April 1942 when Major G.E. Walk, of G Ops Home Forces, wrote that the primary role of the Home Guard was to defend their towns and villages and prevent or delay enemy road movements. However, he was aware that members of the Home Guard considered guerrilla warfare was part of the role, probably because such warfare was being successfully conducted by Russian peasants, and that it was specifically mentioned in the training film, *Defence of a Small Town*. He thought that although the role sounded superficially more attractive and possibly less dangerous than standing firm 'to the last round and last man', it was not suitable for the Home Guard because they were not and could not be trained for it, and that they would be likely to confuse the regular troops.[53] Major Walk's paper appeared in June as an order from the GOC Home Forces, with consequential orders being issued to company commanders that guerrilla fighting by the Home Guard must not be allowed. The overriding principle was that, while there were any men to defend them, there would be no withdrawal from 'nodal points', a term used to describe defended urban areas.[54]

Possibly under pressure from local commands, this position was soon modified and Home Guard Instruction 51, issued in September 1942 compromised by saying that guerrilla activity might be permissible in sparsely populated areas where there were no nodal points and giving details of how to train Home Guards for this role. Clearly the Wintringham effect felt from 1940 was still a feature of Home Guard activities and obviously irked some of the establishment. The popularity of Yank Levy's *Guerrilla Warfare*, published in 1941, would have added fuel to this particular fire. At least one unit in Worcestershire, C Company (Abberley) of the Stourport Battalion, fully intended to assume a guerrilla role in the Teme Valley should the area have been occupied by the enemy.[55]

How to deal with tanks
Although there may have been some doubts in high places about the advisability of having LDVs trained by what some described as 'communist hooligans', (and the staff at Osterley were under surveillance by MI5 who tried to discourage Wintringham's lecture tours), much of what was being taught was not in question. After Tom Wintringham had started his school, the War Office issued Local Volunteers Instruction No 8 – Tanks and Tank Destruction, which contains much of the advice that he was giving on how to tackle enemy tanks. The language of the Instruction is very typical of Wintringham, and he may well have had a hand in its drafting. It advocated that:

> From the moment tanks are located they must be harried, hunted, sniped and ambushed without respite until they are destroyed. Goliath was slain by David's sling, and the lessons of Spain and Finland confirm that tanks can be destroyed by men who have the bravery, resource and determination to do so. The armoured fighting vehicle for all its hard skin, apparent mobility and armament, has serious weaknesses, such as at any moment, at least 90% of the surrounding countryside is invisible to a tank with a closed lid; the guns are incapable of depression to fire at anything at ground level within an approximate radius of 20 feet of the vehicle or elevations above 25 degrees; the vehicle is only mobile as long as its tracks hold out; the exhaustion of crews moving long distances and working for several hours in a closed tank is very considerable (they therefore have to halt and lie about outside their tanks in concealed harbours); the tank is dependent for its supply on local petrol resources, or on its own petrol lorries which are unarmoured and easily set on fire; and that darkness is the greatest ally of the tank hunter.

Various road blocks and obstacles are described, as well as the means to disable a tank or make it stop, so that its crew could be shot. It pointed out that suitable points for ambushes could be found in defiles, villages, towns, cuttings and woods. Diagrams illustrated layouts for ambushes in rural and urban locations.[56]

A number of such tank traps have been identified in Worcestershire, but perhaps the best example was located on the west side of Holt Fleet bridge, where a combination of substantial anti-tank road blocks on the bridge, a steep-sided

This is a gunner's-eye view of the Holt Fleet tank trap from the 6 pounder gun emplacement on the river bank. Enemy tanks approaching from the west would have been held up by the substantial road blocks on the bridge and then be subjected to anti-tank gunfire from the emplacement, as well as grenades and small arms fire from trenches in front of the bungalow, and being blasted with burning liquid from a three barrel flame fougasse battery sited in the bank beyond the Holt Fleet Hotel. It is likely that the LDV would also have had firing positions in the upper floor of the hotel. (Author's photo)

cutting on the approach road, and various defence posts, including a 6pdr anti-tank gun emplacement and a battery of three flame fougasses, would have given an enemy armoured column some serious problems!

As a means of training men specifically to deal with enemy tanks, Western Command introduced the concept of tank hunting sections in an instruction of 23rd September. It recommended that to cope with possible invasion, one or more tank hunting sections were to be formed by each Home Guard battalion. A section was to consist of a leader and nine men and as many spare men as could be trained. The section's armoury was to consist of Molotov Cocktails, a Lewis Gun, rifles, an axe for tree felling and two light crowbars which were to be acquired locally. No transport was deemed to be necessary, although personnel could make use of cycles. No further equipment would be available and carriers for the Molotovs were to be improvised locally. Each section was to operate within a five mile radius and their role was to stalk, surprise and destroy hostile tanks and their crews, so preventing them reaching the larger towns and cities. By then, all battalions had sections formed to deal with parachutists, and the tank hunters were to be trained on similar lines.[57]

General Sir George Weir issues his first local orders

In the first instructions to the Worcestershire LDV, sent out on 12th July 1940, Sir George envisaged that the invasion would be in two stages: landing by parachutists to carry out acts of sabotage and cover a landing by troop carrying aircraft, followed by an attack by considerable forces, possibly including tanks, on some objective selected by the enemy. In the case of a landing by parachutists or small bodies of airborne troops, men already on duty at observation posts or other posts were to act in accordance with their post commander's orders. Other men for whom there were arms were to proceed at once to their allotted posts at vital points, bridges, road blocks, public utility services and other works, towns, villages and at blocks on roads previously selected by local commanders, designed to limit enemy movement to a small area in which he had landed and to contain him until the arrival of regular troops. Men surplus to requirements at fixed posts were to be formed into a mobile reserve under a local commander. On the arrival of regular troops, all LDV were to come under the orders of the officer commanding them. During an enemy attack in force the LDV would again man the posts allotted to them and would act under the orders of the officer commanding the regular troops. He also clarified the circumstances in which church bells should be rung.[58]

Winston thumbs his nose at the Germans

Needing to convince President Roosevelt that Britain was not about to collapse and with one eye on listeners in America, Winston Churchill made another of his morale-boosting speeches on 14th July in which he referred to the armed forces now available for defence in Britain. Behind the regular forces

> ... as a means of destruction for parachutists, airborne invaders, and any traitors that may be found in our midst – and I do not believe there are many, and they will get short shrift – we have more than a million of the Local Defence Volunteers, or, as they are much better called, Home Guard.
>
> Should the invader come, there will be no placid lying down of the people in submission before him as we have seen – alas – in other countries. We shall defend every village, every town and every city. The vast mass of London itself, fought street by street, could easily devour an entire hostile army, and we would rather see London laid in ruins and ashes than that it should be tamely and abjectly enslaved. I am bound to state these facts, because it is necessary to inform our people of our intentions and thus reassure them.

The German response to this broadcast was made by their Minister for Propaganda, Joseph Goebbels, who questioned under what arms: 'Broomsticks or the arms of the local pub, with pots of beer and darts in their hands?'[59]

2   The LDV becomes the Home Guard

In a memorandum sent to Sir Anthony Eden on 28th June Churchill wrote: 'I do not think much of the name Local Defence Volunteers for your very large force … I think Home Guard would be better … the title Home Guard would be more compulsive.'[1]

Anthony Eden tried to resist the change of name for the force, but by 6th July Churchill was more assertive and wrote that 'I am going to have the name Home Guard adopted …',[2] and on 23rd July the Local Defence Volunteers were officially renamed the Home Guard. One local newspaper commented that all must agree that the War Office was right to re-christen the LDV as the Home Guard, and that although the force was little more than two months old, it was now of national importance, the new name expressing more clearly its function as a second line of defence behind the Regular Army.[3] Perhaps in part it was the derogatory comments by the comedian Tommy Trinder that the initials LDV actually meant 'Look, Duck and Vanish' that encouraged this support for a change in the name, although in the initial stages of its life this name was actually quite a close description of the role of the LDV. Weapons were in short supply and there was little more that the LDV could do but to observe and report the presence of the enemy should he come, before taking cover.

Worcestershire Reorganisation

The Army Council Instruction of 1st June 1940, which had required the establishment of LDV battalions, companies and platoons along the lines of the Regular Army, had also set the nominal number of men to each battalion at 1,500.[4] The number of Home Guards enrolling in the Oldbury Police Division area had been so great that the unit far exceeded a battalion's requirements, and was becoming too unwieldy to control. Consequently two additional battalions were formed: Halesowen Battalion, initially commanded by Major Eric Holloway, the former leader of the Cradley unit, and later by Lt Colonel Keene, with its headquarters at the Halesowen Drill Hall; and the Warley Battalion, commanded by Captain T.S. Lancaster MC, with its headquarters initially at Langley Drill Hall. The Warley

Battalion was made up of men from the Warley Woods and Quinton areas of Birmingham, and so the battalion area appears to have straddled the county/city boundary.

The reformed Oldbury Battalion was now commanded by Captain L.C.H. Brown, with a headquarters provided initially by Messrs Albright and Wilson, and comprised entirely of detachments made up of workers drawn from the factories in the area including Messrs Accles and Pollock, steel tube manufacturers; Messrs Albright and Wilson Ltd, then manufacturing Self Igniting Phosphorus bombs; Barlows Ltd London Works; Birchley Rolling Mills Ltd; Brookes (Oldbury) Ltd; Chance and Hunt; Midland Tar Distillers Ltd; F.R. Simpson & Co Ltd; Staffordshire, Worcestershire and Shropshire Electric Co; and William Hunt and Sons (The Brades) Ltd. There may have been others.

Having successfully passed through the police screening procedure, a member of the LDV was issued with an identity card by the Worcestershire Constabulary, but signed by the LDV 'County Organiser', Colonel Wiggin. The later Home Guard identity card shown here on the left, indicates that the police no longer had an administrative role in the force, although their screening of new recruits continued until the Home Guard was stood down in November 1944. (Cards courtesy of John Rowberry)

It has been difficult to pin down precisely when this reorganisation took place. The Warley Battalion history implies that it was at about the time that the force changed its name from LDV to Home Guard, while the Halesowen Battalion history places it in August. No doubt there was a delay in its implementation, but the balance of evidence suggests that it was in August. The Worcestershire TAA meeting of October 1940 certainly records the change in its schedule of battalions.

Dictated by geography and operational requirements, the Dudley Battalion, the Halesowen Battalion and No 1 Company (Wollaston) of the Stourbridge Battalion, were placed under the operational control of the South Staffordshire Zone; while the Oldbury and Warley Battalions came under the Birmingham Zone, although administration of all these battalions would remain with the Worcestershire TAA. In fact, the Oldbury and Warley Battalions and part of the Halesown Battalion area fell within the outer defence line for Birmingham City, as did a significant part of Worcestershire north of Bromsgrove. Consequently, and adding to the complexity of Home Guard affairs in the Birmingham Defence Area, men of the Warwickshire Home Guard battalions based in the southern and western suburbs of the city would garrison many of the defences in that part of north Worcestershire.[5]

Now that the Home Guard battalions in Worcestershire had been reorganised, they were numbered 1 to 12 and are referred to in official documents as, for example, the 1st Worcestershire (Worcester) Battalion Home Guard or the 2nd Worcestershire (Bromsgrove) Battalion and so on alphabetically. Consequently, Dudley is the 3rd Battalion, Evesham the 4th, Halesowen the 5th, Kidderminster the 6th, Malvern the 7th, Oldbury the 8th, Redditch the 9th, Stourbridge the 10th, Stourport the 11th, and finally Warley the 12th. It is assumed that Worcester City heads the list as the 1st Battalion on account of its county town status. Henceforth I shall refer to battalions by their geographical name rather than use the lengthy formal name.

The multifarious character of the Home Guard units

The fact that the Oldbury Battalion Home Guards were composed of factory detachments is one example of the diverse nature and function of LDV/Home Guard units from the outset. Most of the units in Worcestershire, and indeed elsewhere, were described as General Service battalions and would be tasked with manning the OPs, road blocks and static weapons positions, and provide a guard for the vulnerable points within their respective areas of responsibility. Factory units were formed in most of the towns in the county and their role initially was to protect their own factories from attack or sabotage and not participate in the more general defences. The size of factory unit inevitably varied according to the size of the factory workforce: some would be no more than a section, while others, such as Heenan and Froude, in Worcester, would initially raise two platoons, and yet others, such as the High Duty Alloys and the Birmingham Small Arms works, at Redditch, would be large enough to raise a company each. As a variation on factory guards, pit guards were formed by the coal miners, not only in the Black Country, but also at Mamble, to the north-east of Tenbury.

Within the factory units of Home Guard, 'Key Personnel' were appointed to immobilise 'their' factory should it appear that the fight had been lost and the Germans were going to take over the premises. The Ministry of Home Security had required this to be done and since little is known about this aspect of Home Guard affairs and few documents remain to provide clues, it seems likely that the identity of such men would have been a closely guarded secret, known only to the directors of the company. Rather like the members of covert forces, their anonymity would have been paramount if they, or their families, were not to be interrogated and tortured by the enemy to reveal what had been done to disable machinery or where they had hidden key components or raw materials. An example of the arrangements made for sabotaging a works prior to enemy occupation came to light

One of the numerous 'factory' Home Guard units raised in Worcestershire, this is the Enfield of Redditch Company, led on this route march by the Managing Director and Company Commander, Major Frank W. Smith. Note the Royal Air Force wings and medal ribbons on his tunic denoting that he was a man of some military service experience as well as status. (Courtesy of Barry Smith via Mike Johnson)

as a result of a reorganisation of the Warley Battalion in 1942, and a proposal to withdraw the Home Guard from the motor servicing company, Harold Goodwin & Company Ltd, on the Wolverhampton Road, which, like many small garages, was then working for the Ministry of Aircraft Production. The Company Secretary asked for the release of Privates Elliott, Radburn and Leslie from the Home Guard because these three were essential to plans already made for the immobilisation of the depot. Elliott was responsible for immobilising the vehicles and battery charging equipment; Leslie was also responsible for immobilisation of vehicles, as well as the transport to a safe place of vital parts; while Radburn was in charge of denial of access to vital spares and tyres.[6]

Another insight to the role of Key Personnel was given later in an Air Defence Research and Development Establishment (ADRDE) Home Guard instruction issued in August 1941. At this time ADRDE were still located at Christchurch, but issued an instruction to their Home Guard for a review of plans already made for the immobilisation of equipment, machinery, and dispersal of personnel in the event of a threatened attack by the enemy, and, where plans had been completed, for perfecting them as soon as possible. These were to be in two principal stages:

> Stand To – Where conditions were particularly favourable for an invasion, key personnel were to remain on the premises in reliefs and sufficient personnel on hand to ensure continuance of work in spite of temporary disruption of communications and transport.
>
> Action Stations – This order would be given when an attempted invasion was considered to be imminent, i.e. when enemy forces were in motion for an attack on this country. On receipt, military personnel including the Home Guard were to occupy their action stations and ensure that everything was in place to carry out the instructions below.

The plans, which were highly secret, were to be carefully rehearsed and those charged with executive action given clear orders on how and when to act. Juniors were to be deputed to act for them in case they became casualties. Every effort was to be made to carry on working to the last possible moment and there was to be no hasty or premature destruction or immobilisation on account of false rumours possibly spread by enemy agents. The plans were to be explained to the local military commander, and notified to the Regional Commissioner, the former's headquarters being responsible for a decision to put the plans into operation, unless imminent capture was likely when the responsibility would rest with the senior official of the establishment. Due care was to be exercised to prove the authenticity of an order as it was considered quite possible, in the event of a feint attack, that enemy agents might endeavour to create panic by posing as British officers and ordering wholesale destruction.

The plans required that no material or plant would be left in existence at the establishment which could be used against home forces. This could entail destruction or removal of an essential mechanism to a place where retrieval by the enemy would be impossible; removal or destruction of explosives or war materials that the enemy might use; concealment of valuable records or destruction of them if copies were available elsewhere; cutting off gas and electricity supplies; immobilising any transport left on the premises; ensuring that any stocks of petrol or oil did not fall into enemy hands; and removal or concealment of any currency.[7] The cave complex in the Blackstone Rock, near Bewdley, was adapted to provided a secure store for a complete set of duplicate dies for the manufacture of porcelain products by the Steatite and Porcelain Company of Bewdley Road, Stourport, which was then producing material for the Ministry of Aircraft Production. This was a contingency scheme to allow for resumption of production should the factory be damaged by enemy action or temporarily occupied by enemy forces and the production lines sabotaged by the Key Personnel.

Taken at Stand Down in 1944, this photograph is of the Worcester City Post Office Platoon, assembled behind the Sansome Place sorting office. The platoon had the specific task of protecting GPO premises, including the former telephone exchange in what is now the Postal Order pub on the corner of Foregate Street and Pierpoint Street in Worcester. Unfortunately, none of the men have been identified so far.
(Courtesy of the late Colin Jones)

The General Post Office raised sections and platoons from their staff to protect post offices and telephone exchanges throughout the county, the control of these men being conducted from the General Post Office Headquarters in Birmingham, although the units would liaise and train with their local Home Guard General Service battalion. The Post Office Home Guards throughout the Midlands were part of the 24th Post Office Battalion (later to become the 47th Warwickshire Battalion Home Guard) based in Birmingham, and commanded by E.V. Goodrich of Barnt Green. The separate Post Office Home Guard had been formed in view of the need to protect facilities of the GPO which then also operated telephone exchanges.[8] It is likely that Key Personnel would have been appointed to sabotage the telephone system should it be threatened with capture.

Similarly, the Midland Red Bus Company raised sections and platoons in the main towns of the county, as did the Staffordshire, Worcestershire and Shropshire Electric Company, which then ran the larger power stations in the Midlands. Since the BEF had left the majority of its motor transport in the vicinity of Dunkirk, Midland Red buses were earmarked to provide transport for mobile columns, 19 of them being stored at Norton Barracks at one stage for this purpose. It would have been wise therefore to have their drivers in military uniform should the buses have been used in anger! The Worcester City Depot raised No 4 (Worcester) Section, which was part of No 3 Platoon. This platoon area covered a sizeable proportion of Worcestershire, including the Evesham and Kidderminster depots, but also stretched as far as Banbury.[9]

Ted Orchard, writing for a local news magazine produced for the Barbourne, Northwick and Perdiswell area of Worcester, explained the difficulties of serving in the Home Guard as well fulfilling his Midland Red bus driving responsibilities. Late shifts of driving meant that he would sometimes miss, or be late for, 'square bashing' at the Southfield Street Drill Hall, under the supervision of the 'very smart' Sergeant Major Abbot. Apparently buses ran until 8pm and Ted would go straight to the Drill Hall in his blue uniform and peaked cap. On occasions, Sergeant Major Abbot would march the squad down to Pitchcroft for training, and Ted would be required to march separately, on the footpath, because he looked too much like a 'guardsman'. At Pitchcroft, he would be a spectator while the rest of the section were crawling around getting muddy. Occasionally, Ted would be detailed to drive his bus to carry Home Guard units on exercises, including a memorable one to deal with an 'enemy patrol' on the Upton Snodsbury road. The 'enemy' was not found, and Ted was not impressed by the lack of map reading skills of the officer in charge of the Home Guards, who managed to get them lost on the short return journey![10]

The London, Midland, Scottish and Great Western Railway companies also raised separate detachments in Worcestershire which were again controlled from their respective regional headquarters in Birmingham.[11] It was considered that railwaymen were the best people to protect railway installations since they knew the details of what they were guarding, such as the frequency and timing of services, the bridges, the signal boxes, tunnels, and so on, and would be able to relieve the regular forces of the task of guarding them. These men would also know how to immobilise the railways in the event of an invasion, and be better placed to recognise bogus orders and misinformation given by enemy agents, as had happened in France and the Low Countries. Instructions received by telephone would, for example, be treated with great suspicion. Again, Key Personnel are likely to have been appointed.

On 30th July 1940, the status of the Railway Home Guards was regularised by a letter to organisers, stating that Railway Home Guards were to form integral parts of existing battalions and companies, but that they would be given duties in the static defence of railway vulnerable points as agreed with railway liaison officers. Henceforth, a Railway Home Guard was not to be used to guard a non-military VP or be taken to man the defence of towns unless agreement has been reached with the railway authorities concerned. At the same time, Railway Home Guards were not to be left at the bottom of the priority list for arms and equipment, as the static defence of railway VPs was considered to be at least as important as that of villages. Railway units were recognised as performing some of the most arduous and valuable service in the country.

Of particular interest is that the railwaymen of the Worcester City Battalion had the use of an armoured train which was stored in sidings at Shrub Hill Station, although no details of the train have been found.[12]

Within some of the General Service battalions in the county, specialist units were formed, including river patrols at Upton, Worcester and Stourport on the River Severn, although, strangely, no evidence has been found of similar patrols on the River Avon. Later, two Home Guard motor transport units were formed, which were affiliated to the Royal Army Service Corps. Armoured car sections were also formed in some of the county battalions, the Redditch Battalion having at least two such locally-constructed vehicles, at Feckenham and Astwood Bank. There is also evidence that the Eckington Platoon had such a vehicle based upon a tractor. Worcester City Battalion also formed an Armoured Car section, and there is some evidence that a Humber Beaverette was stationed in the Droitwich Road, near Perdiswell Airfield. In 1942, Home Guard Bomb Disposal Units were formed in the county.

On 13th July *The Kidderminster Times* carried an article appealing to huntsmen and riders, and young men desirous of learning to ride, to cooperate in the formation of a mounted corps of the local LDV. Mr Lionel Rowe, the local Hunt Master, also appealed to owners of suitable horses to lend their animals for training inexperienced riders and use by those not owning a horse.[13] There is no evidence that such a mounted unit was actually formed, either in Kidderminster or anywhere else in Worcestershire, or what their specific role would have been in the Kidderminster area. Other counties did form such mounted patrols where there were large tracts of open land that would be difficult or slow to cover on foot or in a vehicle. It is known, for example, that such a force was formed in west Herefordshire, where the Radnorshire Hills were patrolled.

Assembling the Home Guard in an emergency

One of the difficulties with a scattered force, particularly in rural areas where most of the men would not have a telephone, was calling the Home Guard to action. As noted earlier, the ringing of church bells was a specific signal that parachutists had been seen in the locality, but they were not to be used as a general signal that the invasion had begun. The signal to 'muster' to deal with a more general enemy attack would come from Western Command, down through the military hierarchy, by wireless and telephone to the Home Guard battalion headquarters. From there it would go out by telephone and Home Guard despatch riders, in the early days using their own motorcycles, to the company and then platoon commanders. It was the responsibility of each platoon commander to ensure that all his men were informed. Wilf Mound of the Morgan Works unit recalled that this was achieved by the so-called 'snowball' system, whereby the platoon sergeant would tell the next geographically nearest man in his platoon, and then go to the muster point. The

This photograph of part of the Morgan Works Home Guard taken at Stand Down shows Wilf Mound in the middle row. In the back row from the left are Arthur Hodges, the Foreman at the Morgan Works, Gilbert Mathlin, and ? Bannister. In the second row are Ron Mound, Wilf Mound, Walter Cheese and Eddie Williams. In the front row are Lieutenant W.R. Evans, Lieutenant Ted Berrow and Sergeant Bert Rodway. (Courtesy of Stuart Hill)

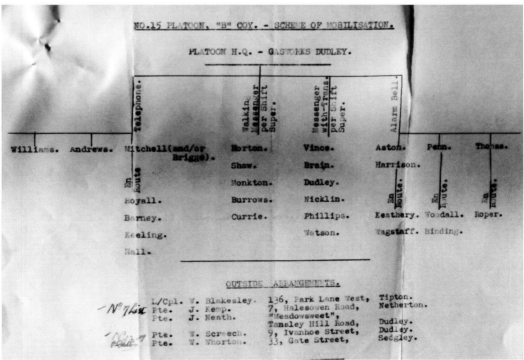

Mustering the sometimes very scattered personnel of a Home Guard unit could be time-consuming. These are the arrangements for No 15 Platoon of the Dudley Battalion, where it can be seen that a combination of telephone, messengers (runners) or men calling on their colleagues was to be used to achieve the muster. (Courtesy of Gwen Harvey)

man he had informed would then inform his neighbour, who would inform his next nearest neighbour, each leaving for the muster point as soon as the message was passed on, and so on until everyone was informed and heading to the muster by the speediest means available. A period of between two and six hours could apparently elapse for a full muster.[14] Apparently, a Sunday morning was when the best muster time could be achieved, but it was unlikely that the enemy could be expected to fit in with that timetable!

Changes of Personnel

Sir Alan Brooke was appointed General Officer Commanding Home Forces on 19th July, in place of General Ironside, who was made up to Field Marshal and retired.[15] Despite the earlier approval of his plans, there had been some criticism of Ironside's arrangements for defending Britain and it was decided to appoint the then Lt General Sir Alan Brooke, who had been a commander with the BEF and had had recent experience of the German blitzkrieg techniques in France, to recast the defence arrangements. He deprecated the fixed lines of defence advocated by Ironside, much preferring a network of defended localities and a more mobile defence force. It would take some time to achieve this change of approach since much of the construction work being carried out in 1940 was subject to contract, and it would be 1942 before the stop-lines were finally abandoned, although many of the other established defences were readily adapted to the new concept.

On 9th August, *The Dudley Herald* carried an article entitled 'Overhaul of Home Guard personnel – Unfit Members to be weeded out'. It reported that a survey of Home Guard was being made with the object of weeding out all who, however keen or experienced, may not have the endurance needed in the event of a large scale invasion. All ranks were concerned in this revision, whether local commanders or rankers. Neither past experience in the services, social position, nor any consideration except that of physical fitness was to affect decisions. The article speculated that the places of the older retired officers in senior positions would be taken by men who had more recent service with the forces. How much this move was influenced by Tom Wintringham is not known, but it chimes well with what he was writing. In Worcestershire, the effect appears to have been minimal, for many of the older officers and men appointed in 1940 were still serving at the Stand Down of the Home Guard in 1944.

On a more positive note, *The Evesham Standard* of that same weekend reported that the Home Guard were now to get free practice ammunition rather than having to pay for it. Over at Kidderminster, *The Shuttle* reported that an increasingly familiar sight in the town was the uniform of the LDV, indicating the increase in enrolments locally.[16] It is clear from this newspaper report that the title LDV would not be forgotten quite so quickly as Winston Churchill would have wished.

Enemy parachutist scares

On Friday, 9th August, Germany's propaganda radio station, the New British Broadcasting Station, mischievously announced that German paratroops would be descending on Britain wearing British Army uniforms captured in France, or as miners.[17] August also saw an increase in air activity by the Luftwaffe in the Midlands and further north. Clearly carried out to unnerve the British defenders and add to any anxiety that may have been caused by the earlier German broadcast, parachutes were indeed dropped, mainly on a five by ten mile strip near Redditch on the night of 16th August. The 11th Battalion, Royal Warwicks, billeted at Hewell Grange, noted that parachutes were dropped at Bentley Manor, Wychbold, Hartlebury, Stourport, Hoo Farm near Kidderminster, Bewdley and Droitwich areas. Fifty-five parachutes were subsequently collected, but no parachutists were found, the event causing increased patrolling activity, notably for the Redditch and Bromsgrove Home Guard battalions.[18]

A number of local newspapers reported that parachutes had fallen in the Midlands during the night of Friday 16th and Saturday 17th August, one of which was found

No 11 Platoon (Stoke Works) of the Bromsgrove Battalion. The mixture of steel helmets and field service caps suggests that this photograph was taken before or after an exercise. Major L.M. Ryland, C Company Commander, stands in the centre front, with Lieutenant Bill Allington (Platoon Officer) fourth from the right in the front row. (Courtesy of Bernard and Olive Poultney)

hanging from some electric cables in such a position that nobody could possibly have been wearing it. In another district, one landed in the garden of an ecclesiastical dignitary and another on a military parade ground. At one Midland town (thought to be Redditch) nearly 50 parachutes had been taken to the county police station by the following Monday, brought in by farmers and Home Guardsmen. Some, it was said, had been stripped of their silk, and one woman stated that people would now be able to get some cheap silk nightdresses at the expense of Hitler. Between 10 and 20 were found largely in open fields in rural areas. In one area church bells were rung to summon the Home Guards to deal with the anticipated parachutists.[19]

Bill Allington recalls that his section found opened parachutes with German markings in the vicinity of Wychbold which resulted in three nights of searching for the supposed parachutists. None were found but the operation almost resulted in an accidental battle between different sections of the Stoke Works Platoon. Bill's section were searching different lengths of the railway line through the area, when they spotted armed men on one of the railway bridges. They were about to open

Cookhill Section of Redditch Home Guard at Stand Down. 2nd Lieutenant E.N. Byrd is in the centre of the front row, with Egbert Ganderton to the right of him. Other members of the Section are back row, left to right: Harry Watton, Walter Bishop, Norman Houghton, Dennis Mark and Len Ganderton. In the middle row, from the left are: Mr Walker, Harold Fletcher, Bill Harwood, Walter Laight, Charlie White, Stan Cooke and Des Tyler. In the front row from the left are: Norman Reynolds, Geoffrey Walker, Ted Beck, and seated to the right of Egbert Ganderton are Harry Bradley and Frank Houghton. (Courtesy of Mrs I. Parr via Mike Johnson)

fire when they realised that the 'enemy' were actually another section of Home Guards.[20]

Egbert Ganderton, of Cookhill, also recalled this period and being alerted by some colleagues that there was a parachute hanging from a chestnut tree in the nearby lane. Egbert took the time to put on his uniform, while the others went directly to the location in their 'civvies'. By the time he arrived, his colleagues were surrounding the area with their rifles at the ready as if they were going to shoot rabbits, rather than deal with a parachutist. They didn't find anything, but a week later, the Chloride and Alco Battery factory at Redditch was damaged by fire and it was rumoured that this was the work of an enemy agent dropped by parachute.[21]

Western Command, wishing to capitalise on the experience gained as a result of the dropping by the enemy of empty parachutes, issued an operation instruction on 22nd August, the purpose of which was to review the immediate action to be taken in the future. The instruction predicted that the enemy might drop agents clandestinely, but that such drops were unlikely except in the close vicinity of a worthwhile objective. It was certain that in combination with the actual dropping of agents, empty parachutes would be dropped, possibly shortly beforehand to draw off troops in a false direction. The instruction explained that the first essential at all times would be to confirm any report of parachutes seen dropping and that no such reports were to be disregarded. Nothing was to absolve the commander of the nearest military unit from taking immediate action to confirm reports and deal with any enemy landed with the utmost vigour. This was declared to be an essential military responsibility, not that of the police.[22]

On 5th September, five more empty parachutes were found on the Lickey Hills,[23] so was it a coincidence that a German parachutist was picked up near Northampton on the following day? After interrogation, his task was established as being to reconnoitre aerodromes and landing grounds near Birmingham.[24]

Factory defence
Home Guard Instruction No 12 1940 dealt with factory defence and was published on 16th August. The object was to guard against sabotage, espionage, ground attack and air attack. In any defensive scheme the tasks of the Home Guard, ARP and fire fighting services were to be carefully coordinated. It was required that there should be no overlap of responsibility and that each element of the defence should understand the duties of the others. In the case of anti-sabotage and counter-intelligence, the first essential was to ensure that no person could enter the premises except by authorised entrances. In the defence against ground attack, defence posts were to be sited to cover, if possible, all approaches to the factory, and these posts should have sufficient protection to allow their manning during an air raid. The actual siting of posts was to depend to a certain extent on the situation of the factory,

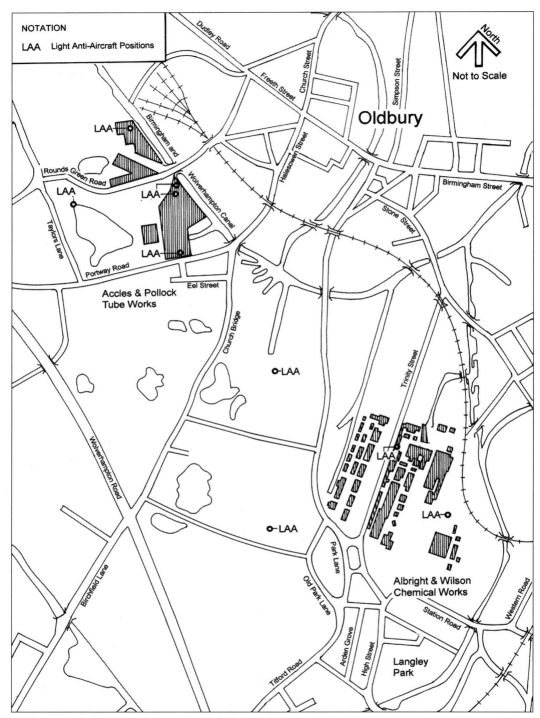

Fig.3 Light Anti-Aircraft defences at Accles & Pollock and Albright & Wilson Works, Oldbury

but some were to be sited within the perimeter, covering the approaches to any vital installations. The design of sunken pillboxes, slit trenches, reinforced cellars, loopholed walls and windows was covered in the instruction, and it was emphasised that both observation posts and defence posts should have good communications with the defence HQ. Preparations for blocking the entrances were to be made, with parties of men detailed and ready for this task. The possible defence of a feature in the immediate vicinity which overlooked and could threaten the factory was also to be considered. Men not otherwise engaged in defence were expected to be accommodated in protected shelters, although the provision of shelters and passive air defence generally was to be the responsibility of the ARP services. Active air defence was normally to be coordinated by the local anti-aircraft unit, but in certain cases dual purpose automatic weapons might be considered as the only means available for anti-aircraft defence. Camouflage of defensive posts and observation posts from the air was to be of the greatest importance.

Bill Hay of the Terry's Factory Home Guard recalls that the anti-aircraft protection for the factory was an aircraft-type Lewis Gun which was looked after by Fred Dean. When a raid was imminent Fred would carry the weapon, slung on his shoulder, to the top of the factory tower where a suitable mounting for the gun, made by Fred, was permanently fixed. After the all clear was sounded, the gun would be carried back down and stored in the armoury. The Lewis gun was fired in anger at the Heinkel which bombed the BSA Works (date not identified). In fact, Bill remembers that just about everyone in Redditch with an anti-aircraft weapon 'had a go' at the Heinkel, including a number of Bofors guns located around the town. Apparently everyone waited until the aircraft had dropped its bomb before firing, but they all missed! Being an aircraft version of the Lewis Gun without the cooling jacket, the Terry's weapon overheated and the barrel 'blued'. Bill recalled hearing Fred Dean saying he would have to get rid of it![25] News eventually reached the Redditch men that the Heinkel was later brought down by a Spitfire.

Another man who remembers firing a factory light anti-aircraft weapon in anger is Geoff Devereux, whom we shall meet again in connection with the Auxiliary Units. After the bombing raid on the Meco works in St John's, Worcester, on 3rd October 1940, when a number of the factory staff and nearby residents were killed and injured, a Browning machine gun had been provided by the Army for factory defence. This was mounted in a sandbagged post on the roof of the main factory building, and Geoff, who was part of the works' aircraft spotting team, was made responsible for its operation during future raids. Apparently, the workforce were normally rather slow in making their way to their shelters when the air raid warning had been sounded, until on one occasion Geoff loosed a volley of shots at a Dornier that was flying up the Severn valley. The effect on the staff was quite dramatic, as they dashed for the shelters. The Managing Director was so impressed that he made his way onto the roof and suggested to Geoff that in future he loosed off a few rounds every time a raid was imminent to get the staff into the shelters![26]

All Home Guard units were required to submit defence schemes for their area of responsibility for approval by the Zone HQ. Those produced for Worcestershire alone must have numbered in the hundreds, if not thousands, but very few have survived to the present day. One of few exceptions is a defence scheme for the High Duty Alloys factory in Redditch, dated 3rd March 1941, which envisaged that enemy action against the factory might take one or more of the following forms: attacks on the works by saboteurs resident in the country; landing by parachutists for sabotage or to cover landings by troop carrying aeroplanes; attack by considerable forces, possibly including tanks, with or without the use of poison gas. The Home Guards and others available for the defence of the factory and its approaches were explained in terms of the fire-power available of 3 shotguns (police), 90 rifles, 1 BAR, 2 Vickers machine guns and 2 Lewis LAA guns.[27] See also Fig.3 for the anti-aircraft defences at the Accles and Pollock Tube Works and the Albright and Wilson Chemical Works at Oldbury.

The policy for Home Guard road blocks
On 3rd September, Western Command set out its policy for the siting and construction of road blocks, although by this time many had already been constructed and were in use. The purpose of the blocks was twofold: firstly, to stop enemy vehicles of all types up to and including medium tanks and secondly, to stop enemy motorcyclists and enemy personnel in captured vehicles from dashing about the country, and to enable civil traffic to be controlled and searched when this might be necessary. The latter could be of a considerably lighter construction, until labour, material and money became available for strengthening them up to stop light and medium tanks.

The instruction declared that the Regular Army had now regrouped sufficiently so that the defence of the country was now based largely on the Army's mobile columns. It was therefore considered to be absolutely essential that roads should not be prematurely blocked, and on important traffic routes that two-way traffic should be possible until the last possible moment. The rapid closing and reopening of gaps to allow mobile columns required practice and the provision of suitable appliances (basically ropes and steel bars!) In the event of an enemy landing, Area Commands were to order the closing of gaps in road blocks, and once gaps were closed, personnel from those provided to defend a block must be stationed at, or very close to the block in order to reopen it for mobile columns and essential military and civil traffic. Personnel were to appreciate that some enemy airborne troops could be dressed in British uniform and be in possession of apparently satisfactory passes. A few words of conversation was reckoned to suffice for

Once a common sight in Worcestershire, anti-tank cylinders were stored on roadsides ready for the Home Guard to create road blocks from the summer of 1940 onwards. Most were disposed of at the end of the war, and the survivors are gradually disappearing as a result of roads being widened and the countryside tidied up. This almost complete set of cylinders has been retrieved from a nearby woodland to form a landscaped display, complete with an interpretation board, on the playing field car park at Finger Post, near Bewdley. (Author's photo)

establishing whether the troops really belonged to the British Army. On the other hand motorcyclists and military motor cars were not to be unduly detained for exhaustive investigation and verification of passes.[28] Subsequently Home Guards were required to learn a few useful phrases of German and British unit insignia, and Home Guard Instruction No 15, entitled *Common German Military Expressions*, was issued on 20th September, listing a number of useful phrases, with a translation and advice on pronunciation.

Given this background, it is small wonder that Home Guards could make life very difficult for the travelling public, and some Army officers were considerably inconvenienced when stopped at Home Guard traffic control blocks. One incident was related by Egbert Ganderton, of the Cookhill Home Guard, which illustrates the point. He and Cyril Buggins were manning a traffic control block, on the main road through Cookhill, near the former bakehouse. The block was typical of the flimsy construction of a traffic control post, consisting of three tubs filled with soil supporting a wooden pole. One night the pair stopped an Army staff car with an officer and an ATS driver. The officer asked Egbert for directions to Hartlebury (probably the Royal Air Force 25 Maintenance Unit) but was refused the information until the officer produced the appropriate pass. The officer protested, at which point Egbert asked Cyril to stand back, cock his rifle and prepare to shoot if the car was driven off! The ATS girl suggested that perhaps the officer should show his pass, which he did reluctantly. From it Egbert could see that the man was a colonel. He had apparently already been stopped by Home Guard three times that night and was getting annoyed by the experience. Egbert was quite clear that he would have asked Cyril to open fire should the car have been driven off without the Colonel having shown his pass.[29] Egbert and Cyril's experience was not by any means unique in Worcestershire and, on occasions elsewhere, shooting did occur and people were killed.

Supplying the Home Guard during an invasion

If the signal 'Action Stations' was given, Home Guards were expected to report for duty with sufficient food and drink to last for 24 hours.[30] By September more expansive arrangements were put in place to supply both civilians and the Home Guard. Under the new arrangements, it was intended by the government that, should invasion take place, civilians were to 'stay put' and the feeding of the population was to continue under arrangements made by the local food controller. This policy was to apply equally to the Home Guard. It was recognised that after an invasion, there would be areas either in temporary occupation by the enemy or where fighting was actually in progress, and that in these areas the normal life of the civil community would be suspended for the time being, and such areas would also give rise to a flood of refugees. Where this occurred and detachments of the Home Guard were involved in the fighting with the Regular Army, they were to be fed by the army units, but reserve supplies to assist in this were being distributed to police stations about the country. At this stage, there was no intention to equip the Home Guard with transport or stores and equipment, because until the supply of the Regular Army was complete in this respect, it would be quite impossible to undertake provision for the Home Guard. As regards ammunition supply for the Home Guard units, because its tactical employment was primarily local and static, their ammunition supply was also to be in local dumps, or in suitably located Command Reserves from which it could be distributed.[31]

These arrangements were modified in June of the following year, when separate provision was made for feeding the Home Guard and various buildings and premises in the battalion areas which could be used as catering establishments had been identified. Food Executive Officers (FEOs) made the arrangements for the food to be made available when needed, but only on purchase by the Home Guard units, funds for which were made available through arrangements with local banks. From October 1941, this would be the normal method of rationing the Home Guard when mustered, although the military authorities had issued 48 hour ration packs, to be kept at battalion or county headquarters, for use until the new system could be put in working order.[32]

Are the Germans coming?

On 7th September, an emergency meeting of the British Chiefs of Staff considered a series of reports on possible German action against the UK. Air photographs had indicated a westerly and southerly movement of barges and small ships to ports between Ostend and Le Havre, which suggested an imminent date for invasion since such craft would not be moved unnecessarily early to ports which were so much more exposed to bombing attacks. Enigma decrypts indicated that the striking strength of the German air force, dispersed between Amsterdam and Brest, had been increased by transfer of 160 long-range bomber aircraft from Norway, and that short-range dive bomber units had been redeployed to forward aerodromes in the Pas de Calais area. Four Germans had been captured on landing from a rowing boat on the south-east coast and had confessed to being spies. They said that they were to be ready at any time during the next fortnight to report the movement of British reserve formations in the area Oxford-Ipswich-London-Reading. In addition, the Joint Intelligence Committee (JIC) concluded that the moon and tide conditions during the period September 8th to 10th were considered to be most favourable for a seaborne invasion on the south-east coast. The indications were that German preparations for invasion were so advanced that it could be attempted at any time. Taking into account the German air attacks, which were at that time concentrated against aerodromes and aircraft factories, the Chiefs of Staff agreed that the possibility of invasion had become imminent and that defence forces should stand by at immediate notice. At GHQ Home Forces there was then no machinery by which the existing eight hours' notice for readiness could be adjusted to a state of readiness for 'immediate action' by intermediate stages. The codeword 'Cromwell' signifying 'Invasion Imminent' was therefore issued by GHQ Home Forces to the Eastern and Southern Commands forward coastal units. It was also issued to air formations in the London area and to the GHQ Reserve, located to the north-west and south-west of London, implying a state of readiness at short notice. The code word was repeated for information to all other commands in the UK.

'Cromwell' was received by the Central Midland Area Headquarters and immediately acted upon. For example, all leave was stopped by the 11th Battalion, Royal Warwickshire Regiment, at Hewell Grange.[33] In Worcestershire all defences were manned on a 24-hour basis for a couple of days, before the crisis passed. Some units misinterpreted the meaning of Cromwell and thought that it meant an invasion had actually taken place. Outside Worcestershire some bridges were blown up, until the matter was brought under control. A redundant canal bridge over the River Teme at Little Hereford, near Tenbury, was also destroyed with explosives

– the ragged stubs of the bridge abutments can still be seen – and although a date for when this happened has not been found, it is assumed to be at this time of high tension.

In some parts of the country certain Home Guard commanders, acting on their own initiative, called out the Home Guard by ringing church bells. This in turn gave rise to rumours that enemy parachutists were landing. There were also various reports, subsequently proved to be incorrect, that German E Boats were approaching the coast. On the following morning (8th September) GHQ Home Forces gave instructions that the Home Guard were not to be permanently called out on receipt of the codeword 'Cromwell', except for special tasks; also that church bells were to rung only by order of a Home Guard who had himself seen at least 25 parachutists landing, and not because other bells had been heard, or for any other reason.

This issue of 'Cromwell' clearly caused a great deal of talk and stir, although no mention was made of it in the newspapers or in parliament. Churchill considered that 'it served as a useful tonic and rehearsal for all concerned'.[34] Nevertheless, 7th September marked a change of tactics by the Luftwaffe, their targets shifting from the airfields of Fighter Command to the bombing of London, and so began the Blitz.

Presumably reacting to the confusion caused by the issue of 'Cromwell' on 7th September, Western Command Operation Instruction No 25 dated ten days later, set out clearly the additional codewords to be used to order the states of readiness for the Home Guard as:

> Ypres – A state of extreme tension existed and parachute landings, especially at dawn, were very possible.
> Cromwell – Invasion believed to be imminent, and parachute landings, especially at dawn were very likely. At the same time, maintenance of industrial output was of great importance.
> Oliver – Invasion had occurred and the enemy was believed to be in range of the area for which Oliver was ordered. At this stage military security was of greater importance than full industrial output. All posts, patrols and lookouts in the area named were to be manned day and night until the situation changed.

It would be 24th September before the 'Ypres' state was lifted in the Midlands,[35] and so the Home Guards' night duty in Worcestershire, and indeed elsewhere, would have been at the heightened state of tension for most of the month. Apart from the incident at Bewdley in late June, this brief period in September was the nearest that many Home Guards came to active service in the early part of the war.

Home Guard dispositions and other affairs

A Western Command order issued in September, commented that undue dispersion was a very noticeable fault in the dispositions of the Home Guard in all command exercises held in 1940. The result had been that garrisons of individual localities had been too weak to do much more than sit in their posts and wait for the enemy to come. The 'Germans' were therefore able to 'winkle' them out easily, especially where the Home Guard posts were on the outskirts of towns rather than in amongst the streets of those towns. It was suggested that this dispersion may be due to a misunderstanding as to the basic object of the Home Guard, which was to obstruct and delay the enemy and help the regular forces to destroy him quickly. This was repeated as the over-riding objective and everything that Home Guard commanders did was to be related to that. A Home Guard commander might, for instance, be given the defence of a village as his particular task, and the inhabitants of the village would probably want him to include the whole village in his defences. However, he was advised that he must ask himself 'What ground must I hold in order to stop the enemy using the roads near the centre of the village?' It was suggested that if he left the outlying parts of the village and only blocked the roads near the centre, the Germans would find it very difficult to turn him out. It was further suggested that the fundamental object of causing delay was best served by using the Home Guards of a village to defend a defile, such as a main road bridge, although it may not necessarily be within the village's perimeter.[36]

The former Drill Hall in Berrington Road, Tenbury, now the town police station, was one of many drill halls taken over by the LDV/Home Guard. From May 1940 to November 1944 this was the headquarters of D Company (Tenbury) of the Stourport Battalion. (Author's photo)

At their annual meeting on 8th October, the County Territorial Army Association noted that the now 12 Home Guard battalions in Worcestershire comprised a total of 19,755 men, a considerable defence force. It appears to have been the peak number in the county, even though nationally the peak was not reached until the end of 1942 at 1,850,757 men. The personnel figures for the individual battalions for this, and subsequent years are tabulated in Appendix 2. To cope with the administration of this burgeoning force, and with the exception of the two most recently added battalions, a civilian administrative assistant had been appointed to each battalion, employed by the TAA at a salary of £300 a year (about £15,000 in today's money), out of which each administrator could employ his own clerical assistant.[37]

The TAA recorded that by October, each Home Guard battalion had been provided with headquarters office and stores accommodation, together with telephones, as had each of the companies making up the battalions. Some of the accommodation had been voluntarily provided, but in other cases had been rented. However, the county had been fortunate in having most of the Territorial Drill Halls available for use by the Home Guard.

The question of the coming winter accommodation for Home Guards was considered to present a difficulty. Although it was expected that occupation of observation posts would be considerably reduced, it was thought essential to keep alive the interest and keenness of the Home Guard volunteers during the winter months, and take advantage of this period to provide training facilities. A programme of requisitioning village halls and other properties was proposed to provide lecture rooms and sleeping accommodation for men on night duty. Perhaps, to follow Goebbels' advice, a number of public houses were also included.

Worcestershire Home Guards relax
In a period when the country was tightening its belt as a result of food rationing, it is interesting to note that on the evening of 17th October, 70 members of the Alvechurch Platoon sat down to a venison dinner at the Red Lion in the village. Major Scott, the A Company Commander, in proposing the toast to Captain Seal, the then Platoon Musketry Instructor who had shot the deer (the section leaders providing the vegetables), also took the opportunity to express his pleasure at being present, and hoped that this would be the first of a series of functions when the platoon came together. He felt sure that this platoon would acquit itself should the opportunity present itself. A concert programme was provided by the various sections of the platoon after the dinner.[38]

Besides introducing us to the infamous Captain Seal, and describing a rather more lavish meal than would normally be available, this example illustrates very well a number of features common to many social events held by the Home Guard across the county and throughout the war, many of them reported in local newspapers. Firstly, it was an opportunity for the officers to thank their men for the effort they were putting into training and duties; secondly, even in those straitened times it was possible, in the country areas at least, for people to gather enough foodstuffs to lay on a supper; and thirdly, significant numbers of people in those days were able to provide entertainment for themselves. Clearly, many people were growing sufficient vegetables in response to the 'Dig for Victory' campaign to have a surplus.

Following this event, and as a consequence of Captain Shaw's comments about Captain Seal's prowess with the rifle in providing the deer, he was ever after known to his Home Guard colleagues as 'Buck' Seal.

Some of the Redditch Battalion Home Guard officers. On the left, holding the telescope, is the infamous Captain J.K. 'Buck' Seal, the Battalion Training Officer, with to the right, Lieutenant R. Ellis, Battalion Catering Officer, Major R. Morom, Battalion Second in Command, Major F.H. Jones, B Company Commander, and Major W.M. Mullins, A Company Commander. (Courtesy of the late Robin Morom)

Biographical note on Captain J.K. Seal of Alvechurch

Captain Seal was one of the outstanding characters of the Worcestershire Home Guard. He came from a Birmingham family and was in Canada when the First World War broke out. He came back to Britain as a private in the 5th Infantry Regiment of the 1st Canadian Division, the first unit to gain a battle honour for the Maple Leaf. He had taken part in all the major battles – Ypres, Vimy Ridge, Somme, Sanctuary Wood and Paschendaele – and was the only officer in his company to survive the operations of September 1918. He finished that war as an Acting Captain and was, by the Second World War, a trichologist in Birmingham, a consulting specialist in diseases of the scalp. He was awarded the MBE in 1944 for meritorious service to the Home Guard, having served as Weapons Training Officer for the Redditch Battalion.[39] His reputation amongst the Redditch Home Guards for strict discipline during live-grenade practice at the range in Pitcher Oak Wood is legendary, and his apparent fearlessness when demonstrating grenades at public events is still remembered by those who witnessed it. His party piece was to set off a live Sticky Bomb and slowly and deliberately walk away, the mighty explosion occurring only seven seconds later.[40]

In this season of Home Guard social events, factory units were also feted by their directors. More often than not, the directors of the company were also the officers of their platoon, and it would obviously be good PR for the directors to thank their men for guarding their factory, in addition to fulfilling their production line duties.

Home Guard bands in the county

The Halesowen Battalion Band claimed to be one of the first Home Guard bands, if not the first, to be formed in the whole of Britain. Major F.P. Smith, previously of the 38th South Staffs Battalion, was credited with raising the band, which was conducted by the Orderly Room Quartermaster Sergeant W.B. Grove. The band was in great demand for leading parades of other battalions of the Home Guard, and by the end of the 1944 season it had completed a record number of engagements throughout the West Midlands.[41] Its first recorded appearance was at the Halesowen Battalion armistice parade on 10th November 1940, when the men marched from the drill hall to the parish church where the band accompanied the singing of hymns and the National Anthem.[42]

Where the Halesowen Battalion led the way, other battalions in the county would follow, with Bromsgrove forming its band in April 1941, Stourbridge in September and Warley in November of that year. Belatedly, the Director General of the Home

Members of the Stourport Battalion Band pose outside the Drill Hall, Lion Hill.
This was one of several Home Guard bands formed in Worcestershire.
Note the guest American clarinettist centre front.
(Courtesy of Stourport Civic Society)

Guard ruled, in January 1942, that there was no objection to the formation of such bands. However, they would receive no financial assistance from the War Office, and the bandsmen, including the bandmaster, were to be found from amongst the men enrolled for combatant duties.[43] A band was formed at Stourport in time for a Wings for Victory parade in the town in May 1943, with one at Evesham appearing in November that year, and the Redditch Battalion leaving it to July 1944 before forming its band.

Home Guards and Civil Defence

After the air Battle of Britain had been fought and won by the RAF earlier in the year, the Luftwaffe started the night blitz of towns and cities throughout Britain. Bombing raids were carried out in the Midlands and further north, generally from the autumn onwards, with the enemy aircraft often over-flying Worcestershire to and from these raids and using the River Severn as a navigational aid. The devastating Coventry raid was experienced on 14th November, but Birmingham and the Black Country were also frequently raided. The more rural parts of the county were not to suffer the weight of bombing experienced further north, although deliberate raids by individual aircraft were experienced by Kidderminster, Redditch and Worcester, causing some casualties.

A memorandum of 5th December sent by the Central Midland Area HQ to the Worcester Sub Area HQ and Town Clerks about Home Guard assistance to the Civil Authorities, explained that the concentrated bombing of towns unaccompanied by other enemy action was now the prevalent activity of the German Air Force and the role of the Home Guard to meet this situation had to be considered. The Emergency Committees in each town were therefore to estimate what work required to be done in order of priority and also labour and material available. It was considered desirable that the Home Guard should fit into the mobilisation scheme, and that the Committee should be told what Home Guards might be available prior to, during and after an attack.

Subsequent Home Guard involvement in civil defence activities is exemplified well by the actions of Sergeant J.V. Jones and E.T.G. Kingsworth of B Company, Warley Battalion, on the night of 11th/12th December, when a land mine caused serious damage to property in the Wolverhampton Road area. The two men carried out their duties, despite the knowledge that their own homes had been severely damaged. They were each subsequently awarded the GHQ Home Forces, Home Guard Certificate for Service.[44]

Renewed threat of invasion

A memorandum dated 23rd December 1940, issued from the Worcestershire Home Guard Zone Headquarters to all the battalion commanders, explained that an attempted invasion was more possible in the next few weeks than it had been just recently (due to the scale and range of the night time blitz) and that the Germans would depend very largely upon airborne troops. It went on to explain that against this form of attack, road and village blocks would be at least as important as the

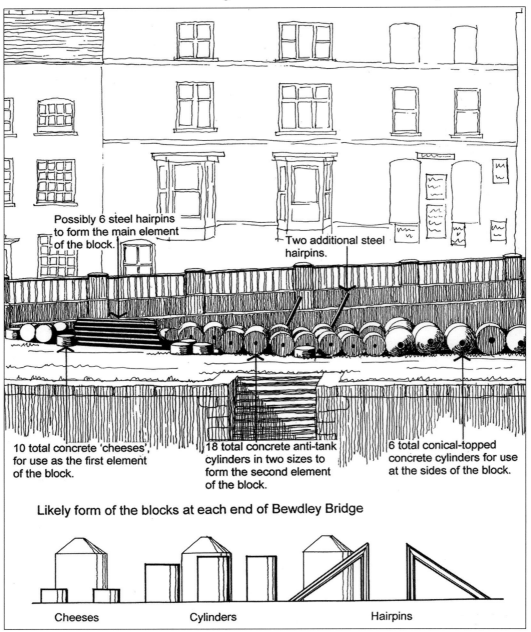

Possibly 6 steel hairpins to form the main element of the block.

Two additional steel hairpins.

10 total concrete 'cheeses', for use as the first element of the block.

18 total concrete anti-tank cylinders in two sizes to form the second element of the block.

6 total conical-topped concrete cylinders for use at the sides of the block.

Likely form of the blocks at each end of Bewdley Bridge

Cheeses   Cylinders   Hairpins

Fig.4 Road blocking materials stored adjacent to Severn Side South for use on the Load Street end of Bewdley Bridge

stop-lines, and that the role of the Home Guard was to contain the enemy troops within the area within which they had landed pending the arrival of mobile columns. Consequently, the memorandum explained to commanders that it was essential that they satisfy themselves on the following points regarding their road blocks and village defence posts:[45]

1) Were the materials for blocks at hand, such as old motor cars, farm wagons, etc? [See Fig.4 for an example of road blocking materials.]
2) Were a sufficient number of trenches dug for the covering positions and were they now fit for occupation?
3) Were bombing pits prepared and bombs at hand? [This reference to bombs generally means grenades, 'bombing' being a First World War term still being used by the veterans of that conflict for the act of throwing grenades.]
4) Were men detailed for the defence of the posts and did everyone know what his job was?

Since poor weather conditions, particularly in the English Channel, meant that an invasion during the winter was unlikely, perhaps this memorandum was an attempt, diplomatically, to pressure some of the Home Guard battalion commanders to finish off their detailed defence works?

Progress on the construction of defences

By the year's end, the Central Midland Area War Diary was able to list, in general terms, the fixed defences that had been created in Worcestershire during the summer and autumn. The main rivers in the county – Severn, Avon and Teme – had been recognised as being natural anti-tank barriers and the river crossings had received particular attention from Royal Engineers and their work parties. The crossings were now provided with substantial road blocks, together with defence positions including gun emplacements, pillboxes and trench systems. Worcester, Kidderminster and Redditch had been designated as 'Anti-Tank Islands' and prepared for all round defence by the respective Home Guard battalions. The key 'vulnerable points' in the county were now graded in importance and the appropriate level of guard provided, although this was not exclusively the responsibility of the Home Guard. Home Defence battalions of the Royal Warwickshire Regiment were also billeted in the county to provide an additional guard at some of the vulnerable points of national importance, including the airfields then existing at Worcester, Pershore and Honeybourne, No 25 Maintenance Unit RAF at Hartlebury, the various petrol storage sites along the River Severn and near Evesham, and both the military wireless stations at Kidderminster and Bewdley, and the civilian radio stations at Wychbold and Evesham. Military Police and the RAF Regiment would later take on some of these responsibilities, while the Royal Navy in Malvern looked after their own sites in that area. The Home Guard were solely responsible for guarding the multitudinous vulnerable points of a more local nature, such as electricity, water and gas supplies, telephone exchanges, and road and rail communications.[46]

Constructed in the summer of 1940, this well preserved Type 24 pillbox covered the ford on the River Avon, near the Fish and Anchor pub at Offenham, and was part of the River Avon stop-line defences. (Author's photo)

3   1941 – The War Office grip tightens

'I heartily congratulate the Home Guard on the progress made by all Ranks since it was established a year ago today … I thank them for the service freely given at considerable sacrifice of leisure and convenience …'.

King George VI , May 1941.[1]

Burgeoning Administration

No doubt influenced by the complex equipment supply arrangements now in place for the Home Guard and the burgeoning paperwork being created, a War Office letter of 22nd January approved the appointment of a full-time Adjutant to each battalion combining the role of Quartermaster, either as newly commissioned Home Guards or through transfer from Regular units. For pay and allowances, they would be attached to the nearest Regular unit or Infantry Training Centre.[2] The Infantry Training Unit for Worcestershire was No 23 Infantry Training Centre at Norton Barracks. Until the appointment of these officers, administration of the battalions continued to be handled by civilian employees of the Territorial Associations.

The TAA report of October 1941 identified those adjutant/quartermasters subsequently appointed as: for the Worcester Battalion, Captain G. Stone; for the Bromsgrove Battalion, Mr N. Morrison (although his appointment had not been approved by October); for the Dudley Battalion, Captain A.V. Rogers; for the Evesham Battalion, Captain W. Fearnside; for the Halesowen Battalion, Captain Beaufort Jones; for the Kidderminster Battalion, Captain E. Gwilliams; for the Malvern Battalion, Captain W.C. Carder; for the Oldbury Battalion, Captain V.J. Fox; for the Redditch Battalion, Captain J. Shaw; for the Stourbridge Battalion, Captain J. Chance MC DCM; for the Stourport Battalion, Captain E. Harris; and for the Warley Battalion, Captain H.S. Kemshead.[3] Most of these men were regular officers transferred to the Home Guard battalions. An exception was Captain Fearnside, a Home Guard and resident of Pershore. He was later to open an artists' supply shop in The Tything, Worcester, a business later run by his son, Ian, in Malvern.

As an example of the administrative load that now befell the battalions, the Central Midland Area Headquarters were informed by letter of 13th March that the Army Council had decided, in accordance with the practice adopted by the Civil Defence Services, to compensate Home Guards who lost income as a result of absence from employment due to Home Guard duties. They were to be allowed up to ten shillings a day maximum (about £25 now), subject to a number of conditions, including the fact that compensation would only be paid to those who had actually suffered financially as a result of interference with their normal employment, including casual workers if they had lost the opportunity of work, but not those who were on unemployment benefits; payment would only be made on receipt of a claim, which included a signed statement from the employer indicating the hours and wages lost; that the claims were certified by a platoon or higher commander that the men were on duty for the time being claimed; and that the battalion commander, in turn, certified that the duty had been authorised by him or a higher authority as a matter of military necessity. The battalion commander could authorise immediate payment of the compensation out of his 'imprest' account, provided the proper procedures had been followed. The TA Association, in turn, were to be reimbursed by the Army Command concerned.[4] Later, it was pointed out in orders that no compensation was admissible in respect of attendance on courses.[5]

As a consequence of the growing complexity in the organisation of Home Guard battalions, HQ companies were formed to incorporate the increasing numbers of specialist officers now being appointed to each battalion. In February 1941, the Halesowen Battalion made plans for such a company under the command of D.H. Brindley, and the Zone Commander gave his approval for its formation on 4th March.[6] However, the Kidderminster Battalion had been first off the mark, forming their HQ Company in November 1940, followed by the Redditch Battalion in February 1941. The process was a gradual one, some battalions leaving the formation of HQ companies until much later, the Oldbury Battalion waiting until early 1944.[7] (See Appendix 4 for a list of HQ Companies and the range of specialist officers employed at Stand Down in December 1944. Appendix 4 also illustrates quite clearly that despite the apparent desire of the War Office for consistency in the organisation of the Home Guard, there was still a wide divergence in the way battalions were organised by their commanding officers.)

An Officer Corps to be formed for the Home Guard
A separate War Office letter of 22nd January informed all Territorial Associations that the volunteer Home Guard officers would receive the King's Commission. Officer establishments were subsequently fixed for Zone HQs and battalions, appointments made and published in Western Command Orders for all battalions. Soon afterwards, formal appointments were also made for Warrant Officer and NCO ranks. For the moment, the 'other ranks' of the Home Guard still continued

to be referred to as 'volunteer', but that would change in due course. Study of Part 2 Orders for the various Home Guard battalions in Worcestershire indicates that the officer appointments were mainly recorded in April and May, with the commissioning back-dated to 1st February 1941 for the purposes of calculating periods of service. Although the creation of a Home Guard officer corps may have been another move to circumvent the German accusation that the men of the Home Guard were *franc-tireurs* and not a legitimate military force, it is also another step by the Army Council, through the War Office, to increase control over the sometimes wayward 'private armies' that some units had become, and recast the image of the Home Guard in the fashion of the Regular Army. It was almost certainly another step by the paranoid War Office to ensure that the Home Guard did not become the People's Army envisaged by left-wing activists such as Tom Wintringham. The spring of 1941 brought to a close the original citizen force and its transition to a branch of the Armed Forces of the Crown.[8]

The Home Guard from C Company of the Redditch Battalion was given extra drill training for royal duties performed on 21st February 1941, when the Duke of Kent visited Redditch. Major Morom commanded the guard, which included Bill Preece, who is the sixth man from this end of the front rank. The final practice for the guard, with bayonets fixed, finished at 1am of the morning of the 21st.
(Courtesy of the late Bill Preece)

The *Dudley Herald* reported the War Office announcement about Home Guard commissioned ranks, explaining that an area commander would be a brigadier; a zone or group commander, a colonel; a battalion commander, a lieutenant colonel; a company commander, a major; and a platoon commander, a lieutenant. Officers were to be commissioned in the rank appropriate to the appointments for which they were selected, and any other form of commission would be regarded as being held in abeyance so long as they retained their commission in the Home Guard. The upper age limit was 65, but selection boards could in exceptional cases recommend the appointment of an officer over that age to be a battalion commander or above. No medical standard was to be laid down, but officers were to have a sufficient degree of mental and physical fitness to carry out their role. Voluntary resignations would normally be subject to three months' notice. Commanders in Chief of all Home Commands were requested to ensure that all nominations of the higher commanders be sent in as early as possible for approval.[9]

George Pitman, who is referred to in the text, is seated at the right-hand end of the front row in this Stand Down photograph taken in 1944. This is part of the Hanley Swan Platoon taken outside their headquarters in what is now the village post office. Other members of the Platoon are: back row, left to right, unknown, W. Rouse, Bill Shipman, S. Edwards, Len Williams, R. Dare, C. Bayliss, George Whitcombe, and ? Long. Middle row from the left are: W. Harwood, Owen Bayliss, G. Dovey, Len Churchill, unknown, Joe Dovey, Harry Harris, and H. James. In the front row from the left are: Jim Dovey, W. Bullock, Sergeant Walter Reynolds, Lieutenant E. Watkinson, Major (retired) Quirke, Sergeant Ted Weildon, and George Pitman.
(Courtesy of Gordon Bennett)

Some changes of Worcestershire Home Guard leaders, now commanders, had already been made from those initially appointed in May 1940. Whilst further personnel changes amongst the commanders would occur, most of the senior officers now in post would remain in the service until the force was stood down in late 1944. Some of the changes that did occur were because the older volunteer officers were caught by the upper age limit of 65. However, age was not always a handicap, and a former member of the Hanley Swan Home Guard, George Pitman, remembers that one elderly warrior, Colonel (his retired rank) Grice-Hutchinson – now commissioned a lieutenant and platoon commander in the Home Guard – would regularly show the younger members of his platoon a clean pair of heels in some of the more strenuous exercises![10] This is just one instance where a retired officer of the Regular Army continued to be referred to by his former rank by his men as he was entitled to be, even though his Home Guard rank was lower.

Defending Urban Areas
With the change of emphasis in defence away from stop-lines to Anti-Tank Islands and Defended Localities advocated by General Alan Brooke, a change of Home Guard training was required to practise the defence of urban areas. Consequently, in the spring of 1941, the War Office issued Home Guard Instruction No 27 which dealt with the defence of urban areas. It was pointed out that in this type of terrain there was excellent cover against small arms fire if the buildings were undamaged, or even if they had suffered from the effects of enemy shelling, bombing or mining. Fighting would take place at short range and therefore shotguns, grenades, revolvers, tommy guns, flame throwers and bayonets were reckoned to be extremely effective, as was barbed wire. Defiles formed by the streets or cuttings of the railways were blockable and easily dominated by automatic weapons or concealed grenade throwers. Movement on the streets would therefore be difficult for the enemy and their tanks would not have the freedom to develop their full powers of manoeuvre and fire.

The instructions described two types of attack adopted by the Germans: neutralisation by subjecting the town to very heavy bombardment and perhaps the use of gas, while the main column bypassed the town, or by infiltration methods which had been developed by them in Spain. It was explained that this form of attack might be preceded by aerial bombardment and then, by capturing three or four buildings well inside the town as first objectives, creating strong points. These would be used as jumping off points 'for eating out' the core of the town.

The general layout of town defences was to consist, firstly, of a defended perimeter or series of defence systems based upon well sited and well constructed anti-tank blocks crossing the main road approaches and designed to trap tanks in defile; concealed posts covering these blocks with small arms fire, grenades and flamethrowers; and

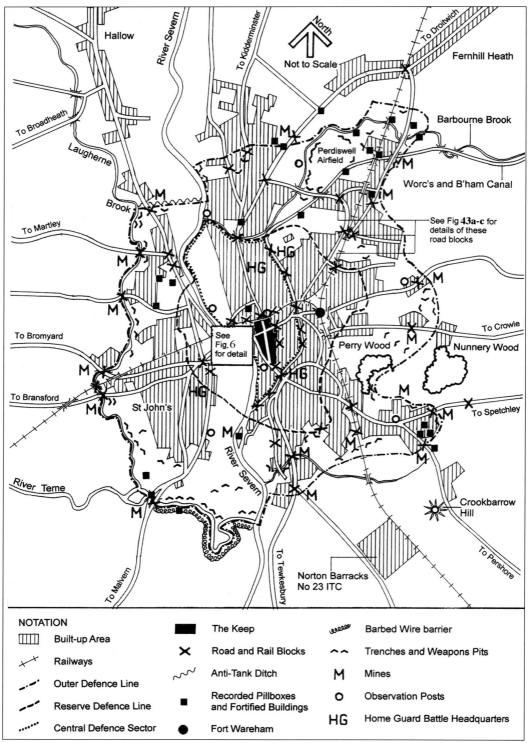

Fig.5 Worcester Anti-Tank Island Defences 1940

subsidiary blocks or bombing posts blocking possible deviations. The second aspect of town defences would be focal points or keeps. The function of the Home Guard in such defences was limited by their numbers and their equipment, but their object was to destroy the enemy, or failing that, to impose delay, forcing the enemy commander to make a new plan whenever he met an obstacle or strong point. Home Guards were asked to remember that five minutes' delay imposed on the leading section of an advance would be multiplied many times over before news of that delay would reach the battalion or brigade commander in charge of the operation. Because Home Guard resources were not available for making every corner into a strong point, defences were to be concentrated on the principal road junctions and main arteries, with important corners or deviation roads being watched by snipers, observers or scouts. (Figs.5 and 6 illustrate the scheme for defending Worcester City for which there has been a good survival of Home Guard defence plans in the Worcestershire Regimental Museum archive.)

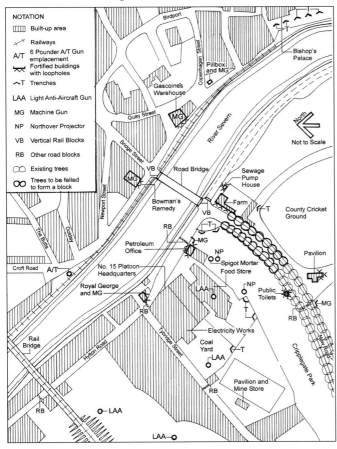

Fig.6 Defence of Worcester Bridge and Electricity Works Vulnerable Point

The instructions put forward the view that, in planning defended posts in urban areas in order to prevent infiltration, it was important that houses on the perimeter which were likely to be the preliminary objective of an attack should be strongly held. Obstacles were, wherever possible, to be sited in defiles where diversions would be difficult to find. If this was impracticable, possible diversions were to be blocked or covered by fire, otherwise the obstacle was ineffective. Every obstacle was to be covered by fire, and to be concealed, for example by siting it around a corner so that the enemy came upon it unexpectedly. Delay could effectively be imposed on the enemy by bluff, such as by stringing blankets across a road as if concealing a minefield, a ruse successfully used in Spain by the Republicans to bring enemy tanks to a halt. Rolls of hessian were issued by the TAA to Worcestershire Home Guard battalions for this purpose. Another bluff, or part bluff, was to lift small patches of tarmac in a road surface and badly roll them down, to make it seem as if each concealed a mine, but perhaps 5 or 10% would actually be mined meaning the bluff could not be called with impunity. A screened defile would not only give the enemy cause to think, but would also cover any movement of the defence, but screens were to be so placed not to mask the fire of the defence. Fire positions could be in pillboxes, sandbagged breastworks, entrenched positions in the open, prepared positions behind loop-holed walls or strong-points, or fire positions built inside houses. In urban areas, locations were best sited at corners where positions could be prepared to face different ways. If necessary, obstructions to the field of fire such as trees, fences and walls were to be cleared. In a city a field of fire down streets of at least 75 to 100 yards was to be achieved. Fire positions were to be proof against small arms fire and be as well concealed as possible.[11]

The Home Guard to have its own medical organisation

From 2nd April 1941, the Army Council authorised the organisation of a medical service within the Home Guard in order to provide casualty treatment in the event of action. The main provisions were that a medical officer, ranked either Captain or Major, should be appointed to each battalion, and that stretcher bearer squads and medical orderlies should be trained, but that this was not to affect the requirement for the men to be trained in the use of weapons or to be called upon to use them. A Regimental Aid Post, if required, was to be established at battalion headquarters and arrangements for the evacuation of casualties was to be reviewed having regard to the requirements of local defence schemes. A list of medical equipment was authorised for each platoon of approximately 100 men.[12] A later Army Council instruction authorised the appointment of company medical officers, and by April 1942, 28 had been appointed in Worcestershire.

Halesowen Battalion had jumped the gun, having already appointed a medical officer in August 1940, as had the Malvern Battalion, which appointed its MO in February 1941, while the Stourport Battalion appointed an MO on the day of authorisation. Local doctors were recruited to fill these posts and their involvement in the Home Guard provided a ready means of not only training stretcher bearers and medical orderlies, but also checking the seriousness, or otherwise, of ailments cited by individuals as a reason for missing parades. By late August of 1941, almost all battalions in the county had a medical officer on their staff. For the Worcester City Battalion this was Dr W.D. Steel, who decided initially not to take a commission; for the Bromsgrove Battalion, Major C.L. Hawkins of Barnt Green; for the Dudley Battalion, Major F.G. Lewis; for the Evesham Battalion,

April 1941 saw the introduction of a medical organisation within the Home Guard and arrangements being made for the treatment of casualties. This would include the appointment of medical officers, the training of stretcher bearers and the provision of first aid equipment. This picture of a field exercise by the Redditch Battalion indicates how stretcher bearers would now accompany the smallest of Home Guard unit operations. (Courtesy of Mr E.P. Grace via Mike Johnson)

Stretcher bearers of the Halesowen Battalion practise their first aid skills on Home Guards during an exercise. (Photo: The Worcestershire Regiment Museum)

Captain J.C. Wilson; for the Halesowen Battalion, Major H.W. Bland, as well as Drs McCarthy and Donnelly; for the Kidderminster Battalion, Major D.G. Dykes; for the Malvern Battalion, Major R.A. Fuller MC; Oldbury Battalion had yet to make an appointment; for the Redditch Battalion, Major N.C. Burns; for the Stourbridge Battalion, Major R.E. Smith OBE; for the Stourport Battalion, Captain Carmichael Mackie; and for the Warley Battalion, Dr W.H. Shilvock, who was already a Home Guard volunteer.

At the Worcestershire Zone HQ, Lt Colonel G. Mackie DSO ADMS was appointed to coordinate the activities of all the Home Guard medical officers in the Zone. Lt Colonel Mackie was already Director of the Red Cross, but by October had organised most of the medical arrangements in the Zone, including establishment of Regimental Aid Posts, the training of stretcher bearers, provision of first aid equipment, and making arrangements generally for Home Guard casualties. The basis of the organisation was the civil defence first aid system. Although each platoon in a Home Guard battalion had a first aid outfit, its casualties were to be taken back to the nearest first aid post of the civil defence organisation. From there they would be taken to the nearest casualty clearing station, and if their injuries were serious they would subsequently be taken, under the civil defence arrangements, to the nearest hospital for treatment.[13]

If a Home Guard suffered an accident or became ill due to Home Guard duty, they were entitled to free treatment by their local doctor in those pre-NHS days. However, in cases of referral to hospital, they were to go to a recognised

---

Biographical note on Lt Colonel (Acting Colonel) G. Mackie

Colonel Mackie came to Malvern in 1907 to act as Medical Officer to 500 boys at Malvern College and to assist in general practice in the town. At about the same time he had also been commissioned as Surgeon Lieutenant in the Royal Artillery. He was promoted to Surgeon Captain in 1908, just before being transferred to the Territorial Force. In 1915 he was selected by Lord Salisbury, the Divisional Commander, to take over command of the Field Ambulances and was gazetted to the RAMC with the rank of Major. On completion of the training and equipment of this unit he was promoted to the rank of Lt Colonel and took the field ambulances to France as part of the 61st (South Midland) Division. He held this command continuously until after the war. He was mentioned in despatches three times, and was awarded the DSO in 1917 on the personal recommendation of his Divisional Commander, Major General Mackenzie KCB. In 1921 he received the Territorial Decoration, after which he was gazetted officer of the Venerable Order of the Hospital of St John of Jerusalem in England. The provision of a medical service for the Worcestershire Zone Home Guard was carried out so successfully that he was asked by the War Office to take command of the development and administration of the Home Guard medical service throughout the country. He was awarded OBE (Military Division) in October 1944 for his work in connection with the Home Guard Medical Service. He died, aged 67, in July 1946.[15]

Emergency Medical Scheme Hospital (EMS), otherwise the War Office might not accept responsibility for payment for any treatment. The following local EMS hospitals were listed: Bromsgrove Cottage Hospital, Dudley Guest Hospital, Kidderminster General Hospital, Kidderminster Emergency Hospital, Redditch Smallwood Hospital, Stourbridge (Wordsley) Emergency Hospital, Stourbridge Corbett Hospital, Wassall Grove Convalescent Home and Barnsley Hall Emergency Hospital.[14]

Home Guard Sectors established

An exercise was held on 19th January 1941 in No 1 Sector of the Birmingham Defence Area to practise the manning and defence of the sector, as well as the intercommunication arrangements and to gauge the operation of the medical services. Sector No 1 included a substantial area of Worcestershire in the Romsley area. Troops involved included the Birmingham Home Guard, Warwickshire Home Guard, a mobile platoon of the 12th Worcestershire (Warley) Battalion Home Guard and the Warwick and Coventry Home Guard. Major R.B. Moss, the Training Officer of No 23 Infantry Training Centre at Norton Barracks, produced the umpires' report after the exercise, and recorded that: 'The keenness shown by all ranks of the Home Guard suggests that we are safe, but certain elementary training is lacking.'[16]

The Birmingham garrison appear to have been the first in the Midlands to divide its area of responsibility into sectors, although they would subsequently be redesignated by the addition of the prefix 'F' to fit into a wider Midlands scheme. It was not until November 1941 that sectors are listed in Worcestershire, when a location statement identified the Home Guard Zone headquarters as being in the Worcestershire TAA Office, Silver Street, Worcester; the L Sector Commander in Wick House, Pershore; M Sector Commander at Norton Barracks; and O Sector Commander at Bank Buildings, Stourport.[17] These sector arrangements were made to provide a more coordinated approach to any Home Guard operations. Henceforth, the hierarchy of Home Guard control and command in Worcestershire would be from GHQ Home Forces to Western Command HQ in Chester, thence to the Mid-West District HQ, on to the Worcester Sub District HQ in Droitwich, followed by the Sector Commands set out below, and then to the individual Home Guard battalions. Exercises involving the Home Guard from this point forward generally involved groups of Home Guard battalions coordinating their response to a threat, while under sector control. The detail of the sector arrangements evolved from that of 14th November 1941, so that by late 1942, L Sector (formed by the very extensive Evesham Battalion area) had been deleted and subsumed into M Sector. For much of the remaining life of the wartime Home Guard in Worcestershire, the arrangements were:

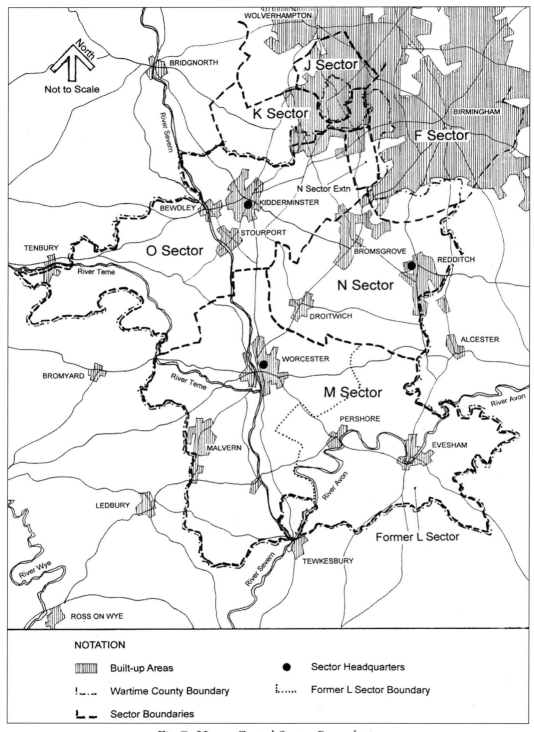

Fig.7 Home Guard Sector Boundaries

M Sector under the command of Colonel V.N. Johnson DSO MC, sharing headquarters with the Worcestershire Zone Commander at the Silver Street Drill Hall, Worcester. M Sector incorporated the Worcester, Evesham and Malvern Battalion areas.

N Sector under the command of Colonel Scothern CMG DSO, sharing headquarters with the Redditch Battalion at the Church Road Drill Hall at Redditch. N Sector incorporated the Bromsgrove and Redditch Battalion areas. On 27th August 1942, it was notified that Halesowen Battalion area would be added to this sector, having previously been part of the Birmingham garrison.

O Sector under the command of Colonel R.W.A. Painter MC, with a headquarters in The Larches, Kidderminster. O Sector incorporated the Kidderminster, Stourport and the Stourbridge Battalion areas, the last less the Wollaston Company. For operational reasons the Wollaston Company area was incorporated into K Sector of the Staffordshire Zone. Reflecting their operational role as part of the Birmingham garrison, Oldbury and Warley Battalions were part of F Sector in the Birmingham Zone, while the Dudley Battalion was part of the J Sector in the Staffordshire Zone (See Fig.7).

The Sector Commanders were made up to full Colonel status in the light of their added responsibilities, being initially responsible for running their battalions as well as the sector headquarters. By late 1942, it was becoming clear that running a battalion and sector command was too much for one man, so the two roles were divided and replacement battalion commanders were appointed. To take one example: at Kidderminster, Colonel R.W.A. Painter MC, who had raised the battalion in 1940, had been appointed the Sector Commander and took on the operational command of the adjoining battalions in O Sector. He subsequently relinquished command of the battalion, his place being taken by Major Clifford Thatcher, who was promoted to Lt Colonel. There were consequential changes in the company structure and command in that battalion. The sector arrangements took some time to evolve and it would be the October 1942 meeting of the TAA before the matter was formally discussed. The process of change continued into 1943.[18]

Exercises organised in 1941 to test the defences in the Midlands
Descriptions of a number of exercises have survived from 1941, which were designed to test the reorganised Home Guard, including coordination with civil defence services and across zonal borders. A few are chosen to illustrate the geographical range of exercises.

A major exercise was held on 24th January 1941. Codenamed VICTOR, it involved mock 'enemy' parachute landings in the vicinity of the Albrighton to Wolverhampton Road, at Kingswood Common, Wrottesley and Chillington Hall, with the objective of disrupting communications. A state of OLIVER was declared (see p.56) and mobile columns from the 12th (Regular) Battalion, Worcestershire Regiment, then billeted in Dudley; from the 307th Holding Battalion in Warwickshire; and from No 23 ITC at Norton Barracks were despatched to tackle them. Home Guard units in Stourbridge, Kidderminster, Bromsgrove, Malvern and Evesham were called out to protect communications in their area, this being emphasised as their first duty during the state of OLIVER. During the exercise, the BBC's facilities near Droitwich (Wychbold) were declared to have been heavily bombed, but were still working, and Worcester Airfield (Perdiswell) was subjected to a gas attack by enemy aircraft.[19]

Home Guard exercises were held in the south of the county on 4th May 1941, to test the defences of the River Severn crossings in the Tewkesbury area, as well as the communication between different battalions. The bridges involved were situated on the border between two different Home Guard battalions and in one case between two different Zones (Worcestershire and Gloucestershire). This was seen as an opportunity to test the liaison between the units concerned. The 'enemy' was provided by the RAF and the 162nd Infantry Brigade, and the defending troops by the 37th Searchlight Regiment RA, the Royal Army Service Corps Depot at Ashchurch, two companies of the 5th Gloucestershire Battalion Home Guard, one company of the Evesham Battalion Home Guard, one company of the Malvern Battalion Home Guard and the 1st Gloucestershire (Tewkesbury) Battalion Home Guard. For the purposes of the exercise it was envisaged that a strong enemy force had landed at Swansea on the Friday (2nd May) with the intention of marching on Birmingham to destroy munitions works. Information purported to have been obtained from a captured document indicated that the enemy intended to land a strong force of airborne troops in the area 10 miles north of Cheltenham and 15 miles west of Winchcombe with the object of capturing the crossings of the rivers Severn and Avon between Ashleworth and Twyning.

At 9am, defending troops were called to 'Action Stations'. At 10am enemy planes dropped parachutes (represented by green flares) west of the River Severn to capture a landing ground (this was probably Berrow Airfield). At 10.30, enemy aircraft troop carriers landed forces equipped with light tanks, which then proceeded to attack the crossings over the River Severn. At 11, a further dropping of parachutes (again represented by green flares) occurred to the east of the River Severn, capturing a landing ground (this was probably Defford Airfield), followed by enemy aircraft troop carriers landing troops who would attempt to join forces with those landed east of the Severn and try to consolidate their positions on the river. At each of the landing grounds, troops were actually landed from the air. Immediately the enemy was reported near, all barricades were placed in position.

Umpires were on duty at the landing grounds, at Haw Bridge and at the Mythe Bridge, while the 162nd Infantry Brigade detailed umpires to supervise the attacking force.[20] It was concluded by the post exercise conference that the Home Guard had

Members of the Redditch Battalion receiving a briefing from a Regular officer, probably the Battalion Adjutant, Captain Hartley, before an exercise. Some are wearing steel helmets representing 'our own troops', while the others who are wearing field service caps would represent 'the enemy'. This was a necessity so the umpires could differentiate between attacking and defending troops during battle simulation.
(Courtesy of Mr E.P. Grace via Mike Johnson)

been well concealed, and while their anti-tank blocks would have been knocked down, they would have imposed considerable delay on the attackers. The 'enemy' (162nd Infantry Brigade) apparently wasted a lot of time on small opposition parties rather than going for main objectives, as the Germans would have done. The siting of Home Guard blocks was criticised, as was the use of concrete defence positions. The involvement of Home Guard units from other areas was praised and cooperation through close liaison was seen as being of the utmost importance. Whilst the Malvern Battalion provided the Cheltenham Battalion with information on the enemy's movements, reliance on telephones was considered to be not good practice and there had been a shortage of despatch riders and motorcycles. The exercise was deemed to have been a big success; it was felt that it was not a question of who won or lost, but a matter of learning from the mistakes that were made.[21]

Major Jewell, commanding the Upton Home Guard Company, was able to report that, after 'The Battle of Tewkesbury' the commanding officer, Colonel Norris DSO OBE of the 1st Gloucestershire Battalion Home Guard, had highly complimented the Bushley and Ripple Platoons (of the Upton Company) for having fought an excellent rearguard action.[22]

Code-named SILVER SCHEME, an attack on Worcester took place on 25th May 1941 as part of a large scale invasion rehearsal, when military units, the Home Guard and every branch of local and civil defences were in action. The scheme was planned to reproduce the conditions that might arise in the event of an invasion, with the combined military and civil defence exercise occurring in a number of areas in the Midlands, but apparently focussing on Worcester. For the purpose of the exercise it was assumed that heavy air raids had taken place from midnight until dawn on several towns, followed by the land attack.

All around Worcester, Home Guards were at their posts to resist the attack and a careful watch was kept on the main roads and the fields, banks and hedges around the city. Towards noon, the sound of firing could be heard as the attackers and defenders, amongst whom were the umpires, established contact. Within the city, some 15 incidents were assumed to have happened, five of them of a major character involving the use of all branches of Civil Defence. All the services were in operation, including the rest centres, communal feeding facilities, information services and billeting, including the re-boarding of persons 'rendered homeless'.[23]

On Sunday, 5th October 1941, Madresfield Park was the scene of 'mimic invasion warfare' by the Malvern Company of the Home Guard. *The Evesham Standard* reporter wrote that if all the companies were as keen and efficient as this one, few fears needed to be entertained as to the way these home defenders would respond to any real test. He thought that it might have been 'Regulars' who were

Being a politician as well as soldier, it behoved Major Kendall to brief M Company for their forthcoming exercise from a 'soap box'. The location appears to be adjoining the farmyard at Madresfield Court. (Courtesy of Sheila Edmonds)

There are at least five Warley Home Guards in the above photograph practising their fieldcraft, while – on the left – some of their colleagues await their turn and look on with a discerning eye.
(Courtesy of Steve Taylor)

'Everything stops for tea.' Men of the Malvern Battalion queue for refreshments during exercises somewhere in the Malvern area. (Courtesy of Sheila Edmonds)

on manoeuvres instead of men who had trained themselves in their spare time from busy civilian jobs. For the exercise, it was assumed that airborne landings had occurred east of the River Severn, that troops from Worcester had been sent to deal with them but they were not yet available, and that a body of German paratroopers, about 70 strong, had landed in Madresfield Park and were seen to move in the direction of Upper Woodsfield Farm. A platoon sent to observe reported that the enemy appeared to have established himself in the vicinity of the farm.

Madresfield Park was considered to be an admirable ground for such an exercise. The attack was started from various points and was rapidly carried out and well coordinated. The defenders succeeded in repelling the attacks until taken by surprise on one flank and overcome. The umpire unanimously agreed that the men had acquitted themselves admirably, both in attack and defence.[24]

Downed aircraft and the handling of prisoners of war

In a memorandum of 13th May from the Central Midland Area Headquarters to the Commander of the Worcester Battalion Home Guard (and presumably all the other battalions), the instructions for handling enemy prisoners of war were set out for the attention of all ranks. It was said that German Air Force personnel who had landed in this country either by parachute or crashed aircraft had been able to remain at large, sometimes for several hours, within sight of troops, Home Guards and civilians. Sometimes they had voluntarily surrendered to totally indifferent bystanders. Once taken, they had been treated as benighted guests rather than enemies, and had been able to destroy maps and documents which would have been of great value to the Army and RAF intelligence in the presence of their captors, who made no attempt to stop them doing so. Such treatment raised their morale, so much so that very little could be gained from their interrogation. This spirit of apathy prior to capture, and camaraderie afterwards was not to be allowed to continue. The loss of documents and poor results of interrogation were seen as serious handicaps to the achievement of air superiority.[25]

For those who found it difficult to rest between patrols, playing cards, commonly pontoon, was a feature of Home Guard duty. Here Corporal Arthur Robins (with spectacles) and other men of the Warley Battalion are playing cards at the Danilo Cinema, their base between night patrols in the Quinton area. (Courtesy of Steve Taylor)

Junkers Ju 88 bombers of the type that crashed at Wychbold and that was shot down at Malvern prepare for a bombing raid. (Courtesy of the late Howard Inight)

Almost 200 aircraft crashed in Worcestershire during the Second World War, but only two were German. The first enemy aircraft came down at night on 12th March 1941, when a Junkers Ju 88 bomber crashed at The Croft, Wychbold. The circumstances are quite bizarre. Piloted by Feldwebel Gunther Unger, the twin-engined aircraft (codes F1+BT) took off from an airfield south of Paris for a raid on Birkenhead. On the approach to the target, the aircraft was attacked by a Boulton Paul Defiant nightfighter and one engine set on fire. After setting the apparently crippled aircraft to fly westwards out to sea, the crew of five men successfully baled out and were captured. The crew had expected the aircraft to crash in the sea soon afterwards, but instead it reversed course and flew southwards to Wychbold where, after clipping the trees near the church, it flew between stables and The Croft, with its wings touching both buildings, demolished a close-boarded fence around the swimming pool and crashed into the adjoining field, just before midnight. The upper floor of the stables at The Croft was the base for the local Home Guards for patrolling the roads around BBC Wychbold, where, at the time of the crash, Bill Allington and some of his fellow Home Guards, who were taking a break between their stints of patrolling, were playing cards. On dashing outside, the men saw that the burning aircraft had disintegrated and amongst the wreckage cylindrical objects could be seen which they took to be bombs. They made a hasty retreat. In the cold light of the following day, the Home Guards and the occupants of the house realised what a fortunate escape they had had from a fiery death. The damage to both buildings was very apparent and part of one wing from the aircraft was lying in front of the stables. As there was no sign of the crew, they were assumed to have perished in the flames. The 'bombs' proved to be oxygen bottles. During all the excitement, however, someone had pocketed the gambling money from the table used for the card play; the Home Guards never did find the culprit.[26]

The second enemy aircraft crashed in the following year. 'A Junkers Ju 88 was brought down by the RAF at Malvern and the crew of four captured', is the short entry in the Worcestershire Sub District War Diary for 31st July 1942.[27] This was Junkers Ju 88 A4 M2+AK of 2nd Kustenfliegergruppe 106 flown by Lt Herbert Gengl with three other crew members. It was shot down in the small hours of the morning by Squadron Leader C.A. Cook and his navigator Pilot Officer McPherson in their Mosquito night-fighter from 264 Squadron. The aircraft wreckage was spread over an area close to the present golf course at Malvern Wells.[28]

Dennis Burrows, then a member of the Malvern Battalion Home Guard Headquarters staff, based at the Golf Club House on the corner of Longridge Road

An early group photograph taken in the winter of 1940/41 on Poolbrook Common, Malvern. The men are: in the back row, left to right, Reg Moss, John Holland, Gilbert Mattin, Bert Hill, Pop Davis, and his son Harry Davis. In the front row are Jack Smith, Bert Jordon, Sergeant Major Tug Wilson, Albert Bird, and Dennis Burrows. (Courtesy of Dennis Burrows)

and Peachfield Road, was part of the force called out to search for the crew of this crashed bomber. The wreckage was still on fire when they reached the site of the crash, although this was quickly put out by the local fire brigade. With his colleague, George Wheelwright, Dennis began searching the nearby woodlands when they heard rustling amongst the trees. They had thought it was the Germans; it wasn't, but they did find a small automatic pistol in its holster together with ammunition. It was in beautiful condition, so Dennis pocketed it for himself. He thought that the weapon had been thrown away by the Germans to avoid being shot while in possession of it. Eventually, Regulars from Norton Barracks turned up and their officer told the Home Guards that if they found anything, it should be handed over. Dennis reluctantly handed over the pistol. The rustling heard in the woods was later found to be an unexploded bomb which was slowly settling into the soft ground. It was subsequently defused and presumably destroyed.[29] Of the German aircrew, Leutenant Gengl was captured by the Home Guard and taken to their headquarters before being treated for his injuries, while the rear gunner was escorted to the local police station by Miss Woodman, an ARP Warden. The fate of the remaining crew is not reported but they are assumed to have been rounded up by the Home Guard.[30]

This incident was apparently the highlight of the Guarlford Home Guard Section's war, the enemy aircraft having flown over the village and been seen quite clearly to be in difficulties. The Section was commanded by Fred George of Priestfields Farmhouse, a First World War veteran. A road block was established on the main road from Malvern to Worcester, at Newland, where a car which had been despatched from Norton Barracks to locate the downed aircraft crashed through it. An enthusiastic member of the Home Guard fired a shot at it, the bullet passing straight through the car, and quite a commotion ensued.[31] This was not the first time, and probably would not be the last, that Regulars showed disdain for Home Guard road blocks in Worcestershire.

Drivers failing to observe signals to stop their cars by night was a reason for deciding, earlier in 1942, that Army and Home Guard personnel whose duty it was to stop road traffic by night, would do so by waving a red light and not a white light in order to reduce danger at road blocks to a minimum.[32] Clearly it had not mattered what sort of light was shown at Newlands, the Regulars were just not going to stop!

Other tasks for the Home Guard
In 1940, the policy was to permanently sabotage or destroy petrol stocks should the invader come and so prevent the sight of enemy tanks filling up at roadside petrol pumps as had happened in France. By 1941, a more considered approach was introduced which reflected the confidence that enemy occupation of any part of

A War Office letter of 1st July authorised the establishment of summer weekend camps for the Worcestershire Home Guard in 1941. Two main camps were organised: at Hewell Grange, near Redditch, and at Tyddesley Wood, near Pershore. Both were extensively used, but the Stourport Battalion organised its own camp at Witley Court which was used regularly until 1944. Here we see the Steatite Porcelain Ltd Platoon, with the ruins of the court in the background. Only Frank Cox, who is receiving a ladle of food, and Bill Allman, seated at the left-hand end of the second bench are recognised.
(Courtesy of Frank Cox)

Britain was likely to be temporary only, but also resulted in greater responsibilities for the Home Guard. It was decided that disruption of supply was preferable and could be achieved by the removal of vital parts from the pumps. Responsibility for disrupting the supply of petrol in any particular area was that of the Sub Area Commander, but if the situation did not allow for this because communication had broken down, the responsibility was delegated to local Home Guard platoon commanders who were expected to act on their own initiative if it seemed certain that pumps would fall into enemy hands. Platoon commanders were therefore required to have a complete list of petrol pumps in their area and squads were to be formed in each platoon for dealing with petrol pumps. All the men in the squad were to know how to remove the vital parts of the pumps, although, where possible, the task was to be carried out by the proprietor of the pumps. So that he could not be held responsible by the Germans, the vital parts were to be hidden by the appropriately named Pump Disruption Squad of the platoon in a location which was to be unknown to anyone but the members of the squad. The squad would then be responsible for refitting the vital parts should it be necessary later.[33]

It was considered very probable that the enemy would try to destroy crops by dropping large numbers of incendiary bombs on ripe cornfields. All observation posts (OP) and patrols were to be alert for fires when alien aircraft were heard in the area, and platoons were to arrange for improvised beaters – bunches of branches or home-made besoms – to be available at each OP with a reserve supply at each platoon HQ. It was emphasised that it was going to be too late to look for these when fires had started! At least two men were to remain at the OPs in the event of fires breaking out in the vicinity.[34]

Home Guard orders stated that small, yellow painted, (high explosive (HE) unexploded bombs (UXBs) might be found in large numbers in all areas. The bombs were considered to be highly dangerous to touch or disturb and when found, the nearest military unit was to be informed immediately of the exact position of the bomb. The Army would then deal it.[35] Similar orders dealt with unexploded projectiles from Z batteries, which could be found on the ground or partially buried. The unexploded rockets could explode if a shadow was cast on them or they were moved, and they were to be roped off to a radius of 10 yards all round and a guard maintained in the vicinity until relieved by Regular troops.[36] Z batteries incorporated simply constructed anti-aircraft rocket launchers. Fig.9 on p.109 illustrates a double rocket launcher, although some were constructed to fire as many as 20 rockets at one time. The rockets could be set to explode at a predetermined time, and a battery of launchers could fill a considerable volume of sky with exploding missiles and were a low-cost, but effective, substitute for heavy anti-aircraft gun batteries. Z Batteries were being introduced as part of the anti-aircraft defences in the Birmingham area, one such battery being located at Cofton, near the Longbridge Factory, just inside Worcestershire, but operated by Warwickshire Home Guards. Another was located near Halesowen.

Crete successfully invaded by German airborne troops
On 20th May 1941, the island of Crete was invaded with the defending Australian, British and New Zealand troops overwhelmed by a German airborne force and forced to evacuate the island. Were it needed, this operation served as a timely reminder of the likely form of the initial attack in an invasion of Britain. However, the high losses sustained by the Germans in this attack, about a third of their airborne troops, resulted in them never again being used in this way, although British defence planners were not to know this at the time.

The occupation of Crete led to a review of airfield defences in Britain, and afforded the Home Guard an opportunity to study the method of attack and apply the lessons learnt to their operational role. It was concluded that the tactics used by the

Germans in Crete confirmed the existing teaching on the subject. The order of events was, firstly, photographic air reconnaissance of the area to be attacked, followed by concentrated dive bomber and fighter machine gun attacks on defence posts in that area. Parachute troops were then dropped on and around the aerodrome selected for attack, followed by air-landed troops from both planes and gliders on and around the aerodrome, after parachute troops had partially neutralised the defenders and cleared the runways for aircraft to land. The enemy also landed gliders and crash-landed aeroplanes on other comparatively level pieces of ground regardless of loss, followed by an advance of all troops to their objective. One of the detailed lessons learnt was the need for mobile fighting patrols to prevent parachutists reaching their arms containers.[37]

Hitler attacks Russia and bayonet standards are issued to the Home Guard

During a broadcast on 22nd June, Winston Churchill informed the nation that, 'At 4 o'clock this morning Hitler attacked and invaded Russia ...'. Just in case anyone thought that the pressure was off those defending Britain, he added that, 'Hitler wishes to destroy the Russian power because he hopes that, if he succeeds in this, he will be able to bring back the main strength of his airforce from the east and hurl it upon this island, which he knows he must conquer or suffer the penalty of his crimes. His invasion of Russia is no more than a prelude to an attempted invasion of the British Isles.' By the 30th June it was reported to the War Cabinet that the Russian position was grave, and fearing a sudden move of German forces from the eastern front, Churchill wanted the British anti-invasion preparations to be in a high state of readiness by September. Clearly influenced by what had happened in Crete only a short time before, he now considered that Britain could face an airborne invasion of perhaps 250,000 parachutists, glider-borne troops, or those from crash-landed aircraft. He considered that everyone in uniform, 'and anyone else who likes, must fall upon these wherever they find them and attack them with the utmost alacrity'. He said that it was the responsibility of the Air Force for the local and static defence of airfields, and that everyone in Air Force uniform 'ought to be armed with something – a rifle, a tommy gun, a pistol or mace'. He thought that 'every airfield should be the stronghold of fighting airgroundsmen, and not the abode of uniformed citizens in the prime of life protected by detachments of soldiers'.[38] In Worcestershire, those detachments were at this stage of the war the 11th Battalion, the Royal Warwickshire Regiment and Home Guards.

It has to be wondered whether Churchill's view that everyone should be armed with something with which to tackle the enemy parachutists led to the issue of the infamous Home Guard pikes, or bayonet standards. A Staff Major at the Worcestershire Zone HQ sent a letter, dated 11th November 1941, to all Company and Platoon Commanders of the 4th Evesham Battalion, in which he said that in the event of airborne invasion, it had been decided that certain personnel should be trained in the effective use of hand grenades and provided with weapons for close combat. An issue of bayonet standards and cudgels was shortly to be made to battalions. It was suggested that these unarmed combat weapons should be allotted to Home Guards not in possession of personal weapons (approximately 4,000 men in Worcestershire at this time), and used for patrol work and village fighting. It was to be explained that recent operations in Crete and elsewhere had shown the low morale of enemy parachutists and other airborne troops immediately after landing, and that they were very susceptible to immediate offensive action. All personnel receiving these weapons were also to be made to understand how the rapid increase in the size of the Army had led to a temporary shortage of personal firearms which would take time to rectify. At the same time they were to understand that such weapons were a useful supplement to the armament of a unit, and not a makeshift alternative.[39] The bayonet standard, which was universally disliked by Home Guards, was quickly consigned to battalion stores and would in any case be followed by the issue of the Sten gun.

Tragedy at Holt Heath

How much additional tension in Britain and increased fear of invasion brought about by the attacks on Crete and Russia, together with training in the use of the bayonet, led to a tragic event at Holt Heath will probably never be known, but on 11th August, Leading Air Gunner Norman Frederick Searle of the Fleet Air Arm, aged 20, died in an ambulance on the way to Worcester Infirmary from a bayonet wound. Gunner Searle was home on leave, and he and his father had been at the Red Lion Hotel. After drinks, they had both left at about 10pm, the son cycling and the father following on foot. When his father reached Pear Tree Walk and had gone about 30 yards, he saw a group of people with the boy on the ground. He was able to ask his son what was the matter and then asked the Home Guards what were their instructions regarding the use of the bayonet, but apparently received no answer. The post-mortem revealed that the cause of death was internal haemorrhage, shock and injury to vital organs by a penetrating stab wound in the upper abdomen. A verdict of accidental death was reached by the jury at an inquest at the Guildhall, Worcester, on 28th August. The evidence given suggested that there had been an altercation during which Gunner Searle was stabbed. The jury consequently added a rider, requesting the Coroner to recommend to the Home Guard authorities that greater care should be taken as to the proper use of the bayonet.[40] This appears to have been the only death of a person at the hands of the Home Guard in Worcestershire, although there could well have been others if good fortune had not intervened, as will be seen later.

The costs of running the Home Guard

At the annual meeting of the Worcestershire TAA on 17th October 1941, the Chairman's report recorded that the costs of running the Worcestershire Home Guard since its inception, a period of 15 months, had been approximately £80,000 (about £4 million in today's money). The two main items of expenditure were subsistence and travelling allowances. The Chairman reminded the meeting of the inadequate capitation grant of £1 (about £50 now) for each Home Guard declared at the previous October's meeting. It was also reported that the 12 Home Guard battalions in Worcestershire now had a total of 18,940 officers and men, a fall of 815 over the previous year. The gross inadequacy of the capitation allowance is quite clear.

Compensation for loss of wages by the Home Guards when mustered was also reported. Wages would be paid at the basic rate of 7 shillings per day, for which no reduction would be made for insurance or feeding, but it would be open to members to claim any balance of actual loss, up to 12 shillings a day or 70 shillings a week, but subject to an appropriate reduction for insurance or feeding then being

This stand down photograph of the Broadwas Platoon of the Malvern Battalion, illustrates very well the standard Worcestershire Home Guard ammunition store, constructed with Anderson shelter sections on a brick and concrete plinth. 80 of these had been supplied by the TAA up to October 1941. This one was located in the back garden of the K Company Commander, Dr Clarke, at Knightwick. Personnel in the back row are from left to right: Ray Light, George Symonds, Reuben Jones, unknown, unknown, Richard James, Bob Gillespie, Ernie Jones, unknown, Brian Winters. Front row, from the left are: Lance Corporal Frank Williams, unknown Corporal, Corporal Jack Saunders, Ernie Wood, Captain Shepherd, Lieutenant Twinberrow, Sergeant 'Coddy' Phillips, unknown Sergeant, Corporal Jack Gale, Corporal Ray Turbutt, Corporal Tommy Higginson, and Lance Corporal Bill Evans. (Courtesy of Margaret Mathews)

made. 70 shillings a week equates to £17.50 in today's money, a pretty mean rate of compensation by any measure and a reflection of just how much a Home Guard was expected to give up if mustered.

Public Demonstrations and Private Celebrations

Earlier in the year, on the evening of 18th May, a Home Guard event open to the public took place in the grounds of The Field House at Clent, and was described as 'interesting' by the local newspapers. As a result a larger demonstration by the Home Guard was held at The Field House on Sunday, 4th August.

These were not unique events, and for the remainder of the war Home Guard demonstrations became very popular entertainment for the public, with units across the county appearing in a succession of events in the following years including Warship Weeks, War Weapons Weeks, Wings for Victory Weeks, and Salute the Soldier Weeks, all organised to persuade the public to invest in savings bonds and help finance the war effort. In addition, and from 1943, Holiday at Home events were organised in most towns as a means of reducing the 'load' on the transport system, both road and rail, which was then being extensively used, notably by the American forces which were coming into Britain as part of Operation BOLERO. Encouraging the population to take their holidays in their own locality consequently meant local authorities laying on and promoting entertainments. The Home Guard would increasingly be used as part of that public entertainment, notably during the latter part of the war.

The winter of 1941/42 saw reports of Home Guard social events in local papers, but these gave rise to concerns about casualties should large numbers of Home Guards be gathered in one place that was subject to a bombing raid. Warley Battalion Home Guard received a Birmingham Zone Order of 14th November to the effect that, until further orders were received, no Military

A poster produced by the Stourbridge Home Guard advertising an event at Hagley to celebrate the First Anniversary of its formation. The event proved to be a great success with the public and was repeated later in the year. (Author's collection)

A few men of the Warley Battalion relax after a strenuous time demonstrating their skills at the Brandhall Cross course, Warley. (Courtesy of Steve Taylor)

Dance or large gathering for pleasure purposes was to be organised within two miles of Birmingham Town Hall during the five nights on either side of the date of a full moon, and during such periods officers and other ranks were to be discouraged from congregating in large numbers at civil functions of similar or non-essential nature between the hours of 7pm and 5 minutes to midnight.[41] This clearly shows that the authorities feared a repeat of the air raid of 14th November 1940, when Coventry was heavily bombed during a period of full-moon.

America enters the war

Early in the morning, Pacific-time, of 7th December 1941, Japanese aircraft attacked the American fleet in Pearl Harbour, destroying four battleships, damaging many other warships, and killing 2,000 American sailors. On 11th December Germany and Italy declared war on the United States of America. This declaration was reciprocated by America.[42] The relief expressed by Winston Churchill that the Americans were now in the war must have been felt by all, (particularly so when American troops began to appear in this country during 1942).

As a result, the Christmas festivities of 1941 might have felt a little more hopeful than those of the previous year. Lt Colonel T.S. Lancaster MC, commander of the Warley Battalion, was not alone in wishing all ranks a Happy Christmas and Prosperous New Year,[43] but the Bromsgrove Battalion went a little further than most other battalions for this Christmas, when orders informed the men that guards and inlying pickets would not be mounted on the night of 25th/26th December 1941. Men who would normally be on duty that night were, however, to notify their platoon commander where they could be found, and be prepared to turn out in the event of an emergency.[44]

4   1942 – A year of change for the Home Guard

'… where the Home Guard is strong and efficient, the new arrangements [for compulsory service] will make very little difference. I cannot imagine any Home Guard resigning who thought that he had a job to do in fighting the Hun if the occasion came.'

From a lecture by Lord Bridgeman, Director General of the Home Guard, to officers of the Worcestershire Home Guard at the end of January 1941.

He was wrong!

Much was to change in the life of the Home Guard during 1942 and it was precipitated by the need for some of the Regular forces to be posted overseas in order to reinforce the troops fighting on the Mediterranean and Far East fronts, while those that remained in Britain, together with the Americans now arriving, prepared for the forthcoming campaign in north-west Europe. The Home Guard was expected to substitute for the Regulars on the Home Front in a number of ways, necessitating increased War Office control and compulsory service.

1st January 1942 saw the formal announcement that Home Guard service would be placed on a compulsory basis in the following month when Army Council Instruction No 151 was published. It was explained that members of the Home Guard were not required to give full-time service or live away from home, except when mustered. Volunteers would now be referred to as Privates and would be subject to military law, with military offences committed while on duty, before and after mustering, being dealt with under the prevailing regulations. Henceforth, a member of the Home Guard who absented himself from duty or parade, before mustering had been ordered, without reasonable excuse, would be subject to a maximum penalty of a fine of £10 (about £500 in today's money) or one month's imprisonment, or both. After mustering had been ordered, absence without leave and desertion would be dealt with under the Army Act. Members could now be ordered to perform a total of 48 hours training and operational duty every four weeks at the discretion of the company commander. After 16th February 1942, members would no longer be able to resign on giving 14 days notice in writing, and applications for discharge were only to be granted if the battalion commander felt there was justifiable cause. However, discharge from the Home Guard would not exempt a man from performing any alternative duty he might be directed to by the Ministry of Labour and National Service.[1]

The calling up of Home Guard officers and NCOs under the Conscription Acts for duties with the Regular Forces was also under consideration. The age for volunteers to the Home Guard remained unchanged (from 17 to 65) but the age of compulsory enrolment was to be the same as that for conscription to the Regular Forces, between 18 and 51.[2]

A study of Part 2 Orders of the various battalions indicates a number of reasons for discharge including:

a) having joined the armed services, usually on reaching the compulsory call-up age for the younger men in the Home Guard, although some volunteered for the Regular Services anyway.

b) changed conditions of employment, including pressure of work, long hours of working, being self-employed and so on, which prevented Home Guard duty. (As an example, Worcestershire Zone Order No 117 of 17th June 1942 drew attention to the importance of Home Guards who were employed in various branches of the food supply chain being placed in a class of members whose sudden withdrawal would dislocate essential food services.)

c) being declared medically unfit or incapacitated through industrial injury, or even Home Guard duty.

d) reaching the upper age limit of 65, although special exception could be, and was, made for some apparently indispensable Home Guards, whose continuing service would be extended on a 6 monthly basis.

e) death (one man of the Bromsgrove Battalion is recorded as being killed while not on duty by an anti-aircraft shell).

f) as being 'unsuitable', Army-speak for being useless. The reason for one man's dismissal is actually recorded as 'useless', another as 'dismissed with ignominy', and a third for being a 'registered conscientious objector'.

Before the watershed date a man would simply be dismissed for not attending parades and training, but after that date such behaviour would result in prosecution, a heavy fine, imprisonment, or one case the imposition of 14 days' hard labour. After that date prosecutions were regularly reported in the local newspapers along with the penalties imposed. This sort of evidence gives the lie to the impression that many people have that serving in the Home Guard was not a serious activity!

From a study of personnel records for the Worcestershire Battalions it is clear that many men did take the opportunity to resign from the force in the months preceding the introduction of compulsory service while they could still take advantage of the regulation that allowed the 14 days' notice period. Major Jewell, in his history of the Upton Company, recorded that 25 men out of a total of 400 took this opportunity, just over 6%.[3] However, the number of new volunteers coming forward for the force meant that some time would pass before compulsory enrolment would need to be invoked in the county.

Western Command Order No 190 of 4th February 1942 set out the hours of compulsory training, which were to be a minimum attendance of four hours on alternate Sundays and two hours in the evening during each week. The subsistence allowance admissible was to be: for a period of continuous duty of less than five hours, nil; for a period of 5 hours or more, one shilling and sixpence (about £3.75 now); and for a period of 8 hours or more, but less than 15 hours, three shillings (about £7.50 now). Any excess over 24 hours was to count as a fresh turn of duty.[4]

Many of the original volunteers were not in favour of the introduction of compulsory service and the more rigid discipline that came with it. In the lower

With the introduction of compulsory service in the Home Guard came the need for accurate record keeping of attendance for duty and training. An official register was produced by the War Office for the purpose, but in the case of the Kemerton Platoon an ordinary notebook sufficed. (Courtesy of Dave Devereux)

ranks protest would take the form of absence from parades, with the consequential appearance before the magistrates, and punishment. Not all officers were in favour either, but left their comments unsaid until later. One was Colonel R.W.A. Painter MC, Commander of O Sector and former commander of the Kidderminster Battalion who, responding to a presentation to him of a group photograph for his service with the battalion, given by his former colleagues in late 1944, said, amongst other things, that he thought that the introduction of compulsory service was 'the biggest mistake ever made'.[5]

The Worcestershire TAA called an extra meeting on 10th April to consider the development and progress of the Home Guard. The first item discussed was the total strength of the force which, on 1st March, was recorded as 17,400 all ranks, a decrease of approximately 1,600 since the previous October, a drop acknowledged as being largely due to resignations of men prior to the introduction of compulsory service. The previous authorised establishment for the county was 19,000 all ranks, but this had now been increased by the Central Midland District to 22,000. There was consequently a shortfall of 4,600, which would need to be made up by either voluntary enrolment or compulsory enrolment.[6]

The first unit in the county to resort to compulsory enrolment of men for the Home Guard in the county was the Redditch Battalion on 13th July. Evesham Battalion followed on 18th July, then the Malvern Battalion on 18th August, and Halesowen, Stourbridge and Stourport in September 1942. Bromsgrove and Dudley battalions had both made compulsory enrolments by the time of the TAA meeting in October, while the Worcester, Kidderminster, Oldbury and Warley Battalions would not need to institute the procedure until the following year.[7]

Bill Allington, who had became a platoon officer in the Stoke Prior Platoon by this time, recalls that not all the men enrolled compulsorily became efficient Home Guards, and that some were 'rum characters'. One man in particular was a real rogue and would regularly slip off whilst on duty, probably indulging in his passion for poaching. The man was finally court martialled for shirking his duties.[8] However, it would be 16th February 1943 before the first man was brought to book for dereliction of duty, when Corporal H. Smith of the Halesowen Battalion was tried by Field General Court Martial, under the provisions of the Army Act, having been accused of leaving his guard while on active service and without orders from his superior. He was found guilty and sentenced to 14 days' detention, the sentence being confirmed by the Sub Area Commander, who remitted the punishment.

The dubious honour of having the first man to be prosecuted in the civil courts for non-attendance at parades, under the new conditions of service for Home Guards, lies with the Evesham Battalion. This occurred on 27th April 1943, when Edward Grove was fined £5 for such non-attendance. Next came an Oldbury man on 12th August, who must have been a volunteer since the battalion did not need to invoke the compulsory enrolment procedure until the following year. The next battalion to prosecute a man for similar offences was Malvern on 24th August, followed by Redditch on 4th November.[9] Later in November, other men of the Redditch Battalion, which seems to have had more than its fair share of uncooperative men, were prosecuted and fined £5. One man was recorded as having missed training parades on 11 separate occasions, while another was threatened with 21 days in prison if the fine was not paid within 14 days.[10] An increase in prosecutions would be reported in the years 1943 and '44.

Representations were made to the War Office to the effect that in many cases men were being enrolled into the Home Guard without their credentials being previously checked by the police as required by the Army Council Instruction of 1940. Failure to carry out the instructions left an opening for undesirable men to enrol.[11] This misdemeanour was prevalent amongst the factory units which had up to now maintained a semi-autonomous approach to Home Guard affairs, and it was probably inevitable when the directors were in many cases also the senior officers of their Home Guard units. In the matter of enrolling their men in the Home Guard, they clearly felt that 'they knew best'. It is possible that the representations to the War Office had been made because George Fletcher, a one-time commander of the British Battalion of the International Brigade, had been appointed as the commander of the Rolls Royce Factory Home Guard Unit![12]

Some of the Home Guard exercises of 1942

Sunday, 8th February, saw a major Home Guard exercise, codenamed SNOWBALL, take place in the Pershore district. Probably influenced by the German attack on Crete in the previous year, this exercise was based upon supposed parachute landings by the enemy in considerable strength at Defford, the enemy having seized the airfield with the intention of effecting further landings. Home Guard mobile columns (see below) from the Evesham, Malvern and Worcester battalions were ordered to attack and retake the position. The Worcester column was established at Ramsden and was to attack the centre, the Malvern column at Wadborough, to attack on the right, while the Evesham Battalion, established to the south of Tyddesley Wood, was to attack from the left. The Worcester Battalion made a direct frontal attack to the north of Besford Court and was heavily engaged, while the Evesham Battalion found a bridge had been 'destroyed' and was forced to cross a brook (Bow Brook). The battalion followed this with a successful attack, drove the enemy from the village (Defford) and were in the course of assaulting the southern boundary of the main hostile position when the time limit for operations arrived. The Malvern column simultaneously attacked the west boundary of the position, where the 'Defford Aerodrome Defence Force', under Colonel Ames, acting as the 'enemy', made a resolute stand. The whole of the Home Guard engaged was under

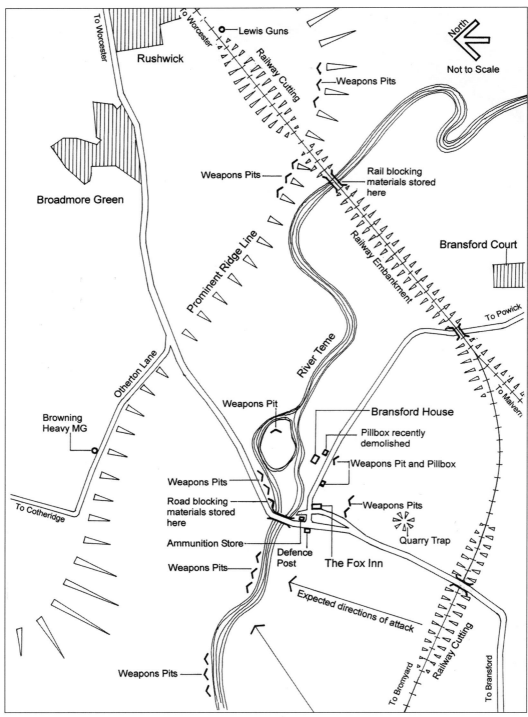

Fig.8 Bransford Bridge defences, based upon a defence appraisal by
Platoon Commander Ashley Break, December 1940

the command of Lt Colonel W.H. Taylor (CO of the Evesham Battalion Home Guard), with Captain Allen, a Regular Army Officer, as Adjutant. Colonel V.N. Johnson (CO of the Worcester Battalion Home Guard) was the chief umpire.[13] What appear to be brick-built defence positions have been recently discovered on the west side of the former airfield.[14]

Another major Home Guard exercise, codenamed GABB, took place on Sunday, 15th February, in south Worcestershire 'to resist an enemy invasion'. The exercise extended in a line from Tewkesbury to Knightwick and worked on the assumption that there had been 'enemy' landings somewhere between Bristol and Pembrokeshire and that the enemy were making a determined advance through to the Midlands. The 'enemy' was represented by the Free French and Belgian forces from Malvern. All Home Guard posts along the line of attack were manned and, in the Worcester area, were under the command of Colonel Gabb, Commanding Officer of No 23 ITC at Norton Barracks. The defending force included two Regular and Home Guard mobile columns.

Operations started at 10am, but there was little activity until noon when it transpired that the 'invading forces' were driving along two lines, one in the Callow End to Powick area, which was thought to be a feint, and another through Leigh Sinton towards Rushwick. Mobile columns attacked in the latter area and a 'heavy battle' developed. The 'enemy' broke through over Bransford Bridge, but the defenders counter-attacked, with the two Regular mobile columns (from Norton Barracks) advancing on the left flank from Crown East, and although the attack was held up by an 'enemy' armoured car 'destroyed' by the defending bombers, the bridge was retaken. (See Fig.8 for the defences around this bridge) A Worcester Home Guard mobile column had an exciting time on the Bransford road opposing the enemy armoured cars, but successfully rolled the enemy back.[15]

A good description of part of this exercise was discovered in a handwritten note in Major Kendall's papers, which provides a wonderful cameo of Home Guard actions:

> During an exercise with Mobile Free French forces, the road block at Leigh Sinton was partly erected with strong words and sweat by members of the platoon.
>
> After viewing the work with some satisfaction, the men of the platoon whose pigeon it was, retired to their respective positions of defence to await the battle.
>
> Some short time elapsed, when armoured forces were reported approaching the village from the direction of Hereford. Not a man could be seen except the local policemen outside his house. On came the vehicles towards the road block. The leading AFV [armoured fighting vehicle] treating the obstacle with contempt continued on its way at fair speed to brush the block aside.

The innocent looking 40 gallon drums, being full of concrete, withstood the assault with such good effect that the AFV ricocheted off a drum, crashed into a brick wall completely demolishing it. The effect of this contemptuous action against the platoon road block brought many faces with broad grins appearing from the most unexpected places.

Instead of a volley of murderous fire being directed onto the unfortunate vehicle, the crew were subjected to curses, ribald jests and riotous laughter from the Home Guard supported by the local policeman. On further examination it was found that the front axle, gearbox, etc. had been completely smashed.

Two officers following closely in a car made a quick appreciation, (too quick) for when turning their car to make a quick getaway, crashed themselves into a telegraph pole, thus completely blocking the road and holding up some 20 lorries and other transport for close on 30 minutes.

Overcoming their momentary surprise, it was felt that this was time for action and the platoon brought their weapons to bear with great effect (according to the umpires). But like all exercises, men prefer not to die, and one Home Guard was to be seen appearing with great care from behind a brick wall, clout a Frenchman on the head with a clod of earth with the words: 'Now will you die you b......!'

Although this story is told with some humour, it does illustrate that the Home Guard road blocks could impose delay on the 'enemy' as they were intended to do, and cumulatively would have disrupted the momentum that German Blitzkrieg techniques had relied upon for success.

Despite the desire of the authorities to replace stop-lines with defended localities and centres of resistance, Exercise AVON was conducted on 23rd February, the objects of which were to test the role of the Home Guard in the defences on the River Avon between Stratford and Bredon; to test the value of the stop-line; and to test communications and control. Those taking part were the Home Guard of L (Evesham) and D (part of Warwickshire) Sectors, the mobile columns of Nos 22 (Budbrook Barracks, Warwick) and 23 (Norton Barracks, Worcester) ITCs, Reconnaissance Units of the Czech Independent Brigade (from Leamington) and the Mobile Companies of the 30th and 32nd Royal Warwickshire Battalions (location not known).[16] Clearly, it would be some time before the concept of stop-lines would die completely!

The formation of Worcestershire Home Guard mobile columns

The exercises above show that the Home Guard was adopting a more aggressive stance by taking the fight to the 'enemy', rather than simply waiting for an attack on the fixed defences constructed in 1940/41 and expecting only the Regular Army's mobile columns to carry out the counter-attack role. However, it was not

Men of the 62nd Mobile Company somewhere in Malvern! The photograph is thought to have been taken somewhere near the Morgan Works, the base for this Mobile Company. It is thought that the officer with the swagger stick is Major G.L. Stone, the Company Commander. Of the other men, the following have been identified. In the back row are: 10th from the right, Reg Hill; 2nd from the right, H. Rowberry; 7th from the right, Peter Rowberry; and 8th from the right, Johnnie Johnson. In the 3rd row are: 3rd from the left, John Rowberry; 6th from the left, ? Garbutt; and 7th from the right, ? Cole. In the 2nd row are: 2nd from the left, Corporal Holt, 3rd from the left, Sergeant Thompson; 4th from the left, Sergeant Sam Beard; and 5th from the right is Jack Sheldon. (Courtesy of Mrs Smith, daughter of Jack Sheldon)

until a Worcestershire Sub Area instruction of 7th April 1942 was issued, that a comprehensive list of Home Guard mobile companies and platoons was recorded. This instruction forms the basis of Appendix 3. The instruction also explains that on mustering, mobile companies were to put their place of assembly in a state of defence and then be prepared to move out if required. Mobile companies were to be organised into three platoons of 40 for counter-attack purposes, the rest to remain in their assembly position. The companies were expected at this stage to move on foot or on bicycles to carry out tasks in their immediate vicinity (i.e. within 5 to 6 miles). They were to move in motor transport only when required further afield. This instruction does not include details of the Dudley, Oldbury or Warley Home Guard Battalions which were part of the Birmingham Defence Garrison. However, it is known from other sources that Dudley Battalion did form a mobile company.[17]

From various Part 1 and 2 Orders it has been possible to establish that the following battalions had designated mobile companies: Bromsgrove Battalion, No 61 Mobile Company, based at the Drill Hall, Bromsgrove; Malvern Battalion, No 62 Mobile Company, based at the Morgan Works, in Pickersleigh Road, Malvern; Redditch Battalion, No 63 Mobile Company, based at the Perkins Factory, Astwood

This group photograph is part of the 64th Mobile Company of the Stourbridge Battalion. It was apparently taken in 1942 at Stambermill, an area of open space to the east of Stourbridge used by the battalion for fieldcraft and battle training. Note that some of the men have webbing and the square ammunition pouches designed specifically for the Home Guard. (Courtesy of Derrick Pearson, who can be seen 3rd from the right in the back row. None of the other personnel have been identified.)

Bank; Stourbridge Battalion, No 64 Mobile Company, based at 13 Coventry Street, Stourbridge; and Dudley Battalion, Mobile Company (number not identified) based at Rosehill School, Titchbourne Street, Dudley.

Transport for the companies was to be in three Midland Red buses, with three lorries as load carriers and two cars. These were to be earmarked beforehand and borrowed for exercises or, in emergency, would be requisitioned from the owners. The role of the columns would be patrolling, ambush and counter-attack within a limited radius. This was intended to be within their sector, and it was not intended that the columns would fight on the move. Their purpose was solely to transport personnel to a threatened point, where they would fight on foot. The late Egbert Ganderton, of Cookhill Home Guard, recalled that the 63rd Mobile Column from Astwood Bank, of which he was a member, participated in an exercise in the Castle Bromwich area, which suggests that the columns could be called out to deal with an enemy attack outside the county where a key armaments factory might be attacked. For this exercise and others he was picked up from his home by lorry.[18]

For Home Guard mustering purposes, an allocation of private cars and load carrying vehicles had been made by Western Command for each battalion and the vehicles duly registered by April 1942. However, in view of the fact that many of these

Promised in April 1942, here we see War Department vehicles which had been delivered to the 62nd Mobile Company of the Malvern Battalion in time for the Third Birthday Parade in May 1943. An Austin 8hp Utility pick-Up, affectionately known as a 'Tilly' leads past Great Malvern Post Office, with a Morris 8cwt truck following. Both are towing Smith Guns. (Courtesy of Sheila Edmonds)

private cars were now wearing out and it was difficult to obtain tyres and spare parts, authority had been given for the issue of 278 War Department vehicles (described as two-seater utility cars or 8cwt trucks) to Home Guard units in the Central Midland District. These vehicles were intended for passenger work, conveyance of stores etc. within the battalions, and the strengths and areas covered by battalions were to be the main consideration in deciding the scale of issue. Also allocated to the Central Midland District were 318 WD motorcycles to be used by Home Guard personnel within the signal organisation. By April, all the permanent staff Adjutant/ Quartermasters at the battalions had received War Department vehicles to assist them in their duties, while the Permanent Staff Instructors who had been, or were about to be, appointed would also receive a WD vehicle or bicycle.[19]

Not everyone treated their WD vehicles carefully and by November of the following year Bromsgrove Battalion found it necessary to draw attention to the avoidable wastage of military vehicles due to both accidents, as a result of excessive speeds, and increased wear and tear. Consequently all drivers of the vehicles and motorcycles were to comply with the speed restrictions imposed by law at all times, the only exceptions being those authorised in an emergency and during training on the written orders of the competent military authority. Severe disciplinary action was going to be taken against drivers for exceeding speed limits and for dangerous driving.[20]

The role of the Halesowen Battalion was still primarily a static one in March 1942, with its road blocks covered by heavier weapons and mutually supporting defended localities, all forming part of a defensive belt around Birmingham and south Staffordshire. Nevertheless, a degree of mobility was implied when, at about this time, a Commando Section was being intensively trained by Captain H.B. Style, the then Second in Command of D Company, who had organised an assault course at The Leasowes, on land lent by Halesowen Golf Course.[21] This was not the only battalion to form a commando unit. The late Morris Jephcott, of the Redditch Battalion, recalled that Major Scott, the A Company (Alvechurch) Commander, also decided to form a striking force or Commando Unit. After suitable tests, including an oral test and a run from Alvechurch to Rowney Green firing range, where live firing was conducted, eight men were chosen from the three platoons of the Company, including Morris, who was appointed Corporal in charge of the Commandos. All were apparently crack shots and carried out extra training for their new role. This included going for runs and learning to swim in the deep end of Major Scott's swimming pool, both exercises in full kit. Morris also spent time with the Regular Commandos undergoing training.[22]

As a reflection of the greater mobility of the Home Guard during 1942, it was ordered by the Worcestershire Zone HQ that no new defence works were to be started unless they were of a minor nature and could be completed by 29th August that year.[23]

Home Guard transport columns formed

By 1942, units of the Royal Army Service Corps (RASC) employed on Home Defence duties were losing large numbers of men who were being transferred to the Field Army, and the Home Guard was seen as a source of manpower with which to supplement the transport needed for active operations in Britain. Twenty-six columns were consequently proposed across the country, with RASC officers providing a full-time adjutant and permanent instructors for each column. Vehicles were to be reserved from civilian sources on the basis that owners or drivers would drive their own lorry, but be members of the Home Guard should they be called out for active service.[24]

Expansion of the Home Guard transport organisation was approved on 27th September 1942, and two of the columns were formed in Worcestershire: No 2343 Worcestershire Home Guard Independent MT Platoon (Worcester) under the command of Captain R.W. Holder, and the No 2244 Worcestershire Home Guard Independent MT Platoon (Dudley) under Captain A.J. Bradley.[25] Both companies had 37 earmarked vehicles available, an equivalent number of drivers, and 14 cooks and artificers.[26] The Worcester Mobile Column referred to in Exercise GABB above was possibly that of Captain Holder and had been used to transport Home Guards from the city out to Bransford, but now its role was being expanded to substitute for the RASC.

The value of the Home Guard Independent Transport Platoons became apparent in the period leading up to D-Day in 1944, when the growing shortage of manpower in the Regular services and the withdrawal of a considerable part of the Royal Army Service Corps (RASC) second line transport, made it necessary to muster the Home Guard Independent Transport Platoons. Although transport units had been intended to operate within a defined area, personnel had been trained so that they could operate anywhere in the UK, should operational requirements dictate.[27]

In a farewell social event held by members of the Worcester MT Platoon, held at the Bridge Inn, Bridge Street, Captain Holder announced that the chief work of the column was little known to the public, with members giving up their Sundays to the removal by convoy of a great number of vehicles from the Midlands to other parts of the country.[28]

Home Guard rights of arrest

In March 1942, the War Office had announced the rights of Home Guards in connection with suspected persons. When in uniform and on duty, they had all the rights and duties regarding arrest and search of suspected persons, and the search of vehicles and premises, possessed by any other officer or soldier. They could stop and question any persons regarding identity and the purposes for which they were in the place where they were found. They could also arrest them without warrant and detain them pending enquiries, although every effort was to be made to report the facts to the police, and wherever possible the actual arrest was to be made by a constable. A Home Guard could also stop and search any vehicle at any place to which the public had access, and he could seize any article found therein which he had reasonable grounds for believing to be evidence of an offence against the Defence Regulations.[29]

Army Cadets and the Home Guard

As a response to a War Office letter of 17th January 1942, setting out the policy for expanding the Cadet Force, the County TAA had set up a Cadet Committee under the Presidency of Lord Cobham, and chaired by General Sir George Weir. Colonel Wiggin, Major C.F. Dyson Perrins and eight others formed the committee, while Colonel Du Sautoy was the County Cadet Commandant. By the time of the TAA meeting in April, it was noted that the Cadet Force had increased in numbers from the pre-war level of 400 cadets to 1,400, in the following units:

Stourbridge King Edwards School – a pre-war unit of 160 cadets, which was now affiliated to the Stourbridge Home Guard Battalion.

Wolverley Seabright School – also a pre-war unit of 60 cadets, which was also affiliated to the Stourbridge Home Guard Battalion.

New units were:

Halesowen Technical School – two companies of 200 cadets, affiliated to the Halesowen Home Guard Battalion.

Upton upon Severn – a platoon of 30 cadets affiliated to the Malvern Battalion.

Redditch – two platoons of 100 cadets affiliated to the Redditch Battalion.

Astwood Bank – a platoon of 30 cadets affiliated to the Redditch Battalion.

Alvechurch – a platoon of 30 cadets affiliated to the Redditch Battalion.

Worcester City – 200 cadets affiliated to the Worcester Battalion.

Stourbridge – 130 cadets affiliated to the Stourbridge Battalion.

Malvern – 30 cadets affiliated to the Malvern Battalion.

Dudley – three companies of 300 cadets affiliated to the Dudley Battalion.

Pershore – a company of 100 cadets affiliated to the Evesham Battalion.

Bromsgrove – a company of 100 cadets affiliated to the Bromsgrove Battalion.

Droitwich – two platoons of 60 cadets affiliated to the Bromsgrove Battalion.

It was noted that the TAA was responsible for claiming grants for cadets between the ages of 14 and 17, and that the cadet forces would in theory also be affiliated to the 7th Territorial Battalion of the Worcestershire Regiment and as a consequence entitled to wear the regimental cap badge. At this time the 7th Battalion was on its way to India, later to participate in the Burma Campaign, and would be able to provide little practical help to the cadets. The 7th Battalion would be reformed back in England in 1947 when it was then able to take the cadet force under its wing.

Articles in *The Kidderminster Times* and *Evesham Standard* of 25th April, explained that the cadets, whose ages range from 14 to 17, received instruction in squad drill and movements, rifle drill, elementary map reading, recognition of aircraft, signalling and field intelligence and that the Home Guard units to which the cadets were affiliated gave help in many ways.

The Army Cadet Force establishments in Worcestershire had enrolled some 2,000 boys by July 1942, and 2,250 by October. By this time, the enrolment into the Home Guard of boys between the ages of 16 and 17 had been proposed under the following conditions:

a) Boys were to be used as messengers only. They were to be enrolled on a scale which would not exceed two per Platoon HQ, two per Company HQ and four per Battalion HQ.

b) No boy would be enrolled without the written consent of his parent or guardian.

c) Preference in recruiting would be given to volunteers who were members of the Sea Cadets, Junior Training Corps or Air Training Corps.

The boys were to be trained in the same manner as other members of the Home Guard, including the use of arms where necessary.[30] However, it would be early January 1943 before the first transfers of cadets to the Home Guard was recorded, with the Malvern and Warley Battalions leading the way. Later that month came the first references to boy messengers (usually cadets) of less than the age of 17 being recruited by Bromsgrove and Malvern Battalions.[31]

Sergeant Hill of the Malvern Company of the Malvern Battalion directs the catering arrangements on Malvern Link Common during the Home Guard Third Anniversary celebrations. One of the cadets attached to the Malvern Battalion for training and use as messenger boys can be seen in the centre of the photograph. (Courtesy of Sheila Edmonds)

Road Safety for marching Home Guards

In the early hours of 23rd April, a motor car collided with a platoon of Home Guards who had been on night exercises, and were marching in threes from Broome towards Hagley. The platoon consisted of 17 NCOs and other ranks under the command

'Somewhere in the Black Country', the Lye Platoon of the Stourbridge Battalion are on a training route march during daylight hours. Marching at night, during the 'Blackout', was fraught with danger, and a Hagley Home Guard was to lose his life as a result of a car running into a marching column in the early hours of the morning of 23rd April 1942. (Courtesy of Dennis Chance)

of 2nd Lt L.A. Parkes and the accident occurred about 200 yards from Thicknall crossroads, knocking down two men. One of these, Thomas Owen Woodhouse, aged 50, suffered a fractured skull and right leg, and was taken by ambulance to Corbett Hospital for treatment. He subsequently developed pneumonia and died on 6th May. The driver of the car and his passenger both said that they had seen nothing until the impact. A verdict of accidental death was brought by the coroner.[32]

A repeat accident almost occurred five days later, when a motorist, George Day, drove between two files of marching Home Guards at about 9.45pm on the Stourbridge Road at Fairfield. Despite being signalled by the Second in Command of the column to stop, the motorist did not pull up or appear to slacken his speed. Fortunately, the marching men heard the warning and broke formation, allowing the car to pass between them before hitting the pavement. Day was charged with driving without due care and attention, fined £2 19 shillings (about £150 now), ordered to pay costs and disqualified from driving for one month.[33]

On 2nd May a Worcester Zone HQ instruction required that it should be impressed upon every officer and NCO who might be in charge of a party of troops moving on the public highway during the hours of darkness, that it was essential to have a look-out man some 40 or 50 yards both ahead and to the rear of the party to warn motorists of their presence and to minimise the risk of accidents.[34]

The anti-aircraft role of the Home Guard

As we have already seen, factory Home Guards in Worcestershire had mounted one or more of their automatic weapons on the roof of their factory to form at least some anti-aircraft defence for their firm. However, manpower shortages in the Regular Army in late 1941 led to a demand for the transfer of 50,000 men from Anti-Aircraft Command to the Field Force, significantly reducing the anti-aircraft cover for Britain.

General Sir Frederick Pile, GOC Anti-Aircraft Command, not wishing to have anti-aircraft guns and rocket batteries unmanned, put forward the idea of utilising women of the ATS and men from the Home Guard to supplement the Regulars of his command.[35] By 1942, training of Home Guards for anti-aircraft duty began and the first indication that this policy was being implemented in Worcestershire was in May 1942, when 43 men were transferred from the Bromsgrove Battalion to the Birmingham Anti-Aircraft Command. More were transferred from the Evesham Battalion in January 1943 to the Gloucestershire AA Command; from the Dudley Battalion to the Birmingham Command in March 1943, together with others from Oldbury Battalion in October 1943 and more in February 1944. Transfers to Z Batteries (rockets) (see Fig.9) were also made from Bromsgrove and Dudley Battalions in September 1942; from Redditch Battalion in

Fig.9 A Z Battery anti-aircraft rocket projector. The battery illustrated could simultaneously launch two anti-aircraft rockets, but launchers capable of accommodating up to 20 rockets were developed. The rockets, or 'unrotated projectiles', were 6ft 4ins long and carried a 22lb warhead up to a maximum of 19,000ft altitude. The rockets would be adjusted to explode at a preset time.

September 1943; and from the Kidderminster Battalion to Glamorgan (presumably as a result of men being moved from work in one factory to another) in August 1944.[36]

An interview of a Home Guard in Tewkesbury, who had been transferred to one of the heavy 3.7 inch calibre anti-aircraft gun sites around Staverton Airfield, indicated that the men were picked up each evening from the centre of Tewkesbury by army lorry and deposited at the gun site. There they would be officered by men of the Royal Artillery, and trained in the use of the gun by the Regulars, taking their place in the gun teams when they had become proficient. After spending the night on the gun site, they would then be returned to Tewkesbury, in time to go to work the next morning![37] It is assumed that the same arrangements applied to those Worcestershire Home Guards transferred to the nearby out of county AA sites.

However, besides the 'leakage' of Home Guards from Worcestershire to anti-aircraft batteries in the Birmingham Gun Defended Area and elsewhere, within Worcestershire itself the following Light Anti-Aircraft Troops were to be formally established in 1944: one troop from the Oldbury Home Guard to protect the Accles and Pollock factory with ten twin light machineguns (LMGs), and with enough men appointed to provide four relief crews for each of the gun positions; at Redditch 'A Troop' was formed to protect the Reynolds Tube factory, with six twin LMGs and four relief crews, and 'B Troop' to protect the High Duty Alloys factory, with four twin LMGs and again four relief crews. In this context, the LMGs were almost certainly pairs of Lewis Guns on anti-aircraft stalk mountings.[38]

Although initially operated by Royal Artillery gunners, the heavy anti-aircraft gun sites at Frankley and Hollywood and the Rocket Battery at Cofton protecting the Longbridge Aero factory, although all located in Worcestershire, were to be eventually operated by Home Guards from the Warwickshire Zone.

The arrival of TRE and ADRDE in Malvern boost the numbers of Home Guards
Late May 1942 saw the arrival in Malvern of many hundreds of scientists and their support staff, as part of the move of the Telecommunications Research Establishment (TRE) to Malvern College,[39] and the Air Defence Research and Development Establishment (ADRDE) from the Dorset/Hampshire area to Pale Manor. Being employed in reserved occupations, many were already members of the Home Guard and were transferred from their respective Dorset and Hampshire battalions, while new staff, recruited from universities and coming direct to Malvern, were compulsorily required to join the Home Guard. Because their work was so very secret and of national importance, the platoons raised by these two scientific establishments tended to operate on a semi-independent basis and, rather like the factory Home Guards elsewhere, provide a defence force largely for their own establishments. Nevertheless their numbers boosted the size of the Malvern

Lieutenant J.B. Walker, Commander of the ADRDE Home Guard unit at Malvern, with some of his men. In the back row, from the left are: unknown, unknown, unknown, Ken Griffin, Tony Black, Les Young and Reg Taylor. In the front row, from the left are: Curly Brown, unknown, J.B. Walker, unknown, and unknown.
(Courtesy of the late Don Tomlin)

Battalion Home Guard substantially and brought the battalion strength to near the planned establishment figure.[40]

The Superintendent of TRE, A.P. Rowe, who apparently was not a great supporter of the Home Guard at TRE because their training would inevitably interfere with their always urgent work in connection with the development of radar, circulated a missive to the staff. This required all the technical staff to state: 'I am employed on vital work at a Ministry of Aircraft Production Research Establishment. My hours of duty are liable to be long and irregular. I have instructions from my Superintendent to state that owing to the shortage of technical experts in the country, my service in the Home Guard is quite impractical since it must of necessity interfere with the important duties to the state which I am required to undertake. The Superintendent asked that, if necessary, reference should be made to Sir Frank Smith, Controller of Telecommunication Equipment.'[41] Nevertheless, TRE did have a large Home Guard contingent which would later be designated as the very aggressive sounding 'T Battle Group' (see Appendix 4).

The summer camps begin and Worcestershire plays host to outside battalions

Approval had been given on 24th March by the Worcestershire Sub District Headquarters for holding Home Guard weekend training camps in the county in 1942.[42] However, it would be some time before camps could be organised, one of the first being that of D Company of the Redditch Battalion Home Guard on 16th May, at Berrow Hill Farm near Feckenham.[43] Home Guard units from outside the county also found it convenient to hold their camps in the Worcestershire countryside. For example later in that month, 50 men of the 29th Warwickshire Battalion Home Guard held their camp at Barnt Green, while the 22nd Warwickshire Battalion held theirs at Weatheroak Hill, near Wythall.[44]

Later, the GPO Home Guard held their training camp on Lickey Hill School playing field at Rednall, when visitors to the camp were the Post Master General, Mr W.S. Morrison MC KC and Major General P.G. Johnson VC CB DSO MC. The former said that it was evident that the GPO Home Guard had reached a fine state of efficiency, and he was quite sure that if invasion came the units would give a good account of themselves.[45]

Home Guard cooks at work! These men of the Malvern Battalion are using a cooker of distinctly home-made appearance. Construction of a field cooker using easily obtained materials would have formed part of the cooks' training. (Courtesy of Sheila Edmonds)

More Home Guard weekend camps were held in a greater variety of locations in Worcestershire during 1942, and by a greater number of units, than the previous year (see Appendix 9 for a list of known Home Guard camp sites in the county), although it was not a happy experience for everyone. Private R.F. Smith from Birmingham was injured while bathing in the river at Holt Heath; he had dived into shallow water and was detained in the Worcester Royal Infirmary, where he was said to be 'very poorly'.[46]

The regular weekend, and apparently popular, summer Home Guard camps brought a demand for hot meals and efficient cooks. Battalion catering officers were appointed as a response not only to ensure the provisioning of Home Guard units on active duty, but also to supply the camps. The need for adequate camp catering was reflected in a Warley Battalion Order of 13th July, which reminded all ranks that names of those attending the camp at Lapal Farm were to reach the Battalion HQ, giving the Catering Officer 14 days notice for arrangement of rations.

Leave granted and reduced duties for Home Guards

Possibly as a result of the expanded role of the Home Guard from this year onwards, what appears to be the first reference to the concept of Home Guards taking leave from duties was made by Halesowen Battalion, when certain officers were allowed leave from duty in July 1942.[47] Granting leave for other ranks would follow, particularly in the Black Country battalions in 1943 and 1944, where it can be appreciated that men working long hours in the munitions industries would want a break from duty to overcome the tiredness being experienced by many Home Guards. Warley Battalion, for example, granted leave of absence for a total of 63 NCOs and privates in batches for periods of up to two weeks during July. Long lists of men allowed leave in August and September were also recorded.[48]

During November, Halesowen Battalion introduced one free Sunday in every month as an apparently welcome innovation during the closing weeks of the year having, in addition to week-nights training, held a parade every Sunday, except at holiday periods, since the formation of the battalion.[49]

Airborne attacks against vulnerable points expected

With the steady expansion of American forces in Britain during 1942 and afterwards as part of Operation BOLERO, the likelihood of the Germans attempting a full-scale invasion of Britain decreased. However, an enemy airborne attack was expected as a measure of counter-preparation against the build-up of Allied armies, and a means of retaliation to raise the morale of the German people. The size and timing of the attack was seen as resting on secrecy and surprise. Consequently defence plans for the Midlands, particularly, would change in emphasis to protecting production, airfields, communications, sources of petrol, stores and dumps, and other vulnerable points, against an airborne attack. While the chances of a seaborne invasion of Britain were now remote, it was nevertheless seen as a possible desperate measure, combined with an airborne action, leading to an advance towards the industrial areas of the Midlands from the east or south-west. The primary role of the Home Guard would continue to be to impose the maximum delay on the enemy by the provision of reconnaissance and fighting patrols, destruction of parachutists within a limited radius, together with action by the mobile companies as ordered. Observation and prompt reporting of enemy movements, providing guides for Regular units, and immobilisation of resources, would all continue as part of its responsibilities. The most favourable time for an attack was now predicted to be in broad daylight, on a weekday, when most of the Home Guards would be at work, and just after the early morning mists in the Severn valley and around the Black Country canals had cleared. As part of the defence planning for the Midlands, an increased scale of guards for vulnerable points was to be organised and codenamed VITGUARD.[50]

A Birmingham Garrison Operation Instruction explained that the VITGUARD policy was to provide a means of defeating any attempt to sabotage factories and to destroy any enemy troops landed by air. All Home Guards except those on duty at anti-aircraft sites were to be available as reinforcements to the vulnerable points guard and mobile companies. Regular troops and US troops were to be treated as reserves.[51]

A sequence of code words was established to bring the VITGUARD troops to readiness and then to action in increasing numbers, as follows:[53]

> STAND TO – when conditions for invasion were favourable.
> ACTION STATIONS – when there was an immediate threat of invasion.
> OLIVER – when Home Guards were to muster.
> BOUNCER – when some Home Guard Mobile Companies were to be provided.
> BUGBEAR – when additional Mobile Companies were to be called out.

Home Guard signals system to be established

Since 1940, the Home Guard had been part of the BEETLE system for gathering intelligence on any enemy attack on Britain, and responsible for passing information to the Observer Corps and local Regular units which, by telephone and wireless, communicated the information to the area commands and onto GHQ. By 1942, the greater mobility of the Home Guard dictated that they too should have a signals capability. In order to provide sufficient staffing arrangements for the Home Guard signals on operations, the Bromsgrove Battalion, for example, ordered that the companies were to train 5% of their personnel for signal duties and that a signal office was to be staffed by trained signallers, while Battalion HQ was to form a signal section of 30 signallers. The Battalion Signals Officer was to be responsible for the training of company signallers.[53] Sector commands would also form part of

The Headquarters Signals Section of the Worcester City Battalion taken at the Southfield Street Drill Hall in Worcester, at Stand Down. Semaphore flags and signalling lamps are prominent in front of the men, while less obviously a couple of the men display their crossed flags signals badges on their sleeves. Of the men, only Peter Whittaker (2nd from the left in the back row), Harold Bramwell (5th from the left in the same row), John Court (3rd from the left in the 2nd row), and William Bramwell (with RSM crowns on his sleeves and 2nd from the left in the front row) are identified. It is assumed the officer sitting in the centre of the front row is the battalion Signals Officer, Lieutenant W.H. Cale. (Courtesy of Harold Bramwell)

the Home Guard signals system, and would be some of the first to receive No 18 and No 38 radio sets on which to train.

In the light of his experience of running a radio shop in Stourport, Home Guard Bill Harper was asked to transfer from the Parsons Chain Company Home Guard unit to the newly formed O Sector Headquarters staff at The Larches, Kidderminster, and train to be a signaller. Most of his subsequent signals work was done on No 18 radio/telephone sets which were carried as a back pack. Plain speech would be used, and although he did learn Morse Code, he did not have any training on the less sophisticated signals flags or lamps. In the event, the wireless sets were usually used at the rifle range for signalling the scores between the butts and the firing points, and occasionally on exercises, when the normal telephone hand set would be used or occasionally a throat mike.[54] The date that radio telephone sets were issued to the Home Guard in Worcestershire is not clear, although Exercise CRACKERS was organised for 30th October 1942, to practise the Central Midland Area and Sub Area staffs, the Home Guard sector staffs, and all Home Guard units in their operational roles, specifically testing signals communications and liaison with the RAF and police.[55] This is an indication of the more coordinated approach to communications needed by the now more mobile Home Guard, and may indicate when wireless sets were first issued.

Home Guards get their own radio programme

At 1.45pm on 27th September, the BBC broadcast the first of a weekly Sunday feature programme, *For Home Guards only*.[56] This is a reference to a topical programme made at Wood Norton and presented by the then Captain Sydney Carter of the Evesham Battalion, during which he and another Home Guard, who would be different every week, would give answers to written queries about Home Guard matters which had been sent to the BBC in London.[57]

Major Sydney Carter, Training Officer of the Evesham Battalion is in the centre of the back row in this group photograph of the training staff taken in 1941 at the Wickhamford Manor Battalion Training School. Note the medal ribbons on many of the staff, indicating a wealth of military experience. (Courtesy of The Vale of Evesham Historical Society)

Biographical note on Major Sydney Carter

Sydney Carter had been farming with his father and at the beginning of the First World War joined the Royal Flying Corps. He served initially as a despatch rider, subsequently becoming an observer in France, and then transferring to anti-aircraft duties in England. After the war he turned to politics, standing as a Liberal, and unsuccessfully challenged Stanley Baldwin for the Bewdley Division in the 1929 election. In later years he was employed by the National Farmers Union at its Stratford office, dealing with agricultural insurance. He was also an experienced broadcaster on countryside matters. He was awarded the MBE in the 1943 New Year Honours list.[58] He joined the LDV in Evesham in May 1940 and rose through the ranks to become the Battalion Training Officer and then the HQ Company Commander with the rank of Major. He served with the battalion until it was disbanded in 1945. This larger than life character lived with his wife on the Broadway Road out of Wickhamford.

Full-time Quartermasters and Permanent Staff Instructors appointed

The full-time Adjutant/Quartermasters who had been authorised by the War Office in 1941, all now Regular officers in each of the battalions, could no longer cope with the increased training demands brought by compulsory service in the Home Guard and the growing administrative complexity of the force. This led the War Office to authorise the appointment of separate full-time Quartermasters (QMs) of officer rank and Permanent Staff Instructors (PSIs) of NCO rank to the battalions. By the time the TAA met on 2nd October 1942, nine QMs had been appointed and a further three recommendations had gone forward. There were to be 19 Permanent Staff Instructors of which 15 had already been posted to the battalions and four more allotted from the Command Pool. The TAA had also continued to give battalions assistance with clerical duties, for which the average expenditure was approximately £50 (about £2,500 today) per battalion per month, although some battalions were much below this figure.

Bridge demolition policy for Worcestershire

In the summer of 1940, any bridge stood the chance of being demolished with explosives to delay the movement of attacking enemy columns, but by 1942 a more selective policy had evolved, set out in the Worcestershire Sub Area Operational Instructions of 31st October. The road bridges listed for demolition were Bewdley, Stourport, Holt and Upton upon Severn, and the railway bridge over the Severn at Worcester. Demolition parties at each bridge were to consist of Royal Engineers supplied by the Officer Commanding No 692 (AW) Company RE, with covering parties, consisting of an officer and 30 men from the local Home Guard.[59]

The road bridges at Worcester, Evesham and Pershore were not included in this list because they carried roads considered to be essential to keep open for use by military traffic, and for use in any counter-attack against enemy forces coming from the south-east or the west. Road blocks on these roads consequently had to be robust enough to stop enemy armoured columns, but capable of being dismantled quickly by the Home Guard garrison to allow Regular and Home Guard mobile counter-attack columns through.

Home Guards receive military honours at their funerals

The War Office had instructed that those men who died while on duty should receive military honours, but that it was a matter for each battalion to decide whether or not it should be a feature of funerals for men who died in other circumstances. Perhaps the comradeship that had developed within the Home Guard was reflected in the fact that at the funeral of Corporal Walter John Brotherton, aged 67, of 85 Vicarage Road, Wollaston, which took place at St James's Church Wollaston on 24th October, he was given full military honours by men of his battalion. Corporal

Brotherton had been a headquarters Corporal attached to the Stourbridge Battalion Home Guard and until shortly before his death took an active part in Home Guard proceedings. He had volunteered for military service at the time of the Boer War, served in the Great War in Egypt and Palestine, been transferred to the reserve at the cessation of hostilities and volunteered again during the present war. Although not accepted by the Army, he had joined the Home Guard. He was a former member of the Staffordshire Volunteers and later the Territorials. Men of the Stourbridge Battalion Home Guard clearly decided that he should have full military honours and preceded the cortège to the church, where guards of honour were formed by officers and men, through which the coffin, draped with the Union Jack, was borne by six corporals. The Home Guard stood to attention at the graveside, whilst the battalion bugler sounded the 'Last Post', after which the officers and men filed past the grave giving a final salute.[60]

Bomb disposal units transferred to the Home Guard
Civilian Auxiliary Bomb Disposal Units had been formed by Ministry of Aircraft Production factories at the end of the Battle of Britain. These units could establish safety zones around unexploded bombs on the factory premises and carry out preliminary excavations, so that Royal Engineer Bomb Disposal Units could more readily deal with the bombs and speed the return to production. At the height of the night blitz in December 1940, the scheme was extended by the War Office to include all factories carrying out government production. The scheme was further extended in June 1941 to allow bomb disposal teams to be an integral part of a factory Home Guard and wear an appropriate badge. By September 1942, it was decided to transfer the pre-existing civilian teams to the Home Guard.[61] A list, dated 15th November 1942, of Auxiliary Bomb Disposal Units being prepared to transfer to the Home Guard, included for the West Midlands:

- a squad of 30 men led by C. Teague at Accles and Pollock Ltd, Paddock Works, Oldbury;
- a squad of 15 men led by M.J. Hayes at the Air Defence Research and Development Establishment (ADRDE), at Pale Manor, Malvern;
- a squad of 16 men led by C.I. Brunt at High Duty Alloys, Redditch;
- a squad of 16 men led by A.W. Phillips at the Royal Ordnance Factory, Blackpole, Worcester;
- a squad of 15 men led by G. Moore at Messrs Stewarts and Lloyds Ltd, Coombs Wood Tube Works, Halesowen; and
- a squad of 16 men led by P.A. Darlington at Tube Products Ltd, Popes Lane, Oldbury.

The primary role of these Home Guard units was bomb disposal within their work premises, with a secondary role as infantry.

Part of the ADRDE Bomb Disposal 15 man squad with Lieutenant Mick Hayes, the Squad Commander, seated in the centre of the front row. The bomb is clearly for effect, having lost its fuse and fins and, presumably, the explosive filling.
(Courtesy of the late Don Tomlin)

Each unit was to form part of the battalion covering the area in which it was formed, with the battalion being responsible for general administration of the unit, for the provision of clothing and personal equipment, for matters of discipline and finance, and for its training. Each unit was affiliated to a Bomb Disposal Company of the Royal Engineers and came under its orders for all bomb disposal operations and bomb disposal training.[62]

Clifford Lord, then an apprentice in the Maintenance and Engineering Department of the Royal Ordnance Factory (ROF) at Blackpole, enrolled in the Home Guard there in 1942 and was invited to join the Bomb Disposal Unit. He recalls Captain Phillips of the Royal Engineers welcoming him to the unit with the words: 'Welcome to the Suicide Squad!' He estimated that by the time he joined there were about 30 people in the ROF Bomb Disposal Unit and their training was very thorough and extensive. It included study of the various bomb types and their characteristics, the effect of blast on buildings, soil types and the need for, and techniques of, shoring up the excavations, removal of fuses, slinging and lifting bombs from the excavations using shear legs and strops, then placing bombs carefully on sandbags in the back of a lorry, and driving very carefully to the destruction site. In some cases it was not possible to remove the fuses and loading such bombs required the utmost care, as did the driving away! Cliff remembers vividly the phenomenon of hairs standing up on the back of his neck and the prickling sensation in his skin when handling live bombs.

The primary task of the ROF Bomb Disposal Unit was to deal with unexploded bombs which might fall in or near the factory site. Fortunately, this did not occur, although Clifford could remember being called to deal with unexploded bombs elsewhere in the vicinity of Worcester. After this intense technical training, Clifford did not care too much for arms drill, although the ROF Home Guard were well trained in the use of infantry weapons.[63]

5   1943 – A continued threat of Paratroop Attack

'The Home Guard might well share the motto of the Royal Artillery – Ubique – for they are everywhere. And if the Nazi villains drop down upon us from the skies, any night on a raid or heavy attack upon the key production centres, you will make it clear to them that they have not alighted in the poultry run, or in the rabbit farm, or even in the sheep fold, but that they have come down in the lions' den at the zoo.'

From Winston Churchill's broadcast from Washington on 14th May 1943

In a letter from the Commander in Chief Home Forces, General J. Pagett, dated 28th December 1942, to all Home Guard commanders, he included:

The Field Army when organised and equipped for the offensive will be a much more powerful and mobile force, whether for the purpose of operations overseas or of defeating an attempt to invade this country. The strength of the Field Army which can be made available for overseas, will, however, be directly related to the state of efficiency of the Home Guard; and, should invasion again be threatened, the Field Army will rely as much as ever upon the system of defended localities held by the Home Guard to check and delay the enemy, and thereby to create the opportunity for decisive counter stroke.[1]

1943 would see the continuing build-up of troops and equipment in Britain for the planned invasion of the continent (Operation BOLERO). Congestion on both the road and rail systems was ameliorated by generally concentrating units of the British and Canadian Field Armies in the east side of the UK, whilst the Americans would be temporarily accommodated in the west of the country – the side on which they arrived, including Wales. In June 1944, and for the same reasons, the Americans would leave for the invasion beaches via the south-west coast ports. Consequently, Worcestershire would see many American troops accommodated as well as the construction of a number of temporary hospitals to handle the post-D-Day casualties in relative quietude. In the short term, these hospital buildings, together with camps that had been vacated by British troops, a number of tented camps as well as requisitioned buildings, were used as short-term accommodation for field units of the American Army. Malvern had a particularly large American presence during this period and later, but most of the large towns in the county would have their contingents. The American supply organisation was concentrated in and around Cheltenham, but impinged on Worcestershire with the construction of a large storage depot at Honeybourne, and the use and expansion of pre-existing facilities such as the Ashchurch depot on the county border with Gloucestershire, and the petrol depots at Stourport. Protection of transport communications and airfields, as well as the increasing numbers of vulnerable points being created in the county, became paramount. All units in the Worcestershire Sub District, including Home Guard battalions, were given a clear indication that the possibility of an airborne attack was still expected in the form of enemy spoiling attacks during the build-up of men and stores for the Allied invasion of the Continent.

The instructions were intended to amplify the existing provisions of Worcestershire Sub District defence plans. All Regular and Home Guard units were therefore to be aware of to whom they should report landings of enemy paratroops, as investigation had shown that this had not always been satisfactory. It was explained that enemy paratroops could land in, on, or near a vulnerable point or airfield for the purpose of sabotage, to act as agents, or to save their lives if their aircraft was damaged; that the paratroop landings were possible by day and night, at dawn or dusk; and that paratroops might jump from below 300 feet with equipment that could include automatic machine guns, mortars, rifles, grenades and bicycles, besides special equipment for demolition purposes, depending upon their mission. Home Guard OPs and patrols were to inform their battalion which would then inform the Sub District HQ.

Local commands were to be responsible for arranging a warning system whereby the transmission of a local alarm could be carried out by phone, runners, and presumably the wireless arrangements organised in the previous year. The local police, civil defence organisation and such vulnerable points as might be directly threatened, would be included in the warning system. Alarms were not to be transmitted by means of sirens, handbells, whistles, rattles or 'stromos horns' (whatever they were). Paratroops were considered to be at their most vulnerable during their descent or immediately on landing, before they had time to orientate themselves, collect their equipment, reform themselves or disperse and hide. It was then that they were to be attacked ruthlessly and vigorously. Rapidity of action and determination to destroy the enemy was considered to be essential for success against what were considered to be the 'really tough types' expected as paratroops. Initiatives by junior commanders, especially of sections and platoons, were therefore to be developed to the maximum. The Home Guard were expected to have admirable opportunities to use their local knowledge in such an action.[2]

As a reflection of the move towards increasing Home Guard mobility to meet the threat of parachutists, 91 officers and men under the command of Captain G.L. Stone were transferred from HQ Company of the Malvern Battalion to the 62nd Mobile Company. A further 38 officers and men were later added from M Company.[3] Concomitant with the increasing mobility and an emphasis on anti-paratroop operations, unit commanders were to make a survey of their areas and were to dispense with all slit trenches, weapon pits, barbed and coiled wire which no longer served any useful purpose. Trenches and weapon pits were to be filled in and wire collected and stored at the unit HQ.[4]

Defending Birmingham in 1943

Operational Orders for the 39th Warwickshire (Birmingham) Battalion Home Guard set out the characteristics of the Birmingham defences, which impinged on north Worcestershire. In the country areas outside the Birmingham defences, the aim was defence in depth within a framework of Anti-Tank Islands and Centres of Resistance. Interspersed among these were mobile columns, some of Regulars, others of Home Guard. The penetration of the Birmingham Defence Area was to be prevented and all enemy troops who attempted such penetrations by air or land, were to be located and destroyed by local enterprise if in small numbers, or by coordinated action if in large numbers.

The Birmingham Defence Area was divided into five main sectors and one reserve sector. The five main sectors consisted of a series of Centres of Resistance (Cs of R) in depth, forming a belt around the city). (Confusingly, all the Cs of R are shown as Defended Localities or 'Studs' on later defence maps for Birmingham, see Fig.10.) The garrison of each C of R was to reflect the size and importance of the area to be held, but would have not less than one Battle Company of three Battle Platoons, and at least a quarter of its strength would be held as a local reserve to counter-attack the enemy in the immediate vicinity, the principle being to counter-attack to retain rather than regain. Defence was to be aggressive at all times. Paratroops which might land in the immediate vicinity (defined as between ¼ and ½ mile) of a C of R were to be dealt with by the nearest troops, static or mobile. Counter-attack between static centres was the duty of reserves located for that purpose outside Cs of R. Patrols from Cs of R were to be limited to small recce patrols, sent out to locate the enemy and to keep touch on the flank. Fighting patrols were to be found from counter-attack reserves, and not from the garrisons of Cs of R. All units were to arrange for sufficient OPs to ensure that all areas within the defences, whether open or built up, were watched for paratroops landing.

Boundaries between sectors and sub-sectors conformed approximately to civil police and ARP boundaries in order to promote liaison with those authorities. The list of mobile companies included No 23 Company found by the 24th Warwickshire

Battalion Home Guard of the Birmingham garrison with an operational role for the Lickey Hills.

Stretcher bearers, with equipment, were to be on duty in each centre to render immediate first aid to casualties. Stretcher cases, and other cases, were to be conveyed to a casualty collecting post. Each C of R was to have its own casualty collecting post which was to be within ½ mile of the battle position. These posts were to provide only essential first aid, warmth and shelter, pending evacuation of the wounded. A dwelling house, or better an ambulance room or first aid post was to be selected.[5] Clearly the Birmingham Garrison had by this time taken to heart the wishes of General Sir Alan Brooke, referred to earlier, and had dispensed with lines of defence. These new defence arrangements were features in some of the Home Guard exercises of 1943.

Some Home Guard exercises in 1943

On the weekend of 6th/7th February, Exercise SAUCE was held, when mobile columns and counter-attack battalions of the Birmingham garrison were involved in an 'attack' on Worcester.[6] These mobile columns and counter-attack battalions were employed again in a second 'attack' on Worcester on 7th September. No details of either of these exercises have been found, but they do illustrate the distance mobile Home Guard units were now expected to move to take on the 'enemy', and how much Worcestershire was still seen as the outer defence for Birmingham.

One of the Birmingham mobile units was the so-called Banshee Squadron, manned by students of Birmingham University at Edgbaston. A former member of this rapid reaction force, John Ralphs, recalled that they were to be transported very quickly to wherever enemy parachutists were landing and attack them before they had had time to form up. For this role, the students would practice embussing and debussing from high-sided lorries. He remembers that debussing the whole section would take 19 seconds from the time the lorry sides were dropped. To achieve this the students would hit the ground running, but woe betide anyone who stumbled because he would have the next man land on him! Because the Banshee Squadron was made up of students who were already members of the University Senior Training Corps they had, unusually for Home Guards, both SMLE service rifles and Bren guns in their armoury.[7]

Men of the Oldbury Battalion were informed that an exercise would take place on the weekend of 6th/7th March. Consequently all centres of resistance and posts in their area were to be fully manned and all officers, NCOs and other ranks would be required to parade, except those who were actually at work.[8] The Birmingham Garrison War Diary explained that, for Exercise BUBBLE, it was assumed that the 'enemy' was already in contact with the outer Birmingham defences in the north and had entered Dudley from the west, where fighting was in progress. No other threat

Responsible for a stretch of the outer defences of Birmingham on the west side of the city, these men of the Warley Battalion prepare for an exercise 'somewhere in the Black Country'. (Courtesy of Steve Taylor)

from the north was expected. To the south-west, 'enemy' columns of up to brigade strength appeared to be approaching, one having reached Bromsgrove, the other Hagley. No indication of their strength at Dudley was given. No other threat from the north-west was apparent. The deductions reached were that: enemy infiltration from Dudley, or for that matter anywhere in the sector, could be expected from midnight onwards, and that no information from police or civil sources could be expected as the enemy were already in occupation.

The intention of the exercise was to stop the enemy penetrating the defences, coupled with the destruction of any hostile troops who succeeded in infiltrating between the Centres of Resistance (Cs of R). To achieve this, the Cs of R were to be occupied. At midnight on the night of 6th/7th March, men, other than those on duty at the outer road blocks, on patrol, or on sentry duty at the Cs of R were to rest undercover, but be prepared to take up battle positions if required. 'Stand To' was to be at 6.30am.

Traffic and pedestrians were to be examined at the outer road blocks during the hours of darkness. Road blocks were to be assumed to be fully blocked throughout the exercise but in actual practice were not to be erected even partially until 7am to avoid accidents; even then they were to be only half blocked. After daylight, no

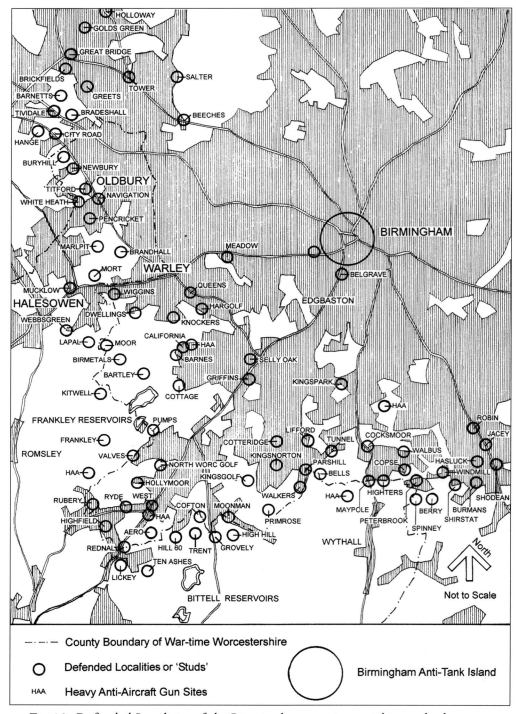

Fig.10 Defended Localities of the Birmingham garrison within and adjacent to Worcestershire

interference with traffic or pedestrians was to be made except for the 'enemy' whose personnel and vehicles were to be identified by field service caps, and yellow crosses on the vehicles. Very active patrolling in the Black Country, from and including Hagley Road northwards, was therefore necessary to obtain early information and prevent enemy penetration between Cs of R during the hours of darkness. Police information from Worcestershire was likely to give an indication of the roads being taken by the enemy, but patrolling would also be needed especially on the minor roads and on the Lickey Hills. The isolated Austin and Birmetals factories (shown as 'Aero' and 'Birmetals' on Fig.10) were seen as potential objectives for the 'enemy'.[9]

No umpires' or directors' report has survived to tell us who 'won', but after the exercise, the Commanding Officer of the Oldbury Battalion thanked all the officers and other ranks for the part they played in it and expressed his appreciation for the excellent turnout of 1,028 from all ranks. He regretted the very small opportunity the battalion was offered for taking part in the fighting. Oldbury patrols had been active throughout the night and day, but apart from occasional brushes, the 'enemy' was apparently reluctant to commit himself to an attack on the Oldbury Battalion.[10] This suggests that both the Dudley and Stourbridge Home Guard Battalions had successfully managed to prevent the enemy from penetrating the outer defences in anything other than 'penny numbers'.

The weekend of 17th/18th April witnessed a county-wide exercise called Operation TRIBE. This exercise, which reflected the increasing defence role of the Home Guard, began in the evening of the Saturday and finished at mid-day on Sunday, and involved Regular troops and the Free French from Ribbesford House. Worcestershire was to be attacked from three directions, the principal thrusts being made against the towns of Kidderminster, Redditch and Evesham. Local newspapers subsequently reported heavy fighting around all three towns, and while Kidderminster was occupied by 'enemy' troops, 'The Keep' at Evesham was held and Redditch too held the attacks apart from the loss of the outskirts of the town. Apparently the umpires had been forced at one stage to separate the protagonists to stop them literally coming to blows! The late Charles Stallard remembered that the men in his unit did indeed come to blows with the 'enemy' as a result of over-zealous actions by a Home Guard Commando unit from Coventry that was 'attacking' Redditch. Over at Bromsgrove, Bill Allington recalls one First World War veteran in his platoon being fairly robust with the Regulars and swinging his rifle like a club against an 'enemy' attack on the Cattle Market, which was protected by the local Home Guard.

At Kidderminster, the 'enemy' commander launched a feint attack on the east side of the town, and followed this up with a heavy attack from the north of the town, which took his forces into the town without very much fighting. He then took up positions in the centre of the town, which were counter-attacked by reserve troops rushed forward by the Free French. A state of siege was achieved in which the 'enemy' could not get out of the town, nor the defenders get in.

During Exercise TRIBE, Halesowen Home Guard was anxious to prove that their town could be held as an Anti-Tank Island. Of the battalion strength of 1,052 men, 777 (74%) reported for duty, which was considered to be no mean achievement for an industrial area. Their task was primarily a static one of manning road blocks supporting Defended Localities, and all were disappointed when none of the 'enemy' came near in the whole 16 hours of the exercise.[11] Although this exercise was primarily about practising the Home Guard in its more aggressive role, it has to be wondered whether the Regular troops involved were also using the opportunity to practise their urban warfare techniques for the forthcoming invasion of Europe.

An unusual basis for discharge of Home Guards
The number of prosecutions for failure to fulfil their Home Guard service obligations during 1943 was significant and in part a measure of the difficulties some Home Guards were experiencing in balancing their work life and service with the Home Guard, as well as the opposing need of the authorities to ensure that the Home Guard was a well trained and efficient force, able to deal with any attacks the enemy might make. Normally Home Guards who were unable to fulfil their compulsory service would be fined or worse, but in late 1943 the Redditch Battalion took a more compassionate approach in some cases, for example when four Privates were discharged on the grounds of hardship.[12] Perhaps this was also an expression of Christmas spirit?

6   1944 – A last call to arms before Stand Down

The possibility of spoiling attacks by the enemy on vital road and rail communications along with petrol depots in order to delay and upset the arrangements for the invasion of the Continent continued to be of concern to defence planners during the first half of 1944. It was expected that an attack might be carried out by special agents who had entered the country secretly, or by parties of paratroops. It was thought that such acts of destruction could be committed at any time, but most probably under cover of darkness, either before or during the initial stages of the Allied invasion.[1]

Lt J.B. Walker, ADRDE Platoon Commander, wrote on 8th February to the Commandant of ADRDE that '… it is not inconceivable that the Home Guard might be mustered during the next six months for some general or more local enemy activity'.[2] The possibility of such actions occurring was also reflected in correspondence between the Mayor of Worcester and Lt Colonel Leicester of the Worcester Battalion Home Guard. The former had written that it was the unanimous wish of the General Purposes Entertainments Committee that the Home Guard should again be invited to arrange a Military Tournament similar to that in the previous year. In his response, Lt Colonel Leicester wrote that it might be necessary to cancel the arrangements at short notice 'because the happenings of this coming summer were likely to be serious and the consequences were not known to anyone'.[3]

The specific tasks for Home Guards in M Sector were set out in instructions of 18th February, and appear to be the only surviving example of sector instructions for this critical period. The following vulnerable points in the M Sector area were considered to be vital for the preparations for the Allied landings. The responsible battalions for manning the various defences on the issue of the codewords BOUNCER or BUGBEAR were listed as:

> No 18 Platoon, Worcester Battalion for the railway bridge over the Severn at Worcester, the railway bridge over the canal at Worcester and the railway tunnel at Worcester
>
> No 15 Platoon, Worcester Battalion for the road bridge over the Severn at Worcester

No 14 Platoon, Worcester Battalion for the road bridge over the Teme at Powick

South Unit, Worcester Battalion for the petrol dumps at Timberdine and Diglis, Worcester

The Evesham Battalion for the railway bridge over the Avon at Fladbury, the railway bridge over the Avon at Evesham East, the railway bridge over the Avon at Evesham West, the railway bridge over the Avon at Defford, the two road bridges over the Avon at Evesham and the petrol dump at Hinton on the Green

The Malvern Battalion for the railway bridge over the Severn at Ripple, the railway tunnel at Malvern, the road bridge at Hawford, the road bridge over the Severn at Holt, the road bridge over the Severn at Upton upon Severn, the road bridge over the Teme at Knightsford, the road bridge over the Teme at Bransford and the petrol dump at Ripple.[4]

This former petrol depot at Saxons Lode, near Ripple, was one of the M Sector Vulnerable Points to be guarded against airborne attack during the build-up for D-Day in 1944. Remnants of this depot can still be seen from nearby roads. By the time this 1960s air photograph was taken, the railway which served the site and the bridge over the River Severn had gone, but the location of both was still clear.
(Courtesy of the Worcestershire Archaeology and Archive Service)

Other sectors were no doubt issuing instructions for similar vulnerable points in their areas of responsibility. It is also significant that Bromsgrove Battalion orders in March made it very clear that in future during all night exercises, all officers – including directing staff, umpires and spectators – were to carry revolvers or a personal weapon.[5] The order is perhaps another indication of the possibility of spoiling attacks by enemy parachutists being expected at any time.

Should an enemy attack on the county be experienced in 1944 the increased complexity of the communication arrangements between sector and Home Guard units, and the availability of wirelesses, is illustrated well by M Sector instructions on intercommunication. These explained that on 'Action Stations' in connection with the codeword BOUNCER (see p.114), the sector headquarters would open at Norton Barracks and personnel to man wireless sets would be found from the sector signals section. Any cadets trained in the use of wireless telegraphy, and who were members of the Home Guard, were to be attached to the sector signals for operations. The sector Signals Officer was responsible for the distribution of sets. The sector report centre for communications was to be at Allesborough Hill, on the Worcester side of Pershore, where a wireless set was to be established, with an NCO in charge of the post. He was to keep in close touch with the Royal Observer Corps personnel who shared the site. The Evesham Battalion Commander was to arrange for the protection of this post and provide two orderlies on bicycles and two despatch riders to distribute messages from the Report Centre. In addition, each Home Guard battalion was to send two despatch riders to the sector HQ at Norton, and the Evesham Battalion was also to send two despatch riders to the Sub District HQ in Droitwich. The sector Signals Officer was to arrange for visual communications (presumably by signals lamps using Morse Code) from Norton Barracks to the HQ of the Malvern Battalion, then at Wheatfields, Callow End, and from Whittington Tump to Allesborough Hill. The Malvern Battalion Commander was to detail an officer to act as Liaison Officer between the RAF HQ at Defford and the sector HQ, while Evesham Battalion was to provide a Liaison Officer for Honeybourne and Pershore Aerodromes. Battalion Commanders were responsible for keeping the closest liaison with the nearest Home Guard troops to their boundary outside the sector area, and also with police stations in their area.

All troops were to carry Celanese Triangles (made of yellow rayon, they were a visual means of signalling to aircraft the location of friendly troops so as to avoid an air attack – Blue on Blue in today's parlance) which would be exposed on the signal of white or yellow Verey lights being given from our aircraft.

GPO telephones were to be used for messages of operational importance, but not administrative messages unless they were urgent, in which case a despatch rider was to be used instead. The telephone systems of the police, railways and Royal Observer Corps (ROC) could be used if other means had broken down. (ROC

Posts in or near the sector were at Ombersley, Himbleton, Powick, Allesborough Hill and Upton upon Severn, and each had its own private telephone lines.) Officers commanding Home Guard battalions were to detail a Liaison Officer or suitable NCO to each ROC post, with transport available to get information to Battalion HQs in case the telephones were out of order.

Halesowen Battalion signallers at work using a No 18 wireless set. Signals exercises were a feature of the last year of duty of the Home Guard. (Photo: Worcestershire Regiment Museum)

When a mobile column was sent out, a Liaison Officer from the battalion was to go with it to report the progress, and any action, to the nearest battalion or sector HQ.[6]

It is likely that similar complex signalling and communications arrangements were being made in other sectors throughout the county in anticipation of raids by the Germans, although similar instructions to those issued in M Sector have yet to come to light.

By 10th April, Worcester Sub Area instructions made it clear that Railway Units of the Home Guard were not going to be available owing to the priority of their normal duties, including moving troops and equipment around the country before and during the landings on the Continent. Consequently the Railway Units were not to be approached by local commands with requests to protect railway vulnerable points. Similarly, Air Ministry Units were not going to be available for protection of their properties. The only troops therefore available for protection of communications within the Worcester Sub Area were the General Service battalions of the Home Guard (presumably because the Regular Field Force troops were far too busy preparing for the forthcoming landings to be involved in such guard duties at this time).

By April, the Sub Area instructions were that the enemy was to be destroyed wherever found and before he could cause damage to communications but that it was considered to be impractical to guard every bridge throughout the length of the more important roads and railways, and so the Home Guard were to provide night guards only on the sites listed below. Preparations for providing those guards were to be made forthwith as this was a much lower level of protection than was envisaged in the M Sector instructions issued only in February. The order for guards to be made available would be issued by the Sub Area HQ, the guards to be in position between 8pm and 5.30am, unless enemy activity rendered it impracticable for the guard to leave at the end of the period of duty.

Clearly watching costs, the Sub Area instructions went on to say that the Home Guard were not to be 'mustered' for the purpose of providing guards covered by this order, and organisers were reminded that under the Home Guard Regulations, the men could not be ordered to perform a total of more than 48 hours training and duty in any 4 week period. Consideration was also be given to their civil employment. Compensation for loss of earnings for periods of duty exceeding 48 hours per 4 weeks was not to be authorised, but lists of volunteers who were prepared to do duty in excess of this period should be drawn up for use if their services were found necessary at a later date. The much reduced range of vulnerable points to be guarded throughout the county was then listed as:[7]

Worcester Road Bridge over the Severn – 2 NCOs and 8 men
Worcester Rail Bridge over the Severn – 2 NCOs and 8 men
Worcester Railway Tunnel – 2 NCOs and 8 men
Worcester Railway Control Centre (Shrubhill) – 2 NCOs and 8 men
Bransford Railway Bridge over the Teme – 2 NCOs and 8 men
Colwall Railway Tunnel – 2 NCOs and 8 men
Holt Fleet Road Bridge – 2 NCOs and 8 men
Upton Road Bridge over the Severn – 2 NCOs and 8 men
Hoobrook Railway Viaduct
Dowles Railway Bridge over the Severn – 1 NCO and 4 men
Bewdley Railway Tunnel – 1 NCO and 4 men
Stourport Road Bridge over the Severn – 1 NCO and 4 men

It is interesting to speculate how much the policy of protecting communications in Britain may have been coloured by the plans for Allied use of the SAS to disrupt German troop and munitions movements behind the lines in France during the subsequent Allied landings in Normandy. The parallels are clear.

It is significant that the Redditch Battalion held VITGUARD Tactical Exercises Without Troops (TEWTS) on 1st February, with A, B and E Companies in the area of the HDA factory, and A, B and F Companies in the area of Reynolds Tubing factory, both factories being of national importance.[8] Such exercises were probably repeated by other battalions, and are another indication that the main enemy threat then was perceived to be against vulnerable points.

Exercise in St John's, Worcester

Exercises in 1944 tended to be small-cale affairs appropriate to the likelihood of dealing only with enemy paratroop spoiling attacks, rather than the more extensive operations envisaged earlier in the war. Typical of these was Exercise SOUTHFIELD, held on 23rd January, when camouflaged defence positions along

Almost certainly taken during a TEWT (tactical exercise without troops), this photograph shows, from the left, Captain Hartley (Adjutant), Lieutenant Colonel Grace (Battalion Commander), and Major Morom (2nd in Command), of the Redditch Battalion, poring over a map during an exercise at Bromsgrove Road Sports Ground, Redditch.
(Courtesy of Robin Morom)

the Laugherne Brook and the River Teme to the confluence with the Severn were occupied against an enemy attack from the west. Recce platoons were sent out to locate the enemy, who were found at Earl's Court Farm, but were deemed by the umpires to have suffered casualties, one platoon being 'wiped out'. Nevertheless, at least some of the defending Home Guards appeared to be conversant with their duties, and the issuing of orders was apparently carried out in a concise and intelligent manner.[9]

Prosecutions for avoiding duty increase

The number of men prosecuted for avoiding Home Guard duty, and whose cases were widely reported in local newspapers, increased during 1944. This may have been symptomatic of general war weariness or perhaps a feeling amongst some that it was only a question of time before victory was secured and that their time in the Home Guard was coming to an end anyway. The first of the Home Guards to be prosecuted during 1944 were three men of the Warley Battalion who were reported as being fined £10 each (equivalent to about £50 each now) for absence from duty in early February. This same battalion would prosecute others later in the month.[10]

In some cases the sentences would be harsher than hitherto as the authorities sought to maintain discipline in the Home Guard. For example, *The Redditch*

Indicator reported that Clifford Jones, aged 20, had pleaded guilty to two charges of absenting himself from Home Guard duties at Alvechurch on 9th and 12th December, and was sentenced to 14 days imprisonment with hard labour in each case, the sentence to run concurrently. He had been previously similarly convicted on 17th February and 27th October 1943, when he was given a serious warning of the consequences if he was again charged and found guilty. Jones pleaded that he was medically unfit for the Army and for Home Guard duties, but in imposing the sentence, the Chairman of the Bench told Jones that he could not defy Authority in this way.[11] What a contrast to the compassion shown at the end of 1943 by the Redditch authorities!

Losses of stores, equipment and clothing

Bromsgrove Battalion noted that there was an alarming increase in the losses of stores, equipment and clothing supplied by the public for use by the Home Guard, those articles most frequently going astray being those which were in short supply in the civilian population or subject to coupon rationing. The attention of all ranks was therefore drawn to the need to look after all items committed to their charge or issued for their personal use. From 29th April, where it was necessary to charge members of the Home Guard for the loss of an item, the full repayment rate (meaning replacement cost plus the appropriate departmental expenses) would be charged.[12]

The archaeology of the Home Guard is gradually disappearing. As an example, most of the once numerous ammunition and explosives stores (over 260 had been provided by 1944) have now disappeared from the county and only a few crumbling structures remain. This example of the standard store used in Worcestershire stood close to Pershore bridges until demolished only recently. (Author's photo)

As a result of a number of War Department vehicles being stolen, a letter was issued by the Worcestershire Sub District HQ on 14th June reminding all ranks of the Home Guard that instructions for the immobilisation of all WD vehicles left unattended for any period, however short, remained in force.[13]

D-Day, 6th June 1944

History tells us that the expected spoiling attacks by German forces during the immediate period before D-Day did not occur, and it is recorded in the Halesowen Battalion history that 'D-Day passed without any call being made on the Home Guard in the Midlands, and each successive phase, after firm establishment of the Normandy bridgehead, strengthened the belief that the job was nearly done and somewhat conflicting statements about the future of the Home Guard were made in the ensuing weeks ...'. However, guards were placed on the Teme Railway Bridge, at Bransford, and at the Colwall Tunnel on the main railway lines to the south-west ports, while others were on stand-by to man a dozen other Vulnerable Points on road and rail communications in the Sub District if required. In addition, both LMS and GWR railway executives had been visited to ensure that special measures of protection were in place against sabotage at central offices, signals offices and marshalling yards.[14]

The Home Guard has difficulty in maintaining its strength

The Worcestershire Sub District War Diary records that the Home Guard had difficulty in maintaining its strength in view of the increasing number of men being taken out of the reserved occupation category. As soon as the landings in France proved to be successful and the production of war materials was adequate for the planned needs, men were 'de-reserved' and became liable for 'call-up' to the Regular forces. In addition, the priority given to anti-aircraft defence in the Birmingham area was increasing the numbers of Home Guards being transferred from ground defence units to anti-aircraft units.[15] One of the Worcestershire Home Guards who was de-reserved was the late Charles Stallard of the BSA Factory Unit at Redditch. He was a pre-war member of the Redditch Territorial

Officers and NCOs of the BSA Factory Home Guard at Redditch. 2nd Lieutenant Charles Stallard, referred to above, is 3rd from the right in the front row. (Courtesy of the Stallard family via Mike Johnson)

Artillery Battery and had been mobilised on 1st September 1939. He was due to be promoted to the rank of Lance Corporal when he received his discharge papers and returned to his work at Redditch. On his return to the BSA factory he joined the Toolroom Section of the works Home Guard and due to his previous, if short, military career, he was appointed Section Sergeant. At that time he would regularly work a 60-hour week, including weekends, with his Home Guard duties on top of that. Subsequently he was recommended for a commission and served as a 2nd Lieutenant until 1944 when, just as he about to get his second 'pip', he received his call up papers for the Regular forces. He was then subjected to his first Army medical and, being found to be missing an eardrum, was sent to the Royal Army Pay Corps where his previous experience was recognised and he became a lecturer in Army Pay Procedures.[16]

Evesham, Dudley and Warley Battalions take leave

The Evesham Battalion was largely drawn from the agricultural community of the Vale of Evesham, so come July 1944 the battalion commander excused the whole battalion from parades, except for necessary maintenance work, to enable the hay crop and fruit harvest to be gathered in. Owing to wet weather it was decided to extend this period of harvest leave until the end of September.[17]

Similarly, and perhaps an indication that munitions production was getting ahead of requirements, two officers and 71 other ranks from A to E Companies of the Warley Battalion were granted leave,[18] while the Dudley Battalion orders made clear that there would be no parades during the holiday week from Sunday 6th August, presumably referring to an established custom of a shut-down of factories for one week, although it is surprising that this was continued during wartime.[19]

The winding down of the Home Guard

For some time the Trades Union Congress had been putting forward the view that it was difficult to convince the average British worker than an enemy invasion was possible, and that it was quite wrong to continue to spend their time on compulsory Home Guard drill and punish men for not doing so. That time would be better spent relaxing from their demanding work. A series of articles in *The Daily Mail* during August 1944 also put forward the view that it was time to relax Home Guard duties.[20] This inevitably caused disquiet in the ranks of the Home Guard, and the orders for the Oldbury Battalion of 22nd August were typical of the response by Home Guard commanders who were trying to maintain discipline in the force against this background of political comment. It was made clear to the men of Oldbury, for example, that the articles were the product of *The Daily Mail* and nobody else, and that GHQ policy was for the Home Guard to carry on its good work until such time as the war situation enabled higher command to allow a relaxation of its duties. The orders pointed out that easing up of duties for men who worked for very long hours in their jobs had already been in operation for over a year, but no general stand down order for the Home Guard could yet be contemplated. The need for keeping ant-aircraft units up to strength was seen as paramount.[21]

The Evesham Battalion Commander used his local newspaper to get a similar message across to both the men and the public at large and, clearly envisaging the Home Guard continuing for some time, went further by issuing a booklet to his men setting out a comprehensive programme from early September 1944 to March 1945, including recruitment, specialist and weapons training, as well as arrangements for conducting proficiency tests. This booklet was seen as a good example of its type and copies were requested by battalions elsewhere in Britain.

A War Office letter, dated 30th August and addressed to all Home Guard commanders, was clearly both an official response to the articles in *The Daily Mail* and support for the actions of local commanders. It explained that the Army Council considered that during the last months the Home Guard had performed a vital service by enabling the Regular forces to leave Britain by providing protection against the danger of potential enemy interference. In its view, that danger had not yet disappeared and it was necessary for the Home Guard to continue until all dangers had passed.[22] Nevertheless there were signs that things were indeed winding down when Redditch Battalion orders of 5th September required all mines to be returned to Battalion HQ forthwith.[23]

The political response to *The Daily Mail* came on 6th September, when the then Secretary of State for War, Sir James Grigg, broadcast a message during which he paid tribute to the service of the Home Guard, but announced that compulsory service for the Home Guard would end on Sunday, 10th September. This must have completely undermined the authority of the Home Guard commanders and confused the other ranks. The actual instructions for the procedure, though not the date for standing down the Home Guard, were received in the Midlands on the same day as Grigg's broadcast. These instructions were also dated 30th August and must have been drafted by civil servants without consulting the Army Council! The War Diary of the Worcestershire Sub District makes no bones about it when recording that 'It was no exaggeration to say that these instructions were received with general consternation by the majority of the Home Guard (certainly 75%) and were considered to be premature as well as being promulgated and drafted in a most unfortunate manner. Special exception was taken to the order with regard to the returning of clothing and boots.'[24]

The parsimonious order for the return of clothing was subsequently rescinded by Winston Churchill, who thought that after four years of largely unstinting effort the least the government should do would be to allow the Home Guard to keep

Warley Battalion headquarters staff manning the telephone and maintaining their messages log. Note the bunk beds for staff covering night duty, and the ubiquitous kettle in the background, tea being the great sustainer of soldiers, then as now. Lengthy headquarters duty would end for many Home Guards in September 1944.
(Courtesy of Steve Taylor)

these items. However, it was not until 5th October that the notification was received that personnel could retain their caps, battledress blouses, trousers, anklets, boots and anti-gas capes, while the retention of greatcoats was still under consideration.[25]

The Home Guard in Worcestershire ceased operational responsibility for the protection of certain vulnerable points on 11th September, resulting in the withdrawal of guards from the GWR in Worcester (this was the Shrubhill complex of engine sheds, sidings and goods yards, and the railway tunnel at Tunnel Hill) as well as Modern Seamless Tubes in St John's; the High Duty Alloys and Reynolds Tubes factories in Redditch, including discontinuance of the light anti-aircraft responsibilities there; Folly Point Aqueduct north of Bewdley; and the Power and Transformer Stations at Stourport. In addition, the manning of telephones at sector and battalion HQs also stopped, and arrangements were made with the County Surveyor to remove anti-tank blocks throughout the county.[26] Stourport Battalion orders further explained that all other Home Guard duties and parades would be on a voluntary basis.[27]

The final orders for the formal Stand Down, but not disbandment, of the Home Guard were received in Worcestershire on 16th October, apparently relieving the uncertainty that had been felt since August. The date would be 1st November. This precipitated a return of ammunition, explosives, mines and fireworks to a depot at Kinlet Hall during the latter part of October, which resulted in a great deal of work for battalion training officers and adjutants in the inspection of munitions to see that all was in good order, and in the right quantities, before acceptance by the Royal Army Ordnance Corps. Also returned were Northover Projectors, Smith Guns, Spigot Mortars, 2 Pounder Anti-Tank Guns, light and medium machine guns, as well as wireless sets that had only just been issued on a generous scale.[28] Dudley Battalion orders noted that the weapons handed in were to be clean and correct in every detail, and include all spare parts.[29] The late Charles Stallard, of the BSA Factory Home Guard, thought that the disarming of the Home Guard was premature and very quickly done. Perhaps that betrayed a basic government distrust of this citizen army that harked back to the early days of the force when men were not allowed to take their rifles or ammunition home with them after duty?[30]

Bromsgrove Battalion orders also made it clear that although the Stand Down came into effect on 1st November, all clothing retained by members remained the property of the War Department, and that disbandment of the Home Guard was not being contemplated at present. Their service respirators were to be retained only so long as respirators were retained by the general public. The same orders recorded that a ceremonial parade to mark the Stand Down was to be arranged for 3rd December.[31] Other battalions were issuing similar orders and it is important to point out that being stood down did not mean the end of the force, which could have been recalled to duty at any time subsequently should there have been an emergency. That did not occur and the force would be finally disbanded a year later.

Members of the Redditch Battalion marching past the saluting base in Church Green during their Stand Down parade. Surely the smartness of these men reflects the standard of soldiering reached by the Home Guard during the Second World War, and deserves a better press than the force often has! (Courtesy of Mr E.P. Grace via Mike Johnson)

The weather on Sunday, 3rd December 1944, matched the mood of many of the Worcestershire Home Guards attending the Stand Down parades. This is the Dudley Battalion in the Market Place, Dudley on that day. (Courtesy of Gwen Harvey)

Worcestershire's Stand Down parades

Sunday 3rd December saw Home Guard Stand Down parades in most of the towns and some of the villages in Britain on a dull and rainy day, which some said matched the mood of the majority of those taking part. The parades were widely and extensively reported in the local press, where they were described as being impressive in character and creating a great deal of interest to those who saw them. Normally a religious service preceded the events or brought them to a close, with expressions of thanks to the Home Guard for its loyalty and devotion to duty from local dignatories and senior officers. Some units presented silverware to the commanding officer as tokens of their appreciation of good leadership. The parades were invariably led by a military band, provided either by the Home Guard battalion itself – there were a number of these in Worcestershire by this time – or by a local military unit. Some parades held a minute's silence for fallen comrades.

That same afternoon, representative contingents of Home Guard throughout the country also participated in a grand parade in London's West End, at which the salute was taken by the king. The Worcester Sub District War Diary noted that 84 other ranks and three officers from Worcestershire attended that parade.[32] Some of the men who went from Worcestershire have been identified and are listed in Appendix 5.

The 4th December saw M Sector HQ at Worcester, O Sector at Kidderminster, and the Black Country sectors close, with paperwork being handed over to the nearest Home Guard battalion HQ. Closure of N Sector at Redditch followed on 9th December.[33]

Home Guards reminisce and consider the future

The release from duty triggered a number of Home Guard social events, where officers thanked their men for the effort they had put into their service, while the men showed their appreciation of the officers, usually with gifts, and the opportunity was taken to reminisce about their service in the force. As examples, on 22nd September, officers of the Kidderminster Battalion paid tribute to the services rendered to the Home Guard by Colonel R.W.A. Painter MC, O Sector Commander, who was the original commander of the battalion;[34] while at Redditch, Lt Colonel E.A. Grace, at a similar event, said that the members of the battalion should take every opportunity of getting together and keeping in touch now that they were working on a voluntary basis, so that they could be sure that they were keeping abreast of events and be ready at all times to take action according to whatever orders might be

O Sector Headquarters staff at Stand Down, the photograph taken in front of The Larches Club House, Larches Road, Kidderminster. In the front row, from left to right are: Captain W.W. Tanser (Transport Officer), Captain G.H. Carter MM (Signals Officer), Captain A.R.T. Ayers (Adjutant), Captain H. Osborne (Weapons Training Officer), Major A.F.R. Godfrey (General List Infantry Training Officer), Colonel R.W.A. Painter MC (Sector Commander), Major A. Allen Knight (Staff Officer), Captain C.R. Millett (Intelligence Officer), Captain J.D. Symes (Liaison Officer), and Captain A. Knight (Staff Officer). (Courtesy of ex Lance Corporal Bill Harper (Signals) who is 4th from the right in the 2nd row. None of the others have been identified.)

issued. He explained that the Home Guard was standing easy but training facilities – ranges, arms, ammunition – were still available and advised the younger members to continue training on a reduced scale. He made it clear that standing down did not mean disbandment, and that the Home Guard could still be recalled at short notice if the military situation required it. As to the future, Colonel Grace said that the formation of rifle clubs, affiliation with Worcestershire Regimental Associations and other options were being considered and he did not anticipate that the spirit of the Redditch Battalion would easily die nor the record of its service be forgotten.[35]

Final Battalion manpower rolls produced

At or around the date of the stand down parades the battalion adjutants produced the final manpower rolls of the Home Guard for the TA Association. The style of presentation and content varied, some battalions including women and boys in their rolls, others not. Appendix 4 sets out, as far as can be ascertained, the battalion structure and the officers serving at that time. At a post-stand down dinner held by the officers of the Evesham Battalion on 18th November, Captain H. Woods, the

MENU

SECTOR SOUP

—

ROAST CHICKEN
BOILED POTATOES   BRUSSELL SPROUTS

—

LARCHES PUDDING

—

COFFEE

TOASTS

H. M. THE KING   Proposed by Col. R. W. A. Painter, M.C.

THE VISITORS   Proposed by Col. R. W. A. Painter, M.C.
                        Response by Col. K. J. Martin,
                                              D.S.O., A.D.C.

THE SECTOR COMMANDER AND OFFICERS
                        Proposed by C.S.M., E. W. Knight
                        Response by Major A. Allen Knight

OTHER SECTOR PERSONNEL
                        Proposed by Capt. C. R. Millett
                        Response by Sgt. H. W. Haywood

ARTISTE

ARTHUR CULPIN   (Deception that Delights : Nipluc,
                        with Jimmy The Cheeky Chappie)

SECTOR PERSONNEL

Colonel R. W. A. Painter, M.C.	Sector Commander
Major A. F. R. Godfrey	General List (Inf) - Training Officer
Major A. Allen Knight	Staff Officer
Capt. A. Knight	Staff Officer
Capt. C. R. Millett	Intelligence Officer
Capt. G. H. Carter, M.M.	Signals Officer
Capt. J. D. Simes	Liaison Officer
Capt. W. W. Tanser	Transport Officer
Capt. H. Osborne	Weapon Training Officer
Capt. A. T. Ayers	Adjutant
C. S. M. E. W. Knight	

Sjt. A. E. Neale	Intelligence Section
Cpl. K. S. H. Bazley	" "
Pte. C. H. Taylor	" "
Pte. D. D. Leigh	" "
Pte. B. H. Dakin	" "
Pte. T. H. Kimberlee	" "
Pte. A. W. Waring	" "

Sjt. H. W. Haywood	Signals Section
Cpl. F. G. Humphries	" "
L/Cpl. W. D. Harper	" "
Pte. J. P. Naughton	" "
Pte. F. W.Woodings	" "
Pte. A. W. Hunt	" "
Pte. G. B. Jones	" "
Pte. A. L. Willsmere	" "
Pte. G. Green	" "
Pte. S. Knowles	" "
Pte. J. H. Powell	" "
Pte. H. S. Helmore	" "
Pte. T. J. Davies	" "
Pte. S. T. Coleman	" "
Pte. C. Morris	" "

Cpl. J. C. Killey	D. R.
Cpl. W. J. Smith	D. R.

O Sector Stand Down Dinner menu and sector staff List. The event was held at the Black Horse Hotel, Kidderminster on Friday, 1st December 1944, and was one of many such events held through out the county at about this time. The menu seems to reflect austerity Britain and is in stark contrast to the venison dinner held in Alvechurch in October 1940. (Courtesy of Bill Harper, who attended the dinner)

Battalion Adjutant, gave some very useful statistics for the battalion, which might well reflect the experiences of most battalions in the county. 4,273 men had served in the battalion, of whom 423 had been called up into the Regular forces, 26 of their number dying on active service. 720 had been compulsorily enrolled, while of the 2,393 who were enrolled in 1940, 40% were still on the roll. The maximum strength of the battalion was 2,238 and the minimum 2,028, with 138 serving officers.[35]

Home Guards eligible to join the
Worcestershire Regiment Old Comrades Association
In a memorandum of 12th December to members of D Company (Tenbury) of the Stourport Battalion, the Company Commander wrote that all members of the battalion were eligible to join the Worcestershire Regiment Old Comrades Association on payment of a membership fee of 5 shillings (£2.50 now). Any man who had been a member of the Association for not less than 13 months could apply for assistance in the form of a grant or loan not exceeding £100 (£5,000 in today's money) if the necessity arose. No man who was recommended and was eligible within the rules of the Association was apparently ever refused assistance. The type of help given was: to start a business; to pay arrears of rent; to meet doctors' bills; to buy furniture; to educate children; to emigrate to the dominions and colonies; and assistance after illness. He urged every member of D Company to become a member of the Association, for even if they were never likely to need help themselves, the subscription would help some Worcestershire comrade who was not so fortunate. In order to maintain the friendship and fine spirit of comradeship which had animated the Home Guard for the previous 4½ years, a scheme was also afoot for the formation of local branches of the Association to carry on social activities, including one in Tenbury.[36]

But the year ended in tragedy
On Christmas night, 46-year-old Sergeant George Simpson of Evesham died in Barnsley Hall Emergency Hospital, Bromsgrove, where he was found to be suffering from poisoning. He had served in No1 Platoon of A Company, of the Evesham Battalion and was apparently a very popular and efficient NCO. His sister, of Barnt Green, with whom he had been staying for the Christmas holidays, said at the subsequent inquest that he was an old soldier and had taken his war very seriously, and that he had seemed very restless and worried since the last parade. His landlady, at Evesham, confirmed that he had been noticeably depressed since the Home Guard had stood down, and that he had missed the companionship. The inquest reached a verdict of suicide while the balance of his mind was disturbed. He was buried at Barnt Green.[37]

1945 and Afterwards

In the years when our Country
was in mortal danger

L.W. SHAWE

who served   24.9.41   to 31.12.44

gave generously of his time and

powers to make himself ready

for her defence by force of arms

and with his life if need be.

Following Stand Down, certificates were issued by the Territorial Army Association, in the name of the king, to those men who had provided satisfactory service, giving the dates of the individual's service. In this instance at least, the end date is strangely inconsistent with that which would later appear on the individual's record of service on his enrolment form. (Courtesy of the late Leyland Shawe)

Members of the Malvern Home Guard were invited to attend a special meeting on 2nd February 1945 to consider forming an Association and to establish a constitution. The activities of the Association were to be confined to those of a social nature, and there was an intention to form a rifle club.[1] By January 1946, it was reported that the Home Guard Association had not been very active, thought to be due to the necessity for members to settle down and adapt themselves to the transition from war to peacetime conditions. This appears to have been the last newspaper report of the Malvern Home Guard Association, which seems, like old soldiers, to have just faded away.

Despite the apparent failure to establish a Home Guard association in Malvern, 24 Home Guard rifle clubs had been formed in the county and recognised by the Worcestershire TAA by June 1945.[2] These are listed in Appendix 7. A number of individual sections, platoons or companies also organised annual reunion dinners, the last being reported in 1952 for B Section of No 1 Platoon of the Malvern Battalion.[3]

In special recognition of the services rendered by officers and ex-officers of the Home Guard, it was decided by the War

Office, in March 1945, that officers whose service had been satisfactory would be granted honorary rank on the disbandment of the Home Guard. The rank given would be the highest that had been held for a minimum of six months.[4]

Home Guard disbandment

The disbandment of the Home Guard finally took place on 31st December 1945.[5] This occurred with hardly a mention in the press, and no ceremonies, the stand down parades 12 months earlier having been the last major public celebration of the Home Guard. After a minimum of three years satisfactory service, members were entitled to the Defence Medal, but the majority did not bother to claim their medal in 1945, perhaps a reflection of the fact that most wanted to pick up the strings of peacetime living again. In Worcestershire, the only unit that appears to have marked the disbandment of the Home Guard was the Dudley Battalion, which laid up its colours in St Thomas's Church (Top Church) at Dudley. The creation of Battalion Colours in Worcestershire seems to have been unique to this battalion.

The last act for the Dudley Battalion was to lay-up its colours in Dudley Top Church (St Thomas's) in December 1945, after a final parade to mark the disbandment of the Home Guard. Major Hedley Porter, standing at the back, commanded the Colour Party. The battalion was the only one in Worcestershire which appears to have acquired colours. (Courtesy of David Wesley-Smith)

The threat of war in Europe returns

While the former members

To qualify for the Defence Medal, a Home Guard had to serve for a minimum of three years. However, the medal had to be claimed and proof provided of the period of service before the medal would be issued by the Army Medal Office. Many Home Guards who qualified simply did not bother to apply at the end of the war. (Courtesy of the late Bill Preece)

of the wartime Home Guard were settling back to a relatively peaceful life in austerity Britain, Winston Churchill was expressing disquiet as early as 1946 about the communist dominance behind the so-called Iron Curtain, although at the time he did not believe that Soviet Russia desired war.[6] However, deteriorating relations between the Western Allies and Soviet Russia, reflected in the blockading of Berlin and the consequential Berlin Airlift in 1948, brought the spectre of a return to war in Europe. In a note of 7th December 1948, the War Office considered that it was a Russian aim to first eliminate Britain as an Allied base by air bombardment coupled with attacks against sea communications, to be followed by a full-scale invasion which would be accompanied by internal communist inspired subversive activities designed to achieve that aim. The possibility of communist inspired sabotage attacks highlighted the need to guard key points in Britain. It was therefore thought that a force similar to the Home Guard could be raised to take over some guard duties from the Regular forces, as well as to man road blocks to control civilian movement. Once trained, the Home Guard could be used to supplement the anti-aircraft defences of the UK, supplement the minimum counter-attack defences provided by the regular forces and provide assistance to the Civil Power in the maintenance of internal security.[7]

Endless discussions about the need for, and form of, a reconstituted Home Guard carried on throughout the late 1940s until November 1950, when the Defence Committee finally agreed that a Home Guard was needed, but that it should not be formed until the early stages of an emergency, and that to begin with it should not exceed a strength of 200,000.[8] This was announced by the Labour Minister of Defence, Emmanuel Shinwell, later in the month. The intervention of Chinese forces in Korea in the winter of 1950-51 brought a renewed sense of urgency to defence planning, with the pro-Home Guard lobby on the Conservative benches putting forward the view that the Russians could overrun Western Europe in a matter of weeks, giving Soviet forces forward bases from which to attack Britain by airborne and seaborne forces. It was considered that if war broke out there would be insufficient time to train and equip the Home Guard.[9]

While out of office, and in a letter to Lord Trenchard in March 1951 regarding the development of a long-range bomber force and fighters, Winston Churchill expressed concern at the possibility of 'large scale paratroop raids – twenty thousand or so – where our troops are out of the country, or sent away, and we have no Home Guard …'.[10] The Conservatives were re-elected to power on 25th October 1951 and with Winston Churchill once again Prime Minister this gave new impetus to the formation of the Home Guard.

The statutory basis for the revived Home Guard was the Home Guard Act of 1951, passed on 7th December, which confirmed that the force would again form part of the Armed Forces of the Crown. It was to be unpaid and men were not required to give fulltime service, live away from their homes, or carry out duties in connection with an industrial dispute, except when mustered. It was to be mustered only in defence of the UK against an actual or apprehended attack. Within the War Office, the Director of the Territorial Army and Cadets was responsible for coordination of all Home Guard matters. Each military district or sub-district could include one or more sectors comprising Regular troops and Home Guard, under a commander who could be an officer holding a Regular or Home Guard commission, with the rank of Colonel. Sectors were to consist of not less than two Home Guard units. All local organisation and administrative control was again to be through the Territorial Army Association, which had by then been renamed the Territorial and Auxiliary Forces Association (TAAFA).

Home Guard progress in Worcestershire

By January 1952 it was reported that considerable progress had been made in setting up the framework of the Home Guard in Western Command, including the raising of five battalions in the Worcestershire area. Every battalion had been filled on a cadre basis with an average strength of 50 men, all the volunteers for service coming forward in advance of a general appeal for members. Experienced officers of the wartime Home Guard were among them, while others were ex-Regular and TA officers. The selection of suitable adjutant/quartermasters for each of the Worcestershire battalions was also well advanced. The five Worcestershire battalions were:

> 1st Worcestershire (Oldbury) Battalion commanded by Lt Colonel T.C. Fillery, with the headquarters at the police station, Oldbury;
>
> 2nd Worcestershire (Kidderminster) Battalion, the CO of which was expected to be appointed shortly, with the headquarters at The Shrubbery, Kidderminster;

3rd Worcestershire (Droitwich) Battalion, commanded by Lt Colonel J.T. James TD, with the headquarters at the TA Centre, Droitwich;

4th Worcestershire (Pershore) Battalion, commanded by Brigadier J.H. Sykes, with the headquarters at the TA Centre, Pershore; and

5th Worcestershire (Worcester and Malvern) Battalion, commanded by Lt Colonel A.R. Harrison TD DL, with the headquarters at The Avenue, Worcester.

Registration for membership of the Home Guard started on Saturday, 19th February 1952; it entailed filling in a special pre-paid post card, available at all post offices, and sending it to the War Office. The cards were then forwarded to the county TAAFA concerned, which would then sort them out according to units, inform applicants of the names and headquarters of the local battalion and then forward the cards to the battalion commander concerned. From these cards, the battalion commander could select for interview likely candidates for his cadre.[11]

By late February 1952 it was clear that while some Home Guard units in the Midlands had achieved more than the target recruiting figure for a battalion cadre, throughout the country as a whole there had been no great response to the recruiting appeal. A positive response was most marked in the industrial areas, such as Kidderminster, where the cadre was up to strength, but more difficulty was being experienced in the rural areas.[12]

Regulations for the 'new' Home Guard issued

On 14th March 1952 the War Office issued the regulations for the 'new' Home Guard, which explained that there would be no fixed war establishments, but battalions would average 1,500 men of all ranks. Sections would normally consist of 25 men and might be divided into squads under a leader. Normally there would be four sections in a platoon, four platoons in a company and four companies to a battalion. The peacetime battalion establishment was to be a cadre of 50 men for administrative purposes, which would facilitate rapid expansion in an emergency. Close cooperation was to exist between the Home Guard and Cadet forces, especially in war, when responsibility for training cadets would pass from the Territorial Army to the Home Guard.

The main tasks for the Home Guard were likely to be: defence against airborne raids; defence against small scale seaborne raids; anti-sabotage protection of key points; assistance to civil defence; and defence against invasion. In an emergency, the Home Guard would assist in Civil Defence in accordance with plans made by local commanders. Each Home Guard was to undertake a minimum of 15 hours training and/or duty in a period of three calendar months, and was to attend an annual weapons firing course at a range, but other training was to depend on local conditions. Training and duty included that required in connection with

Civil Defence, which could be authorised by the appropriate military authority. Training and duty would as far as possible be arranged so as not to clash with a member's normal employment and would be subject to military law. The order to muster was to be given by the Commander in Chief, UK Land Forces, or by delegated commanders. When mustered, a Home Guard could be required to serve continuously and live away from home.[13]

Churchill introduces the Defence Estimates to the Commons

On 5th March 1952, Winston Churchill introduced the Government's Defence Estimates to the House of Commons, stating the forces required both as a deterrent against aggression and to afford some measure of defence should war come. He was concerned about the condition of home defence, especially against large scale attacks by paratroops, and pointed out that Britain had moved, or had decided to move, all its Regular divisions out of the island; consequently the Home Guard had been revived and revitalized. At first he felt unable to provide the Home Guard with uniforms or even with greatcoats or boots, but he decided 'upon consideration to draw upon our mobilisation reserves to the extent necessary to clothe at least the first 50,000'.[14]

Progress in Worcestershire

TAAFA noted that Worcestershire was divided into two sectors, North and South, with a total of five battalions. North Sector, comprised of the 1st Worcestershire (Oldbury) Battalion, commanded by Lt Colonel T.C. Fillery, with Captain J.A. Groves as Adjutant/Quartermaster; the 2nd Worcestershire (Kidderminster) Battalion, commanded by Lt Colonel E.G. Wallace, with Major H.G.B. Jordon as Adj/QM; and the 3rd Worcestershire (Droitwich) Battalion, commanded by Lt Colonel J.T. James TD, with Captain R.J. Birch as Adj/QM. The South Sector was commanded by Brigadier J.H. Sykes, and comprised the 4th Worcestershire (Pershore) Battalion, also commanded by Brigadier Sykes, with Major A. Stephens as Adj/QM; 5th Worcestershire (Worcester and Malvern) Battalion, commanded by Lt Colonel A.R. Harrison TD DL, with Lt Colonel F.A. Morris as Adj/QM, who had seen a great deal of service on the North-West Frontier. At this stage, no commander had been appointed for the North Sector. Commanding officers had made considerable progress in selecting their cadres, enrolment of which was to have started about 1st April, but was delayed pending the issue of the conditions of service. The number of *registrations* received at the date of the meeting was: Oldbury Battalion 57, Kidderminster Battalion 74, Droitwich Battalion 42, Pershore Battalion 20, Worcester and Malvern Battalion 97, totalling 299. It was not then known how many of these would accept the conditions of service or who would in fact prove to be suitable for enrolment in the cadres.

Men and one women of the Stourbridge Company of the 1st Worcestershire (Oldbury) Battalion of 1950s Home Guards. They are wearing the standard British Army battledress uniform and black berets of the time, with the Worcestershire Regiment cap badge. The Officers and NCOs are also wearing the Worcestershire Regiment collar dogs on their lapels. Only two of the men in this photograph can be named: Thomas Chance, who is 4th from the right in the 2nd row, and Jack Lewis to the right of him.
(Courtesy of Dennis Chance)

At the TAAFA association meeting of 31st October 1952 it was reported that since the last meeting, Lt Colonel C. Thatcher was to command the Kidderminster Home Guard Battalion, in place of Lt Colonel E.G. Wallace who had resigned with effect from 25th August. It was also noted that battalions had made progress with the formation of their cadres and while these were not at the full strength of 50, all company commanders and most platoon commanders had been appointed. It was considered that these cadres were now going concerns and had been able to start training. The strength of the force on 15th October was recorded as follows, it being noted that there had been further enrolment since that date: the Oldbury Battalion comprised 40 men; the Kidderminster Battalion, 57; the Droitwich Battalion, 41; the Pershore Battalion, 122; and the Worcester and Malvern Battalion, 124 plus one woman. (These figures must refer to individuals who had registered but were not all enrolled.)

It was reported that Western Command were proposing to the War Office that Home Guard cadre battalions should be issued with uniforms, and that the establishment of cadres should be increased up to 75. At the following meeting of the TAAFA on 24th April 1953, it was reported that these two suggestions had been approved, but with authority to increase the cadre strength to 100. Since the last report the following appointments had been notified: Lt Colonel E.A. Redfern TD to command the North Worcestershire Sector; Major J.H.L. Beard TD to command the Bromsgrove Battalion in place of Lt Colonel J.T. James TD, who had resigned; and Lt Colonel O.W.D. Smith was to command the Pershore Battalion, Brigadier J.H. Sykes continuing to command the South Sector. In addition, it was reported that the War Office had given approval for the issue of white metal lapel badges to enrolled members, and to those members on the Reserve Roll of the Home Guard.[15]

Development of the new Home Guard

Lists were to be prepared of transport which could be requisitioned in an emergency for the movement of 100 men, together with motorcycle despatch riders, for each company area and battalion headquarters. This is an indication that the role of the Home Guard was to be relatively mobile in the next conflict. A 3-ton lorry could accommodate 18 to 20 men with full equipment, arms and ammunition. About six 3-tonners were therefore to be earmarked in each company headquarters area for the rapid movement of a mobile column. Motor cycles were to be earmarked on the following scale: Battalion HQ, 4; each company, 2; and headquarters, 12. Sections

Men of the 1950s Home Guard march past the Guildhall, in Worcester, following a service in the Cathedral, and as part of a recruiting drive in May 1953. This contingent is the Worcester and Malvern Battalion, led by Major Kendall, who is giving his 'trademark' left-handed salute. (Courtesy of Sheila Edmonds)

of platoons mounted on cycles were seen as extremely effective mobile patrols. The lists, when completed, were to give the locality and number of vehicles and other transport that could be made available for each company and platoon area in an emergency.

A list to be prepared for the Kidderminster Battalion gives a general indication of the company areas, which were: Battalion HQ and A Company covering Kidderminster itself; B Company covering the Stourbridge, Lye, Hagley, and Belbroughton area; C Company covering the Stourport, Great Witley, Martley, Hartlebury, Crossway Green area; and D Company covering the Bewdley, Rock, Mamble, Lindridge, Tenbury Wells area.[16]

These men of the Worcester and Malvern Battalion show off the numerous trophies won at the Altcar firing ranges in September 1955. There has been a long-established and strong military shooting tradition in Worcestershire which is reflected in this photograph. The team members in the back row from the left are: Major W.F. Taylor, Captain W.C. Allington, Lieutenant C.J. Holloway, and Lieutenant R. Lunn. In the front row are Lieutenant S.M. Guinan, Sergeant H.W. Bramwell, Sergeant J.L. Morgan, and Sergeant J.A. Rowberry. Captain Allington, Sergeants Bramwell and Rowberry had all served in the wartime Home Guard. (Courtesy of Bill Allington)

Kidderminster Battalion records also show that a number of men had been classified for shooting with the Sten gun and rifle for the training year 1953/54 at three levels: 1st Class Standard; Marksman Standard; and 2nd Class Standard. In addition shooting competitions between companies and individuals had taken place at the Hampton Lovett range. The miniature (.22) range at The Shrubbery, Kidderminster, had also been made available to the battalion as well as a small number of dummy No 36 grenades for training purposes. The use of the short range at RAF Halfpenny Green and the North Worcestershire Rifle Club range at Cookley was also being sought. By this time, the War Office had also ruled that members on the Reserve Roll, those who would have been available for inclusion in the force should there have been an emergency, could attend the lectures, training films, demonstrations and TEWTs if they wished.

Difficulty in recruitment

By the autumn of 1953 the total number of Home Guard volunteers had increased by only 2,800 nationally over the previous seven months, and overall it was just over a third of its intended establishment. In addition, some of those who had joined in 1952 were coming to the end of their two-year commitment. The Opposition were pressing for abolition of the force, while the economic situation was leading to the likelihood of defence cuts.[17] Consequently at a Cabinet meeting of 29th October 1953, the future of the Home Guard was under discussion. Sir David Maxwell-Fyfe thought that to disband it would have a discouraging effect on the recruitment to the Civil Defence services, which themselves were seriously understrength. When all the ministers had spoken, Churchill concluded that it was clearly the view of the Cabinet that the Home Guard should be retained, adding that 'The decision to retain it should be announced boldly'.[18]

A recruiting drive had been organised in Western Command from 16th to 30th May, the main objects being to bring cadre battalions up to their establishment and to increase the numbers on the reserve roll, particularly in those areas in which Home Guard battalions had a special and important task. The local press in Worcestershire had apparently been very helpful in publicising the Home Guard and approaches had been made to a large number of firms in the battalion areas. Displays of arms and equipment in shop windows throughout the county were also organised, as well as parades and church services in Worcester and Kidderminster. It was also reported that the enrolment of women up to 4% of the personnel of all Home Guard battalions had been authorised.[19]

Manpower strength of the Home Guard in 1955

By 19th April 1955, the manpower strength of the Home Guard in Worcestershire was:

Oldbury Battalion – 1 permanent staff officer, 1 part-time female, 27 enrolled officers, 29 enrolled ORs, and 163 enrolled reserves.

Kidderminster Battalion – 1 permanent staff officer, 1 part-time female, 21 enrolled officers, 38 enrolled ORs, 3 enrolled females, 311 male reserves, and 2 female reserves.

Droitwich Battalion – 1 permanent staff officer, 1 part-time female, 20 enrolled officers, 38 enrolled ORs, 97 male reserves.

Pershore Battalion – 1 permanent staff officer, 1 part-time male, 26 enrolled officers, 64 enrolled ORs, 102 male reserves.

Worcester and Malvern Battalion – 1 permanent staff officer, 1 part-time female, 32 enrolled officers, 52 enrolled ORs, 422 male reserves, 3 female reserves.[20]

The last days of the 'new' Home Guard

Winston Churchill tendered his resignation as the Prime Minister on 5th April 1955, and was replaced by Sir Anthony Eden. With the main political proponent of the Home Guard throughout its history now gone, and the continuing austerity measures being applied in Britain, it could only be a matter of time before the post-war Home Guard was stood down. In addition, the development of the hydrogen bomb and new missile delivery systems made a conventional land war in Europe less likely, leading to a major defence review of which the outcome was to be substantial cuts in the Regular Army and in the reserves. Consequently, on 20th December 1955, the Minister of Defence announced that the Territorial Army was being scaled down to two Divisions and that the Home Guard would no longer be needed, but that their standing down did not actually mean disbandment.[21] Meanwhile, and despite the political background, Home Guard training continued in Worcestershire during 1955.

By 8th June 1956, all those who were on the cadre had been transferred to the

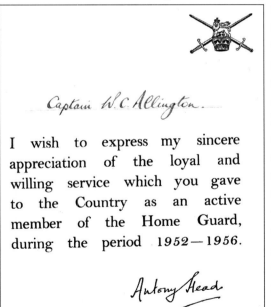

Captain W. C. Allington.

I wish to express my sincere appreciation of the loyal and willing service which you gave to the Country as an active member of the Home Guard, during the period 1952—1956.

Antony Head

The War Office,
London.

*Secretary of State
for War.*

A certificate of service was again issued by the War Office to those men who served in the 1950s Home Guard. (Courtesy of Bill Allington)

Home Guard Reserve Roll and all the officers, less a small cadre, had relinquished their commissions. However, commissioning documents were ready so that in an emergency those officers willing and required could be commissioned and take up their duties immediately. All clothing and equipment had also been handed in.

The duties of the small remaining cadres were recruiting for and maintaining the Reserve Roll, and keeping up-to-date all arrangements for mobilisation and operational plans. This included attendance at conferences and exercises authorised by the District Commander. Four of the five Home Guard battalions in Worcestershire had also formed rifle clubs.[22]

A War Office letter addressed to Western Command, discussed by the November 1956 meeting of TAAFA, made it clear that the Army Council considered that the Home Guard would still have a most valuable role to play in the defence of the country in a total war, and that the Associations might have to accept the responsibility of holding extra stores and equipment for the Home Guard so that these could be issued with the least possible delay in the event of mobilisation.

The Home Guard finally ceased to exist, however, as a result of a statement by the Secretary of State for War on 31st July 1957.[23]

PART II

More detailed aspects of the Home Guard in Worcestershire

8   The Home Guard goes underground

The GHQ Auxiliary Units formed in the Second World War were intended to provide, within the framework of the Home Guard organisation, small bodies of men especially selected and trained, whose role it was to act offensively on the flanks and in the rear of any enemy troops who may have obtained a foothold in this country. Their action was to be particularly directed against tanks and lorries in laager, ammunition dumps, small enemy posts and stragglers. Their activities would also include sniping.[1]

The GHQ Auxiliary Units were given their deliberately vague name to deceive the Germans should the term be inadvertently used in any radio transmission or in 'loose talk'. The patrol members were secretly recruited and given the classification 'Most Secret' to secure, as far as possible, their own and their family's safety, since they were going to be clearly acting contrary to the normal conventions of war. However, they were to operate in uniform, with a rank structure, and under military control. Contrary to popular belief, they were a military, not a resistance, organisation. Nevertheless their covert night operations would mean that they could expect short shrift from the Germans if caught. Recruitment and training of Auxiliary Patrols was under the control of Intelligence Officers, the process starting in the areas thought to be most likely to be invaded first – Kent, Essex and Suffolk. Recruitment then spread northwards, just inland of the east coast up to Scotland, and westwards to Devon and Cornwall, as well as along the south Wales coast.[2]

Clearly forming part of the extensive military defences covering the south-west approaches to the important armaments and aircraft manufacturing factories in the West Midlands, patrols were also recruited in both Herefordshire and Worcestershire. A more comprehensive account of the GHQ Auxiliary Units in the two counties can be found in *The Mercian Maquis*, also published by Logaston Press. The opportunity is taken here to provide more detail about the men of the patrols, based on more recent research.

Recruiting for the Auxiliary Units
The recruitment of men to become part of the Auxiliary Units appears to have begun in Worcestershire in the late summer of 1940. Not all members were recruited from

The Broadheath Scout Hut before the Second World War, with some of the members of the Scout Troop, and later members of the 'Samson' Auxiliary Patrol, painting the hut. Geoff Devereux is on the ladder, Rob Boaz at the bottom of the flag pole, Ron Seymour standing in front of the window and Arch Clines on the roof. The hut has long since been replaced by a house overlooking Broadheath Common, but the yew tree still stands alongside the road. (Courtesy of Geoff Devereux)

the Home Guard, but all would become part of the Home Guard and be provided with a uniform. However, the first complete patrol was formed primarily from Senior Boy Scouts from Broadheath, who were already members of the Worcester City or Malvern Battalions of the Home Guard. Geoff Devereux, who was the first individual to be recruited by Captain John Todd of the Intelligence Corps, was appointed as leader of this patrol. Early written records for the Auxiliary Units in Worcestershire have not survived, if indeed there were any, but interviews with surviving patrol members suggest that this first patrol included Rob Boaz, Arch Clines, Val Clines, Joe King and Ron Seymour. Half a dozen men appears to have been the normal size of an Auxiliary patrol in Worcestershire. Their task was to carry out night attacks against any German forces which had occupied an area of about 20 square miles around their operational base (OB). Until their underground OB had been constructed near Broadwas, the patrol's training was conducted in their scout hut which adjoined Broadheath Common. Here, lectures were given by Captain Todd on the use of explosives, with Geoff, who had been in the OTC at Worcester Royal Grammar School, giving instruction to his scouting friends on the use of firearms, and Peter Price, a pre-war boxer and son of a prominent butcher in Worcester, providing training in unarmed combat. Later the patrol members would attend the Drill Hall in Silver Street, Worcester, and Norton Barracks for some of their training. To maintain the secrecy surrounding the patrol and its intended purpose, and to put the curious off the scent, the members of the patrol would declare that they were a scouting unit along the lines of the original Baden-Powell Army Scouts for message carrying purposes. This seems to have been accepted.

The Todd method of recruiting Auxiliers

Geoff Devereux was working as a student apprentice at the Meco factory along the Bromyard Road, in Worcester, in 1940, when he received a telephone call from Captain John Todd, who asked him to come to his car by the factory main gate. After a short drive into the countryside they stopped, and Geoff was asked to swear on a Bible that he would abide by the Official Secrets Act. He was then informed that Winston Churchill was convinced that the Germans were about to invade Britain and that, as a matter of urgency, a guerrilla force was to be recruited to harass the invaders. He was informed that he had been highly recommended and Todd asked if he would be prepared to recruit and lead a local operation. Geoff was left in no doubt that his life expectancy after a successful occupation of the locality by German troops would be about 15 days. He met Todd the following day with his list of potential recruits, without reference to the individuals concerned, and some time afterwards these were approved after being vetted. Geoff was then coached in the methods of secretly recruiting them. Geoff is fairly convinced that Todd had approached Major D.A.N. Asterley, the Powick Company Commander of the Malvern Battalion Home Guard, and the then headmaster of the nearby Aymestrey School, for him to be picked out as a potential leader. Since General Sir George Weir, the Worcestershire Home Guard Zone Commander, also visited Geoff at the Meco Works, which caused quite a stir at the factory, it seems likely that he too was fully aware of the Auxiliary patrols in the county.

Training at Coleshill and construction of an Operational Base

The Meco Works in St John's, Worcester, was bombed on 3rd October, during the course of which incident Geoff Devereux was wounded in the backside. This is significant, because four days later he was given a very uncomfortable lift as a passenger in Captain Todd's car, down to the village of Highworth, near Swindon, and dropped off outside the infamous post office run by Mabel Stranks. Here he went through the now well known, but then secret, procedure to gain access to the Auxiliary Units Headquarters and training facility at Coleshill, situated in the countryside to the east of Highworth. Over several days, he was trained in the use of explosives, grenades and other weapons, as well as experiencing operating out of an underground OB at night. Coleshill Park is now run by the National Trust, although access to the training site is limited.

On his return from Coleshill, Geoff was shown his newly completed, and well camouflaged, OB in Sneyds Coppice, close to the A44 between Cotheridge and Broadwas. Both the coppice and the OB have now gone. However, Geoff had carefully chosen the site so that from there the patrol could have attacked German forces laagering at night in the lay-bys along the main road, or on the commons at Broad Green and Broadheath. Any enemy fuel or ammunition dumps in the vicinity would have been fair game for an attack, as would the railway line that used to follow the River Teme, and would almost certainly have been used by German forces to transport troops and equipment up into the Midlands from the south Wales ports. The patrol would have used delayed action explosive packs to carry out the night attacks in order to give themselves time to return to their operational base. Their aim was not to confront the Germans but to lay their explosive charges and get away as quickly as possible.

Taken in February 1941, this photograph shows the Intelligence Officers and Headquarters Staff at Coleshill House, near Highworth. Captain John Todd, who was the Intelligence Officer responsible for recruiting and training Auxiliers in the counties of Monmouthshire, Herefordshire and Worcestershire from 1940 to 1942, is standing in the 3rd row and is 3rd from the left. By this time Colonel Gubbins has left to take control of SOE and Colonel Major has replaced him as the Commanding Officer. He is in the centre of the front row, with his 2nd in Command, Lieutenant Colonel Beytes to the left of him. The names of the remaining personnel are given in The Mercian Maquis. *(Courtesy of the late Miss E.M. Wilmot, formerly Captain Todd's ATS Secretary)*

The design of the OB was generally as shown in Fig.11, and appears to have been the standard form of structure used in Worcestershire. Geoff was impressed with the quality of construction and camouflage of his OB, and this somewhat mollified his concerns that it could become a death trap for the patrol. The OB at Sneyds

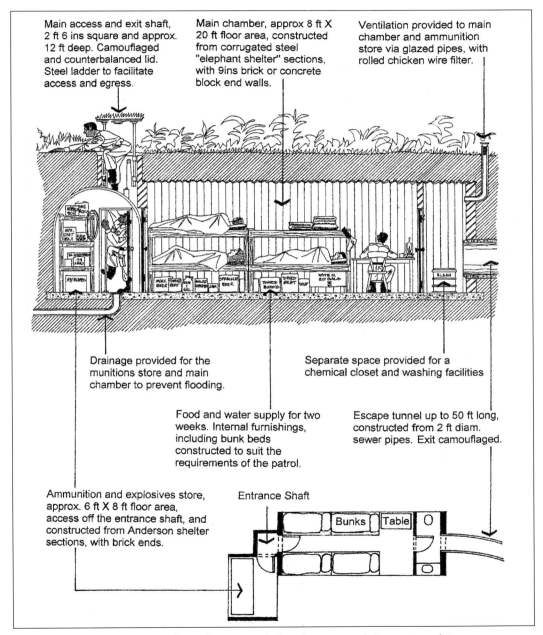

Fig.11 Section through a typical Auxiliary patrol Operational Base, based upon the design of the Alfrick base

Coppice incorporated an explosives store, as did some of the other OBs in the county, but other patrols chose to store their munitions separately, probably when the difficulties of storing things like the Self Igniting Phosphorus (SIP) Bombs, which were prone to deterioration, became apparent.

The OBs were normally constructed by Royal Engineer and Pioneer teams who would be posted in from elsewhere, specifically because they would have no local knowledge. They were briefed to tell any inquisitive locals that they were examining possible anti-aircraft gun sites, apparently a common cover story. Nevertheless, the locals did occasionally discover the sites and an alternative OB would have to be built. This happened at Crowle, where the first OB in Bow Wood was discovered, largely because the foliage planted over the structure to camouflage it had died. An alternative was built in Stanley Wood.[3]

The other Auxiliary Patrols
Geoff Devereux recalled that the only other Auxiliary patrol he was aware of was under the control of Sergeant Roger Smith from Crowle who, when he was not creeping about the countryside at night with his patrol members, farmed at The Commandery, to the east of the village. The extensive acres around the farm, together with the farm buildings, provided plenty of opportunity for training. It is likely that this was the second patrol to be formed in Worcestershire and, in due time, it was to form part of a semi-circle of patrols a short distance from and partially surrounding Worcester Anti-Tank Island. All in all, evidence of eight patrols of Auxiliaries being recruited from the Home Guard in Worcestershire has now been found and their putative areas of operations are shown diagrammatically on Fig.12.

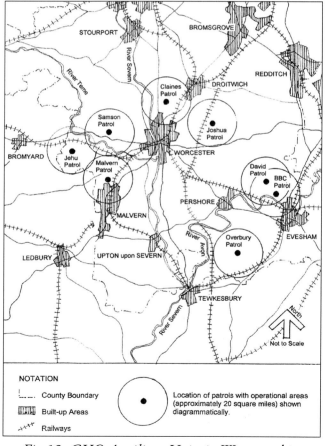

Fig.12 GHQ Auxiliary Units in Worcestershire

164

The bulk of the Worcestershire Auxiliary patrols appear to have been located in order to disrupt an enemy attack on Worcester, notably from the west, and then to frustrate an advance on Birmingham from both the south and west. Their close proximity to railway lines also implies disruption of enemy troop and munitions movements in much the same way as SOE were to do in France after D-Day. However, some of the patrols had clearly defined tasks to perform should the Germans have come. A patrol led by Sergeant Alec Fernihough, who farmed at Radford, would have had the task of disabling German aircraft occupying Pershore Airfield, and so their OB was located on Bishampton Bank, a wooded ridgeline which overlooks the airfield.[4] Alec Fernihough was promoted to Lance Corporal in March 1941, so it is likely that this was the approximate date that this patrol was established.

A patrol about which little is known was recruited at BBC Woodnorton, and it is easy to imagine what their primary task would have been. This patrol certainly involved the then Chief Engineer at the complex, William Bruce Purslow, and a William Harley. Who better than the Chief Engineer to sabotage the transmitters at Woodnorton? Bruce Purslow was also the initial leader of the BBC's 300 man strong X Platoon of the LDV and so he had a dual role. There is hearsay evidence that their OB was located in the woods overlooking Woodnorton, but nothing has been found apart from the very obvious remains of an above-ground standard Anderson shelter based Home Guard ammunition store.

The Auxiliary Patrol located at Overbury was originally led by Sergeant Thurston Holland-Martin, who lived at Overbury Court. That he was not promoted to Sergeant until June 1941 suggests that this was one of the last patrols to be formed in the county. Their OB was on the southern slopes of Overbury Hill, and unusually was built by estate workers. It is likely that their task was to observe any enemy troop movements coming up from the south-east into the county and disrupt rail traffic on the line between Evesham and Tewkesbury. For observation purposes, the Overbury Patrol would use Parson's Folly on top of Bredon Hill, from where they had a hidden telephone link back to their OB.[5]

All of the patrols in south Wales, Herefordshire and Worcestershire were given biblical codenames to avoid the need to use a geographical title and risk the location of the patrol being compromised. Most of the codenames for the patrols in Worcestershire have been identified from interviews with patrol members. Others have simply been forgotten, or it has not been possible to find and interview members of them. The patrol names, where known, are shown on Fig.12 and listed in Appendix 8.

In the event of an invasion

The signal for the Auxiliary Units to become operational was, according to Geoff Devereux, 'The balloon has gone up', at which point he would gather together his patrol and move into their OB, not telling anyone that they were going or where. They would literally vanish from the face of the earth! There they would live underground, only coming out to carry out scouting patrols for potential targets, and then prepare their explosives for the attack back at the OB. Time delay pencils would be used to detonate the explosives and enable the patrol to return safely to the OB. Although they were not intended to confront enemy forces, they were nevertheless well armed so that the men could if necessary fight their way out of a corner. Tony Barling, for example, recalled receiving a Thompson Submachine Gun, well before his brother, who was a Major in the Royal Marine Commandos, received his! For personal protection the men were supplied with a revolver of some sort, most in Worcestershire having the American .38 Smith and Wesson. For the silent despatch of enemy sentries, the Fairbairn-Sykes fighting knife was supplied to most men, although some of the Auxiliers, notably the Broadheath boy scouts, supplied their own sheath knives. Besides the sabotage of enemy installations and communications, the Auxiliaries had a number of other tasks to perform in the event of an invasion. This included the ambush and assassination of enemy officers and assassination of informers and collaborators. Each patrol was issued with a .22 rifle with silencer and telescopic sight, ostensibly for this purpose, but more likely intended for shooting enemy guard dogs and providing game for the pot! Geoff Devereux recalled receiving a plain brown envelope from John Todd which was to be opened only when the patrol became operational. He never did find out what was in it, although his successor, the late Sergeant Val Clines may well have done, but we shall now never know. Perhaps, as elsewhere, amongst the more conventional orders for the operational tasks to be undertaken by the patrol, there was a list of local people to be 'dealt with'![6]

Coordination of the patrols in the event of an attack

Initially, John Todd coordinated the activities of the Auxiliary Units in Worcester-shire, arranging both their training and supply of armaments and explosives. He would have been responsible for re-supply of the patrols should the Germans have occupied the area, which would have tested his ingenuity! However, Thurston Holland-Martin of the Overbury Patrol appears to have taken on some of this responsibility from June 1941, and a number of ex-Auxiliers remember Overbury Court and the Holland-Martin estate being a focus for meetings and training. One of the quarries on Bredon Hill, for example, was regularly used for revolver shooting and explosives practice. In 1942, Thurston Holland-Martin left the UK and moved to South Africa, and Basil Tadman, the Overbury Estate farm manager, was promoted to the rank of Sergeant and would lead the Overbury Patrol until Stand Down in 1944.

The van Moppes brothers enter the arena

By the summer of 1941, Auxiliary Patrols were made less independent and brought more within the military establishment through the appointment of Group Commanders. In August 1941 two Dutch diamond merchants, Lewis and Edmund or 'Gug' van Moppes, were commissioned as Lieutenants in the Malvern Battalion Home Guard, and are presumed to have been appointed as Group Commanders for the patrols at the same time. (As a later example, Roger Smith, the leader of Joshua Patrol at Crowle, was promoted to 2nd Lieutenant and appointed as a Group Commander.) Thereafter, the focus for meetings, training and social events for the Auxiliaries moved to Wolverton Hall, near Peopleton, where the van Moppes ran their industrial diamond supply business. Here, the Auxiliers would stay overnight, carrying out practice night patrols in the grounds and receiving other training, including small bore shooting on a temporary range there. The meals supplied by the van Moppes were noted for their excellence. With the increasing central control came the introduction of foot drill to their training, something that was not enthusiastically received![7]

Changes in personnel and administration

Despite the intended secrecy for the Auxiliary Patrols and their operational control by GHQ, it has been something of a revelation to find that their administration was handled by the parent Home Guard Company, then Battalion HQs, and any

Wolverton Hall, wartime base of the van Moppes diamond processing company and headquarters of the Auxiliary Patrols in Worcestershire from 1941. The group photograph that appears on page 170 was taken on the terrace and steps in front of the door.
(Courtesy of Susie Elliot)

personnel changes in the patrols from 1941 to 1942 were clearly listed in Part 2 Orders for all in the Home Guard parent units to see. Promotions had to be authorised by the battalion commanders and these orders were normally displayed on the Battalion and Company HQs noticeboard. Perhaps it was only in the first, and most critical year, 1940, that the extremes of secrecy were applied and only John Todd knew the details of each patrol? Although the change of administration in 1941 appears to have been part of a national policy towards the Auxiliary Units, Worcestershire appears to be unique in having surviving copies of the Home Guard Part 2 Orders as supporting evidence of this change. As early as August 1940, Colonel Colin Gubbins, in command at Coleshill, and Major Peter Wilkinson, his second in command, were concerned about the risk to security of the Auxiliary Units being compromised, and the latter proposed an 'inner circle' of covert forces. It is not clear whether this idea was proceeded with because both men were transferred to SOE soon afterwards, but it might just explain the other covert forces described in *The Defence of Worcestershire*.

However, it was from Part 2 Orders that the existence of a Malvern Patrol was discovered when men were listed as being discharged in December 1941 as surplus to establishment of the Malvern Company and Auxiliary Unit (see Appendix 8).[8]

7TH WORCESTER (MALVERN) BN. HOME GUARD.

Part Two Orders: No. 35. dated 22nd October, 1941.

No.	NAME	Coy.	Particulars of Casualty
1) Aux. Patrol (attached 7th Worcs. (Malvern) Bn. Home Guard Hqrs:1.10.41.			
3527/2	Lt. L.E. Van Moppes)		
3550/2	Lt. E.M. Van Moppes) Ombersley		
3528/2	Vol V. Poland)		
3310	R.V. Clines Sgt.	Powick	
3293	R.H. Boaz	"	
3190	W.A. ing	"	
3274	A.V. Clines	"	
3197	P. Lester Cancelled	Patv Porders. No 52.	
3255	Sgt. G.A. Devereux	"	
3677	Vol. R. Smith	Crowle	
3693	J. Wythes	"	
3679	J.I. Thomas	"	
2147/D	J.E. Badger	"	
3686	M.F. Huband	"	
3685	A.J. Holt.ng.	"	
3424	A.S. Barleen	Frightwel	
3416	G. Dalley	"	
3389	R.F. Mason	"	
3437	W.F. Jauncey	"	
3447	A.G. Jeynes	"	
3476	W.J. Plaskett	"	

This example of Part 2 Orders of the Malvern Battalion Home Guard of October 1941 indicates that the high level of secrecy surrounding the Auxiliary Units had not been maintained. (Courtesy of the former Army Medal Office)

The location of their OB has not been identified, although there is some hearsay evidence of an underground structure being sited in the woodlands just to the south of the Hereford Road, at Storridge. This would seem to be a good location for a patrol to observe an enemy advance along the western approaches to Worcester, and then attack their supply chain. Malvern Battalion Part 2 Orders also reveal a number of changes to the personnel in the other patrols.

With effect from 1st October 1941, the Auxiliary Units in the Malvern Battalion area were transferred from their Home Guard Company Rolls to Battalion HQ administration,[9] presumably to improve security. The Evesham Battalion were a little slower off the mark in transferring their Auxiliers from Company administration to the Battalion, it being January 1942 before Part 2 Orders listed the transferred men.[10]

It is likely that the planned secrecy surrounding the existence of the Auxiliary patrols was still being severely compromised by having the details so readily available to the rest of their parent Home Guard battalions, and so on 22nd September 1942, we find the Evesham Battalion men being transferred to TAA administration. It is interesting to note that the two BBC engineers from the previous list are missing; perhaps they were released from duty to concentrate on their 'day job'. It was the Malvern Battalion which was slower off the mark this time, it being 19th November before we see orders removing the Auxiliers from the roll of the Malvern Battalion.[11] Henceforth the administration of all the Auxiliary Units in Worcestershire passed to the Territorial Association head offices in York. However, before this major change in administration in 1942, it is possible to trace from Part 2 Orders the departure of Geoff Devereux and Rob Boaz from the Samson Patrol to the Regular services, as well as the discharge of P. Lester, and their replacement in part by John Boaz and later, Peter Wright and Peter King. Names which do not appear in any of the Samson Patrol lists are the late Ron Seymour and the late Joe King, who were members of the patrol in the early days, before Ron was transferred to an anti-aircraft unit in the Gloucestershire Home Guard at Staverton, and Joe joined an anti-tank regiment in the Regular Army.

The Alfrick Patrol also experienced a number of personnel changes, with Sergeant Tony Barling joining the Parachute Regiment and later dropping into Arnhem and becoming a POW. George Dalley was made up to Sergeant and took his place. This patrol also lost John Barker, Chris Bullock, Bill Jauncey and Fred Mason quite early on, to be replaced by Peter Bussey, Jim Griffin, Horace Phillips and Bill Plaskett. Horace Phillips also left in due course to rejoin the Knghtwick Company, leaving a very depleted patrol. Dick Philips's patrol at Claines also experienced a number of changes in personnel, but because the majority of men in the remaining patrols in Worcestershire were recruited from the farming community, and were in reserved occupations, there was less change of personnel. The changes, and the dates where known, are included in Appendix 8.

A last call to arms

Rather as the Home Guard was called to arms to protect Vulnerable Points during the critical period before and during the D-Day landings, so volunteers were called for from the ranks of the Auxiliary Units to undertake the task of protecting military installations along the south coast against possible sabotage raids by the enemy. A number of men volunteered from the Worcestershire patrols and travelled down to the Isle of Wight by car and Army lorry to spend a couple of weeks night-patrolling

The Group Leaders, Sergeants and some of the Worcestershire Auxiliaries at Wolverton Hall, taken at Stand Down in 1944. In the back row, from the left are: Jack Badger (Joshua Patrol), Hubert Jackson (Claines Patrol), Andrew Green (Claines Patrol), John Hartwright (Joshua Patrol), 'Packy' Packwood (Overbury Patrol), and Corporal Arthur Allen (Jehu Patrol). In the 3rd row, from the left are: Tom Harwood (David Patrol), Colin Curnock (David Patrol), Jim Holt (Joshua Patrol), Horace Roberts (Claines Patrol), Jim Griffin (Jehu Patrol), Bill Plaskett (Jehu Patrol), Peter Bussey (Jehu Patrol), and Reg Wilkinson (Overbury Patrol). In the 2nd row are: Sergeant John Wythes (Joshua Patrol), Sergeant T.G. Dawe (Quartermaster, Wolverton Hall), Sergeant Basil Tadman (Overbury Patrol), Sergeant Val Clines (Samson Patrol), Lieutenant Edmund 'Gug' van Moppes (Group 1(a) Leader), Captain Lewis van Moppes (Group 1 – Worcestershire – Leader), 2nd Lieutenant Roger Smith (Group 1(b) Leader), Sergeant Dick Philips (Claines Patrol), Sergeant 'Alec' Fernihough (David Patrol), and Sergeant George Dalley (Jehu Patrol). In the front row are: Noel Huband (Joshua Patrol), Ernie Shervington (David Patrol), Harold Plain (David Patrol), Corporal Harry Curnock (David Patrol), Corporal Vincent Poland (Claines Patrol), and Corporal Ivor Thomas (Joshua Patrol). (Courtesy of the late Colin Curnock)

around munitions dumps and protecting the vital above-ground installations of the PLUTO petrol pipeline to Normandy. Fortunately the anticipated enemy raids did not take place, and the greatest excitement was caused by a potentially lethal accident with the notoriously unreliable Stens with which they were issued and an exploding V1 missile. It seems very likely that the Auxiliers who did not go to the Isle of Wight would have had a similar role in relation to Vulnerable Points in this county during this critical period. Although no evidence for this has been found for Worcestershire, Auxiliary Units elsewhere were acting as recce patrols for the local Home Guard as part of the VITGUARD operations.[12] The fact that John Hartwright of Joshua Patrol was not recruited until May 1944 tends to confirm that the Auxiliary Units were still seen as having an important role to play at this late stage of the war.

Measuring just 5/8ths of an inch from top to bottom, this lapel badge was issued at Stand Down in 1944, and together with a letter of thanks, is the only tangible evidence that the recipients had been members of the GHQ Auxiliary Units. The numbers on the badge refer to the three battalions of Auxiliaries formed: 201 in Scotland and northern England, 202 in the Midlands and Wales, and 203 in the south of England. (Courtesy of the late John Thornton)

Stand Down

Due to the intended secrecy surrounding their existence, the Auxiliers could not be indulged with a grand parade, or any form of public display when they were quietly stood down in late November 1944, although their existence was acknowledged in an article in *The Times* in 1945. Instead, the members of the patrols received a letter of thanks from General H.E. Franklyn, the Commander in Chief of Home Forces, and Colonel F.W.R. Douglas, the last commander of the Auxiliary Units, based at Coleshill. The men were issued with a small lapel badge as the only other memento of their service. They were also eligible to receive the Defence Medal, if they had performed the minimum of three years' service in the Auxiliary Units, but most did not bother to claim it. Like the more conventional Home Guards, those Auxiliaries still serving at Stand Down were not formally discharged until 31st December 1945 as a consequence of the disbandment of the Home Guard, but were discharged by the TAA York which had taken over the administration of all Auxiliary Units in 1942 to restore some of the anonymity that had been lost when administered by local Home Guard battalions.

After the patrols were stood down, Royal Engineers were intended to collect up the unused armaments and destroy the OBs, but this did not always happen and caches of grenades and explosives, and the occasional revolver, still come to light at intervals. Of those OBs not destroyed, most have now succumbed to the effects of dampness on corrugated metal and have collapsed.

Hospitable to the end, the van Moppes brothers organised a few social evenings for the ex-Auxiliers from Worcestershire at the Shuthonger Hotel, north of Tewkesbury,[13] before moving their diamond processing business from Wolverton Hall to Basingstoke.

Bernard Lowry, one-time Regional Co-ordinator for the Defence of Britain Project, climbing down the entrance shaft of the Jehu Patrol operational base on a wet day in 1999. This is one of the few surviving pieces of Auxiliary Unit archaeology in Worcestershire.

9　Women and the Home Guard

In his broadcast of 14th May 1940, Anthony Eden had clearly asked only for men between the ages of 17 and 65 to volunteer for service with the LDV, but from the outset women too had wanted to join the new force. However, despite the efforts of Labour MP Dame Edith Summerskill to promote the concept, there was a general view in the War Office and Parliament that women should not bear arms and that, in any case, there was a need for women to work in other aspects of the war effort including Civil Defence, munitions production, nursing and voluntary work. Frustrated by the official view, many women joined rifle clubs in order to learn to shoot, while others formed their own home defence corps, starting in the London and Bristol areas. Despite the lack of support from the government, the movement quickly spread to the rest of Britain, becoming a national organisation called the Women's Home Defence Corps under the chairmanship of Dame Edith Summerskill.[1]

Training for the new force included range practice with firearms, unarmed combat, fieldcraft, anti-gas drill, first aid, construction of defence works and field cooking. To reflect their combative intentions, the Corps developed their own shield-shaped badge, complete with crossed rifles and a pistol together with the initial letters WHD.

Despite the War Office view, women had been employed by the Home Guard in Worcestershire from the outset, one example being at Upton upon Severn. Major Jewell established his Company Office in the police station and Mrs

The Women's Home Defence Corps badge reflects the intention of members to become involved with armed conflict with any invader, much against the advice of the War Office. (Courtesy of Gwen Harvey)

Women's Home Defence Corps at range practice near Watford. Of note are the Home Guards standing behind the women, and the use of .300 P17 rifles and one SMLE, although most are using .22 rifles. Clearly some men supported the involvement of women in a combatant role, enough to lend them their full-bore rifles! (Courtesy of Gwen Harvey, who can be seen in the centre of the front row of standing women, 11th from the right)

Phillips, the wife of the local police inspector, was appointed to help with the clerical work, which she apparently continued to do until the stand down of the Home Guard.[2]

During 1941, discussions took place between the War Office and the Women's Voluntary Service about their cooperation with the Home Guard for clerical work, cooking and other miscellaneous services deemed suitable for women, on the understanding that there was to be no formal recognition of the WVS and no enrolment in the Home Guard.[3] Sir James Grigg, the then Secretary for War, was of the view that the only acceptable arrangements for women having any role in the Home Guard were those with the Women's Voluntary Service. As late as April 1942 the government were considering suppressing the Women's Home Defence Corps as being outside the law as an armed force.[4]

Nevertheless, there were signs of a thaw at the War Office in a memorandum dated 24th August 1942 which, while maintaining the policy of not enrolling women as combatants, accepted that there were ways in which women could be of assistance to the Home Guard in non-combatant roles, including clerical work,

Until 'nominated' women were admitted to the ranks of the Home Guard, the War Office encouraged the Women's Voluntary Service to help the force with non-combatant work, including driving, catering and clerical duties. Here a WVS member is helping a Malvern Home Guard with catering during an exercise in Madresfield Park. (Courtesy of Sheila Edmonds)

manning telephones, motor driving and 'other miscellaneous odd jobs'. The memo recognised that the driving of vehicles, telephone work, and other employment with the Home Guard was already being undertaken by WVS members, but it was considered that where the WVS were not available wives, sisters and female friends of Home Guards would be willing, and anxious, to give some assistance without becoming members of the force. Implying, perhaps, another reason for not having women in the Home Guard, the memo raised the financial implications of full enrolment, including the supply of free uniforms, subsistence, allowances, compensation for injury, disability pensions, compensation for loss of earnings and travelling expenses.[5] In War Office correspondence of October 1942, the question of women being enrolled in the Home Guard was dealt with again. The view was still that women should not be formally enrolled in the force, but that a limited number should be allowed to register for employment in support roles, the correspondence making it clear that no uniform would be issued and only a brooch provided.[6]

Clifton upon Teme Home Guard ignore the War Office

In October 1942, Lt H.R. Winn formed a Women's Section in No 13 Platoon at Clifton upon Teme. In an apparent act of defiance of the official view, they were also enrolled in the Women's Home Defence Corps and provided with uniforms paid for with money raised by Lt Winn. He apparently had to put up with a considerable amount of leg-pulling about his Women's Section, but apparently never had occasion to regret forming it. Half the Section was trained to give first aid, under the instruction of Mrs Thompson; the rest were trained in signalling by Private W.C. Sanders, who had been invalided out of the RAF and had subsequently joined the Clifton Home Guard. Under his tuition, the section reached the high standard of eight words a minute, the Stourport Battalion Signals Officer claiming he had not seen better signalling in the Home Guard. The involvement of the Clifton women in both first aid and signalling, the provision of uniforms and the wearing of Womens Home Defence Corps cap badges were all outside the War Office recommendations, and indicates very clearly the degree of independence that had been a feature of some Home Guard units throughout their history.[7] Joan Warren (née Enion) was one of the Clifton upon Teme Section, and recalled that their training began with a signalling lamp and learning Morse Code, and that the Section Signallers became proficient at both

Despite the edict that they should not have a uniform or have signals or first aid training, the Commander of the Clifton on Teme Home Guard Platoon contrived to provide his 'nominated' women with dark blue uniforms and have them practise the banned roles. Here the signallers are wearing field service caps and first aiders' berets. In addition to the standard issue plastic Home Guard brooch, the women here are also wearing the Women's Home Defence Corps badge on their headwear.

The photograph was taken at Stand Down, outside the Lion Hotel at Clifton. In the back row, from the left are: Mrs Winn, Mrs Thompson, Mrs Mary Mitchell, Mrs Burford, and Mrs Mabel Turner (née Millward).

In the front row, from the left are: Nora Saunders, Mrs Joan Warren (née Enion), Lieutenant Henry R. Winn, Clifton Platoon Commander, Josie Thompson and Muriel Kirkman. (Courtesy of Joan Warren)

The 'official' plastic lapel brooch supposed to be worn on the civilian clothing of women serving in the Home Guard, but a number of Worcestershire Home Guard commanders contrived to supply 'their' women with more appropriate uniform. (Courtesy of Malcolm Atkin)

Four very smartly uniformed ladies of D Company (Wollaston) of the Stourbridge Battalion Home Guard. Note the use of the standard brooch as tie pins. From left to right: Dot Davies, Margaret White, Betty Davies and Sheila Borroughs. (Courtesy of the Wollaston Local History Group)

sending and receiving signals, although she was unaware of the operational requirements of the section should there have been an emergency. Apparently the Women's Section were not expected to do drill, although she remembered the men of the Clifton Platoon being drilled in the road near the village hall, which was used as a headquarters. The uniform issued to the Clifton Section was dark blue (probably Civil Defence battledress) with the First Aiders wearing blue berets, and the Signallers two-tone forage caps, which may be a dress version of Worcestershire Regiment field service caps.[8]

In March 1943, 11 women were recruited to form a Women's Section of U Company, Upton upon Severn, who were trained in telephone and clerical work and received some instruction on map reading.[9]

The War Office go a step further

As has often been the way with Home Guard affairs, the War Office responded belatedly to what was becoming a fait accompli and by October 1943 agreed, half-heartedly, that 5% of the existing ceiling for men could be filled by women registering with, but not enrolled in the Home Guard. For this duty, they would be given a brooch and, where necessary, compensation for injury, but there was to be no training in arms.

In the following April, Lord Bridgeman, Director General of the Home Guard, in a memorandum to all commands again set out the official footing for employment of women to assist the Home Guard. He confirmed that they would be restricted to non-combatant duties and training in weapons would be forbidden. Duties were to be confined to clerical work, manning of telephones,

cooking and service of food, and driving of vehicles, including War Department or G Licence vehicles on authorised journeys. They were not to be employed in intercommunication (signals) in the field or first aid. Women would be 'nominated' for employment and listed by the Home Guard commander. The scheme was entirely voluntary and did not exempt women from other part-time service which the Ministry of Labour or National Service might require, or performing fire prevention duty. No uniform was to be supplied, but a badge in brooch form was to be made available.[10]

Evesham Battalion employed 'nominated' women in its signals platoon, although not in uniform apart from their plastic brooches. Note the lavish supply of radios available by the time of this Stand Down photograph of December 1944.
(Courtesy of The Vale of Evesham Historical Society)

By 30th September 1943 a total of 125 women were employed in Worcestershire's Home Guard as follows:[11]

Worcester City Battalion, 30 out of a ceiling figure of 82
Evesham Battalion, 17 out of a ceiling figure of 53
Halesowen Battalion, 12 out of 23
Malvern Battalion, 25 out of 53
Redditch Battalion, 37 out of 79
and Stourbridge Battalion 4 out of 15.

For the remaining battalions in Worcestershire, which had yet to nominate women to their personnel rolls, the ceilings were set at:

44 for the Bromsgrove Battalion,
23 for the Dudley Battalion,
64 for the Kidderminster Battalion,
14 for the Oldbury Battalion,
23 for the Stourport Battalion,
and 13 for the Warley Battalion.

The terminology used by some Home Guard battalions in describing women employed by them clearly caused consternation in the War Office, and in

February 1944 the Director General, in a memorandum to all commands, made it clear that the correct term for them was 'Nominated Women'. Such terms as Women Auxiliaries, or Home Guard Auxiliaries, or other expressions (presumably Women Home Guards) were to be discontinued forthwith![12]

Stand Down

It is not known how many 'nominated women' participated in the Home Guard Stand Down parades on 3rd December 1944, but at Worcester the women in the parade were given a hearty cheer by spectators.[13] At Stourport, the Clifton Section helped the WVS provide refreshments at The Haven Cinema for the marching troops after the parade![14]

After it was all over, and to mark the contribution women made to the Home Guard, a certificate of service was issued by the Territorial Associations. War Office inconsistency and confusion was apparent in the certificates when the women were referred to as 'Women Home Guard Auxiliaries' despite the earlier edict.

Women, although few in number, seem to have been more readily accepted by the authorities in the 1950s Home Guard (see Chapter 7).

I have received The King's command to express His Majesty's appreciation of the loyal service given voluntarily to her country in a time of grievous danger by

as a Woman Home Guard Auxiliary.

The War Office, London.

Secretary of State for War

'Nominated' women of the Home Guard received a certificate of service from the War Office, but unlike the menfolk of the force, this was issued in the name of the Secretary of State for War rather than the king. (This unused example of the women's certificate is courtesy of Tim Norton.)

10   Training the LDV/Home Guard

The LDV was probably the first organised British military force to be sent out on operations with the possibility of active engagement *before* it had been trained, properly clothed or armed! With an enemy invasion expected soon after their formation, the first priority of the LDV was to patrol their locality and man their observation posts, defence posts and rudimentary barricades. There was little time for any training in this initial period of high alert, and heavy reliance was put upon the old soldiers in the organisation to show the inexperienced men and boys how to conduct themselves. Patrolling and observing would be carried out in pairs with one experienced man accompanying an inexperienced colleague. Bill Allington, then a young and untrained volunteer, and a member of the Stoke Prior Platoon of the LDV, recalls night patrolling on Dodderhill Common with Corporal Hailes, a one-legged veteran of the First World War. Dawn was approaching and the nightingales started to sing in the beech woods which covered the common then as they do now. This was a new experience for Bill, who stopped to listen and placed his rifle against a tree. Corporal Hailes took exception to this and, clearly influenced by his experiences in the trenches on the Western Front where dawn attacks could be expected, roundly told Bill off for dropping his guard: 'Don't you realise that the Germans could appear at any time?'

Bill's Section Commander, Major Kay, was another veteran of the Great War and a member of the family which ran Kays mail order company in Worcester. Being an officer 'of the old school', he was apparently very strict about his section's night patrolling and observation duties and would carry out inspections at unexpected times. Woe betide any volunteer who did not carry out the correct challenge procedure, although it is reported that he did give the men on duty a sporting chance to look alert by tapping his swagger stick on a nearby stile or fence before making an appearance. The Germans would not have been so understanding, but the inexperienced men quickly learned what was expected of them, some apparently quicker than others. Bill was soon made a corporal, responsible for the men manning an observation post in the grounds of what was then Sir Hugh Sumner's house, located on the top of the hill at Rashwood, to the north of Droitwich. This house is now a nursing home, and the grounds around it provide extensive views of the countryside to the east, over what is now the M5. Major Kay made one of his surprise visits and was not properly challenged by one of the night pickets. Being now the NCO responsible, Bill was taken to task by the Major and when Bill subsequently asked the culprit for an explanation, the reason given was: 'I part knowed the Old Bugger!' Clearly familiarity with the officers was not going to be tolerated or accepted as an excuse for not carrying out the proper procedures.

Later, Major Kay also arranged for his section to have drill training at Wychbold Village Hall from RSM Smith, formerly of the Coldstream Guards but in 1940 part of the training staff at one of the OCTUs then based in the War Office buildings at Droitwich. This element of military training was considered necessary to inculcate discipline in the men, to ensure a prompt response to orders and familiarity in handling a rifle.[1] However, there were those, both within and outside the LDV, who thought that drill was not an appropriate use of the limited time that the volunteers could give to training, usually one or two nights a week and Sunday mornings.

Tom Wintringham was particularly scathing about what he saw as outdated training methods and, through a series of articles in the summer of 1940 and into 1941, put forward the notion that, to meet the Blitzkrieg techniques of the Germans, the LDV/Home Guard should be taught the lessons learned the hard way by the International Brigade in Spain. There the Germans, who were fighting with General Franco's Nationalists, had practised their new tactics and utilised their modern weapons and equipment, while for their part the volunteers of the International Brigade fighting with the Republicans had developed what they considered to be effective methods of countering the German 'Blitzkrieg' weapons and tactics. Instead of drilling, Wintringham considered that the LDV/Home Guard should be learning about the manufacture and use of their own weapons; the use of explosives; the art of fieldcraft; the shortcomings of tanks and how to counter them; and the tricks and tactics used by the Germans. He claimed that such things could be taught in a few days, for he had already played a part in teaching them to the British volunteers of the International Brigade, which he considered was the best unit in the Brigade.

Home Guard training schools
The first dedicated training school for the LDV was established by Tom Wintringham at Osterley Park. For training staff he recruited Hugh Slater who had been in Spain and, amongst other things, was an expert in destroying tanks; a couple of Spaniards who could handle explosives; Roland Penrose, an expert in camouflage; Stanley White, an expert in field craft, Wilfred Vernon, who could improvise mines, grenades and other destructive devices; and 'Yank' Levy, who

taught unarmed combat and silent killing. For LDV/Home Guards who were looking for something more than simply watching for enemy parachutists, patrolling and practising drill, the Osterley Park courses offered the opportunity to learn 'ungentlemanly warfare'. The courses were an immediate success and constantly oversubscribed. Men from the Regular services, including the Brigade of Guards, the Armoured Corps, some of the infantry regiments, and even a Naval Shore Establishment, sneaked onto the course to learn Wintringham's new ways of war. At this point, the LDV was leading the way in formulating defence thinking – a far cry from Captain Mainwaring's 'Dad's Army'!

It is not known how many LDVs from Worcestershire attended the school at Osterley, but one man who did was Sydney Carter from the Evesham Battalion. He later wrote that he came back full of enthusiasm and proceeded to teach the Osterley methods throughout the battalion. For this purpose, he would have almost certainly had a copy of the small training manual, *The Home Guard Can Fight*, written by Wintringham. It was packed with good advice on fighting the coming

Here men of the Redditch Battalion are undergoing indoor training in what appears to be a schoolroom. The presence of aircraft recognition models, including an American Flying Fortress, indicates a late war period, and the map on the blackboard suggests that a map reading exercise is being conducted. This may be one of the Intelligence Courses held at Redditch County High School.
(Courtesy of Mr E.P. Grace via Mike Johnson)

battles, being a summary of the lectures given at Osterley Park. Sydney Carter was subsequently to be appointed as the Training Officer for the battalion and would reach the rank of Major. Ironically, Wintringham and his friends were prevented from joining the LDV at this time as being known communists, although in fact they had been disowned by both the Communist Party and the International Brigade Association.[2]

By the Autumn of 1940, a worried War Office was becoming concerned about the influence the courses at Osterley were having on the LDV/Home Guard. It was reluctant to give the LDV/Home Guard an irregular role and disliked the idea of amateurs being trained in guerrilla warfare. LDV/Home Guard units were consequently told not to attend the Osterley School. One War Office Staff Brigadier, clearly harking back to his earlier days of soldiering, made it clear to the organisers of the school that the Home Guard had one simple role: to man their defence posts and stay there. Using scarce materials to construct their own weapons or indulging in guerrilla tactics was not acceptable.

The fact that the Osterley School was run by former members of the Communist Party also raised the fear in government circles of an armed insurrection by at least some of the more left-wing factions of the Home Guard, who they were concerned might have been indoctrinated by the tutors at the school. An insurrection, they feared, might occur if the legitimate government lost even temporary control of part of the country following a German invasion. This may also be an explanation for the reluctance of the War Office to allow Home Guards to take home their rifles and ammunition in the early part of the war – a point not lost on some former Worcestershire Home Guards when they were quickly disarmed in 1944, well before the war was over. This fear must have increased when it was appreciated that Tom Wintringham and Lord Hulton had made a direct and successful private appeal to citizens of the United States to donate arms and ammunition to them in the summer of 1940 through the Committee for the Defence of British Homes.[3]

The effect of all this was that the War Office took over the running of the school at Osterley and then closed it down. It was replaced by the War Office's own establishment, No 1 GHQ Home Guard School at Dorking in Surrey, where many Worcestershire officers and NCOs would later undertake week-long courses. Two further schools were subsequently established, No 2 GHQ Home Guard School at Moncrieff House, in Scotland, and No 3 GHQ Home Guard School at Stokesay Court, Onibury, near Craven Arms.[4] At the latter school, potential Worcestershire Home Guard officers received training in Junior Leadership. One of these was Bill Allington, who recalls that the students were accommodated in Stokesay Court. When visiting the Court for an auction of furniture and effects some time after the war, he was surprised to find that the doors in the Court still had the various notices put there by the Home Guard School staff during the war. Officers and potential

The ever-so-slightly superior pose struck by the Sergeant in the background compared with the more relaxed Home Guards suggests that he was a Regular soldier and one of the Permanent Staff Instructors attached, in this case, to the Malvern Battalion. Here he is supervising Browning Machine Gun practice at the West Malvern Range. Note the 200 yard marker post beyond the men. (Courtesy of Sheila Edmonds)

officers would receive training in the handling of Battle Companies in Attack and in TEWTs, while NCOs received lessons in Orders, Squad Commands and Snap Decisions. Onibury also ran Sniper Courses. The students did not escape night duty while staying there, and were expected to provide a guard on the road bridge over the River Severn at Onibury!

Western Command Weapons Training School at Altcar, on the Mersey Estuary north of Liverpool, was also made available from June 1941 for Home Guard training. There, Worcestershire officers and NCOs were trained and qualified as instructors and would return to their battalions able to supervise training in the use of a wide variety of weapons.[5] The lessons learned at the national schools consequently filtered down to locally established Home Guard schools.

One of the problems found by Home Guards was making the time to attend such courses when there was already Home Guard duty to be done, and many of the men were working in demanding reserved occupations. Nevertheless, compulsory training for Home Guards was ordered in February 1942 and a minimum attendance at training courses was required of four hours on alternate Sundays and two hours in the evening during the week. Consequently, local training opportunities became necessary. Since the first winter of 1940/41, battalion and company headquarters, village halls and schools were already being utilised for indoor training. That usage would intensify as the war progressed. A list of both national and local training schools used by members of the Worcestershire Home Guard is included in Appendix 9, which indicates that there was no shortage of opportunities for the enthusiastic members to train as the war progressed.

An example of winter training was held in January 1941, when the 11th Battalion Royal Warkwickshire Regiment at Hewell Grange arranged map reading instruction for selected candidates from both the Redditch and Bromsgrove Battalions. In February, the same battalion organised a TEWT for the Bromsgrove and Redditch Battalions, this being a reflection of the desire of the War Office to bring the training of Home Guards more into line with that of the Regular Army.[6] No details of the latter scheme are recorded but it was almost certainly an indoor exercise, where a table holding sand or cloth was used to simulate battlefield topography, Regular Army instructors then taking the Home Guards through a series of battlefield manoeuvres and coaching them on the appropriate responses. The exercise would now be called wargaming.

The full-time adjutants appointed to the Home Guard battalions in 1941 were expected to help with training, as well as deal with the increasing administrative tasks. With the introduction of compulsory service for the Home Guard in 1942 and the need for training the influx of inexperienced younger men, two and sometimes three Permanent Staff Instructors (PSIs) were attached to each Home Guard battalion from 1942. These were Regulars of Sergeant rank, although they were normally promoted to temporary Warrant Officer (WO) rank, unpaid, while with the Home Guard, presumably to give them some seniority over their Home Guard NCO colleagues.

Besides the expanded training curriculum, not least as a result of the increasing variety of weapons becoming available to the Home Guard, recruit training was introduced by the battalions, whereby men would receive basic training before being posted to the companies. Recruit training included various forms of drill and the Empire Test for rifle firing, essentially where the recruit had to obtain a reasonable grouping with five shots at 200 yards. Clothing and equipment was issued only after the recruit had successfully passed through this training, presumably to save retrieving the kit if the man proved to be 'unsuitable' and was discharged. Many of the 17-year-olds were to reap the benefit of this early training when conscripted to the Regular services aged 18, or later if they had been employed in a reserved occupation. They would then be given a letter of introduction by their Home Guard battalion commander, which included an explanation of their military training, to show to the authorities when reporting for duty with the Regular forces. One can imagine that despite the letter the arrogance normally displayed by the Regulars would have been very forcibly expressed by NCO squad commanders to any ex-Home Guards on the parade square!

The threat of a gas attack always a concern

The possible use of gas during any attack by the Germans meant that Home Guards had to be capable of recognising and dealing with the more common gases, as well as being proficient in the use of their respirators. Most battalions had a building in which the men could train, commonly an air raid shelter with a door at each end, through which they could grope through a gas cloud, wearing their respirators. Redditch Battalion, for example used an air raid shelter sited just south of Birchfield Road, while at Malvern a mobile facility was temporarily sited at the Winter Gardens.

Gas training took several forms and included wearing gas masks during other forms of training to acclimatise the men to wearing the equipment, and to ensure that the face mask did not become misshapen through over-long storage in the haversack. Here we see Redditch Home Guard having their masks checked by a Quartermaster Sergeant and Corporal before an exercise. Note also the leather Sten magazine pouches worn by the two nearest men as well as the standard Home Guard canvas rifle ammunition pouches.
(Courtesy of Mr E.P. Grace via Mike Johnson)

By 1942, when perhaps those in authority thought that a full-scale enemy invasion was less likely, it was expected that the Germans might use gas canisters dropped from aircraft to disrupt British war production. Home Guards were required to carry respirators in the alert position, i.e. on their chests, when on patrol, on guard duty, training or on tactical exercises. To intensify anti-gas training, respirators were to be worn by all personnel at least once a week for a period of 15 to 30 minutes during training, both indoor and outdoor, and when on the march, to ensure that all ranks were accustomed to wearing respirators when carrying out their duties.[7]

Unarmed combat for Home Guards

Possibly as a response to the proliferation of handbooks published on hand to hand combat and clearly aimed at the Home Guard, in December 1941 the 'Military Correspondent' of *The Bromsgrove, Droitwich and Redditch Weekly Messenger* wrote

The winter of 1941/42 saw an introduction of unarmed combat training for Home Guards, although the Auxiliaries had been practising this art since the previous year. Books on the subject were readily available, including those illustrated here. James Hipkiss was able to demonstrate his particular skill to members of the Redditch Battalion. (From the Author's collection)

about the subject. He explained that during the coming winter, those members of the Home Guard who specialised in unarmed combat were to follow the programme suggested by the War Office Military Training Directorate. This recommended a course of 12 periods of 10 minutes each on the subject. The programme included exercises in attacks, holds, and releases, as well as endurance training, practice in swimming, and certain muscle developing sports. The endurance training was to be undertaken in order that men should become fit enough to conserve wind and strength for accurate marksmanship after duties involving strenuous activity. Thus a run of a quarter of a mile uphill or through woods in full kit at top speed should leave the specialist in unarmed combat unimpaired as a marksman.

The programme was described as severe, and in most cases it was the younger men – youths of between 17 and call-up age – who were picked to learn the lessons. Instruction was to be given by members of the Army Physical Training Corps where they were available, or by many of the ex-instructors who were giving their services to their local units. Speed, efficiency and ruthlessness were the prime essentials in this form of close combat. The commando units formed by some of the Worcestershire battalions also practised what was being advocated by this military directive.

Robin Morom, son of Major R.C. Morom of the Redditch Battalion, recalled, as a young boy, witnessing a demonstration of unarmed combat put on by members of the Headquarter Company at the Drill Hall in Church Road. At the same time, the HQ was being visited by a number of officers from the Kings Norton Home Guard. Instruction was being given by a sergeant, a local Redditch butcher, who was demonstrating the various methods for dealing with a knife attack, for which a rubber knife was being used. After watching for a while, one of the Kings Norton officers asked if he could have a try and in Robin's words proceeded to 'tie the sergeant in knots'! It transpired that the officer was James Hipkiss, a pre-war British Empire judo champion and author of instruction books on the subject of unarmed combat.[8]

Musketry and grenade training

The widespread issue of American rifles in July 1940 and the availability of more ammunition, together with a wider issue of grenades, allowed musketry practice and grenade training to be carried out by the Home Guard from the late summer onwards.

One man who had experience of musketry training in both the Home Guard and the Regular forces was Derrick Pearson of the Stourbridge Battalion. Derrick recalled that he and his colleagues were taught musketry by a couple of ex-First World War 'Old Sweats', who knew how to shoot. Apparently these men were known as 'Sixpenny Soldiers' after the extra sixpence a day they were paid for being able to achieve a high standard of excellence. From these experts, he was able to learn about aiming off for wind, as well as estimating the lead on a moving target, and so reached a high standard of shooting. After being called up he received Regular Army training at Norton Barracks and took part in shooting competitions against other 'squaddies' where everyone put in a threepenny bit, the winner pocketing the kitty. After winning the kitty several times, Derrick was disappointed to find the competition was 'dropped'! He was in no doubt that the standard of shooting taught by the 'Old Sweats' of the Home Guard was much better than the instruction in the Regular Army. He also considered the 18-inch bayonet issued to the Home Guard to be a much more useful weapon for parrying another bayonet than the 6-inch spike with which he was issued later for the campaign in north-west Europe.[9]

That Derrick's experience was not unique was reflected in a late war Home Guard Circular which noted that: 'In early 1944, a group of distinguished soldiers were watching a party of RAF Regiment men firing on an open range. A leading aircraftsman got down with a Mk IV rifle on a 200 yard firing point. The order to start firing was given and at the end of sixty seconds a spectator holding a stopwatch called time. The LAC cleared his rifle and stood up. He had put thirty-nine rounds into the target. One of the old soldiers, all of whom were astonished by his performance, asked the LAC where he had acquired his skill. His answer was, "It's mainly the teaching I got in the Home Guard before I was called up".'[10]

Members of the Evesham Battalion, under the direction of Captain Collett,
practising their 'musketry' at the Tyddesley Wood Range, near Pershore.
(Courtesy of The Vale of Evesham Historical Society)

Musketry becomes seriously competitive

Competition shooting increasingly became a feature of Home Guard life as the war proceeded, and again in the 1950s. Many Worcestershire Home Guards had been enthusiastic marksmen from the moment sufficient ammunition for practice became available in 1940. Sydney Carter, the chronicler of the Evesham Battalion, remarked that it 'was good to see the almost childish joy with which many of the old soldiers cuddled the rifle to their cheeks and got going again'.[11] Many of these men had learnt their skill in the Great War, when the British Army was recognised as the best exponent of musketry in the world at the time, and the Worcestershire Regiment was reckoned to be the best of the best.

A sniper competition at the Kingsbury Range, Warwickshire, in July 1941, appears to have been the first of its type, and would have been more than simply demonstrating a very high standard of target shooting. Ten men from the Oldbury Battalion are recorded as attending this competition.[12] Western Command Weapons Training School at Craven Arms provided sniper courses which included: open range rifle shooting including zeroing; observation, training and use of binoculars; judging distance; elementary and advanced field craft; personal camouflage; selection, construction and camouflage of snipers' hides; sniper exercises and field firing ranges.[13]

However, the Home Guard were not always the best shots, *The Malvern Gazette* reporting on a rifle shooting match between Malvern Post Office Ladies Rifle Club and No 3 Platoon of the Malvern Home Guard which, in a keenly contested match, resulted in a win for the ladies. Major Kendall, the officer commanding the Malvern Company Home Guard, in congratulating them on their splendid victory, hoped the teams would have the opportunity of meeting again.[14] The fact that the post office ladies of somewhere like Malvern were fielding a competitive shooting team suggests that militaristic ladies were more widespread than the War Office would have liked! While there was no mention of the fact that these ladies were in any way connected with the Women's Home Defence Corps, there was a clear enthusiasm for shooting and no shortage of skill at arms.

There seems to have been a particular emphasis on competitive shooting matches at Kidderminster which probably stemmed from the fact that the first Battalion Commander, Lt Colonel Painter, had previously shot competitively at Bisley. As an example, an inter-company shooting competition was held by the Kidderminster Battalion under apparently ideal conditions at the Sutton Park Range on 11th June 1942. The light was good, with very little wind, ensuring keen competition and good scoring. Each team consisted of 10 riflemen, two Sten-gunners, and 'bombers' (a name used during the First World War for grenade throwers), who worked under the direction of a team captain, the teams having to make a number of advances whilst firing at special targets.[15] This report is interesting in that it confirms the

Warley Battalion men were in trouble on more than one occasion for the irresponsible use of rifles. This picture suggests that at least some had a fairly casual approach to the way they handled, and pointed, 'their rifles'! (Courtesy of Steve Taylor)

availability of Sten Guns at this date in Worcestershire. The exercise was repeated later in the year when the conditions were different and was so organized as to bring into play the lessons of recent months. It was reported that the accuracy of the shooting 'left nothing to be desired and would have brought any enemy under a truly withering fire'.[16]

Not everyone behaved themselves on the rifle ranges and the Birmingham Zone HQ had to remind the trigger-happy Warley Battalion that the owners of the Tanhouse Quarry Range had been put at a loss and considerable inconvenience when old oil drums supplied for their excavators were used as targets. Apart from the fact that the Home Guard were guests of such places, units were asked to remember that new oil drums could only be obtained by the return of the old drums.[17] The Warley boys were in trouble again when it was reported that the firing of service ammunition had taken place under unauthorised circumstances and without adequate precautions being taken for the safety of the public. The orders emphasised the necessity of not firing live ammunition, whether miniature or service, except on authorised ranges and with adequate precaution for the safety of the public.[18]

Country Life magazine sponsored a national Home Guard miniature (.22 calibre) shooting competition in 1942. There were over 400 entries, and Kidderminster Battalion, which had been top scorer in the Worcestershire Zone and second in Western Command, tied for 10th place. Malvern and Halesowen Battalions also

A number of temporary firing ranges were established by the Home Guard throughout the county. These Redditch men are using a playing field 'somewhere in Redditch' for this purpose. It is possible that this is the 200 yard range created at the rear of the HDA Works. (Courtesy of Mr E.P. Grace via Mike Johnson)

entered teams and gained 66th and 107th places respectively.[19] The *Country Life* competition was promoted again in 1943.

By 1944 an extra dimension to simulate battle conditions had been added to rifle competitions in time for an inter-battalion contest for O Sector at the Ribbesford Range. The course, for teams of 10 men under the command of an officer or senior NCO, involved an approach march of three miles in 'anti-aircraft formation' to the range (spread out on each side of the road, providing less of a target to air attack and a greater chance of finding a ditch in which to shelter in the event of such an attack), the maximum time allowed being 50 minutes. On arrival at the range, the teams were issued with 13 rounds for each man, and the team then doubled to the 200 yards firing point, crawling the last few yards into the firing position. Here they had to fire five rounds at small camouflaged targets, which were exposed for a limited period, recharge magazines and advance to the 100 yards point, where they fired another five rounds. The last stage was a double to within 20 yards of the butts, where ground targets were exposed, at which each man fired three rounds from the hip. This apparently exciting contest, at which there was consistently good shooting, was won by the narrowest possible margin by No 14 Platoon of the Stourbridge Battalion, just beating No 21 Platoon of the Kidderminster Battalion, with No 2 Platoon of the Stourport Battalion a close third.[20] Other sectors in the county held similar elimination competitions, culminating in a competition between M, N and O Sector teams held at the Perry Wood Range, Worcester, on 8th October 1944, which was won by N Sector's No 9 Platoon of the Bromsgrove Battalion.[21]

In Worcestershire, a number of established and temporary firing ranges were employed by the Home Guard for weapons training and competitions. These are listed in Appendix 9.

Grenade Ranges

Live grenade throwing ranges were created at a number of locations throughout the county, sometimes in disused quarries where the flying shrapnel balls and casing fragments could be contained. Initially, however, the purpose-built grenade range at Norton Barracks was used for training some of the Home Guard battalions and Auxiliary Units, under the supervision of Regular officers. Later, Home Guard instructors who had had previous experience became qualified to supervise grenade practice, and selected men were trained, usually at Altcar or Norton, to run courses elsewhere in the county.

Artillery and Sub-Artillery Ranges

With the handing over by the Royal Artillery of 6pdr Hotchkiss guns to the Home Guard in the spring of 1941, a local live firing range was required for them to practise using them. The issue of Northover Projectors and Spigot Mortars in 1941, and

Malvern Battalion grenade practice. This location has not been identified, but it is likely that this scene depicts some sort of distance throwing competition with a dummy grenade. Grenades having a potentially lethal range of about 100 yards, it would be unlikely that the men in the background would be quite so relaxed if this were live practice! (Courtesy of Sheila Edmonds)

later still Smith Guns, added demands for sub-artillery training ranges in the county. Live firing of the 2 Pounder Anti-Tank Guns, also issued to the Worcestershire Home Guards, was carried out under the supervision of Royal Artillery staff at Borth on the west coast of Wales, or at Umberslade in Warwickshire. The 1950s Home Guard was issued with the standard infantry 2 inch mortar, but to practise using this weapon the men had to travel to Halfpenny Green Airfield in Shropshire. The various firing ranges for artillery and sub-artillery used by Home Guards in Worcestershire are listed in Appendix 9.

Home Guard Camps

A generally popular way of fulfilling the training needs of Home Guards was to organise weekend summer camps. Here the men could actually escape, for a short time anyway, the demands of trying to combine work and duty and, in the case of the older men, also running a home and family. Some commanding officers suggested that the men might like to give up part of their annual holiday for this purpose. One can only imagine the furore that this must have caused at home!

A War Office letter of 1st July 1941 authorised the holding of the first weekend camps for the Home Guard in Worcestershire. These camps seem to have begun on the weekend of 9th/10th August, when Home Guards 'from Worcestershire' were reported by local newspapers to have had an interesting and instructive time. The main camps that year were located at Hewell Grange and Tyddesley Wood, and both were apparently extensively used by Home Guard units. A subsistence allowance had been authorised to cover the cost of messing.[22] However, the Stourport Battalion chose to organise their own camps in the grounds of Witley Court in that and subsequent years.

The length of the Home Guard camping season expanded in later years, as did the number of sites being used, and the range of activities undertaken. This is well illustrated by an Evesham Battalion camp training schedule, set out in an undated paper by Major Sydney Carter, the then Training Officer of the Evesham Battalion, and probably predates the 1943 camping season. The Evesham men were going to be very busy!

> Battle Drill – Platoon flanking attack drill will be taught at camps. It is hoped to arrange a demonstration of live firing over a section at one or more camps.
> Own Rifle – Each man will fire five rounds from his own rifle of 100 yards application.
> In the event of the man not having a good score, his rifle will be tried by a well-known good shot, and if then not satisfactory, will be labelled and set aside for accurate zeroing. Pln Cdrs and NCOs are asked to see that rifles are examined and thoroughly dried before coming to the range.

Sten Gun – NCOs and men in possession of Sten Guns will fire five rounds deliberate at 50 yards, and if there is sufficient ammunition, fifteen rounds in bursts at 30, 20 and 15 yards respectively. Each man should bring 20 rounds of ammunition and four magazines.

TEWT – Officers and NCOs will be divided into syndicates and a simple problem will be set. The object of this TEWT [Tactical Exercise Without Troops] is to introduce the idea to those not familiar with the procedure, with a view to carrying out more ambitious TEWTs during the winter months.

Mine Laying – Each platoon will lay a minefield of 60 mines, and at each camp it is hoped to explode one mine to show the effect.

Camouflage – Methods of camouflaging machine guns and blacker [a reference to the Blacker Bombard or Spigot Mortar] will be shown, and personal camouflage will be dealt with.

Gas Mask Shooting – Men will wear gas masks, and fire five rounds grouping at 100 yards with P14 rifles. [Surely by 1943 this must mean P17 rifles.]

Distance Judging – The appearance method and halving method will be demonstrated.

Note – It is requested that the men in camp be divided into 6 platoons of 32 men each or such less number as convenient. Pln officers and NCOs for the camp should be appointed, who will be responsible for seeing that their platoons arrive at the right place at the right time, where they will come under the control of Bn Instructors. Bn Ins will wear a brassard. In the event of it being wet, arrangements have been made to hold lectures and demonstrations etc in huts.[23]

Camping could be a dangerous business!

One accident appears to have occurred during a weekend camp at Weatheroak where battle training was being practised by men of the Redditch Battalion. Bromsgrove Battalion orders blandly record that a Home Guard was injured by the blast of a blank cartridge being fired at close range in his direction, but this seems to have been the result of a bit of horseplay. The names of those involved have been omitted to save embarrassment, but apparently the Home Guards were sitting around in a circle after one of the exercises, indulging in the usual banter, when one man, as a joke, threatened to shoot another in the crotch. The victim told his friend not to be such a bloody fool, but he fired anyway and caused much damage to his friend's private parts, resulting in a spell in hospital. Consequently, it was ordered that no firing at the opposing side in an exercise was to take place within 50 yards.[24]

The expanded camping activities of the Home Guard brought with it a need for trained cooks, and a number of training courses were organised in the county both at Norton Barracks and by individual battalions. When women were nominated to

Members of the Malvern Battalion 'enjoying' an alfresco meal at one of their weekend camps. The officers seem to take it all very seriously, and the Regimental Sergeant Major, nearest the camera, has that 'don't mess with me' look that goes with the rank.
(Courtesy of Sheila Edmonds)

serve with the Home Guard, many attended the camps and brought their cooking skills with them, apparently to the delight of the men. A list of known Home Guard camp sites is included in Appendix 9.

That some Home Guards were not well versed in the ways of the countryside was reflected in later orders, when all ranks were warned against the dangers of drinking from springs or other natural water supplies, unless such supplies had been analysed and declared fit for consumption.[25]

As if there were not enough matters to be concerned about in wartime, a case of Foot and Mouth disease was reported in Powick on 21st June. Consequently no military training was to be held within 2 miles of the outbreak. However, these restrictions were withdrawn on 10th July.[26] Was the lifting of restrictions a result of mistaken diagnosis or was the outbreak in wartime controlled more efficiently than the one that happened relatively recently?

Fieldcraft and battle training

This form of training sometimes entailed using extensive areas of open countryside, but this sometimes caused a conflict of interest at a time when it was also necessary to increase food production. Reports were made of unnecessary damage to farmland caused by troops in training as a result of which, in 1942, Home Guard instructions made it clear that the responsibility for avoiding unnecessary damage rested with officers of all ranks, and that NCOs and men had also to appreciate their responsibilities.

Attention was drawn to the following points: oil was not to be drained from mechanised vehicles onto pastureland; more gaps were not to be made in hedges than was absolutely necessary; where they were made, temporary blocking repairs were to be made immediately to prevent stock straying; vehicles were not to be parked with exhaust pipes close to hayricks or stacks of straw; cable and wire was not to be left on the ground for stock in the field was to be thought about; vehicles were not to be turned abruptly on grass fields because grass was a crop; fencing stakes were not to be cut for firewood because stock would soon find the weak spot and break out; firing was not to be carried out in the immediate neighbourhood of animals, or to cause them unnecessary fright which would affect their breeding capacity; rabbit netting around plantations and fields was there for a purpose and if it was damaged by vehicles or troops and not repaired, the rabbits would soon find out; gates were to be shut between fields; arable fields with growing crops should be avoided, but if such a field was to be crossed common sense was to be used; thatching on ricks was not to be disturbed, but if it did occur, the farmer was to be informed immediately or the rick could be damaged; and finally, the farmer was to be thought of as the Home Guard's host and a partner in helping to win the war. This order was to be repeated every quarter and officers and NCOs were to be responsible for their men being fully conversant with its contents.[27]

The concept of Battle Drill was introduced into Home Guard training during July 1942 as a means of teaching the principles of movement supported by covering fire, with a final assault on the enemy by a flank attack.[28] Initially it was introduced as a drill which could be practised on the parade ground, the first reference to it in the county appearing in Stourport Battalion Part 1 Orders of 9th July. These refer to a squad parading to demonstrate the drill for the various companies, under the instructions of the Training Officer. However, it would be September before the first two parts of a five volume set of Home Guard Instruction No 51 *Battlecraft* and *Battle Drill* were published by GHQ Home Forces, explaining the new system of tactical training. The remaining volumes of the Instruction were published in early 1943. Part I, entitled *Introduction and Battlecraft* described Battle Drill as 'hard training for hard men whose role is to go out and hunt the enemy' and was to be practised by young and fit Home Guards. The instructions made it clear that those Home Guards described as the older steadier men were not going to be called upon to achieve such feats of physical endurance since theirs was not a mobile role.[29] This advice did not appear to stop the elderly men of Worcestershire from participating!

Later, the training was to include Battle Innoculation in order to accustom men to the sudden noise of battle. In the First World War it been possible to put a man in a quiet sector of the line until he was experienced enough to judge for himself the comparative dangers of shot and shell. It was going to be impossible to do this with the Home Guard, so the noise of battle had to be produced artificially. It was emphasised that the main object was for each man to learn for himself that noise was harmless. Instructions explained three different schemes: men lying in the open; troops under cover; troops in the open and subject to live firing. All firing of live ammunition was to be controlled by an officer or warrant officer.[30]

In an apparently 'meritorious performance', men of the combined Welland and Hanley Swan Battle Platoon won the Worcestershire Sub District 'Platoon in Attack' competition on 26th September 1943. In the back row, from the left are: John Allison, Don King, Bill Weaver, Joe Bullock, Dick Hart, Pat Oliver, Dennis Barnes and unknown. In the 3rd row, from the left are: Harry Somers, Fred Carter, Raymond Hill, Ernie Rouse, Charlie Wheeler, and John Lewis. In the 2nd row are: Sergeant Walter Reynolds, Lance Corporal George Pitman, Lieutenant Grice Hutchinson (Colonel retired), Major M.F.S. Jewell, Lieutenant E.C. Watkinson, unknown, Sergeant Ted Weildon, Alec Dare, and Jim Dovey. In the front row are: Sergeant Hubert Preston, Frank Hill, Ken Lawrence, Vernon Reece-Pinchin, Sergeant Mike Hill, Harold Webb, and Lance Corporal Bill Shipman. (Courtesy of Gordon Bennett)

Men of the Evesham Battalion negotiate their 'Battle Innoculation' course at The Dingle, Elmley Castle, complete with explosions and live overhead firing. This experience was not for the faint hearted or unfit! (Courtesy of The Vale of Evesham Historical Society)

Evesham Battalion established a battle inoculation course as early as 1943 at The Dingle, Elmley Castle, on land owned by General Sir Francis Davies. There, the men were divided into squads, each squad making an assault up the side of the hill. Machine gun fire would be directed as close to their heads as safety would allow, while mines exploded around them and they themselves fired live ammunition at targets set in various locations on the hill. Captain Collett, who had adapted a Browning Machine Gun mounting to carry a Hotchkiss Light Automatic, fired many thousands of rounds during these exercises; 'firing to miss 'em', as he described it.[31]

A battle innoculation course was also established by the Bromsgrove Battalion in a wooded dingle to the south of the rifle range at Hampton Lovett. Bill Allington, who was qualified to supervise the training here, recalls that the explosive charges of gun cotton were wired back to a control panel and, by pressing appropriate buttons, a varying pattern of simulated shell fire could be arranged. The Home Guards would make their way around a course, through the trees and marked by white tapes, with explosions going off around them. The Americans also used these woods for training purposes and often left their booby trap wires strung between trees. As was also the case with their grenade training, the Americans seemed to be somewhat careless about clearing up afterwards. This training facility was apparently constructed by the Regular Army.[32]

That the Halesowen Battalion travelled all the way to Hampton Lovett to undertake battle innoculation exercises, which were apparently well attended, suggests that there were possibly only a few courses laid out in Worcestershire for this sort of training.[33]

Clearly there was the chance for things to go wrong on a battle innoculation exercise and safety procedures would have been paramount. A demonstration of Battle Innoculation was therefore laid on for Home Guard Commanders by No 23 ITC at Norton,[34] while the battalion adjutants, to help meet their responsibility for overseeing training, could attend the Western Command Weapons Training School at Altcar. Here the syllabus included: fuses and their initiation; service explosives; making up charges; the theory of small arms fire; conduct of practices and safety precautions.[35]

The principles of fire and movement by a platoon in attack were still being taught to the 1950s Home Guard, often using a cloth model of a piece of terrain and the TEWT system. Such an action was seen as having six phases: advance before contact; making contact; recce appreciation and planning; issue of orders; the attack; and reorganisation.

Training with the Regulars

Second Lt O'Neill, Sergeant Everall and Corporal Hadley of the Warley Battalion attended Home Guard Training with the Field Force from 8th to 15th July 1942.[36] This seems to have been the first occasion when men from the Worcestershire Home Guard would spend a week training with the Regulars, but this was to become a feature of future training. Under this scheme, Chris Bayliss of the Bushley Platoon was attached to a unit providing lookouts on the white cliffs overlooking St Margaret's Bay, near Dover, where the men were accommodated in a small cave, cut out of the limestone near the top of the cliffs, as a shelter. From there they could observe Germans on the north coast of France who, in turn, were watching them![37]

Winter training in 1943

An instruction issued by the Commanding Officer of Worcester City Battalion Home Guard on 25th August referred to the recent summer's training showing good progress in the powers of command, section leading, discipline, drill and battlecraft, but commented that, with few exceptions, weapons training had not progressed as it should. It was pointed out that in battle the chief aim was to kill the enemy and to do this it was necessary to close with him. The main essentials were seen as battlecraft and use of weapons, both having to be perfect to achieve success. All commanders were to keep this in mind when arranging training that winter. Training in making a plan for attack and defence and issuing verbal and written orders were to be the first essential for all officers. They were to study the use of weapons in supporting their troops in battle, and moving troops to assemble for attack by both day and night. NCOs were also to be given plenty of training in making a plan for attack and defence, giving verbal orders, and moving troops at night. The men were to concentrate on battlecraft in street and open country along with weapon training, but also train in patrolling at night. For specialists a complete replacement team was to be trained. Officers commanding units were to select suitable men to be put through a course under a specialist officer or NCO in signalling, stretcher bearing, despatch riding, intelligence, field engineering, and use of the machine gun, Smith Gun and Spigot Mortar. Arrangements were also to be made in each company for 10 NCOs and men to go through a course in rescue work and civil defence duties.[38]

Chris Bayliss, of the Bushley Platoon of Malvern Battalion, was one of the men chosen to train with the Regulars on the south coast. He can be seen standing at the right-hand end of the back row of this Stand Down photograph taken in what was then a field opposite the church at Longdon (now covered with housing). He is wearing a civilian shirt and tie. Other people recognised in the photograph are front row, left to right: Jack Palmer, Norman Rayer, unknown, Fred Rayer, Henry Peters, Ernie Pendry, ? Spry, John Woodward, Alf Matty, unknown. 2nd row from the left: Corporal 'Tango' Bisley, ? Healing, Corporal Bob Lane, Corporal R. Daniels, Corporal R. Griffiths, Captain Morgan, Major M.F.S. Jewell, 2nd Lieutenant Woodward, Corporal T. Hardcastle, Harold Weeks, George Bloxham, ? Jeynes, and B. Williams. 3rd row, from the left: Brian Bainbridge, ? Fowler, unknown, Jack Fowler, Alan Jones, Fred White, Bob Lodge, Reg Bayliss, ? Starting, T. Lane, F. Cosier, Tom Parker, unknown, D. Hart, unknown, and George Peters. Back row, from the left: Bob Lawler, Fred Lane, Fred Radley, J. Guilding, unknown, T. Lowe, Graham Watkins, unknown, B. Peters, F Radley, Charles Bayliss, and Chris Bayliss. (Courtesy of the late Chris Bayliss)

Books, pamphlets, play acting and training films

The Malvern Gazette of 23rd November 1940 reported that a Home Guard Manual, compiled by ex-Warrant Officer/Instructor Southworth RSM of Sevenoaks Battalion Home Guard, had been published by Ruberoid Company Ltd of Stonehouse, Gloucestershire costing sixpence (about £4 now), and covering rifle drill, squad, platoon and company drill, signals, range practice, scouting, fieldcraft and how to construct road blocks. This was but one of many Home Guard books and instruction manuals which could be purchased, so there was no shortage of advice for the enthusiastic Home Guard. Publications were to come from a number of sources: from Tom Wintringham and his ex International Brigade friends such as Hugh Slater (*The Home Guard for Victory*) and Yank Levy (*Guerrilla Warfare*); from left-wing journalists who had reported on the Civil War in Spain, such as Langton Davies; the from the many retired officers, often described as 'blimps', putting over the more conventional methods of training for battle. The left-wing publications tended to be more lively and dealt with the irregular methods of warfare, whereas the 'blimps' emphasised operational training and drill. On top of this came the regular issue of War Office instructions specifically for the LDV/Home Guard which totalled 68 between 1940 and 1944, usually on a restricted supply basis down to platoon commanders.[39]

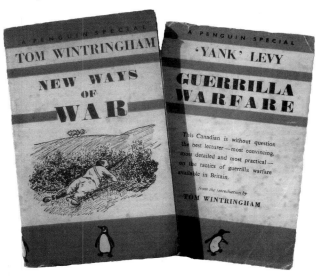

A combination of official Home Guard instructions and published books, available over the counter, including those written by Spanish Civil War veterans, meant that an enthusiastic Home Guard was not short of advice on how to prepare for invasion. The two shown here were especially popular and dealt with irregular forms of warfare. (Author's collection)

In pre-war Army training, the belief that 'to be told was to be taught' held considerable sway, and this was reinforced by the notion that the louder the shout the deeper the impression on the poor victim's mind! As part of British Army wartime reforms, it was established that 'showing how' was far more effective than 'telling how', and that the demonstration would beat the lecture every time.[40] Reflecting this change, on the evening of Sunday, 4th May 1941, a play called *Up Guards and at Em*, was enacted at the Worcester Theatre Royal. It had been devised by staff of the

Western Command Headquarters, with material from several lectures for the Home Guard embodied in this novel method of instruction. Home Guard representatives from a wide area came to see it, as well as members of other forces. Orders that had been found on an actual enemy parachutist formed the basis of a blitzkrieg plan discussed by two officers of the German Army. In the first act, the scheme was revealed by two parachutists giving a clear indication of what Britain's defenders could expect to meet in an invasion. The Germans would be armed with rifles, pistols, tommy guns and grenades, and some would be in British battledress and ordered to spread false information. There would be other disguises too, and in the play one of the enemy was dressed as a nurse carrying a basket that contained a couple of bombs! These would be the vanguard, each member of which would have definite objectives. Next would come the troop-carrying planes and others carrying light tanks.

The play was apparently very capably presented, with humour, and dealt with the Home Guard counter-measures and the invasion itself, the capture of a Fifth Columnist and the questioning of a captured parachutist commander. At the conclusion, General Sir George Weir said he hoped that members of the Home Guard present would remember what they had learned from the play, and that they would have the opportunity of seeing the company which had presented it in Worcestershire again.[41]

An experiment in this method of instruction was also organised by the Redditch Battalion, when a two-act play by Major A.E. Grace, then the Second in Command of the battalion, was enacted before an audience of Home Guard officers at the Union Club, Redditch on 2nd March 1943. In the play, the Battalion Commander, the Adjutant and the Intelligence Officer considered the meaning of 'appreciations' of an operational problem, explaining that this was reviewing the tasks, terrain, personnel, resources and administration, and deducing from them an operational scheme. In the second act, the Battalion Commander discussed the same fundamentals with the Company Commander whose company had been assigned a specific task. From this review and deductions, a scheme was built up, step by step on a large scale map, providing a practical solution to a problem.[42]

Training films were often shown to the Home Guard at the local cinema, which would be temporarily requisitioned for the purpose. The first evidence of these being shown was to Halesowen Home Guards at the Lyttleton Cinema on Sunday, 22nd March 1942. Other battalions were subsequently shown training films in the local cinemas which could then be found in most of the towns in the county. 1944 saw training films concentrating on urban fighting including *Home Guard Fighting Series, No 7 – Clearing a Street* and, pertinently for some battalions in Worcestershire, *Ammunition Accidents – They need not happen!*[43]

Swimming canals with their kit on

With a number of canals in the Black Country, it was very likely that men would have to swim across or along them during active operations, although swimming in the poorly maintained and heavily polluted wartime canals would have been a distinctly unhealthy occupation. Nevertheless, it was brought to the attention of officers that a demonstration of swimming in uniform and carrying equipment would take place at 3pm on 29th March at Nechells Swimming Baths, situated at the corner of Nechells Park Road and Aston Church Road.[44]

Travelling Wings visit Worcestershire

To reduce the cost and amount of travelling by individuals from the various Home Guard battalions to Home Guard schools, the concept of Travelling Wings of Regular officers was introduced to bring the latest training methods to their locality. The first reference to such training was when a Travelling Wing visited the Kidderminster Battalion, from 20th to 25th July 1943, and officers and senior NCOs were given lectures, witnessed demonstrations and themselves carried out exercises. On the Sunday, the public turned up in large numbers and were able to witness what might happen if street fighting occurred. It was reported that the spectators were intrigued at the sight of troops in full battle order, wearing rubber-soled shoes, who literally walked up the sides of houses with the agility of a cat. The scaling of high walls seemed a mere bagatelle, and much credit was given to the many old soldiers who vied with the younger hands in taking on these seemingly impossible feats. Another impressive sight was the clearing of a row of houses in which the 'enemy' was strongly posted. After effecting an entry in the prescribed manner, our troops in the face of strong resistance, managed to get the enemy (complete in German uniform) out into the open.[45] The Travelling Wings visiting the Worcestershire area came from the No 3 GHQ Home Guard Training School at Onibury in Shropshire.

Stourport Battalion orders later that year recorded that a Travelling Wing report had found the standard of training in the battalion to be satisfactory, although 'appreciations' and orders still required considerable practice, and the weekend exercises showed that squad fire control and fieldcraft generally needed attention. 'Battledrill Mindedness' also needed to be overcome, as there was a tendency to allow this to trump elasticity of thought and action.[46]

Town or street fighting

A number of town fighting facilities were established in Worcestershire, some of which are listed in Appendix 9. The principal venue in the Midlands for this form of training was, however, located in the Bristol Road in Birmingham, when the sort of antics described above would be taught. This form of fighting, like so many other aspects of Home Guard training, became the subject of competition. One was attended by Stourbridge Home Guards on 3rd May 1942, when a score of Belgians had a very busy day. Taking the role of the enemy in German helmets and tunics, they fought five battle platoons of the Central Midland District Home Guard from 8.30am to 5pm. The object of the mock battle was to establish a winning team from entrants representing all Home Guard battalions in Staffordshire, Warwickshire and Worcestershire, the five platoons competing already having gained the top places in a Central Midland District competition.

The scene of the battle was a bombed area of the city. The Belgians were supposed to be German parachute troops who had fought their way into this area and taken up defensive positions in the partially wrecked houses. It was the job of the Home Guard to destroy the armoured cars the Germans had captured and turn the enemy out of the houses. A Battle Platoon from the Stourbridge Battalion, under the command of 2nd Lt G.R. Reading won.[47]

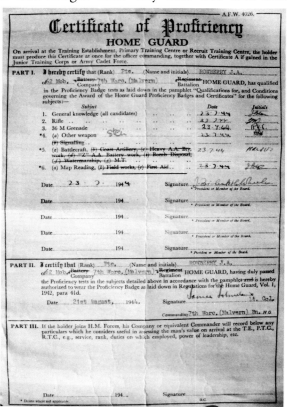

Home Guard Proficiency Tests

Army Council instructions introduced the concept of Home Guard Proficiency Badges on 16th April 1941,[48] and it was the Malvern Battalion that was first off the mark in this county, when one man passed the appropriate test on 29th July. Redditch Battalion followed a month later. For most battalions in Worcestershire, Part 2 Orders record the most significant numbers of men passing the test from 1943 onwards. For example, orders of the Halesowen Battalion listed 38 'other ranks' as having passed the Proficiency Test in February 1943, and that the tests included: map reading, patrol and sentry duties, leadership and discipline, elementary drill, and use of

This Home Guard Proficiency Certificate, issued later in the war, indicates the range of tests undertaken by John Rowberry of the Malvern Battalion, the dates when the tests were taken, together with an authorisation to wear the Proficiency Badge. Its value to those going into service with the Regular forces is also indicated. (Courtesy of John Rowberry)

the Browning Automatic Rifle, Browning Heavy Machine Gun, Spigot Mortar and Lewis Gun.[49] The wearing of a proficiency badge (see Chapter 12) gave recognition of a Home Guard's proficiency and encouraged the men to reach a high standard of training. The issue of a certificate was also seen as being of value to those members of the Home Guard who would go on to serve in the Regular services. The test was changed in 1943, when it was required that a man would undergo an oral examination before a tribunal of officers in general knowledge, the rifle, the 36M Grenade and battlecraft, as well as one of the following: BAR, Sten Gun, Lewis Gun, Browning Machine Gun, Vickers Machine Gun, Northover Projector, Spigot Mortar, Signalling, and either map reading, fieldwork or first aid. Practical range tests with chosen weapons and throwing live grenades would form part of the examination.[50]

Operational training for the Auxiliary Units
Most of the patrol leaders from Worcestershire appear to have gone to Coleshill for their initial training and while there they would have been provided with a copy of *The Countryman's Diary*, essentially an instruction manual for the saboteur. On their return the leaders would then pass on the lessons to the remainder of their patrol. They would also receive training from John Todd and instructors at Norton Barracks and at the Drill Hall in Silver Street, Worcester. Once the men had their OBs, they would experience living in them at weekends and occasionally weekdays, and practise their night attacks on potential vehicle and tank laagers, using their local knowledge of the landscape and their fieldcraft skills. The Boy Scouts from Broadheath were well versed in fieldcraft, and since the majority of the other patrols were recruited from the farming community, creeping round the fields at night would have been second nature to them anyway. As cover they would dress in their Home Guard uniforms, but would wear plimsolls for patrolling or their rubber-soled boots. The use of live explosives in training caused some difficulties since loud bangs in the middle of the night would inevitably result in questions from the locals. John Wythes, later the Sergeant of the Joshua Patrol in the Crowle area when Roger Smith was promoted to become a Group Leader, told me that when they used explosives, the locals seemed to be satisfied when told that it was German bombers jettisoning their bomb loads after raids into the Midlands. Some of the farming members of the patrols would later find their explosives useful for blowing up tree stumps when clearing land for cultivation![51]

Training schemes with the local Home Guard later became a significant part of the Auxilier's life, and Ron Seymour, of Samson Patrol, who worked at the Meco factory in St John's, recalled two schemes involving the Home Guard in the Bromyard Road area of Worcester. One involved testing the guard on the road bridge over the Laugherne Brook, by the patrol creeping up to the bridge in the dark with the intention of laying dummy explosives – they failed and were caught! Another involved entering the Meco factory at night by devious means and leaving dummy explosives on the machinery. This was carried out at the request of the Managing Director, who was anxious to test the factory guard, so he too must have been aware of the existence of Samson Patrol, despite the desire for secrecy. In this exercise Samson Patrol was more successful and the dummy explosives were successfully installed without the guard being aware.[52] Similarly John Wythes recalled an 'attack' on a road bridge, probably the one over Bow Brook near the Coventry Arms at Upton Snodsbury. Coincidentally, the pub was also the headquarters of the local Home Guard.

The Holland-Martin estate at Overbury was a focus for training by a number of the Worcestershire Auxiliary Patrols from an early date, including pistol shooting and explosives practice in one of the quarries. The local training focus changed to Wolverton Hall when the van Moppes were appointed as Group Commanders, and the Auxiliers would practise for the competitions which were encouraged between patrols at local and national levels. A number of Worcestershire men recalled travelling to Coleshill to compete against teams from across Britain. Some of these competitions are described in *The Mercian Maquis*; they seem regularly to have involved a night approach to an objective while being stalked by the training staff from Coleshill. Overall, the Worcestershire patrols did rather well in these tests and on most occasions 'held their own'. After John Todd was transferred to SOE in 1941, to help plan the invasion of Madagascar, Captain Sandford, of Eye Manor, near Leominster, a senior officer in the Herefordshire Home Guard, was appointed as the Intelligence Officer for the Herefordshire and Worcestershire Patrols. He had been commissioned as a 2nd Lieutenant in the Intelligence Corps in July 1941, but had kept his Home Guard rank. In consequence, Herefordshire also became a focus for Auxiliary training and a number of Worcestershire men recall travelling to Eye Manor and Holmer. Later, Captain Lloyd Bucknall RA, from Bullingham Barracks, Hereford, took on the role of Intelligence Officer, meaning training in Herefordshire would continue for the Worcestershire men.

'Travelling circuses' of officers from Coleshill visiting Worcestershire became a feature of later Auxiliary Unit training in Worcestershire. These must have been along the same lines as the Travelling Wings from the GHQ Home Guard School at Onibury.

11   Arming the LDV/Home Guard

In the early days of the LDV, the military stores were scoured for any weapon that could be used. Bill Allington recalls that the SMLE rifle he was issued with had come from the Downes School OTC, near Bath. In those early days almost anything would be turned into a weapon; at Evesham, one man even turned up with a piece of four by two timber studded with six inch nails, which he described as his Hun Buster! Many of the improvised weapons drew their inspiration from the night-time trench raiding weapons developed by the British soldier during the Great War, no doubt remembered and replicated by the 'old sweats' who were amongst the first to join the LDV.

In stark contrast to some of the improvised weapons available in the early days, some Home Guard units in the Midlands later had the most unlikely armaments available. For example, and probably uniquely, the Austin Aero Factory at Longbridge had two pilots in its Home Guard unit who had the use of two Hawker Hurricane fighters, supplied by the Ministry of Aircraft Production. These were kept on the works airfield at Cofton, on the edge of Worcestershire.[1] The Birmingham Carriage Company Ltd provided their Home Guard unit with six fully armed tanks, while the Karrier Motors unit had six armoured cars.[2] The nearest that any of the Worcestershire battalions came to this level of sophistication were the home-made armoured cars of the Inkberrow and Feckenham Platoons, the armoured tractor at Eckington, and a Humber 'Beaverette' supplied to the Worcester City Battalion.

The Birmingham Small Arms shadow factory at Redditch, amongst other armaments, was producing the BESA and Browning Machine Guns. Inevitably, perhaps, and uniquely, some of these found their way onto the works Home Guard unit armament inventory, together with lavish supplies of ammunition. Apparently some of the BESAs were mounted on vehicles to provide a mobile attacking force.[3]

However, before those levels of sophistication in Home Guard weaponry were reached, it was the supply, at a cost, by the American Government of more than a ¼ million rifles and 77 million rounds of ammunition to Britain on 10th July 1940, that really began to see the LDV evolve as a credible fighting force. More rifles and automatic weapons would come later.

By October 1940, the TAA was able to record that the following weapons and quantities had been issued to the Home Guard in the county:[4]

6,530 Rifles .300 (these were the American Pattern 17 rifle)

534 Rifles Ross (this is a Canadian supplied .303 rifle)

128 Rifles Private (these are likely to have been mainly .22 sporting rifles)

436 Shotguns (these will have been local weapons collected by the police)

8 Hotchkiss Machine Guns (these were ex-WWI tank weapons)

30 Browning Machine Guns (these were American .300 calibre weapons)

152 Browning Automatic Rifles (these were American .300 calibre weapons)

12 Lewis Light Machine Guns (both .300 and .303 calibre, these were largely WWI aircraft stock)

Missing off this list are 249 SMLEs and 300 Enfield Pattern 14s, all .303 calibre rifles, which were noted on the list for October 1941 (see below), but had surely been issued in the summer of 1940.

By March 1941 the Worcestershire Home Guard were required to surrender their .303 calibre rifles (a figure of 14,000 was mentioned but this seems unlikely) with .300 calibre weapons being issued in lieu. A start was also made in the issue of Thompson Submachine Guns and ammunition on a 1,300 rounds per gun scale. The idea was that the Home Guard would be concentrating on .300 calibre weapons, while the Regular Army used .303. Clearly this did not happen on the scale envisaged, because as late as May 1941 the Redditch Battalion issued orders describing the means of distinguishing between the American and British-made arms. On the American rifles, this was to be in the form of a red band, 2 inches wide, to be painted around the barrel and woodwork, with .300 stencilled in black; while British rifles were to have a green band and stencilled .303.[5] More compelling evidence that .303 rifles were still on Home Guard inventories was recorded by the TAA in October 1941, when the following figures were given:[6]

249 .303 calibre SMLE rifles (Interviews with ex-Home Guards and photographic evidence suggests that at least some units kept their SMLEs for the remainder of the war. It seems that nothing is straight forward about Home Guard accounting!)

300 Pattern 14 rifles

564 Ross rifles

12,494 Pattern 17 rifles

40 .22 calibre rifles

436 12 bore shotguns

25 16 bore shotguns

70 Thompson Submachine Guns

202 Browning Automatic Rifles

32 Browning Machine Guns

12 Hotchkiss Machine Guns (calibre not given)
31 Lewis Guns (calibre not given)
94 Northover Projectors
1 Flame Thrower
550 Rifle Grenade Dischargers
564 Ross bayonets
9,676 USA bayonets for the P17s
750 Bayonet Standards

Grenades and Mines
27,792 M36
16,800 Self Igniting Phosphorus
310 M73
60 Sticky Bombs
180 Practice 36
346 Anti-tank Mines
50 Drill Mines

Ammunition
79,743 rounds of .303
916,778 rounds of .300
814,430 rounds of .22
56,000 rounds of .45 Thompson SMG (800 rounds per gun)
82,500 rounds of 12 bore lethal
2,500 rounds of buck shot
9,300 Northover cartridges
1,440 rounds of .38
2,330 rounds of .45
150 rounds of .32

The last three items are listed as revolver ammunition, yet there are no revolvers listed in the inventory. Home Guard accounting again? That revolvers were available was implied in Bromsgrove Battalion orders of 20th December 1941, when it was ordered that these weapons were not to be carried on exercises or on duty by NCOs and men, except Company Sergeant Majors, Despatch Riders and transport drivers who were in possession of them. It was also pointed out that it was necessary for all Home Guards to hold a firearms certificate for privately owned revolvers! It is interesting to note that there were many more .45 rounds for the First World War version of the MK VI Webley revolver than that for the more modern, and lighter .38 Mk IV Webley. This may reflect that there were many privately purchased .45 Webleys in the hands of ex-First World War officers, or that the Mk VI, which is significantly heavier than the Mk IV, was not favoured by the Regular Army, and was issued to the Home Guard instead.[7]

Three of Bennett's Dairy Home Guards show off their Pattern 17 Enfield rifles (in this case of Springfield manufacture) to Land Girls employed on the company's farm at Lower Wick. (Courtesy of John Bennett)

Not mentioned in the list are the Belgian manufactured Mauser rifles that certainly were issued in Worcestershire.[8] These had either been brought into the country by the remnants of the Belgian Army that had managed to escape from Dunkirk, or were part of a shipment originally intended for the Spanish Republicans but seized by the British Government. All were apparently rechambered for the .300 ammunition to be compatible with other Home Guard weaponry, which probably delayed the issue of these rifles.[9]

The American Committee for the Defence of British Homes

Quite separately from the arms supplied to Britain by the American government, concerned Americans established the Committee for the Defence of British Homes, which made appeals to civilians to donate arms, ammunition and binoculars for the British cause. Some donors provided cash for the purchase of additional weapons and ammunition. The response from across America was generous and the loaned weapons – rifles, Thompson Submachine Guns, pistols and shotguns – started to arrive in Britain in early 1941. Some shipments were lost to U-boat action in the Atlantic but by the time the appeal ended in June 1942, the Committee had supplied over 25,000 weapons and over 2 million rounds of ammunition. Weapons donated

Lieutenant Russell, Weapons Training Officer of the Evesham Battalion, aims one of their Hotchkiss Machine Guns, while Company Sergeant Major Allcock prepares to feed one of its unique 20 round strip magazines. The photograph was taken at one of the battalion camps at The Dingle, Elmley Castle. Note the privately owned lorry used by the battalion in the background, with its distinctive white painted edges to the mudguards, a necessity during the 'blackout'. (Courtesy of The Vale of Evesham Historical Society)

by individuals had a label attached giving their name and address, and some of the Home Guard recipients sent letters of thanks to the donors. The majority of these weapons were not returned to their original owners at the end of the war and some of the more unusual have ended up in the hands of collectors.[10]

Using his connections, including Edward Hulton, Tom Wintringham was instrumental, with the help of his wife Kitty, in encouraging the establishment of this American committee. The War Office, fearful that a private gun running exercise such as this might be a prelude to an armed insurrection, ensured that control was established over the reception and distribution of these armaments by having them delivered to Army Depots and to the Ministry of Aircraft Production. Wintringham was later to complain that none of the revolvers donated had reached the Home Guard.[11]

By October 1942 the TAA was able to report that new weapons issued in Worcestershire included 2,000 Sten Carbines and ammunition and the 3 inch calibre Smith Gun. A further issue of Sten ammunition had been made during early 1943, by which time the TAA held one Sten per every five men. There had also been a further issue of Smith Guns. With the increased quantities of ammunition issued, the question of storage had become a serious problem. Apparently following an explosion in the Western Command, instructions were issued that ammunition and explosives were to be dispersed as widely as possible, with active steps taken to requisition suitable accommodation together with increased provision of ammunition shelters away from other buildings.[12] It was at this point that the comment was made facetiously by some wag in the Halesowen Battalion that 'By this time the Battalion was armed with rifles, EY rifles fitted with Cup Dischargers, Browning Automatic Rifles, Sten Machine Carbines, Hotchkiss Machine Guns, Browning Medium Machine Guns, Lewis Guns, Northover Projectors, Spigot Mortars, and a choice of grenades. Webbing equipment, face veils and gas capes supplemented the earlier issues … all the Home Guard was short of was a hand cart to carry his burden into action.'[13]

For convenience and comparison, the description of the weapons which follows has been divided into the following categories: improvised weapons, explosives, flame devices, grenades, rifles, pistols, edged weapons, automatic weapons, sub-artillery and artillery.[14]

Improvised Weapons

A number of examples of weapons carried by men who did not possess a firearm during the early days of the force have come to light, but the use of most of them would have required the men involved being 'up close and very personal' with their victim. Bill Bainbridge of the Bushley Platoon remembered being on duty with only a pitchfork with which to tackle enemy parachutists. The plan was to attack the enemy troops before they had time to find their weapons containers. Not surprisingly, he and his colleagues found those early days particularly tense and frightening! The bayonet standard (inspired by Winston Churchill in 1941) would have been little better for dealing with enemy parachutists.

Dennis Burrows of the Malvern Company recalled that Albert Bird of his unit carried a stick with which to beat the Germans. He claimed that he had carried the same stick during the Great War, but since he had become a prisoner quite early in that conflict, the young men in his unit suggested that it had not got him very far! The then 16-year-old Bill Hay of Terry's unit of the LDV at Redditch, had only a chair leg tied to his wrist with string as his weapon with which to go on patrol. Questions were asked about this under-age lad being on duty at all, but Phillip Terry, his commander and a director of the company, apparently turned a blind eye to it in the light of Bill's keenness.

Egbert Ganderton of Cookhill was issued with a length of cheesewire which, together with a couple of home-made wooden handles, was fashioned into a garrotting wire. A number of interviewees have mentioned having this weapon, and a number armed themselves with a long hat pin. The idea was to creep up behind a sentry and either loop the garrotte around his neck and pull it tight, or press the pin into the victim's neck, just behind the ear. Lengths of wire were also to be used to deal with enemy despatch riders: stretched across a road between two trees and at an appropriate height, it would be difficult to see at night and could decapitate a motorcyclist travelling at speed. Coils of steel wire for this purpose were supplied to the Auxiliaries, and no doubt the less well supplied LDV would have obtained their wire from local hardware stores or a farmer.

In his book, *New Ways of War*, Tom Wintringham described how to make grenades out of gas pipe connectors and explosives obtained from the local quarry operatives. He was also a keen advocate of the jam tin bomb, a simple weapon comprising a tin packed with explosive, together with odd bits of metal to form shrapnel, and a short piece of slow-burning fuse poked through a hole in the tin to detonate the device. Before properly designed grenades such as the Mills Bomb became available to the British front-line soldiers in the Great War, the jam tin bomb had been a very popular means of attacking the enemy. However, experimenting with unauthorised explosives could be a dangerous business, sometimes with fatal results (see Appendix 2). Another Wintringham device was the homemade mortar costing 38 shillings 6 pence which utilised a length of boiler tube and fired a jam tin bomb. It was described in the *Picture Post* magazine before their construction by amateurs was banned by the government. Some LDV/Home Guards who had access to industrial chemicals and a knowledge of chemistry were intending to manufacture their own explosives utilising nitric acid, sulphuric acid and cotton waste, or a mixture of saltpetre, fertiliser or weed killer.

Strangely, Tom Wintringham did not recommend the use of the Molotov Cocktail, because he believed it had limited effect and was dangerous to the user. In Spain they had used jam jars filled with petrol and half a blanket or a curtain wetted with petrol to set fire to the rubber idler wheels on which a tank ran. Nevertheless, following General Ironside's advice to the LDV, the Molotov Cocktail was produced in great numbers as a viable device with which to tackle enemy tanks, and before more powerful and sophisticated grenades became available. Another method of disabling tanks mentioned in LDV instructions, which would require great courage to carry out, was to jam a length of steel rail in the driving sprockets and bring the vehicle to a halt, after which the crew could be roasted with petrol bombs or shot as they tried to escape their tank. This method had apparently been successfully used in Spain against the same light tanks still being used by Germans in great numbers in 1940. Hanging lengths of material, usually hessian, across a road to obscure what might be behind, and placing upside-down soup plates across a road to simulate mines were a couple of techniques used in Spain to bring tanks to a halt, at which point the men with the steel rails and petrol bombs would leap into action! 5,632 yards of hessian had been issued by the TAA to Home Guard units in Worcestershire by October 1941, suggesting that the technique was going to be used here.

Before General Ironside's promised leopard-killing or lethal shotgun rounds reached the LDV, men were modifying the standard buckshot sporting cartridges to improve their lethal capacity, by either partially cutting around the circumference of the cardboard cartridge so that the lead shot and the end of the cartridge remained in one solid lump when fired, or removing the shot and mixing it with molten candlewax before pouring the mixture back into the cartridge. The mixture would solidify and again remain as a solid lump when fired! All these variants were contrary to international law.

Explosives

Tom Wintringham and his fellow Osterley instructors were instrumental in encouraging the LDVs to obtain blasting gelignite from local quarrymen. When made up into small packs with insulating tape, together with a short length of slow burning fuse, this could be used to break the tracks of a tank – another technique that had been successfully used by Spanish miners during the Civil War. In 1942, Bromsgrove Battalion orders drew attention to the fact that the local purchase of explosives, ammunition and pyrotechnics by Home Guards was prohibited, and attention was drawn to the Army Council Instruction 2616 published in Home Guard information Circular No 33 which explained that when explosives were carried, whatever their weight, neither the driver nor any of the personnel accompanying the vehicle were permitted to smoke.[15] Official issue of explosives to the Home Guard was initially limited to small quantities of gun cotton for use in detonating faulty live grenades that had not exploded on the practice range, and it was as late as 1944 before sufficient quantities of the same material were available to 'arm' the Battle Innoculation facilities described earlier. It was the Auxiliary Units who had preferential treatment as far as explosives were concerned, with substantial quantities of the newly developed 'plastic explosive' made available to them. Geoff Devereux remembers Captain Todd delivering about 100lbs of plastic for use by Samson Patrol for sabotage and demolition work, together with the complementary detonators, time pencils, fuse wire of various types and booby trap switches.

Flame Devices
The Molotov Cocktail

One of the most basic of weapons utilising flame was the Molotov Cocktail referred to above. It is still used world-wide against armoured and soft-skinned vehicles by insurgents and rioting crowds. In June 1940, General Ironside directed that Molotov Cocktails should be provided as early as possible at all road blocks manned by military personnel. He said at the time that it was immaterial what the actual pattern of the bomb was, provided that it proved to be efficient in practice. Six

Molotov Cocktails were considered to be sufficient to disable a tank. However, there was a need for the bombers to be close to or well above the tank to be effective. The most vulnerable parts of a tank were identified as the engine louvres, or around the driver's, gunner's or other observation slits. The instructions claimed that a bomber who remained cool and chose the right moment to throw his bombs should have no difficulty in disabling a tank! Petrol bombers were recommended to coordinate their attack with other weapons and remain out of sight until the tank was within range, the idea being to surprise the enemy, even at the expense of a good field of fire. Home Guards under training were instructed in tank recognition using silhouette pamphlets.

A pint beer bottle was recommended for use as a Molotov, scratched or etched on the outside to facilitate its breaking, with 'Royal Flaming Wax Vestas' matches fixed to the outside of the bottle. These were to be struck before throwing the device. Difficult to throw accurately, being quite large and too shiny to grip well, practice was required against moving targets, but apparently it didn't matter whether the device was bowled, lobbed or thrown, so long as it broke![16] The type of bottle used for the Molotov was apparently critical and there is evidence that C Company (Abberley) Home Guard used ginger beer bottles, which did not break readily enough when thrown against an old car in Walsgrove Quarry.

One of the best operational bombing posts identified so far in Worcestershire was the slit trench on top of the high bank close to and overlooking the road, opposite the Fleet Hotel at Holt Fleet bridge (SO 823 633). Here enemy tanks could be readily pelted from above, having been brought to a halt by the road block on the bridge. Even one disabled tank in the defile here would block the road for an indeterminate time if it were kept under small arms fire.

The efficiency of Molotov Cocktails was reported to the Home Guard in June 1941, when the Commander in Chief Middle East was quoted as saying that enemy tanks which had penetrated the perimeter of the Tobruk defences had been destroyed by Molotov Cocktails.[17]

Perversely, the Molotov Cocktail was withdrawn from use by the Home Guard later that same month to be replaced with the SIP grenade, the men being advised to dispose of the Molotovs either by burying them or practice throwing.[18]

Flame Traps and Fougasses

The Flame Trap was simply a 40 gallon drum, or drums, of flammable liquid placed in a roadside bank from which gravity would carry the fuel down to the road surface, via a hose or hoses. To activate the device, a tap would be turned on and the road surface flooded with fuel, which could be ignited by a Verey light or a Molotov Cocktail thrown onto the road. Again an AFV or soft-skinned vehicle would need to be brought to a halt by a road block in a defile for the weapon to be effective.

A Flame Fougasse was a variation on the Flame Trap, but the fuel would be projected from barrels placed in a roadside bank by a small charge of explosive, usually gun cotton (see Fig.13). The Fougasse would be electrically detonated from a protected position some distance away. Until needed, the explosive charge, electrical detonators, cabling and battery would be kept dry and stored together in a box at the Unit HQ responsible for firing the Fougasse; the battery was to be tested monthly. When fired, one Home Guard officer in Worcestershire described it as 'Five minutes of fiery hell!' A demonstration of the Flame Fougasse was given at the British Sugar Corporation gravel pits, Stourport Road, Kidderminster, at 10.30am on 2nd November 1941,[19] an indication that Flame Fougasses were now installed, or about to be so, in the county. Documentary evidence and eyewitness accounts confirm that Flame Fougasses were installed at the following locations in Worcestershire, and there were probably others:[20]

Cofton. In the defile in Grovely Lane at SP 012 765.

Fladbury. Adjoining the Jubilee Bridge at SP 001 455.

Holt Fleet. In the road cutting on the Holt Heath side of Holt Fleet Bridge, at SO 824 632, where a three-barrel fougasse was emplaced.

Kidderminster. The location for this fougasse has not yet been identified but the defile formed by the cutting at Hoobrook (SO 837 744) would seem likely.

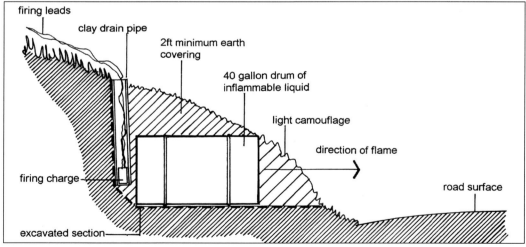

Fig.13 Roadside installation of a Flame Fougasse. When fired, the Flame Fougasse would project a sheet of flame 10 feet wide and 30 feet long, sufficient to disable any tank and its crew which stood in its way. A similar, but simpler device, was the Flame Trap, where flammable liquid would be released from the barrel via a tap and hose, using gravity to spread it over the road surface. A Verey Light Flare or Molotov Cocktail would then be used to ignite the fluid. Both means of attacking a tank would require it to be brought to a halt by a road block, preferably in a defile.

Pershore. In the road cutting at Avonbank on the Comberton road, at SO 953 446.

Redditch. In The Holloway at SP 047 674.

Worcester. Near the Ice Works in the Bromyard Road, St John's, where there is a suitable defile at SO 828 542.

Worcester. London Road, in the defile formed by the cutting on either side of the climb up to Spetchley Road, at SO 864 538.

The Flame Thrower

There is documentary evidence of one of these being supplied to the Home Guard in Worcestershire, although which type is not specified. Two types were commonly supplied or developed elsewhere, the Harvey Flame Thrower and the so-called Home Guard Flame Thrower. The latter was simply a 40 gallon drum of fuel with, commonly, a 60/40% mix of petrol and diesel, the fuel being projected along a hose via a rotary hand pump, all mounted on a two-wheeled trolley. In use from a fixed emplacement, the device had a range of about 15 yards and the flame could be maintained for about two minutes. The Harvey Flame Thrower was more portable, and relied on a cylinder of compressed gas to project the fuel, via a hose. Although the Harvey Flame Thrower had its defects, it was considered by the Home Guard establishment to have a good chance of being effective when properly sited and concealed, particularly in defiles which tanks must use. The anti-tank rifle was considered to be hardly comparable![21] Since examples of the Harvey Flame Thrower were used for the defence of Tewkesbury during an exercise in May 1941, it seems likely that the same device was supplied in Worcestershire.

Grenades and Mines

The wide range of grenades issued to the Home Guard are listed on the certificates issued to NCOs completing courses at Altcar qualifying them to supervise the throwing of live grenades and dealing with blinds. They are:

No 36M Grenade

Also known as the Mills Bomb after its designer, the 36M Grenade had its origins in the First World War as both a hand-thrown grenade or fired from a cup discharger fitted to a rifle after attaching a 2½ inch base plate to the grenade. It could also be fired from the Northover Projector. Originally developed with a 7-second fuse to allow the use of a rifle discharger, the British Expeditionary Force of 1940 discovered that the Germans were throwing back the hand-thrown grenades, so a 4-second fuse was quickly developed. The 36M Grenade was used extensively throughout the Second World War in all theatres by the British Army, and issued in some quantity to the Home Guard. The grenade weighed 1¾lbs and was filled with Baratol explosive.

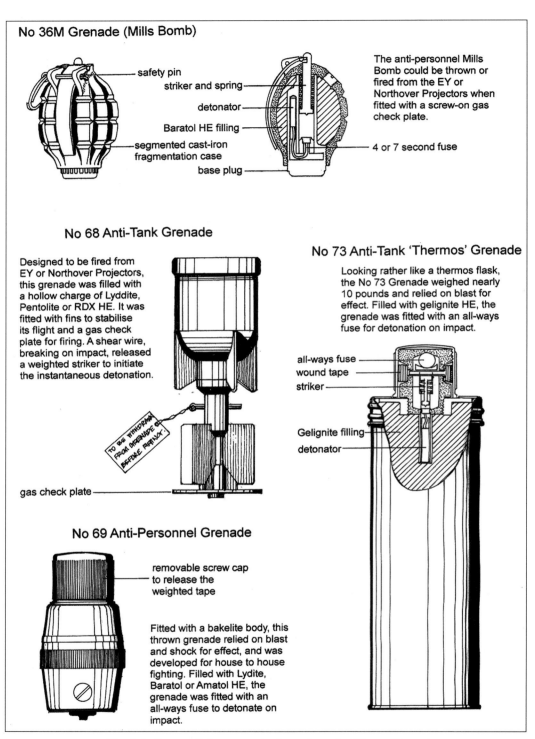

No 36M Grenade (Mills Bomb)

safety pin
striker and spring
detonator
Baratol HE filling
segmented cast-iron fragmentation case
base plug

The anti-personnel Mills Bomb could be thrown or fired from the EY or Northover Projectors when fitted with a screw-on gas check plate.

4 or 7 second fuse

No 68 Anti-Tank Grenade

Designed to be fired from EY or Northover Projectors, this grenade was filled with a hollow charge of Lyddite, Pentolite or RDX HE. It was fitted with fins to stabilise its flight and a gas check plate for firing. A shear wire, breaking on impact, released a weighted striker to initiate the instantaneous detonation.

TO BE WITHDRAWN FROM GRENADE BEFORE FIRING

gas check plate

No 73 Anti-Tank 'Thermos' Grenade

Looking rather like a thermos flask, the No 73 Grenade weighed nearly 10 pounds and relied on blast for effect. Filled with gelignite HE, the grenade was fitted with an all-ways fuse for detonation on impact.

all-ways fuse
wound tape
striker

Gelignite filling
detonator

No 69 Anti-Personnel Grenade

removable screw cap to release the weighted tape

Fitted with a bakelite body, this thrown grenade relied on blast and shock for effect, and was developed for house to house fighting. Filled with Lydite, Baratol or Amatol HE, the grenade was fitted with an all-ways fuse to detonate on impact.

Fig.14 Some of the grenades issued to the Home Guard

On explosion, the segmented cast iron casing would break into quite large pieces that could inflict serious wounds up to a range of 100 yards. Home Guard training ranges took this risk into account, and men were advised to take cover behind the breastworks immediately after throwing a live grenade. An average range for the thrown 36 Grenade was about 25 yards, although with practice this could be increased to 30 yards or further for particularly strong men.[22]

Despite its longevity and proven design, the use of the 36 Grenade was not without its risks. As a result of an accident in 1942, the circumstances of which were not recorded, it had been decided that grenades would not be kept primed. Consequently, all men were to be trained to prime grenades rapidly, and in an emergency individuals would be told to do this. In the case of mobile columns, arrangements were to be made to do this on receipt of orders to move, while the column was preparing to turn out. The same procedure was to be applied to defended localities when the commander considered the situation demanded it.[23] Priming the 36 grenade, or indeed any of the main types of grenade issued to the Home Guard, was a particularly hazardous operation since even the heat of a human hand could set off the fulminate of mercury igniter, with the loss of at least some fingers. Bill Allington recalled that this happened to one of his friends in the Bromsgrove Battalion.[24]

No 68 Rifle Grenade

The 68 Grenade was designed from the outset to be used from a rifle cup discharger and was the first hollow charge, anti-tank weapon to be issued to the British Army. The grenade became available from May 1940 onwards but was issued to the Home Guard in the following year. The grenade could also be fired from the Northover Projector, but fired from a cup disharger it had a range of about 100 yards. Weighing a little more than a 36M grenade, at almost 2lbs, the 68 was provided with fins to improve its accuracy in flight and filled with a variety of explosives, including Lyddite, Pentolite or RDX.

No 69 Grenade

Designed to rely on blast and shock for effect, this grenade had a bakelite casing and weighed only 13½oz. Fitted with an 'all-ways' fuse, it exploded on impact and was to be used primarily in house-to-house fighting. The grenade had several alternative explosive fillings, including Lyddite and Baratol, and the fuse was primed in flight by a length of weighted tape that would be released by unscrewing a cap. The tape would unwind and remove the pin during flight. The dangerous nature of grenades to their handlers was brought home to the Warley Battalion, which suffered a number of accidents after both 69 and 73 grenades were thrown and failed to detonate. Because these grenades were fitted with the all-ways fuse, they were very sensitive to shock and were to be destroyed in situ by a qualified officer.[25]

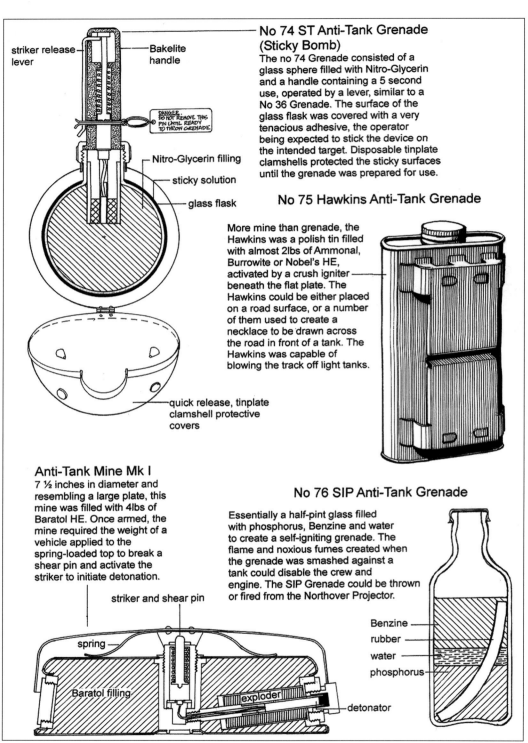

No 74 ST Anti-Tank Grenade (Sticky Bomb)

The no 74 Grenade consisted of a glass sphere filled with Nitro-Glycerin and a handle containing a 5 second use, operated by a lever, similar to a No 36 Grenade. The surface of the glass flask was covered with a very tenacious adhesive, the operator being expected to stick the device on the intended target. Disposable tinplate clamshells protected the sticky surfaces until the grenade was prepared for use.

striker release lever

Bakelite handle

DANGER DO NOT REMOVE THIS PIN UNTIL READY TO THROW GRENADE.

Nitro-Glycerin filling

sticky solution

glass flask

No 75 Hawkins Anti-Tank Grenade

More mine than grenade, the Hawkins was a polish tin filled with almost 2lbs of Ammonal, Burrowite or Nobel's HE, activated by a crush igniter beneath the flat plate. The Hawkins could be either placed on a road surface, or a number of them used to create a necklace to be drawn across the road in front of a tank. The Hawkins was capable of blowing the track off light tanks.

quick release, tinplate clamshell protective covers

Anti-Tank Mine Mk I

7 ½ inches in diameter and resembling a large plate, this mine was filled with 4lbs of Baratol HE. Once armed, the mine required the weight of a vehicle applied to the spring-loaded top to break a shear pin and activate the striker to initiate detonation.

striker and shear pin

spring

Baratol filling

exploder

No 76 SIP Anti-Tank Grenade

Essentially a half-pint glass filled with phosphorus, Benzine and water to create a self-igniting grenade. The flame and noxious fumes created when the grenade was smashed against a tank could disable the crew and engine. The SIP Grenade could be thrown or fired from the Northover Projector.

Benzine
rubber
water
phosphorus

detonator

Fig.15 Some of the grenades and mines issued to the Home Guard

No 73 Grenade

Weighing nearly 4lbs, of cylindrical form and about 10 inches long, the 73 Grenade looked very much like a thermos flask and was generally known by this name. Intended for use against armoured fighting vehicles or soft skinned vehicles, this heavy grenade was to be hand thrown, when the range would be about 12 yards, or dropped from buildings. Filled with 3¼lbs of gelignite, the grenade relied on blast for effect and, like the 69 grenade, was fitted with an all-ways fuse for explosion on impact. Again, the fuse was primed in flight by an unwinding weighted tape. The short range of the weapon meant that the operator had to throw it, or drop it, from cover. Against tanks it was recommended that it be thrown against their tracks.[26] A cut-down version of this grenade was used by the Czech agents sent from Britain to assassinate Heydrich in Prague in 1942.

No 74 or ST Grenade

Designed for use against armoured fighting vehicles and generally called the Sticky Bomb by Home Guards, the 74 or ST Grenade comprised of a glass globe containing 1¼lbs of nitro-glycerine attached to a wooden handle containing a 5-second fuse. The fuse was activated on releasing a lever similar to that on a 36 Grenade. The glass container was covered in stockinette coated with birdlime which, when the grenade was in storage, was covered by a thin tin-plate casing. Prior to being thrown a pin would be pulled, releasing the two clam-shell like halves of the metal cover that would then drop away, exposing the sticky surface of the bomb. The operator would then get in close to a tank and throw the grenade so that the glass smashed against the armour. The explosive would then spread out over the armour plate before detonating. Alternatively the operator could run up to the tank and stick it on the armour. Either method would require a high level of courage! Relying on blast effect, the Sticky Bomb was capable of penetrating armour plate of just a little less than 1 inch and severely damaging thicker material.[27] Experience had shown that the thrower of the ST Grenade needed to take cover from both the explosion and possible metal splash from the target, and in the opposite direction to that which the handle of the grenade pointed. Audiences at demonstrations were therefore not allowed to be within 100 yards of an exploding ST Grenade. These characteristics make all the more remarkable Captain Seal's party piece at public demonstrations on the Redditch Golf Course (see p.59).

No 75 Hawkins Grenade

Named after its designer, the Hawkins Grenade was actually an anti-tank mine and relied on the tank running over it to crush the acid-filled igniters contained within the casing. The Hawkins could be buried in a suitable location, skilfully thrown to land in front of a tank or, most efficiently, used in necklace form and pulled across the road in front of a tank. In this case a number of Hawkins mines would be tied at intervals along a length of cord. The necklace would be hidden on one side of the road, while the operator would hold the end of the cord in a slit trench on the other side. On the approach of the tank the necklace would be pulled across the road in front of the tank. Experience of their use in North Africa showed that the Hawkins Grenade was capable of breaking the track of a Panzer III.

No 76 SIP Grenade

Developed by SIS and really a sophisticated Molotov Cocktail, the Self Igniting Phosphorus or AW Bomb, as it was sometimes called after its manufacturers, Messrs Albright and Wilson of Oldbury, was a half-pint glass bottle filled with a lethal mixture of phosphorus, benzene and water. A small length of rubber would be included which would dissolve in the benzene to create a sticky mixture. This was intended to make the contents stick to armour plate when the bottle was smashed against a tank, while the phosphorus would ignite on exposure to the air, setting fire to the benzene and giving off a toxic white smoke. Supplied in boxes of 24, they had to be stored and handled with care. It was advised that they were stored away from other munitions and somewhere shaded since phosphorus melted at little more than the boiling point of water! A metal crown cork sealed off the bottle when in store, but these would rust over a period of time resulting in the danger of self-ignition. For this reason many AW Bombs issued to the Home Guard and Auxiliaries were buried in remote places for safety, to await discovery by some unfortunate person years later. Caches of AW Bombs are still being found more than 60 years after their burial, and only recently a store of bombs was ignited when air raid shelters were being demolished at the former BSA works in Redditch.

Two thicknesses of bottle were used by Albright and Wilson for their AW Bombs: a thin-walled version for hand-throwing and a thicker version for firing from the Northover Projector to reduce (but not eliminate) the incidence of bottles breaking in the barrel. The different bottles were identified by using green crown corks on those to be fired from the Northover, and red for the hand-thrown version. When used with the Northover, a cardboard ring was pressed over the neck of the bottle to prevent it sliding out if the barrel of the weapon was depressed and a rubber washer placed between the bottle and the propellant to absorb some of the shock when fired. Although issued to the Regular Army during 1940/41, the AW Bomb was primarily a weapon of the Home Guard.

It was found that after Northover Projector practice on meadowland, sheep were dying from ingesting the toxic residue left after live firing of the SIP bomb. The broken glass could also pose a threat to cattle if they ingested it, and so Home Guards were asked to exercise great care when choosing practice grounds for this bomb.

No 77 Grenade Mk 1

This was a hand-thrown phosphorus grenade designed to replace the SIP Bomb. It had a small metal canister jacket and the contents were activated by an all-ways fuse. Warnings were issued to Home Guards that if air was admitted to the filling, this grenade would burst into flame immediately, whether primed or not. As far as possible these grenades were to be stored and transported separately from other types of ammunition.[28]

Anti-Tank Mine Mk I

Described by one Home Guard as an explosive dinner plate, this steel encased circular device was intended to be either placed on road surfaces where enemy tanks were expected to pass, or in ground where tanks or other vehicles might divert to avoid obstacles. 350 of these anti-tank mines had been issued by the TAA to the Home Guard in Worcestershire by 1941, the majority apparently being set aside for use in the Worcester Anti-Tank Island defences.

Small Arms
Shotguns

It was the Americans who developed trench fighting with the shotgun to a fine art during the Great War, even to the extent of using experienced clay pigeon shots to fire at and detonate hand grenades while still in the air. When used against German soldiers, the high casualties from the use of shotguns loaded with buckshot led to the German authorities threatening to shoot any American soldier taken prisoner and armed with a shotgun or carrying cartridges.[29] The shotgun was again to come to the fore as a weapon of war in the summer of 1940, particularly in rural areas, where almost every household would own one. The weapon was commended to the LDV/Home Guard for close quarter or street fighting, some being 'sawn off' to improve their portability. Home Guard Instruction No 28, *Weapons – Notes on the use of shotguns and spherical ball ammunition*, explained that these cartridges were accurate enough for their purpose up to 100 yards and were lethal up to half a mile. In training, therefore, every care was to be taken to ensure that they were fired against a safe background. With the majority of guns the aim with this ammunition up to 50 yards could be as good as point blank, but at 100 yards you had to allow for a drop of the shot of approximately one foot.

Rifles

The rifle synonymous with the Home Guard was the American manufactured Enfield Pattern 1917, usually referred to as the P17, but it was not always so and in the early days of the LDV the men were anxious to get their hands on anything that fired a bullet. A miscellany of types was issued, although generally of .303

calibre, including the Short Magazine Lee-Enfield (SMLE), the Enfield Pattern 14 and the Canadian Ross rifle, all from the First World War period and supplied from government arms stores and cadet units. Added to these were the privately donated rifles handed into the police which were of many calibres, including the elephant gun from Croome Court mentioned on p.25, but the most commonly loaned weapons were sporting guns of .22 calibre. Later, Mauser rifles were issued to at least some Redditch Home Guards to add to the variety.

The SMLE and Enfield Patterns 14 and 17

The SMLE was familiar to the 'old sweats' of the Home Guard and considered by them to be the best of the lot, but is that true? Before the SMLE was produced, it was usual to supply the British Army with two rifles: a long rifle for infantry use and a short carbine for the cavalry. The SMLE was designed as a compromise to standardise the manufacture and issue of rifles from 1903 onwards for both the infantry and cavalry, but it was shorter than the ideal for accurate shooting at long ranges and the sighting arrangements were apparently not easy to use. Its prime advantage was that it had a 10-round magazine – most other service rifles had only 5-round magazines – which allowed the British Army to achieve a rate of aimed fire exceeding that of most other armies, a performance that led the Germans to believe that in the early battles of the First World War they were facing machine guns!

The 1950s Home Guard were issued with the standard for then SMLE Mk IV, which had been developed and issued during the Second World War to supplement, and eventually supplant, the earlier Mk III.

Part of the Stourbridge Company of the Oldbury Battalion 1950s Home Guard during an exercise. The prone riflemen are using SMLE No 4 Mk 1 rifles, while the standing men have Sten Machine Carbines. (Courtesy of Dennis Chance, whose father stands 2nd from the right)

Concern about both the accuracy of the SMLE and the lengthy manufacturing time involved, allied to the increase in demand for rifles prior to the First World War, led the Enfield Company to design an alternative rifle for rapid production, with a longer barrel than the SMLE, Mauser bolt action and an aperture sighting arrangement. Many thousands of these rifles, chambered for the standard British .303 cartridge, were produced under licence in America as the Enfield Pattern 14, together with a 17 inch sword bayonet similar to that of the SMLE. The rifle proved to be extremely accurate and, with the standard aperture sights, could outperform the SMLE, even if the latter was fitted with a telescopic sight, over long ranges. Consequently it became a favourite weapon of the British snipers during both world wars, and for competition shooting. However, despite its accuracy, the weapon was not widely issued in the Great War. It was considered by its critics to be badly balanced, too heavy and unwieldy, and had just a five round magazine. Consequently some were sold to the White Russians in 1919, while others found their way to government stores, until reissued in the summer of 1940.

In an almost mirror situation, America was also short of rifles when it entered the Great War in 1917 and, although their standard service issue rifle was the .300 Springfield, it was convenient to put the British designed Enfield back into production, but re-chambered for their standard .30/06 Springfield rimless cartridge. Well over two million of the Enfield .300 Pattern 17 were produced by the Remington Company and its subsidiary Eddystone, as well as the Springfield and Winchester companies. Replaced by the Garand, these weapons found their way into stores in America. It was this model of rifle that the British government purchased from the Americans in large quantities in the summer of 1940 and again in the spring of 1941. Many Home Guards receiving their first P17 rifle recall the problems of removing the particularly stiff grease within which the weapons had been embalmed by the Americans.

The P17 rifle with the .30/06 cartridge had a muzzle velocity of 2,700 feet per second, about 400 feet per second higher than the SMLE. With this velocity, windage and drop could be ignored up to 200 yards, and at 1,000 yards the drop was less than ten inches, so it was much more accurate than the SMLE.[30]

Small Bore Rifles

The P17 was also issued to the Auxiliary Units, but for silent sniping and for shooting rabbits to supplement their food supplies once they went underground, each patrol also received a .22 rifle. After 1942, the .22 Winchester Model 74 became available, fitted with silencer and telescopic sights. It had a 15-round magazine. Even using the more powerful long .22 cartridge, its effectiveness as a sniper weapon was limited to about 100 yards maximum. The rifle would be issued to the best shot in the patrol, but many Auxiliers doubted the ability of this weapon for sniping,

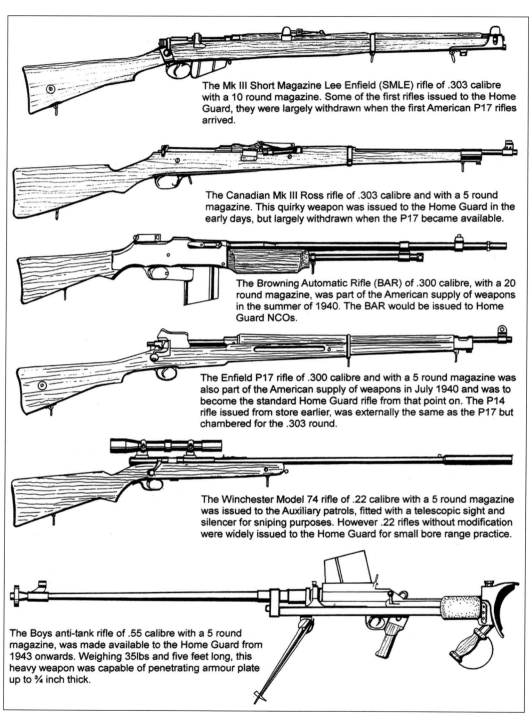

The Mk III Short Magazine Lee Enfield (SMLE) rifle of .303 calibre with a 10 round magazine. Some of the first rifles issued to the Home Guard, they were largely withdrawn when the first American P17 rifles arrived.

The Canadian Mk III Ross rifle of .303 calibre and with a 5 round magazine. This quirky weapon was issued to the Home Guard in the early days, but largely withdrawn when the P17 became available.

The Browning Automatic Rifle (BAR) of .300 calibre, with a 20 round magazine, was part of the American supply of weapons in the summer of 1940. The BAR would be issued to Home Guard NCOs.

The Enfield P17 rifle of .300 calibre and with a 5 round magazine was also part of the American supply of weapons in July 1940 and was to become the standard Home Guard rifle from that point on. The P14 rifle issued from store earlier, was externally the same as the P17 but chambered for the .303 round.

The Winchester Model 74 rifle of .22 calibre with a 5 round magazine was issued to the Auxiliary patrols, fitted with a telescopic sight and silencer for sniping purposes. However .22 rifles without modification were widely issued to the Home Guard for small bore range practice.

The Boys anti-tank rifle of .55 calibre with a 5 round magazine, was made available to the Home Guard from 1943 onwards. Weighing 35lbs and five feet long, this heavy weapon was capable of penetrating armour plate up to ¾ inch thick.

Fig.16 Rifles issued to the Home Guard in Worcestershire

even with the heavier bullet. Doubt was also expressed about the use of telescopic sights which were not robust, easily knocked out of adjustment, and were mainly abandoned. Before the Winchester 74 became available, the Auxiliaries were issued with a variety of .22 weapons, including Remingtons and Martinis.

Unmodified .22 rifles were also made widely available to the Home Guard for musketry training on the 25 yard indoor ranges that were provided in all of the drill halls, or could easily be arranged in the local quarry. The .22 was also to serve on with the rifle clubs formed by the Home Guard after Stand Down, when their full-bore rifles had been withdrawn.

The Ross Rifle

The Ross rifle was of Canadian manufacture and used by their troops at the beginning of the First World War. Problems with the jamming of the otherwise simple push-pull bolt action in the mud and dust of the Western Front led to its withdrawal from service and replacement with the British SMLE. The Ross was also heavy, at almost 10lbs weight, and cumbersome. It had a 5-round magazine for the standard .303 rimmed cartridge, but being a long rifle it was accurate. One disconcerting feature of the Ross was that if the bolt was incorrectly fitted after cleaning, and this was quite possible, the next discharge would drive the bolt backwards into the firer's eye with fatal results! The Ross rifles were returned to stores between the wars, but in the summer of 1940, together with their short 10 inch bayonet, were gratefully received by the LDV/Home Guard.

Cup Discharger or EY Rifle

Essentially a service rifle adapted to project grenades, this was a hang-over from the trench warfare of the Great War, reintroduced in 1940. The cup discharger was a short tubular device mounted onto the muzzle end of a service rifle to enable a grenade to be launched over a far longer distance than it could be thrown. The grenade would be placed into the cup, after removing the safety pin, where the gas pressure from a blank ballistite cartridge would be utilised to project the grenade. In Home Guard hands, either a 36M Grenade, fitted with a 7-second fuse and a screw-on metal disk to fit the cup discharger diameter, or the 68 Anti-Tank Grenade, where the disk formed part of the grenade, could be used with the device.

Initially, substandard SMLE rifles fitted with cup dischargers were issued to the Home Guard. Later the P17 rifle was adapted for use when it became known as the EY rifle. Some ex-Home Guards claim that the letters were an abbreviation of 'EmergencY', but in fact it derives from the initials of the inventor, Edwin Youle. The back pressure created in the barrel from firing the EY rifle was such that it required both the barrel and supporting wooden structure to be bound with wire to prevent the barrel from expanding or the butt from fracturing.

The Cup Discharger, or EY Projector, being demonstrated to members of the Redditch Battalion, with the Sergeant Instructor inserting a No 68 Anti-Tank Grenade. The EY Projector cups here have been fitted to American P17 rifles, where wire binding around the barrel and stock is apparent, as is the clear marking that these are .300 calibre weapons. (Courtesy of Mr E.P. Grace via Mike Johnson)

Boys Anti-Tank Rifle

Named after Captain Boys, one of the principal designers of the weapon, this rifle had a calibre of .55 inch and fired a steel-cored bullet at a muzzle velocity of 3,250 feet per second. The rifle weighed 36lbs, was 5 feet long and had a top-mounted 5-round box magazine. Introduced in 1937, the rifle was capable of penetrating the armour of any tank in service then, at a range of up to 250 yards. Later, it was much criticised for being inadequate, but the Boys could still make itself felt in 1940, if used in the appropriate circumstances. The Boys was capable of penetrating all parts of the armour of the German PzKw I, the armour on the sides or rear of a PzKw II, but with the PzKw III or IV it was recommended that fire should be aimed at vulnerable points such as the junction of turret and hull or gun mantle to jam them, or the tracks. It was reckoned that a trained man could fire 9 rounds a minute and that a two-man team was required, one to observe for the firer.

Some 10,000 Boys rifles were made available to the Home Guard in 1943, who found that despite having a strong recoil spring and a well padded butt, the recoil was massive. Home Guards who have fired this weapon describe how they were pushed back some eight or nine inches with each shot, when firing from the prone position.[33] Derrick Pearson of the Stourbridge Home Guard considered the Boys to be extremely accurate, but so powerful it could only be fired in practice on the range at Norton Barracks. Its ability to penetrate masonry and its accuracy would have made it a very useful weapon for dislodging snipers from the upper storeys of buildings and would have been devastating against soft-skinned vehicles. As such the Boys could be said to have been a precursor of the long range, large calibre, high velocity, sniper rifles used by the British Army today.[34]

Which of the Home Guard battalions in Worcestershire were issued with the Boys is not known, although the Stourbridge Battalion clearly had one, and there is photographic evidence that the Evesham Battalion did too.

Pistols and Revolvers

At the insistence of Winston Churchill, revolvers were issued to Auxiliary Units in the summer of 1940. Most of the hand guns issued in Worcestershire were of American origin and the majority received the .38 Smith and Wesson, although Colt .32, 'Colt Police Positive' and 'Official Police', and other makes were made available from a large consignment of arms purchased by the British government from the United States or provided by the American Committee for the Defence of British Homes. Geoff Devereux, for example, received a .32 Beretta automatic pistol, while Roger Smith, at Crowle, was issued with the same calibre revolver. For those Auxiliaries with a .38 they were, in some cases, issued with the 'special' high-power cartridge with a soft lead bullet, modified by the men to become a dum-dum by filing off the tip, although the use of such ammunition was clearly outside the Hague Convention on arms.

Home Guard officers also carried sidearms, although precisely what is not readily apparent as only the holster shows in most photographs. The issue of .455 revolver ammunition during 1941 suggests that the heavy, and not very popular, Webley and Scott service revolver was made available to at least some of the Home Guard officers in Worcestershire.

Edged Weapons and Coshes
Bayonets
Mention has already been made of the bayonets supplied with the various rifles. However, the combination of the long P17 rifle and the 17 inch bayonet, when fitted, would seriously challenge the height of some of the smaller Home Guards when standing to attention! Nevertheless, this length was, as noted earlier, to make it a much better weapon for bayonet fighting than the shorter spike bayonet later issued to the British Army, and would certainly outreach the short bayonet issued to the Wehrmacht.[37] As a result of the danger of accidents occurring during training

---

Theft of weapons and ammunition

The Malvern Gazette reported a case where a 14-year-old boy had taken a revolver and ammunition. It was described as a boyish prank, and the boy appeared in Malvern Juvenile Court on 20th April 1943, charged with stealing 23 rounds of .38 ammunition valued at 4 shillings (about £10 now). Home Guard Sergeant Major Richard Kemys owned the .38 Colt revolver and a quantity of ammunition which he kept in a workshop. The boy made a statement that he took the revolver and ammunition, went to the common and fired one shot and another boy fired a second shot. The next day he returned the revolver. The case was dismissed on payment of costs. However, Sergeant Major Kemys was charged with not keeping the revolver in a secure place and fined £1 (about £50 now).[35]

This was clearly not an isolated case because later in the year Army Council Instruction No 987 drew attention to a large number of cases of theft of firearms. The attention of all ranks was consequently drawn to the necessity of safeguarding at all times weapons issued to them, especially revolvers. Special care was to be taken during railway and other journeys. All such weapons when not with the individual were to be kept under unit arrangements. Disciplinary action was be taken in all cases of losses which were the result of negligence.[36]

with the bayonet, one Home Guard battalion issued an edict that on no account would bayonets be fixed during field training by any member of the Home Guard. It was clearly a dangerous weapon!

One of the points Tom Wintringham made, and a clear dig at the veterans that were now running and training the LDV, was that against men with automatic weapons and grenades, the bayonet was useless. He was concerned that the same infantry tactics were being taught as had been used at the battle of Blenheim. Wintringham's view had been coloured by the fact that in Spain the long bayonet issued with the Moisin Nagant rifles had been designed to be permanently fixed in battle, making it unwieldy to use. (Ironically, Wintringham was wounded at the Battle of Jarama after ordering a bayonet charge!) He also pointed out that the British service rifle fired less accurately with the bayonet fixed than it did with the bayonet removed. Instead he recommended a stout knife for hand to hand fighting.

Pikes or bayonet standards

Influenced by the fear of a paratroop attack, and apparently at the instigation of Winston Churchill, Home Guard battalions were issued with the pike in 1941. Although many Home Guards still did not have a personal weapon at this stage, the issue of the pike drew much criticism, and might have been better received in the early days when weapons were in really short supply! Called officially 'Bayonet Standards', 750 were issued in Worcestershire and they apparently went straight into store, carrying them being judged as just too embarrassing! However, one battalion hit on the novel idea of making miscreants carry a pike on parade as a punishment. The standard form of the pike was a SMLE or 1917 issue steel bayonet welded into a piece of round steel tube. One is known to survive in Worcestershire and is on display in the Regimental Museum.

Knives

The shortage of weapons for the Home Guard in 1940, and the emphasis given in popular publications to unarmed combat and knife fighting, led to many Home Guards producing their own fighting knives. Albert Toon, of the BSA Home Guard, utilised the hardened steel of a broken industrial hacksaw blade, ground to a suitable shape, sharpened and fitted with a riveted-on wooden handle, and many others must have been produced by similar means.

Fairbairn-Sykes knives, designed for use by the Commandos, were widely issued to the Auxiliary Units for the silent killing of enemy sentries, but some were to find their way into the hands of the Home Guard, one I know of being won in a shooting competition.

Coshes and Clubs

Developed as a close-quarter trench fighting weapon during the First World War, the cosh or club was introduced again in 1940 as a means of dealing with German sentries. We have seen how one Evesham LDV created his own version of the club with a nail studded piece of timber (see p.209), but the official version was a lead weighted and studded ash club, known officially as a 'knobkerrie'.

Automatic Weapons

Although some Home Guard units elsewhere in Britain were issued the Bren Light Machine Gun, there is no evidence that these were made available to the wartime General Service battalions of Home Guard in Worcestershire, with one exception. This was Crowle Company, which shared duties with the Regulars of No 23 ITC from Norton Barracks, and had emplaced a Bren on an anti-aircraft mounting on Whittington Tump.[38] Brens were, however issued to the 1950s Home Guard.

Another rare automatic weapon in the Worcestershire Home Guard was the standard British Army .303 Vickers Heavy Machine Gun, although they were issued to General Service Home Guard battalions elsewhere. The exception was the High Duty Alloys factory in Redditch, which had two. They were probably supplied by the Ministry of Aircraft Production and may have been the air-cooled version. However, there is good evidence that the following types of automatic weapon were issued to the Home Guard in the county:

Joe King, of Samson Patrol, clutching his 'shellelagh' or cosh, one of a number of hand to hand fighting weapons issued to Auxiliary Units. (Courtesy of the late Joe King)

The Besa Machine Gun

This was a Czechoslovakian designed, air-cooled machine gun of either 7.92mm or 15mm calibre and came from the same factory in Brno that had produced the original Bren Gun. Adopted by the British for use in tanks, an arrangement was made in 1936 for both calibres of the weapon to be produced by the Birmingham Small Arms Company. This production was later moved to their factory in Redditch. The name of the weapon derives from **B**rno, **E**nfield and B**SA**.

The weapon utilised a canvas belt feed for the ammunition and was capable of variable rates of fire, either 500 or 700rpm. Not unnaturally, the weapon was adopted by the BSA Home Guard at Redditch for both ground defence and LAA use. Ammunition was in, apparently, plentiful supply. It is not known whether any of these weapons reached other Home Guard units in the area.

The Browning Automatic Rifle

Usually referred to as the BAR, this was part of the batch of weapons purchased from America in 1940 and was one of the first automatic weapons issued to the Home Guard. Designated the M1918, after the year of manufacture, it had been designed as an assault weapon to be fired from waist level, while slung from a shoulder strap. A 20-round magazine was fitted from beneath the breach, which caused some awkwardness and delay when changing magazines. A 40-round magazine was also available.

The weapon was very heavy at over 17lbs and capable of firing the standard American .300 ammunition at a rate of 500 rounds a minute. When set at automatic fire, it would empty the magazine in 1½ seconds. This rate of fire also caused severe overheating and jamming. Home Guards were therefore recommended to fire the weapon in single shot mode and use automatic fire only in an emergency. It was said that this would not only avoid wasting ammunition but would also disguise the fact that an automatic weapon was present on the field of battle, until the enemy was too close to do anything about it! Fired from the shoulder as a conventional rifle, from the standing or prone position, the weapon was extremely accurate. The Americans continued to use the BAR until after the Korean War.

Over 200 BARs were issued to the Home Guard in Worcestershire, but opinions vary about its qualities, some claiming that it was a very efficient weapon and one even saying that it was better than a Bren. Others, however, found it to be too heavy, one Worcestershire Home Guard apparently threatening to throw his away during an exercise because it had become too heavy to carry![39]

The Hotchkiss Machine Gun

This weapon had an interesting origin, having been designed by an American, Laurence Benet, who had taken over the Hotchkiss Arms Company in France when the founder died. Wanting a light automatic weapon that could be carried by cavalry, the British government purchased the rights to manufacture what became known as the Hotchkiss Machine Gun Mk I. Modified to take the standard .303 cartridge, the Hotchkiss was put into service with the cavalry in 1916, but it was also used in the female version of the British Mk IV tank.[40] The weapon weighed 27lbs and had a rate of fire of 500rpm from a 30-round metal strip rather than a canvas belt.

The weapon was still in use with the British cavalry at the start of the Second World War and some found their way to the Home Guard in 1940, possibly those salvaged from scrapped tanks and put into storage. A dozen Hotchkiss machine guns

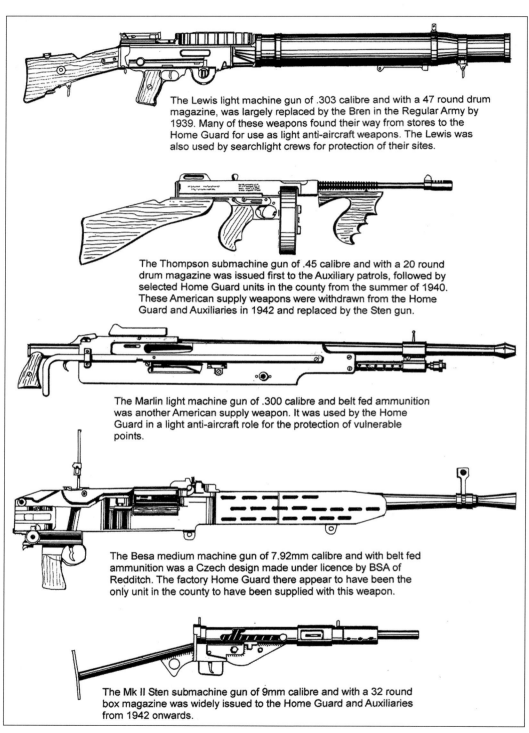

The Lewis light machine gun of .303 calibre and with a 47 round drum magazine, was largely replaced by the Bren in the Regular Army by 1939. Many of these weapons found their way from stores to the Home Guard for use as light anti-aircraft weapons. The Lewis was also used by searchlight crews for protection of their sites.

The Thompson submachine gun of .45 calibre and with a 20 round drum magazine was issued first to the Auxiliary patrols, followed by selected Home Guard units in the county from the summer of 1940. These American supply weapons were withdrawn from the Home Guard and Auxiliaries in 1942 and replaced by the Sten gun.

The Marlin light machine gun of .300 calibre and belt fed ammunition was another American supply weapon. It was used by the Home Guard in a light anti-aircraft role for the protection of vulnerable points.

The Besa medium machine gun of 7.92mm calibre and with belt fed ammunition was a Czech design made under licence by BSA of Redditch. The factory Home Guard there appear to have been the only unit in the county to have been supplied with this weapon.

The Mk II Sten submachine gun of 9mm calibre and with a 32 round box magazine was widely issued to the Home Guard and Auxiliaries from 1942 onwards.

Fig.17 Automatic weapons issued to the Home Guard

were issued to the Home Guard in Worcestershire and the Evesham and Halesowen Battalions were two of the recipients.

The Lewis Gun

This was a portable air-cooled machine gun, originally designed by Colonel Isaac Lewis of the US Coast Artillery and manufactured by the Birmingham Small Arms Company during the First World War. Weighing only 26lbs, the weapon was eminently suitable for use in aircraft, with the characteristic tubular air cooling jacket removed to lighten it still further. The Lewis Gun was manufactured in the standard .303 calibre, with the ammunition carried in a shallow drum magazine mounted over the breech of the weapon, which gave the gun an uncluttered appearance. However the breech mechanism was complex and the gun was prone to jamming for any one of eleven reasons.

The British Army retained the Lewis Gun until 1939, until replaced by the Bren. In addition to its ground or aircraft use, the weapon could also be used in a light anti-aircraft role, when it would be mounted on a simple steel tube post and provided with a clamp-on anti-aircraft fore-sight that incorporated a simple aiming off device for moving targets. Fortunately, the redundant weapons had been put into store in 1939 and were available for re-issue to both the Home Guard and LAA units of the Regular Army and the Navy in the summer of 1940. At least 30 were issued by the TAA to the Home Guard in Worcestershire, but many more were issued from Air Ministry stores for LAA use at Ministry of Aircraft Production factories and on the airfields in the county. American manufactured and supplied Lewis Guns of .300 calibre also found their way to the Home Guard in Worcestershire.

The Marlin Machine Gun

This was another American weapon from the First World War period, being designed and produced by the Marlin-Rockwell Corporation of Connecticut for the US Navy. Of .300 calibre, the weapon was light enough, at 22½lbs, to be used in aircraft. By 1930 the weapons had been put into store, but were shipped across to Britain in 1940 to be issued to both the Home Guard and Merchant Navy for LAA use. The number issued in Worcestershire is not known, other than the fact that the Worcester City Battalion had eight on two quadruple mountings protecting the city power station, and another pair mounted on the Worcester Sheet Metal Company works, in the former Tram Depot in Hylton Road, St John's.[41]

The Thompson Submachine Gun

The infamous 'Tommy Gun' of gangster fame was designated the M1928 by the Americans, who supplied substantial numbers of them to Britain in 1940. Of .45 calibre and fitted with either a 50-round drum magazine or a 20-round box

Ron Seymour of Samson Patrol aims his patrol's Thompson Submachine Gun while training near Bransford Bridge. The weapon is not fitted with a magazine, although both drum and box magazines were provided for use by the patrol.
(Courtesy of the late Ron Seymour)

magazine, it was capable of firing at a rate of 800 rounds per minute. The weapon was well made and reliable, if a little heavy at over 10lbs.[42] The Auxiliary Units appear to have been the first to have received this weapon, one being supplied to each patrol. Since the Auxiliaries were not intended to confront the Germans, the weapon was to be used only for protection should the patrol have to fight their way out of trouble. By March 1941 the Thompson had been issued to the General Service battalions of the Home Guard.

By August 1941 it was recognised that the continual stripping and assembly of the Thompson Submachine Gun for instructional purposes could cause serious damage to the main spring and was liable to put the gun out of action. Owing to the difficulty of replacing the spring correctly, the stripping and reassembly of the Thompson was only to be carried out by an armourer or other qualified individual.[43]

Some 70 of these weapons were issued to the Home Guard in Worcestershire in 1941, but notification that they were to be withdrawn and replaced by the Sten Machine Carbine came in February 1942, much to the disappointment of both Auxiliaries and Home Guards.[44]

Sten Machine Carbine

Produced at a unit price of less than £3 (about £150 now), the Sten was said by some to be the ugliest and nastiest weapon issued to the British Army. Imitation is said to be the sincerest form of flattery, and since the Germans found it appropriate to copy the Sten towards the end of the war, perhaps it was not so bad after all! It was relatively light at less than 7lbs weight and compact at only 30 inches long. In fact it was a most successful weapon for close quarter fighting and, apart from a few idiosyncrasies, served the British Army well throughout the remainder of the Second World War and into the 1960s. Both the Mk II and more simplified Mk III versions were supplied to both the Auxiliaries and Home Guard, to replace the much loved Thompson. The first Stens reached the Home Guard in Worcestershire on 19th March 1942 and would eventually reach almost parity with the number of rifles issued.[45]

Of 9mm calibre and fed by a side mounted 32-round box magazine, the Sten was capable of firing at a rate of 550 rounds a minute, although in theory also capable of firing single shots by moving a change button.[46] It was subject to a number of faults: it would occasionally 'run wild' and fire off the entire magazine, would remove the tips of the fingers if the firer was careless enough to let them enter the return spring slot while firing, or would jam completely if the magazine was pushed in too far.

The Sten was considered to be more appropriate for use in urban areas than in the countryside, and so a higher proportion of Home Guards in towns received them. It was necessary as a consequence to make adjustments in the distribution of Stens and rifles between town and country units. Stens were primarily issued to Home Guard NCOs.

Browning Heavy Machine Gun
Designated the M1917, after the year of manufacture, this was another American supplied weapon of .300 calibre. Water-cooled and mounted on a tripod similar to

Malvern Battalion men operating an American supplied water-cooled, .300 calibre, Browning Machine Gun at the West Malvern Range. (Courtesy of Sheila Edmonds)

the British Vickers machine gun, its distinguishing features were the mounting of the ammunition box on the side of the weapon and a pistol hand grip. With several Brownings firing on an area, the maximum usable range was about 4,000 yards, with 2,500 yards as the maximum effective range for a single gun. The rate of fire for this weapon could be varied from 60 rounds per minute up to a maximum of 550rpm, although 125rpm was the norm.[47]

Over 30 Browning heavy machine guns were issued in Worcestershire, although the detailed distribution is not known.

Sub-Artillery

This was a term applied to a number of rudimentary artillery-like but portable weapons issued to the Home Guard during 1941 and 1942. Three weapons came into this category: the Northover Projector, the Spigot Mortar and the Smith Gun.

The Northover Projector

Officially described as a 'smooth bore breech loading weapon of simple design', the Northover Projector was described by many Home Guards as being like a stove pipe mounted on a tripod. Costing about £14 (about £700 now) to manufacture, it was designed by a Home Guard officer, Major H. Northover, and worked on the principle of a small cannon, using a small charge of black powder to project various grenades. Primarily an anti-tank weapon with a fighting range of 50 to 150 yards,

Battle stations on Malvern Link Common being occupied by Malvern Battalion men during a public demonstration in May 1943. In the foreground is a Northover Projector and crew, while in the background and to the left, is a Spigot Mortar on a portable mounting, and crew. (Courtesy of Sheila Edmonds)

,it was best employed in an ambush covering a road block or tank obstacle, or any route a tank might take to bypass an obstacle. The Northover required a crew of three to operate it.

The ammunition for the Northover Projector could be one of the following:

Incendiary, using the SIP Grenade with the green cap, described earlier. The maximum range for this ammunition was 200 yards but a more effective range against armoured vehicles was 75 to 100 yards.

Fragmentary, using the 36M Grenade. In this case the safety pin was withdrawn before the grenade was pushed into the breech, where the barrel kept the fuse activating lever in position until fired. The recommended ranges were as for the SIP Grenade.

Anti-Tank, using the No 68 Grenade. Again the safety pin was removed before pushing the grenade into the breech, tail to the rear! The maximum range for this grenade was 150 yards, but the effective range was the same as the other grenades.

The suggested method of employment against an armoured vehicle was:

At 80 to 100 yards range, fire one or two No 68 Grenades in order to stop a tank. It was reckoned that an average crew could hit a tank every time from 80 yards.

Fire two or three SIP Grenades to set the tank on fire.

If the crew of the tank attempted to get out or an infantry counter-attack develops, fire 36M Grenades.

The cardinal principle for the Northover crew, set out in instructions, was to 'hold fire', presumably to the last minute, because the white smoke given off by the weapon when fired would give away its position, though the instructions do not say this! Despite its simplicity and shortcomings, the Northover Projector was apparently loved by the Home Guard.[48] Over 90 Northovers were issued in Worcestershire.

The Northover Projector, firing the SIP bomb, was prone to having the bottle break in the barrel and the phosphorus igniting. Treatment for anyone suffering burns consisted of removal, under water, with a clean rag and a match-stick, of the small fragments of phosphorus which had become embedded in the skin. The burnt part was then to be kept under water or a thick pad soaked in water applied until medical aid was available. On no account were oil or oily dressings to be applied.[49]

The Blacker Bombard or 29mm Spigot Mortar

Described as quite a devastating piece of sub-artillery, it would apparently have made a pretty mess of any tank receiving one of its direct hits. It was, however, not easy to arrange for live firing of this weapon as the danger area of the burst was 400 yards.[50]

The weapon was initially called the Blacker Bombard after its designer, Lt Colonel L.V.S. Blacker, a Territorial Army officer who had been experimenting with such weapons for some time. It was primarily an anti-tank weapon, although it could also be used in an anti-personnel role using a lighter bomb. The weapon projected the bomb from a long steel rod which gave direction, rather than from a barrel, although the use of a large diameter tube over the spigot, to protect the crew from blast, gives the impression of a large calibre weapon.

The Spigot Mortar required a crew of three to operate it from either a fixed concrete pedestal or a portable mounting, comprising four long horizontal steel arms with spade grips to dig into the soil. Both mountings incorporated a stainless steel pintle and circular steel plate, upon which the weapon could be pivoted.

The ammunition for the Spigot Mortar comprised an egg-shaped bomb, which together with a tube and circular stabilising fin was over two feet long. The tube fitted over the long 29mm diameter steel spigot. Several types of bomb were made available for the Spigot Mortar:

One of the more enduring examples of Home Guard archaeology is the fixed concrete Spigot Mortar mounting with the tell-tale stainless steel pintle for locating the weapon. Heavily reinforced with a steel spider, the mounting is almost indestructible, and most were simply buried at the end of the war. This is one of the most accessible examples in Worcestershire, and can be seen at the entrance to the Eckington Bridge Picnic Site. (Author's photo)

- A 20lbs anti-tank round, containing 9lbs of Nobels 808 explosive and a percussion fuse. This had a maximum range of 400 yards, although a range between 75 and 200 yards was considered to be best. A maximum rate of fire of 12rpm was possible, although 6rpm was more normal but, rather like the Northover, it gave off a lot of white smoke when fired and so would have quickly given away its position.
- A 14lb anti-personnel high explosive round. This had a range of up to 950 yards, when its high trajectory would reach 600 feet before plunging down to the target in true mortar fashion.
- An inert practice anti-tank round, filled with concrete and weighing 15lbs.
- A drill bomb, identical to live rounds but filled with sand.

It was emphasised that Spigot Mortar practice bombs were not to be used for drill or demonstration purposes other than on open ranges, and that they were clearly marked with a yellow band on bomb body and tail tube.[51] It is significant

An unidentified gun team of the Redditch Battalion exercise with their Spigot Mortar on a portable mounting. The Terry's Factory Unit from Redditch won the N Sector competition for this weapon at Hampton Lovett in November 1943. (Courtesy of Mr E.P. Grace via Mike Johnson)

that this order was issued in Worcestershire within a very short time of a sergeant of the Tewkesbury Home Guard dying after being hit by a Spigot Mortar bomb accidentally fired during indoor practice at Healings Mill, Tewkesbury.

The first information and details of the allotments of this weapon to be made to the Home Guard were received by the Worcestershire Sub District HQ on 2nd May 1942.[52]

Bill Hay, a former Terry's Home Guard, recalls a Spigot Mortar firing competition at Hampton Lovett where a Redditch Battalion team put one shot through the bull without touching the surrounding white ring. Apparently Captain Seal, who was managing the team, thought that this was pure luck, so the team put the next shot through the same hole in the bull and were able to carry off the championship.[53] This experience gives the lie to criticism that the Spigot Mortar was a crude and inaccurate weapon.

The Smith Gun

Designed by a Major W.H. Smith of the Trianco Toy Company, this was a smooth bore weapon of a little over 3 inches calibre with a low muzzle velocity of around 350 to 400 feet per second. As with the other pieces of Home Guard sub-artillery, the Smith Gun was capable of firing either anti-personnel or anti-tank rounds, the design of which were apparently based on the standard infantry mortar round. Production problems with the ammunition's fuses delayed the supply of the weapon until 1942, when it was issued to the RAF Regiment. They found it to be dangerous to use, with at least one of their number being killed operating it.[54] I have found no evidence of the Worcestershire Home Guard rejecting the weapon as being dangerous!

In an anti-personnel role the Smith Gun could be fired to ranges of up to 650 yards by indirect fire, but it would have been more normal to engage targets at shorter ranges. In the anti-tank role the effective range was 200 yards or, with moving targets, 100 yards, but in this role the gun was considered to be less effective than either the 2pdr Anti-Tank Gun or the Spigot Mortar.

In the hands of a competent four-man crew the Smith Gun had a high rate of fire of up to 25 rounds per minute. In addition, the weapon with its ammunition limber, which together weighed about 8¾cwts, was capable of being towed behind a small car and apparently even a motorcycle. Unhitched, the gun could be manhandled quite readily in both built-up areas and accessible areas of countryside. One major disadvantage of the weapon was that it was conspicuous and difficult to hide, and the narrow tyres restricted its mobility on rough ground, too.

One of the Malvern Battalion Smith Guns, with ammunition limber and crew. The gun and limber could be towed behind a small vehicle and then manhandled into their firing position, where gun and limber would be turned on their sides to provide some protection for the crew. The crew here from the left is: Corporal Woodward, of Woodward's Coaches, Walter Handy, Reg Hill, Johnny Johnson, Bert Cheese, Peter Rowberry and Sergeant Sam Beard. (Courtesy of the late Sam Beard, son of Sergeant Beard)

Three types of ammunition were provided for the Smith Gun, each coming as a complete round, with an all-ways fuse, propellant and percussion cap:[55]

An 8lbs anti-personnel round comprising a cast iron casing, that would fragment when the amatol filling exploded. This round was also effective against buildings and would create a hole in 9 inch brickwork sufficient for a man to crawl through.

An anti-tank round similar in construction to the 68 Grenade. This projectile was fitted with four fins to provide stability in flight. Said to be effective against armoured vehicles up to 200 yards range, it could also penetrate 80mm of armour plate at 50 yards. It too was effective against buildings and could create a hole 2 feet in diameter in 9 inch reinforced concrete.

An inert practice round was also provided.

The first Smith Guns arrived in the Worcestershire Sub District on 6th June 1942 for issue to the Home Guard. Ten more arrived on 1st July for the Home Guard, four of them for issue to mobile columns.[56]

Mortars

During the Second World War the Regular infantry issue mortars were not part of the Home Guard inventory of weapons in Worcestershire, although the 1950s Home Guards were trained in the use of the standard 2 inch infantry mortar. It is not known whether any of the Wintringham design home-made mortars were constructed in the county.

Artillery

Two forms of artillery are known to have been issued to the Home Guard in Worcestershire, both for an anti-tank role.

The Hotchkiss Mk II 6pdr, 6cwt, Quick Firing Gun

Designed in the late 19th century as an anti-torpedo boat weapon for use in the superstructure of Dreadnought battleships, the weapon was later supplied by the Admiralty for use in the side sponsons of Mark IV male tanks, from 1917 onwards.[57] In this role the Hotchkiss was used in an anti-personnel weapon firing a 6lb shrapnel shell up to a range of more than 5,000 yards. Manufactured, under licence, by the Armstrong Whitworth Company of Newcastle on Tyne, it was to this company that the government turned in 1940 to recondition several hundred examples of the weapon that had lain in store since the tanks had been scrapped. Having left the majority of their 2pdr Anti-Tank Guns in France, the Royal Artillery were provided with the Hotchkiss as a stop-gap anti-tank weapon firing a solid shot. Issued to the 62nd Anti-Tank Regiment, some 16 of these weapons were deployed in the Central Midland Area, of which seven are known to have been used in fixed

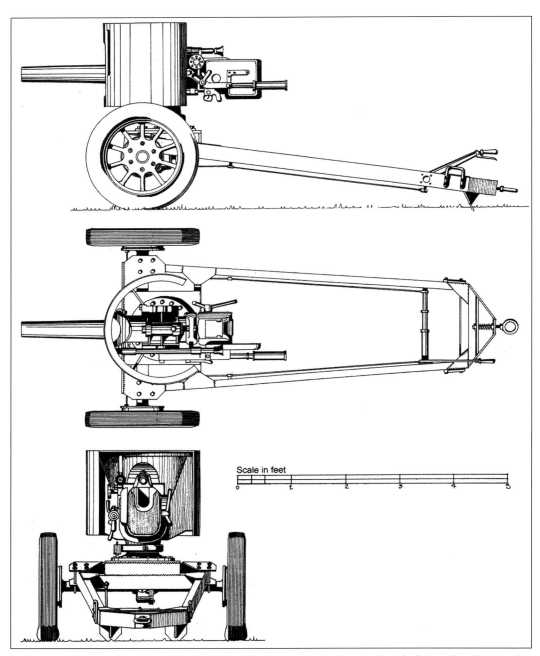

Scale in feet

Fig.18 The trail-mounted Hotchkiss 6 pdr gun. These were handed over by the 62nd Anti-Tank Regiment to some of the Worcestershire Home Guard in the spring of 1941. The trail utilised easily sourced mild steel channel sections and plate, welded together and mounted on an Austin 12 car axle and wheels. Firing solid 6lb shot, the quick-firing Hotchkiss would have been more than capable of dealing with the generally light German tanks of 1940/41.

emplacements at river crossings on the Severn and Avon stop-line,[58] while others had been supplied with a crudely constructed chassis to provide towable mobile artillery (see Fig.18).

Although Home Guard units in Worcestershire received live firing instruction on the Hotchkiss as early as August 1940 on the range at the British Camp Reservoir, the guns in the fixed emplacements were not handed over by the 62nd Anti-Tank Regiment until the spring of 1941. Consequently the Evesham, Malvern, Stourport and Worcester City Home Guard Battalions became responsible for the emplaced guns at Pershore, Evesham, Upton upon Severn, Holt Fleet, Stourport and Worcester. With a relatively low muzzle velocity of 1,350 feet per second, but firing a solid shot, the weapon would have been capable of disabling the lighter German tanks of 1940/41. The quick firing ability of the weapon was put to good effect in practice by one Worcestershire Home Guard team, trained by an ex-naval gunner, who managed to get off 8 shots in 10 seconds. That was fast by any standards![59]

The Worcestershire Sub District HQ War Diary for 2nd January 1942 recorded that it had been decided that the Home Guard 6pdr Hotchkiss guns were to be made mobile and work on the fixed emplacements was to be halted.[60] The history of the Upton Company Home Guard notes that in February 1942, the Upton Platoon 6 Pounder Team were highly praised for their part in firing practice for all teams of the battalion at Malvern.[61] It seems from this that the Home Guard at Upton had not wasted any time in extracting the 6 Pounder Hotchkiss gun from its emplacement in Fish Meadow, and mounted it on a mobile trail. It is not known how many gun teams the Malvern Battalion had, but there was certainly one other gun at Holt Fleet Bridge which was also made into mobile artillery.[62]

This emplacement appears to be the last surviving, unaltered, Hotchkiss 6 pounder position in the West Midlands, and can be found at the side of Holt Fleet Bridge. It is located on the east side of the River Severn and faces west, reflecting the function of the Severn stop-line to deal with enemy attacks into the Midlands from the west and Wales. (Author's photo)

2 Pounder Anti-Tank Gun

This was the standard anti-tank weapon of the British Army at the beginning of the Second World War and it apparently performed well against the lighter German tanks of 1940 in France. The majority of the guns, over 500 of them, were left in France with the rest of the heavy equipment when the BEF were evacuated from Dunkirk. Well engineered, the gun had a calibre of 1.57 inches and fired a solid armour piercing shell of 2.4lbs. It was a relatively heavy gun, weighing some 1,850lbs and would require a powerful vehicle to tow it. An efficient gun crew could fire up to 22rpm and the effective range was 600 yards. Capable of penetrating 53mm of armour plate at 500 yards, the 2pdr became inadequate as an anti-tank weapon when the heavier German tanks were introduced at the end of 1941. Replaced by the Royal Artillery first with the 6pdr and then later the 17pdr Anti-Tank Guns, the now redundant 2pdrs were handed over to the Regular infantry regiments in mid-1942 and a few found their way into the hands of some Home Guard battalions.

Any 'new' weapon issued to the Home Guard was well received. A number of Worcestershire battalions of Home Guard are known to have received 2 Pounders, including Worcester City, Redditch and Warley. Eric Doughty of the Worcester Battalion, and a member of the Heenan and Froude 2 Pounder gun team, recalled that a gun team went to north Wales for a training scheme and actually beat a Regular Army gun team in firing at a moving target.[63]

Members of the Worcester City Battalion demonstrate their 2 pounder Anti-Tank Guns at the New Road Cricket Ground during a 'Holiday at Home' event. The groundsman was apparently not best pleased when the gun teams sank the spade grips of the gun trails in the hallowed turf. (Courtesy of the late Mr A.E. Doughty, who can be seen with his arm outstretched in the nearer of the two gun teams)

12 Uniforms, Badges and Flashes

Despite Eden's promise in his broadcast on 14th May 1940 to supply a uniform to volunteers, it would be some time before a full set of battledress and accoutrements would become available to the men.

This is an early version of the LDV armband, or brassard, which has a distinctly home-made appearance. This will have been quickly replaced with a War Office supplied version in khaki cloth with printed black lettering but that, in turn, would have been superseded by the 'HOME GUARD' armband in late July.
(Courtesy of Malcolm Atkin)

Major Kendall, at his pep talk to the Malvern LDVs in the Winter Gardens towards the end of June 1940, and in an effort to engender the confidence of the public in the force and in themselves, said that despite the lack of uniforms he expected a degree of 'spit and polish' when on parade. He thought that uniforms would arrive in a week or so – he was optimistic to say the least![1] Initially therefore the men would parade, or go on observation or guard duty, in their civilian clothing, with no more than an armband and an identity card signifying that they were in the LDV. Some of the armbands had a distinctly home-made appearance.

The first items of uniform issued to the Home Guard in Worcestershire, as elsewhere, were field service caps, the Halesowen unit receiving theirs on 26th July. This unit's history usefully lists the arrival of these and other items of uniform during 1940:[2]

    26th July – 86 field service caps.
    16th August – 684 denim overalls, 275 greatcoats, 525 blankets, 690 field
        dressings, and 230 LDV arm bands.
    25th September – 939 pairs of boots, 440 haversacks, 192 battledress.
    8th October – 260 leather anklets, 380 belts.

On 22nd August 1940, a letter from the Adjutant of B Company (on Parsons Chain Company headed paper) to the Company Quartermaster listed the equip-

After armbands, the first item of uniform to arrive for the Home Guard in Worcestershire, as elsewhere, was the Field Service Cap. The buttoned side panels could be folded down and re-buttoned under the wearer's chin to cover the ears and back of the neck. A peak for the cap, seen here beneath the cap badge, could also be folded down. The cap badge of the Worcestershire Regiment was issued from August 1940 onwards to reflect the affiliation of the Home Guard to the county regiment.
(Courtesy of the late Wilf Mound)

ment to which Home Guard volunteers were entitled, as and when available. It comprised a suit of denim overalls, service respirator, two eye shields, anti-gas ointment, steel helmet, field dressing, greatcoat, pair of boots, pair of gaiters, haversack and two armbands. Blankets were to be issued at a rate of one for every two men and groundsheets at one for every four men. The Adjutant thought that many of the Company's volunteers would not want to draw army boots, which seems a strange comment to make.[3]

It was reported to the Worcestershire TAA meeting of 8th October that some 16,500 denim suits and 2,100 battledress suits had been issued, together with other items of equipment, including a few steel helmets, so that at least some of the Home Guards in the county could take on the appearance of soldiers.[4] However, it would be October 1942 before webbing equipment was issued to the Home Guard.

The denim overalls were the standard British Army working wear of blouse and separate trousers and are remembered for their ill-fitting qualities and shabby appearance. Some of the men were pleased to receive the standard battledress later in the year, although it would be well into 1941 before everyone had this uniform and could take on the appearance of the Regular soldier. Early group photographs of the Worcestershire Home Guard show a mixture of denim and serge uniforms being worn. However, the denim overalls should not be disparaged totally, because during the summer the denim was appreciated as being cooler and less itchy than the woollen serge. It is no coincidence that the denims were also worn by some of the D-Day assault troops during the hot June weather of 1944.

With the War Office sanctioning the designation of battalion commanders, company commanders and platoon commanders in June 1940, rank insignia was also approved. For the battalion commander this was to be four dark blue stripes worn on the epaulettes of the uniform; for the company commanders, two blue stripes; and for platoon commanders one blue stripe. Section commanders (the equivalent rank of sergeants) were to wear three chevrons of the usual army pattern on the left arm, and squad commanders (the equivalent of corporals), two chevrons. Saluting was left to good sense and taste as a matter of courtesy, although the men were apparently not bound to salute at this stage.[5]

The 3rd August 1940 saw the formal affiliation of the Home Guard to the county regiments and confirmation that the Home Guard was to wear the badges of the county regiments in whose area they served. It was reported that the Home Guard had welcomed the granting of badges, as it was felt that this would give them the status appropriate to their duties.[6] In the same month, the War Office announced that the issue of an official tie by the Home Guard authorities was being considered.

To coincide with the granting of the King's Commission to Home Guard officers, battalion orders in February 1941 explained that officers were expected to provide

Major Morom of the Redditch Battalion invites the Duke of Kent to inspect the Honour Guard in February 1941. Major Morom's two rank stripes (blue tape) can be seen on the epaulette or shoulder strap of his great coat. These Home Guard officers' rank tapes would be replaced by conventional Regular Army pips and crowns later that month. (Courtesy of the late Robin Morom)

themselves with conventional badges of rank, as laid down by formal instructions, as soon as possible and that the existing blue shoulder stripes were to be discontinued.[7] As a result, shoulder pips and crowns replaced the blue tape stripes on the epaulettes previously used to denote rank. NCOs were also now to wear the conventional stripes of lance corporal, corporal and sergeant.

February 1941 saw the Worcester City Battalion being informed by the Zone HQ that steel helmets (Grade 2) in sub-standard mild steel were being made available. These were apparently distinguishable from the standard military issue steel helmet of hardened steel by having three small holes punched in each side of

'Home Guard' shoulder titles were issued in May 1941, while the battalion codes and numbers were issued later in the summer. 'WOR' represents Worcestershire and the '7', the Malvern Battalion. (Courtesy of the late Leyland Shawe)

the brim. No chin straps were provided with this issue and it was suggested that a suitable attachment should be improvised, at no cost to the public![8]

'Home Guard' shoulder titles were introduced from 18th May 1941 and the brassards, or armbands, were to be withdrawn. By this time, most men would have received the standard battledress uniform to replace the denim suits issued during 1940 and so, with their shoulder titles, they would take on a similar appearance to that of the Regular forces. Later in the summer, additional cloth identification flashes were issued for wearing on the upper sleeve on Home Guard uniforms denoting the county allegiance and battalion number. These symbols of recognition would be necessary for the large scale operations in which the Home Guard now found itself involved, including test musters, simulated battle manoeuvres, exercises and route marches, as well as church and War Weapons Weeks parades and other public events in the larger towns. They also reflected the more structured organisation of the force. The soldierly bearing of the Home Guard was becoming apparent for all to see.[9]

The cloth flash showing the county allegiance of Worcestershire was 'WOR' in dark blue lettering on a buff coloured patch with, immediately below it, the relevant battalion number of 1 to 12. Although the issue of flashes had been announced in April 1941, the actual date of issue in Worcestershire has not been identified. However, it certainly appears to have been before the 27th August, the date that

Oldbury Battalion Part 1 Orders made it abundantly clear that the practice of wearing uniform without Home Guard shoulder titles and flashes was to stop. Home Guard Instruction No 1920/41 issued with a War Office letter of the 28th August also dealt with the display of these flashes, and pointed to the fact that some Home Guards were still not wearing them correctly. The regulations were: that shoulder titles and regimental flashes signifying the county and battalion number were to be worn on both sleeves of the battledress and greatcoat, with the shoulder title one inch below the seam of the shoulder, and the regimental flash half an inch below the bottom edges of the shoulder title. The battalion number was to be immediately below the lettering of the county, with no space being permitted between the letters and the number. Both titles and flashes were to be sewn on under private arrangements and at no expense to the public!

It was decided in 1943 that the clothing of cadets enrolled as messengers should carry no shoulder titles, but that two Home Guard armbands would be worn, above the elbow on each sleeve of the greatcoat, and that greatcoats were to be worn only when actually on guard duty.[10]

The range of equipment and clothing issued to Sergeant Frank Devereux of No 7 Section, No 21 Platoon (Kemerton), Evesham Battalion by 1942. (Courtesy of Dave Devereux)

Theft of Home Guard clothing and equipment

It must have been a great temptation in times of clothing coupons and rationing to use Home Guard uniform items or other equipment for everyday use, and even declare that they had been lost! It is therefore significant that the Redditch Battalion brought it to the notice of the men in Part 1 Orders that greatcoats cost nearly £3 (about £150 today); Haversacks 6 shillings (about £10.50 today); and serge capes £2 (about £100 now).[11] This problem was clearly becoming serious because in August 1941 a court of enquiry was to be arranged by Captain J.R. Wright to look into the loss of 10 pairs of trousers in transit from Worcester.[12] Later in the same month, *The County Express and Dudley Mercury* reported that the theft of a haversack and seven bandages from a Home Guard depot at Halesowen led to two boys, aged 11 and 14, being brought before the Juvenile Court. Although the boys admitted the theft, it was said that they had been helping out acting as casualties for the ambulance section of the Home Guard and were keen and interested in ambulance work. It was thought that in their enthusiasm for the work, they had taken the articles in order to practise methods. Although the bench said that it was wrong of the boys to take advantage of the position which they had been given by the Home Guard, the case was dismissed on payment of costs by the two boys (or their parents perhaps?).[13]

It was noted in August that some members of the Oldbury Battalion were wearing greatcoats and boots when not on duty. Part 1 Orders made it clear that this practice was to cease! It was also reported that of the 770 denim suits issued, only 264 had been returned to the headquarters, the order for which had been issued on 6th May 1941.[14] It is believed that the denims were required for the growing Regular Army as working fatigues. Clearly there was still a temptation to supplement the civilian clothing allowance by wearing Home Guard kit when off-duty.

Home Guard badges

Possibly concerned that some uniforms were taking on the appearance of a boy scout with a sleeve full of specialist badges, it had been decided by the Warley Battalion Commanding Officer in 1941 that no badges other than those officially approved by the War Office would be worn by the Home Guard. The next month the Warley Battalion orders were more emphatic about wearing unauthorised badges, and specifically mentioned that the badge of the Army School of Physical Training was not authorised in the Home Guard. It was also pointed out that there was no rank of Staff Sergeant in the Home Guard, so a crown over three stripes must only be worn by the Quartermaster Sergeant of each company. Any Sergeant Instructor at present wearing the crown over stripes was to remove the crown.[15]

Despite the Warley Commander's concerns, over the life of the wartime Home Guard a slow accretion of additional badges was authorised by higher authority, starting with a Western Command Order of 8th July 1942, which made it clear that

Major A.E. Grace (later Lt Colonel and Redditch Battalion Commander) presents medals to the winning team from A Company (Redditch Town) after a First Aid competition held at Redditch County High School in October 1943. They are wearing their Red Cross sleeve badges in the prescribed manner. This was one of the many competitions organised for the Home Guard during the last two years of its existence to test military skills and keep interest in the force high. The team, from the left are: Private Crook, Private Edwards, Lance Corporal Pye, Private Teague and Lance Corporal Simcox, the team leader. (Courtesy of Mr E.P. Grace via Mike Johnson)

the proficiency badges authorised for wear by members of the Home Guard were for privates and NCOs below the rank of Sergeant who had passed the appropriate test. The 1 inch red diamond Proficiency Badge was to be worn on the lower part of the right sleeve of the battledress blouse and not to be worn on the greatcoat. Secondly, those who had passed the necessary examination and who had been awarded the badge of the St John Ambulance Brigade and St Andrew's Ambulance Association, or the British Red Cross Society, could also wear such a badge on the lower part of the battledress blouse sleeve. Officers and other ranks who had been awarded the regulation flying badge after service with the RAF could wear their wings, when their qualification had been duly confirmed. However, the RAF Observers badge was not to be worn. Post Office personnel engaged upon essential defence communication or upon important Post Office work, could wear a small blue and

white diamond flash one inch below the point of the shoulder.[16] The authorisation that Red Cross proficiency badges could be worn was a direct reflection of the appointment of medical officers to the Home Guard, with the express intention of training other ranks in the techniques of first aid and stretcher bearing.

When the civilian Bomb Disposal Units were transferred to the Home Guard from November 1942, a special badge was approved for issue to personnel of these units who had performed not less than 24 hours' bomb disposal training. The small cloth badge, which displayed crossed bombs in yellow on a red background, was to be worn on the <u>left</u> sleeve below the elbow, with the bottom of the badge 5 inches above the bottom edge of the sleeve.[17]

In this close-up of an unidentified member of the ADRDE Bomb Disposal Unit of the Malvern Battalion, the distinctive yellow on red crossed bombs badge of the unit can be seen on the man's (wrong) sleeve, as well as four service chevrons, each representing a year's service in the Home Guard. Note also the British Army webbing gaiters being worn by this man, probably reflecting the association of the Bomb Disposal units with the Royal Engineers. (Black leather gaiters were issued to the majority of Home Guards.) (Courtesy of Sheila Edmonds)

From August 1943, it was decided that Home Guards who had been issued with the Silver War Badge would be allowed to wear them above their medal ribbons on their battledress. The badge was issued to men who, during the First World War, had been discharged through sickness or injury which had prevented them from returning to service. (Courtesy of Malcolm Atkin)

Despite the earlier attempts to restrict the number of badges being worn, the authorities decided that the Silver War Badge, issued to members of the Regular Forces in the First World War who had been discharged from service owing to disability, could now be worn on the left breast of the battledress blouse. The badge was to be worn immediately above the space normally occupied by medal ribbons.[18]

On 9th March 1944, it was announced that NCOs and men who were wounded in the last war were now entitled to wear a red bar to denote this. Platoon Commanders were to verify the claims and forward claimants' names through Company headquarters to reach Battalion HQ by 25th March.[19]

In recognition of service undertaken by the Home Guard and other defence services since 3rd September 1939, a Home Guard circular of 1944 described the wearing of wound stripes and service chevrons. Wound stripes were to be narrow gold braid 1½ inches in length and worn vertically on the left sleeve of the battledress blouse. They were to be issued in respect of each wound or injury sustained while on duty as a direct consequence of enemy action. Small service chevrons, printed in red on a khaki background, were now allowed to denote the length of service during the Second World War. One chevron was to be issued for each completed year of service.[20] During this last year of Home Guard duty, the wearing of skill at arms (crossed rifles) and signallers (crossed flags) sleeve badges was authorised, subject to a maximum of two only on the individual's sleeve.[21]

Auxiliary Units

The Auxiliary Units were issued with the same denim and then battledress serge as the Home Guard to give them a degree of anonymity and legal protection, but with the conventional Home Guard receiving county and battalion number flashes unlike their Auxilier counterparts, the Auxiliaries stood out as different and their disguise of masquerading as Home Guards would be compromised if they were caught after an invasion. Coincidental with the move of administrative responsibility for them from the local battalion headquarters to the TAA in York, it was decided that the Worcestershire Auxiliaries would wear the county flash, WOR, and the number 202.

1950s Home Guard

In the initial stages the Home Guard clothing was to consist of a brassard and steel helmet. Badges of rank were to be painted on the helmets and brassards would carry the regimental flashes. The uniform subsequently issued was battledress, with black beret or bonnet, khaki shirt, collar and tie and was to be worn only when on parades or duties. The arm title 'Home Guard' in white lettering on a red background was to be worn one inch from the top of each sleeve of the battledress blouse, with a subsidiary title signifying the county and battalion number half an inch below the bottom edge of the arm title. The number was to be located centrally below the county letters.

Proficiency badges were again to be a diamond-shaped piece of red cloth, each side measuring 1 inch, with a bar of the same material 1 inch long by ¼ inch wide placed horizontally a ¼ inch below the lowest point of the diamond. Additional bars could be added spaced at ¼ inch intervals. The badge was to be worn on the left sleeve of the battledress blouse, the bottom of the badge being 6 inches from the bottom edge of the sleeve. Skill at Arms and Signallers badges for those qualified to wear them were to be worn on the left sleeve, or if a proficiency badge was also worn, half an inch above that badge. No member could wear more than two of the badges mentioned above. Those who had passed the qualifying examination and been awarded the Badge of St John's Ambulance Association, the St Andrew's Ambulance Association or the British Red Cross Society could wear any two such badges on the right sleeve of the battledress blouse. However, First Aid badges were to be obtained privately and were not to be worn by members above the rank of corporal.

As in the 1940s, officers and other ranks of the Home Guard were not allowed to attend public meetings in uniform, although they could in civilian dress.[22] The drafters of the Act establishing the new Home Guard had clearly looked up the records relating to the wartime Home Guard and were able to include many of the details relating to service and uniform that had evolved over the four years of the war.

The white on red shoulder flashes of the 1950s Home Guard, the number 5 denoting the Worcester and Malvern Battalion. (Courtesy of Bill Allington)

Conclusions

Opinions do vary about the value of the Home Guard, some saying that they would not have coped with the German methods of waging war. Others, including some of the leading Spanish Civil War veterans, thought that the force would have been eminently suitable for dealing with the techniques of the German Blitzkrieg, especially if trained to use irregular methods of fighting. Ultimately, success might have been in terms of simply slowing down the advance by providing resistance in depth (something the French were not able to do in May and June of 1940), however self-sacrificial that might have been. It is often not realised just what a body of experience there was within the ranks of the Home Guard; a good percentage of them had already been 'shot over', some as recently as in France prior to the Dunkirk evacuation in late May and early June 1940,[1] and many of the older Home Guards, having already beaten the Germans once before in 1918, had every intention of doing so again.

During many interviews, more than a few Home Guards have said to me that they, and the defence structures put in place, would not have been able to stop the Germans had they invaded Britain. It is likely that they were unaware of the totality of the defence arrangements and their view will have been coloured by knowledge of only their small part in it. The 'need to know' policy was very much in evidence then. Certainly, the numerous traffic control road blocks, manned by many Home Guards who have expressed this view, would not stop an armoured column for one moment, but then they were not meant to. Initially, the role of many LDV/Home Guards was to deal with any Fifth Column threat and marauding enemy parachutists, possibly in disguise, and their lightly constructed road blocks were simply for traffic control and making checks of anyone travelling the roads, particularly at night. Later in the war there were many other road blocks constructed that would have given the Germans, in their generally light tanks, cause to stop! With enough of these more robust blocks, each imposing delay, any momentum that the enemy had hitherto relied upon to achieve success would have been lost, and used up valuable fuel and ammunition supplies. Delaying the enemy forces became the key role of the Home Guard and their orders were to fight in these generally static positions to 'the last man and the last round!' There was to be no repeat of the Continental campaign of retreat after retreat, even where troops had successfully held the enemy. Most Home Guards, however, were well aware that, if the Germans had come, their static role was not going to be easily survived. With the widespread publicity given to the LDV/Home Guard in 1940 it can be argued, as indeed it was by many Home Guard officers, that Hitler was dissuaded from invading by the clear message that there was a defence in depth. Equally the Home Guard was a clear indicator to Roosevelt that Britain was not going to submit easily, and was therefore worthy of material support. From 1942 onwards, when the possibility of full-scale enemy invasion had gone, they were prepared for a more mobile role against possible enemy nuisance raiding, at the same time allowing Regular forces to concentrate on preparing for the D-Day landings and largely absolve them from home defence duties.

In recent years, so much myth and misinformation about the force has been put forward by the media and people who were not involved, or perhaps were there but have forgotten the real story, that the Home Guard is now often portrayed as a not viable or serious military force, and instead is the butt of jokes. It is appropriate, therefore, to look at some of the contemporary wartime evidence for guidance as to its real value.

On 27th May 1940, the day that he was appointed Commander in Chief of Home Forces, General Ironside recorded in his diary that he was 'glad to see that the parashooters, as they are now called, are going well. Not only will they be a body of good stout people, but they will be able now to get us a good deal of information that has been denied us so far.' Two days later he wrote '… we shall get those LDVs going. Static defence in each village by blocks and information going out from there. And thousands of Molotov Cocktails thrown from the windows of houses. That might settle the tank columns. We just want the courage of men. Nothing else matters. No defence is any good if the men behind it leave it and run away. The old LDVs won't do that.'

On 6th June 1940, after his meeting in York with the Local Defence Volunteer leaders, General Ironside recorded that he had had a good meeting with people who 'are mad keen but want coordinating'. By 9th June he wrote that he had the greatest belief in the strength of the LDVs, given that they had had only a little time for organisation. 'We have an inexhaustible supply of experience and courage in the country. I hope the leadership will be all right.'[2]

An official view was recorded by a Home Guard Sub-Committee of the Army Council, which reported as early as the 9th October 1940 that:

> The Home Guard have for the most part proved their efficiency for the important military duties assigned to them and have thus established their

value as an essential part of our system of Home Defence. There is no doubt moreover, that their value will steadily increase with fuller training and better equipment, and that they may play a still more valuable part next year, by enabling us to release a large proportion of the Field Army for service in other theatres. We hold therefore, that on strictly military considerations alone, everything possible should be done to maintain their keenness and increase their self-confidence.[3]

The then Secretary of State for War, Sir James Grigg PC MP KCB KCSI, in his foreword to John Brophy's book *Britain's Home Guard*, added a different point of view when he wrote, in 1945, that: 'It does not matter that the emergency for which they were created has never in fact arisen. The threat was there, and there can be no doubt that the existence of the Home Guard is one of the main reasons why the threat was never carried into an actual invasion.'

But what did other military forces think of the Home Guard? The Home Guard was investigated quite closely, in early 1941, by representatives of the Massachusetts Committee on Public Safety, who subsequently reported their findings to the US War Department in Washington. Their findings are of great interest to anyone studying the Home Guard, but the comments made to them by senior British military personnel and by those of some of the occupied countries are particularly pertinent.

For the British, General Sir Alan Brooke had this to say:

The Germans have developed a strategy of infiltration which results in battlefields not being confined to front lines of the opposing forces. To meet this strategy and its accompanying tactics, there must be a widely dispersed force to take the shock of the enemy's primary attacks. Consequently, the most modern defensive strategy involves just such a force as the Home Guard and its function is just as important to the organisation of the defence of a country as the functions of any of the other forces such as the regular army.

For the Polish, an interview with Major Dowdrowsky and Colonel Torks, of Polish forces in Britain drew the comments that:

Fifth Column activities and landing of parachute troops without opposition, which completely disrupted lines of communication and disorganised the rear of the Polish Armies, would have been minimised by the existence of such a force as the Home Guard.

For the Norwegians, interviews with Mr Trygve Lie, General Fleisher and Major Peterson provided the view that:

... by the surprise of its initial attack on Norway, Germany was able, by the employment of very few troops, to obtain an advantage Norwegians, and the British acting with them, were never able to overcome. They seized all the aerodromes in southern and central Norway, every port, where heavy material could be landed, the termini of Oslo to Trondheim, Oslo to Bergen and Oslo to Kristiansand, highroads and railways, the chief cities and most of the magazines and depots of the Norwegian Army. They seized control of the communications system of the country, including the telephone and radio. This situation created such confusion throughout the country that the Norwegian effort was paralysed. All this resulted from the effort of small numbers of German troops who could have been met successfully, particularly in the initial stages, by such an organisation as the British Home Guard.

General Fleisher, who was part of the Norwegian Military Commission and Commander in Chief of the Norwegian forces in Britain, but before the occupation of Norway had been the Commander of the Norwegian Northern Army, took the view that, 'had Norway had a force similar to the British Home Guard, there would have been an entirely different picture'. He believed that the Germans could not have successfully taken Norway.

For the Dutch, Captain Schoonenburg, said that:

The German campaign in Holland was characterised by extensive Fifth Column activities, combined with such an extensive use of parachute troops and airborne forces as had never before been witnessed in warfare. The Germans were able to accomplish certain very definite military missions through the employment of these methods. In the first place they were able to seize and hold certain strategically important points, such as the Moerdyke bridge, the Waalhaven Aerodrome at Rotterdam, etc... In the second place, they were able to create all over Holland, in the rear of the front line, so many small engagements that they prevented the Dutch reserve troops from being used as previously planned. Most of the Fifth Columnists, parachute troops and airborne detachments were ultimately wiped out by the Dutch, but the effort of one whole army corps in accomplishing this was such that it was exhausted, dispersed and could not be used as planned. Properly organised and equipped, local military units such as the British Home Guard would have prevented the Germans from accomplishing both of the above results.

For the French viewpoint, the Committee representatives interviewed General Eastwood, General Sir Robert Bridgeman, Colonel Shortt, Lt Colonel Elias-Morgan, Lt Colonel Wouters and a French officer of the Division Legere Motorise (DLM), whose name was not given because his family were still in occupied France. It was recorded that:

The Panzer division, after the breakthrough, proceeded at will and without resistance all over the rear of the armies, creating a confusion and disorganisation which contributed largely to the ultimate German success. The civilian population fled in great disorder and blocked all the roads so that the defending armies were tremendously handicapped. Such a static force as the Home Guard, completely covering the rear areas would have served to eliminate these two factors which contributed greatly to the success of the German Blitzkrieg.

As a result of their interviews, the Committee representatives reported that an analysis by the High Commands of the British and those of the invaded countries came to two conclusions: that the only way to meet the German offensive tactics of penetrating the defence with their Panzer divisions and air forces, was by the use of like forces in the 'counter-offence', and secondly, the corollary that to give the 'counter-offence' opportunity to go into action effectively, a complementary strategically static, local defence force needed to be organised. In order not to disrupt production, this force had to be raised locally from the producers of the country volunteering part of their free time for this service. A local force, through the use of its peculiar knowledge of the terrain, could, it was felt, if properly instructed in the use of that terrain for defence, be effective against the most modern German equipment. A force organised in a similar way to that of the British Home Guard was therefore a strategic necessity in modern warfare. The tactics which followed from its particular function were then analysed, and the report also covered the weapons and methods of dealing with tanks being taught to the Home Guard, including evaluating the relative efficiency of the various types of road block.

One of the significant conclusions reached by the Americans was that they themselves were not immune to the German weapons of sabotage and espionage – the Fifth Columnists: 'How better could a country be protected against these weapons than to have a force whose primary purpose is the protection of its country, and reaches into every city, town and village, into every home, office and plant?'[4] It seems that they were impressed by the Home Guard and so perhaps should we be.

By 1944, many Home Guards felt that they were so well trained and prepared for battle that they should be given the opportunity to fight side by side with the Regular Army in the planned assault on the Continent. Sir Smedley Crooke, Conservative member for Deritend, asked the Secretary of State for War whether he would give consideration to the proposal.[5] There is no evidence that any Home Guards actually achieved this ambition, but the thought indicates that they were willing to take on the Germans in battle. Some in Worcestershire took matters into their own hands. Geoff Devereux of Sampson Patrol, having trained as an Auxilier in 1940, considered that the Germans were not going to come. Wanting to put his

263

training to good use, he joined the Grenadier Guards and had a very active war. A number of other Auxiliers took the same view, including Tony Barling of Jehu Patrol, who joined the Parachute Regiment as a medical officer, was captured at Arnhem, but served again after the war.

Despite their protestations and threats about the formation of the LDV in 1940, the Germans too would, in the autumn of 1944, call upon their old and very young men, and those employed in civilian trades, to form the *Volkssturm* when the fatherland was threatened by Allied forces approaching from both the east and the west. All German men between the ages of 16 and 60 and capable of bearing arms were liable for service. This last levy by the Nazis yielded several million more men and boys, and apparently some women, to construct and man the defences on the home soil of Germany. Unlike our Home Guard, some 100,000 Volkssturmann were to fight alongside the Wehrmacht on the 'front line', about 10% of whom died and many more of whom were wounded and/or taken prisoner. The Germans also recruited, trained and equipped the equivalent of our Auxiliary Units. Called the Werewolves, these men and some women would go into action once an area had been occupied by the Allies.[6] It is said that 'plagiarism is the sincerest form of flattery'!

Elsewhere in Europe, covert resistance to the enemy began after occupation, and until the Germans formed their Werewolves, Britain had been unique in recruiting, equipping and training such a force *before* an invasion! What can be concluded about the Auxiliary Units and other resistance organisations in Worcestershire and elsewhere? Would they have given a good account of themselves had there been a German invasion of Britain? Winston Churchill certainly thought so, holding the view that 'these units in the event of an invasion, should prove a useful addition to Britain's regular forces …' and wishing to be kept informed of progress in their formation.[7] General Andrew Thorne, one of the proponents of the Auxiliaries, thought that if he was pushed back to the GHQ Line … any delay or interference by irregulars operating against German supply routes and concentration areas would, even to a negligible degree, improve the chances of repelling an attack.[8] Colonel Gubbins, the first commander of the Auxiliaries, thought that they would have justified their existence, although to what extent would have been dependent on the circumstances. Because Auxiliaries were all volunteers, their existence had cost the country virtually nothing, yet with their arms and training he thought that they would have given a good account of themselves in the invasion areas. He recognised that their usefulness would have been short-lived, because they would either have quickly used up their supplies or been hunted down and eliminated.[9]

Peter Fleming was one of the first Intelligence officers appointed by GHQ with the task of forming Auxiliary patrols, in his case in perhaps the most critical area of XII Corps in Kent and East Sussex. He was of the opinion that they would

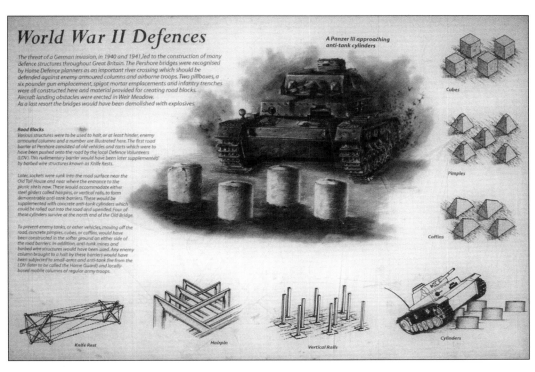

World War II Defences

A Panzer III approaching anti-tank cylinders

The threat of a German invasion, in 1940 and 1941, led to the construction of many defence structures throughout Great Britain. The Pershore bridges were recognised by Home Defence planners as an important river crossing which should be defended against enemy armoured columns and airborne troops. Two pillboxes, a six pounder gun emplacement, spigot mortar emplacements and infantry trenches were all constructed here and material provided for creating road blocks. Aircraft landing obstacles were erected in Weir Meadow. As a last resort the bridges would have been demolished with explosives.

Road Blocks

Various structures were to be used to halt, or at least hinder, enemy armoured columns and a number are illustrated here. The first road barrier at Pershore consisted of old vehicles and carts which were to have been pushed onto the road by the local Defence Volunteers (LDV). This rudimentary barrier would have been later supplemented by barbed wire structures known as Knife Rests.

Later, sockets were sunk into the road surface near the Old Toll House and near where the entrance to the picnic site is now. These would accommodate either steel girders called hairpins, or vertical rails, to form demountable anti-tank barriers. These would be supplemented with concrete anti-tank cylinders which could be rolled out into the road and upended. Four of these cylinders survive at the north end of the Old Bridge.

To prevent enemy tanks, or other vehicles, moving off the road, concrete pimples, cubes, or coffins, would have been constructed in the softer ground on either side of the road barriers. In addition, anti-tank mines and barbed wire structures would have been used. Any enemy column brought to a halt by these barriers would have been subjected to small-arms and anti-tank fire from the LDV (later to be called the Home Guard) and locally-based mobile columns of regular army troops.

Cubes

Pimples

Coffins

Knife Rest

Hairpin

Vertical Rails

Cylinders

World War II: Gun Emplacement

This panel illustrates what might have happened if Britain had been invaded by the Germans in 1940 or 1941 and an enemy column had penetrated inland as far as Pershore Bridges.

Defence would have been conducted firstly by the Home Guard and then later by a mobile column of regular troops from either Worcester or Evesham.

The defence feature illustrated is a six pounder anti-tank gun emplacement. This emplacement survives within the adjoining pumphouse and originally housed a Hotchkiss 6 Pounder Quick Firing Anti-Tank Gun. The field of fire from the emplacement was sufficient to cover the bridge approaches from Worcester, Evesham and the Combertons as well as the bridges themselves. Behind the emplacement can be seen the remains of an infantry trench which was formerly connected to the emplacement in order to provide an escape route for the gunners.

A Spigot Mortar

View from the gun emplacement

Worcestershire County Council has provided interpretation boards at the Pershore Bridges Picnic Site in order to help visitors to understand the significance of the surviving structures which can still be seen there. (Author's photos)

have struck some useful blows before 'melting away in the white heat of German ruthlessness'. However, he found it difficult to find fault with Churchill's estimate of Auxiliaries being a useful addition to the Regular forces.

The recruitment of other forms of resistance groups may be puzzling in view of the War Office stance that they did not advocate Home Guard guerrilla activity.[10] Nevertheless, there is good evidence that such groups and individuals did exist in Worcestershire, and it has to be assumed elsewhere in Britain. A distinction therefore needs to be drawn between the War Office responsibility for conducting warfare in Britain while regular forces were still operating, supplemented by the activities of the Auxiliary Patrols, and the responsibilities of SIS for organising any resistance after any enemy occupation. This resistance would be by civilians, would be unattributable and still remains cloaked in mystery. The existence of another level of organised resistance was, perhaps, indicative of the high morale that existed in some quarters at the time, with many people considering that they were going to at least 'Take one with them', as Churchill had advocated, and, it seems, by whatever means available.

The 1950s Home Guard was a shadow of its former self, and really did not get going as a viable defence force before it was axed as being unaffordable in the then austerity Britain. Perhaps had the Russians been occupying most of Western Europe as the Germans had done in 1940, the force would have been better supported by volunteers and a more grateful government.

Some sites and buildings associated with the Home Guard have been shown in photographs in this account to illustrate specific points, but there are other sites, buildings, structures and features which were associated with the force, and can still be seen from public places in Worcestershire. There is, however, a slow removal of these as a result of new development and agricultural processes. While some structures have been the subject of interpretation panels or small notices provided by the County Council, or local organisations, to identify their connection with the past, it is hoped that by drawing attention to others, the process will be continued. By so doing we will ensure a lasting memory of those momentous days and a job well done by the Home Guard.

Appendix 1

Roll of Honour

Early information indicated that eleven men of Worcestershire who served in the Home Guard died while on duty although they were not identified,[1] while the Commonwealth War Graves Commission lists the graves of nine men who died while serving. Casualties who have been identified so far, and their grave locations where known, are listed below. Where the circumstances of their deaths can be established, this has been added. However, the author will be more than pleased to add information in order to make the Roll of Honour as complete as possible. Contact with the author should be made via the publisher.

Archer, Leslie Charles. Private in the Evesham Battalion. Son of Albert Thomas and Agnes Kate Archer and husband of Hilda Doris Archer. Died 24th January 1943, aged 42. Leslie Charles Archer, of Beaconsfield, Kemerton, suffered a broken neck when a lorry in which he was riding overturned on a sharp corner between Conderton and Beckford. He and his colleagues were travelling to grenade practice at Hinton-on-the-Green. The lorry was considered to be overloaded and had just driven down a slope. Death by misadventure was recorded. He is buried at Kemerton Cemetery.[2]

Beechey, Dennis Noel. Volunteer in the Evesham Battalion. Son of Arthur and Harriet Beechey of 69 Bewdley Street, Evesham. Died on the night of 13th/14th September 1941, aged 17. Buried in Evesham Cemetery. He was accidentally shot by a colleague at Evesham police station where an armed guard was mounted each night. Instructions were issued that rifles were not to be loaded except in an emergency. Neither of the youths concerned had had instructions in loading and unloading their rifles. Reginald Barrett was attempting to show Beechey how to load and unload a rifle and appeared to have put ammunition in his rifle. He was unloading when it went off. The jury brought in a verdict of accidental death.[3]

Castles, Thomas William George. Sergeant in the 1st Middlesex (Staines) Battalion Home Guard. Died 11th September 1942. Buried in Oldbury Cemetery.[4]

Chaplin, Frank. Lieutenant in the Bromsgrove Battalion. Son of George and Anne Eliza Chaplin and husband of Marjorie Elizabeth Chaplin of Bangor, Caernarvonshire. Died 14th May 1944. Buried in Wychbold churchyard. The sudden death occurred of Lieutenant Chaplin while acting as an umpire at a Home Guard exercise, near Redditch. Bill Allington, who was with him at the time, confirms that he suffered a heart attack. Lieutenant Chaplin had been a member of the Honourable Artillery Company during the First World War. He had joined the LDV in 1940 and had been instrumental in forming two Home Guard units elsewhere in Britain, before taking command of the No 13 Platoon of the Bromsgrove Battalion, at BBC Wychbold, where he was an engineer.[5]

Evans, Cumming Benyon. Corporal in the Malvern Battalion. Son of Frederick Whitfield and Mary Evans of Swansea, and husband of Hilda Alexandra Evans of Bello Squardo Mansions, Foley Terrace, Malvern. He had a two-year-old son. Corporal Evans collapsed while on Home Guard manoeuvres in Blackmore Park, on 31st May 1942. He was given first aid before being taken home by car, where he died soon afterwards, aged 37. He was employed as an accountant at the Midland Bank, Malvern, and was a keen member of the Worcestershire Golf Club. He had been at the bank as usual on Saturday and seemed in good health when he left home for Blackmore Park. Home Guards acted as bearers at his funeral on 4th June, at Malvern Cemetery. He does not have a Commonwealth War Graves Commission headstone.[6]

Kent, Raymond. Corporal in the Worcester City Battalion Home Guard. Son of Charles and Diana Kent and husband of Ellen Kent. Died 15th June 1941, aged 30. Buried in Astwood Cemetery, Worcester. Corporal Kent was accidentally shot dead while on exercise near Perry Wood, when a live round was mixed with dummy rounds being used in a sighting test, at which he was an instructor. Corporal Kent was a draughtsman with the Heenan and Froude Company and lived at 64 Belmont Street, Rainbow Hill, Worcester.[7]

Kettlety, Alfred Reginald. Private in the Fernhill Heath Platoon of the Malvern Battalion. Husband of Florence May Kettlety of Twerton on Avon, near Bath. He was living at 180 Bilford Road, Worcester and was employed as a clerk. He died on Sunday, 7th March 1943, aged 38, while being conveyed to Worcester Royal Infirmary by ambulance. He had collapsed while on parade after participating in a field exercise and respirator drill at Hurst Lane Fernhill Heath. He is buried in Haycombe Cemetery, Bath.[8]

Morris, Ernest Gilbert. Private in the Malvern Battalion. Living at 24 Madresfield, he was married to Ellen Morris and was the father of two young children. He was employed as a farm labourer at nearby Lower Woodsfield Farm. He died during the night of 10th January 1942, aged 39. Private Morris was cycling along Gloucester Drive, returning to duty in Madresfield Park, when he attempted to ride across a cattle grid and fell between two iron frames, struck his head against a concrete wall of the ditch, and was drowned in the water below. The Coroner brought in a verdict of accidental death. He is buried in Madresfield Churchyard.[9]

Richards, Howard Walter. Volunteer in the Oldbury Battalion. Son of Walter Howard and Phoebe Richards and husband of Evelyn Alice Richards of Morton, Shropshire. Died 14th July 1941, aged 41. Buried in Lodge Hill Cemetery, Birmingham.[10]

Slater, Lionel. Private with the Dudley Battalion. He was employed as a pit guard at a Dudley colliery and had only recently joined the Home Guard. He was drowned while on guard duty at the colliery in the early hours of 19th February 1941.[11]

Woodhouse, Thomas Owen. Private with the Stourbridge Battalion, a gardener aged 50, of Bromsgrove Road, Hagley, succumbed to injuries sustained in a road accident. He had been admitted to Corbett Hospital with a fractured right leg and a fractured skull, subsequently developed pneumonia and died on Tuesday, 6th May 1942. 2nd Lt L.A. Parks was in charge of a platoon of 17 NCOs and other ranks engaged in night exercises and were marching from Broome towards Hagley in the early hours of the morning, when a car collided with the back of the column. Two men were knocked down, including Private Woodhouse. The driver, and his passenger, claimed they had seen nothing in the blackout, until the collision occurred. A verdict of accidental death was brought by the Coroner. The officers, NCOs and men of the Hagley Home Guard provided an escort and pall-bearers at his funeral service at Hagley Parish Church, followed by interment in the churchyard there.[12]

Others who died as a result of Home Guard activities, although not necessarily on active duty were:

Pearce, Charles Samson. Corporal. Aged 29, of 13 Mount Street, Hasbury. Married, with one daughter, he was member of the Halesowen Battalion. He died on the way to hospital on Wednesday, 17th June 1942, following an explosion in his garden shed while experimenting with explosives extracted from shell cases. As a member of the Pioneer Section, he was expected to know about explosives and had apparently become very interested in this branch of work. A verdict of accidental death was brought by the coroner. He was buried with military honours after a service at Halesowen Parish Church.[13]

Solon, Oswald Arnoux. Aged 32, of Ronkswood Cottage, Newtown Road, Worcester. He was found shot in his office at Messrs Alley and McLellans premises, Bromyard Road, Worcester, where he was employed as assistant works manager and, as a member of the works Home Guard, was in charge of the weapons and ammunition. It was thought likely that he had been cleaning an automatic rifle which dropped and discharged twice into his body. An open verdict was brought by the coroner.[14]

Military honours for Home Guard casualties

The Central Midland Area HQ notified Home Guard battalions, on 12th June 1941, that an officer or member of the Home Guard who died or was killed while on duty was entitled to a military funeral, provided that the ceremony was carried out by the Home Guard and that officers and men attended in a voluntary capacity. Conversely, if he died while not on duty, then he would not be entitled to the ceremonial of a military funeral, although it was appreciated that his fellow members of the Home Guard would wish to show respect for him on such an occasion.[15]

Appendix 2

Personnel statistics

	Oct 40	Oct 41	Mar 42	Oct 42	Sept 43	Sept 43	Dec 44
Worcester City Bn	2,382		2,025	2,185	2,140	2,202	1,937
Bromsgrove Bn	1,797		1,372	1,415	1,359	1,307	1,234
Dudley Bn	1,885		1,342	1,550	1,364	1,236	1,172
Evesham Bn	2,045		1,802	2,091	2,194	2,095	N/A
Halesowen Bn	1,313		1,046	1,148	1,026	1,096	1,006
Kidderminster Bn	1,104		949	1,057	1,057	968	950
Malvern Bn	1,690		1,827	1,898	2,010	2,193	2,124
Oldbury Bn	955		1,395	1,560	1,549	1,790	1,558
Redditch Bn	1,871		1,514	1,774	1,863	1,825	1,627
Stourbridge Bn	1,540		1,414	1,556	1,442	1,500	1,514
Stourport Bn	1,198		1,470	1,460	1,470	1,478	1,419
Warley Bn	1,975		1,100	1,306	940	901	804
County totals	19,755	18,940	17,148	19,000	18,414	18,591	13,408 *

* less Evesham

The figures in this table represent the totals of officers and other ranks for each of the Home Guard battalions in Worcestershire. Unfortunately a breakdown into the battalion figures of the total for October 1941 is not available, but it is clear that the peak of enthusiasm for serving in the Worcestershire Home Guard was reached in 1940. It is also clear how much the planned introduction of compulsory service had reduced the overall numbers by March 1942, even though the Malvern and Stourport Battalions seem not to have suffered in this way. The figures were restored somewhat by compulsory enrolment, but never reached the peak of 1940.[1] The figures for December 1944 have been assembled from Part 2 Orders of the various battalions and may not be entirely accurate. Given incomplete figures for the Evesham Battalion, if one assumes a total for that battalion of around 2,000 officers and other ranks, the total for the whole county would have been down to between 15 and 16,000. This is perhaps a reflection of the loss of men to the anti-aircraft units and those released from reserved occupations and called-up to the Regular Forces.

Appendix 3

Order of Battle in 1942

Worcestershire Zone Home Guard Headquarters (non operational)

Commanded by Colonel W.H. Wiggin DSO TD, with its HQ at the TA Centre in 16 Silver Street, Worcester.

Worcester Battalion

Role: garrison for the defence of Worcester City Anti-Tank Island.

Commanded by Lt Colonel V.N. Johnson DSO, with its HQ at 16 Silver Street, Worcester. The battalion, which comprised 22 Platoons, was at that time divided into the North Unit, commanded by Major W.G. Avery, with its HQ at St George's Tavern, and further divided into the A Sub Unit, commanded by Captain H.V. Edge, sharing the St George's Tavern HQ, and B Sub Unit, commanded by Captain F.J. Barclay, with its HQ at The Vauxhall Inn; South Unit, commanded by Major J.E.E. Goate, HQ not identified, comprising of C Sub Unit, commanded by Captain G.C. Clarke, with its HQ at the Metal Box Factory, D Sub Unit, commanded by Captain R.C. Wareham, with its HQ at the Heenan and Froude Factory; and the West Unit, commanded by Major J.H.P. Waterhouse, with the HQ at the Bell Inn, St John's. This was also the HQ of the E Sub Unit, commanded by Captain F.W. Taylor.

Bromsgrove Battalion

Commanded by Lt Colonel J.T. James TD, with its HQ at the Drill Hall, Recreation Road, Bromsgrove, the battalion comprised four General Service Companies incorporating 20 Platoons.

A Company, commanded by Major B.G. Holt, with its HQ at Blackwell Golf Club, less No 4 Platoon, was to provide a Mobile Company based at the Golf Club, with a counter-attack task for Hewell Grange. No 4 Platoon was to garrison the Defended Locality at Chadwick.

B Company, commanded by Major J.T. Bridge MC MM, with its HQ at Watt Close School, Bromsgrove, less No 8 Platoon, was to garrison the Defended Locality at Whitford Hall and act as battalion reserve. No 8 Platoon role was to be mobile and was based at Blackwell Golf Club, with a counter-attack task for Hewell Grange.

C Company, commanded by Major L.M. Ryland, less Nos 11 and 13 Platoons, was to provide a Mobile Company based at the Wagon Works with a counter-attack task for the BBC (Wychbold). No 11 Platoon was also mobile and based at The Croft, with a counter-attack role for the BBC, while No 13 Platoon was to garrison the BBC Defended Locality.

D Company, commanded by Major C.F.D. Dyson Perrins, with its HQ at Droitwich Drill Hall, was to garrison the Defended Locality at Droitwich.

It has not been determined which of the above Mobile Companies became No 61 Mobile Company based at the Drill Hall Bromsgrove.

Dudley Battalion

Commanded by Lt Colonel A.R. Tanfield, with its HQ then at Rose Hill Schools, Tinchbourne Street, Dudley. The battalion comprised six General Service Companies incorporating 24 Platoons. Role not determined, but the battalion did have one Mobile Company and there were Defended Localities within the battalion area.

Evesham Battalion

Commanded by Lt Colonel W.H. Taylor, with its HQ at Wick House, near Pershore. The battalion comprised six General Service Companies incorporating 22 Platoons.

A Company (formerly No 1), commanded by Major H. Davenport-Price, with its HQ at Walker Hall, Evesham, less Nos 2 and 3 Platoons, was to garrison the Defended Locality at Evesham. No 2 Platoon was to be mobile but based in Evesham, while No 3 Platoon was to garrison the Defended Locality at Harvington.

B Company (formerly No 2), commanded by Major Lees-Milne, with its HQ at Wickhamford Manor, had the following tasks: No 5 Platoon to garrison the Defended Locality at Broadway, No 6 Platoon to be based in Evesham, No 7 Platoon based at Honeybourne Aerodrome, and No 8 Platoon based at the Fish and Anchor, Offenham.

C Company (formerly No 3), commanded by Major R.C. Lees, with its HQ then at No 66 Bridge Street, Pershore, had the following tasks: Nos 9 and 22 Platoons were to garrison the Defended Locality at Pershore, Nos 10 and 12 Platoons, based at Eckington, were to be mobile with a counter-attack task for Defford Aerodrome, while No 11 Platoon was to garrison the Defended Locality at Bredon.

D Company (formerly No 4), commanded by Major R.H. Stallard, with its HQ at Throckmorton Court, had the following tasks: Nos 13 and 15 Platoons were based at Pershore Aerodrome, and Nos 14 and 16 Platoons were to garrison the Defended Locality at Fladbury.

E Company (formerly No 5), then commanded by Major Disney, with its HQ at Wood Norton, had the following task: Nos 17 and 18 Platoons were to garrison the Defended Locality at BBC Wood Norton.

F Company (formerly No 6), commanded by Major H.J. Cotton, with its HQ at The Bungalow, Hinton on the Green, had the following tasks: Nos 19 and 20 Platoons were to garrison the Defended Locality at Beckford, and No 21 Platoon was to garrison the Defended Locality at Bredon.

Halesowen Battalion

Commanded by Lt Colonel B.J. Keene, with its HQ at the Drill Hall, Grammar School Lane, Halesowen. Role: garrison the Defended Localities around the south-west side of Birmingham.

Kidderminster Battalion

Commanded by Colonel R.W.A. Painter, with its administrative HQ at Kingsley Buildings, Vicar Street, Kidderminster, and Battle HQ at the Larches Club, Foley Park. The battalion comprised five General Service Companies incorporating 11 Platoons. Role: garrison for the defence of Kidderminster Anti-Tank Island.

HQ Company commanded by Major A.A. Knight, with its administrative and Battle HQ at 110 Park Lane, Kidderminster.

A Company commanded by Major O. Davies, with its administrative and Battle HQ at Rosemere, Chester Road North, Kidderminster.

B Company commanded by Major H.T. Viney, with its administrative and Battle HQ at the BSC Factory, Stourport Road, Kidderminster.

C Company commanded by Major W.H.X. Smith, with its administrative HQ at Land Oak Garage, and its Battle HQ at Highfields, Hoo Road, Kidderminster.

D Company commanded by Major J.G. Anton, with its administrative and Battle HQ at The Briars, Habberley Road, Kidderminster.

Malvern Battalion

Commanded by Lt Colonel P. Tyrwhitt DSO, with its HQ at St Andrew's Golf Club, Longridge Road, Malvern Wells. The battalion comprised six General Service Companies incorporating 27 Platoons.

HQ Company, commanded by Major H.E. Day DSO MVO, with its HQ at St Andrew's Golf Club.

M Company (Malvern), commanded by Major W.J.C. Kendall, with its HQ at Lyttelton House, Great Malvern. Static defence provided by No 1 Platoon based at the Wyche Cutting, No 2 Platoon based at Cowleigh Park, and No 3 Platoon based at the Hollybush. No 4 Platoon had the role of Mobile Reserve. (The numbering of these platoons does not equate with other sources, but it was probably the No 4 Platoon reserve from which men were drawn to form the 62nd Mobile Company.)

U Company (Upton upon Severn), commanded by Major M.F.S. Jewell, with its HQ at the police station, Upton upon Severn. The platoons are not specified, but their role was to garrison the Defended Localities at Upton upon Severn, Longdon and Saxons Lode (the Ripple Petrol Depot), and provide a mobile unit based at Severn Stoke, with a counter-attack task for Defford Aerodrome.

P Company (Powick), commanded by Major D.A.N. Asterley, with its HQ at Crown East Court. The platoons are not listed, but their role was to garrison the Defended Localities at Powick and Bransford.

K Company (Knightwick), commanded by Major E.H. Clarke, with its HQ at Woodford House, Knightwick The platoons are not listed, but their role was to garrison the Defended Locality at Knightsford Bridge.

O Company (Ombersley), commanded by Major W. Wynn, with its HQ at Rae's Garage, Ombersley. The platoons are not listed, but their role was to garrison the Defended Locality at Holt Fleet, and provide a mobile unit based at Hawford Bridge, with a counter-attack task at Holt Fleet or Fernhill Heath.

C Company (Crowle), commanded by Major H.P. Rushton with its HQ then at Phepson Manor. The platoons are not listed but two mobile units were based at Spetchley and Norton Hall, with counter-attack tasks at Pershore and Defford Aerodromes respectively.

Oldbury Battalion
Commanded by Lt Colonel L.C.H. Brown, with its HQ at the Albright and Wilson Works, Oldbury. The battalion comprised seven General Service Companies incorporating 23 Platoons. Role: garrison the Defended Localities on the west side of Birmingham.

Redditch Battalion
Commanded by Lt Colonel A.E. Scothern CMG DSO, with its HQ at the Drill Hall, Church Road, Redditch. The battalion comprised four General Service Companies incorporating 12 Platoons. The Redditch factory units are also listed below and their role, at that stage, would have been factory defence

A Company, commanded by Major W.F.P. Scott, with its HQ at Walker's Stores, Alvechurch. The platoons are not listed, but their role included a mobile unit with a counter-attack task at Hewell Grange.

B Company, commanded by Major R.C. Morom, with its HQ at Redditch Drill Hall. The platoons are not listed but their task was to garrison Redditch Anti-Tank Island.

C Company, commanded by Major J.F.S. Mellor, with its HQ at the Cooperative Hall, Headless Cross. The platoons are not listed, but their task was to garrison Redditch Anti-Tank Island.

D Company, commanded by Major F.M. Twist, with its HQ at the Perkins Factory, Feckenham Road, Astwood Bank. The platoons are not identified, but their role was to provide a Mobile Company (this became the 63rd Mobile Company) with a counter-attack task at Pershore Aerodrome.

HDA Unit commanded by Captain E.R. Bannerjee, with its HQ at the HDA Works, Windsor Road, Redditch.

BSA Unit commanded by Major E. Hodgetts, with its HQ at the BSA Works, Ipsley, Redditch.

Enfield Unit commanded by Major F.W. Smith, with its HQ at the Enfield Works, Windsor Road, Redditch.

Reynolds Unit. Details not identified.

Monochrome Unit commanded by Lieutenant J.L. Barnes, with its HQ at the Monochrome Factory, Ipsley, Redditch.

Britannia Batteries Unit. Details not identified.

Stourbridge Battalion
Commanded by Lt Colonel Laughton-Goodwin, with its HQ at George Street, Kidderminster. The battalion comprised four General Service Companies incorporating 36 Platoons.

A Company (formerly No 1), commanded by Major F. Gilbert MC, with its HQ at The Oaks, Worcester Road, West Hagley. The platoons and their role have not been identified.

B Company (formerly No 2), commanded by Major G.G. Watson, with its HQ at Stone Manor, Stone. The platoons are not listed, but their role was mobile with the counter-attack task of reinforcing C or D Companies. From this Company would come the 64th Mobile Company.

C Company (formerly No 3), commanded by Major G.S. Chadwick, with its HQ at Caswell's shop, Cookley. The platoons are not listed, but they were to be mobile with a counter-attack task at 25 MU Hartlebury.

D Company (formerly No 4), commanded by Major F.A. Hejl, with its HQ at The Barn, Wollaston. The platoons are not listed but their role was to be mobile with a counter-attack task at the crossings on the River Severn.

E Company, commanded by Major A.B. Clibbery, with its HQ at The Grove, Norton. Platoons. Role not identified.

F Company commanded by Major W.C.I. Walton, with its HQ at The Post, Ham Lane. Platoons. Role not identified.

Stourport Battalion
Commanded by Lt Colonel J.A.D. Perrins MC, with its HQ at Bank Buildings, Stourport. The battalion comprised six General Service Companies incorporating 22 Platoons.

A Company (Stourport), commanded by Major A.L. Thomas, with its HQ at Stourport Drill Hall. The platoons are not listed, but their role was to garrison the Defended Locality at Stourport (West).

B Company (Stourport), commanded by Major H. Richardson MC, with its HQ at Stourport Drill Hall. The Company comprised factory platoons formed by Parsons Chain Company (No 2 Platoon), Steatite Porcelain Company, the SW&S Power Station, and Baldwins Works, and their role was to garrison the Defended Locality at Stourport (East).

C Company (Abberley), commanded by Major G. Ashton, with its HQ at Abberley Hall. Platoons not identified but they were to be mobile, although their counter-attack role is not specified.

D Company (Tenbury), commanded by Major H. Bentham, with its HQ at the Drill Hall, Berrington Road, Tenbury. The platoons are not listed but their role was to garrison the Defended Locality at Tenbury.

E Company (Bewdley), commanded by Major H. Goodwin, with its HQ at St George's Hall at Bewdley. The platoons are not listed but their role was to garrison the Defended Locality at Bewdley.

F Company (No 25 MU RAF Hartlebury), commanded by Major F.B.H. Stokes, with its HQ at No 25 MU. The platoons are not listed, but their role was to garrison the Defended Locality at RAF Hartlebury.

Warley Battalion

Commanded by Lt Colonel T. Lancaster MC, with its HQ at High Tor, Berry Hill Road, Quinton. The battalion comprised six General Service Companies incorporating 12 Platoons but no details have been found. Role: to garrison the Defended Localities to the west of Birmingham.[1]

Appendix 4

Battalion structure and officers in December 1944

The figures below do not always tally but are, for the time being, the best that can be achieved from surviving Battalion Part 2 Orders. Unfortunately, the surviving orders are not always complete or were not accurately kept by the battalion adjutants, or even presented in a consistent way. Some battalion stand down rolls are more informative than others and it has not been possible to establish the platoon structure for some battalions with any accuracy. However, where possible the platoon arrangements have been supplemented with information from official unit histories and end of war newspaper reports of social events.

1st Worcestershire (Worcester City) Battalion
Battalion HQ – Southfield Street Drill Hall, Worcester

Battalion Roll – 1,937 officers and other ranks, 30 nominated women and 16 boy messengers. Capt A. Shelly Creake seconded to the Army Cadet Force. Supernumerary: Capt H.N. Jacobs. Permanent Staff Instructors: Sgt Maj A.W. Abbot (South Staffs Regt) and Sgt G. Tanker (Lancashire Fusiliers).

HQ Staff
15 officers and 19 other ranks
Bn Cmdr – Lt Col P.A. Leicester
Bn 2nd in Command – Maj W.G. Amery
Bn Adjutant – Capt G.H. Stone
Assistant Bn Adjutant – Lt H.P. Meadows
Bn Medical Officer – Maj W.D. Steel
Bn Weapons Training Officer – Capt W.J. Denton
Bn Training Officer – Capt A.H. Evans
Bn Intelligence Officer – Capt L.L.S. Lowe
Bn Chemical Warfare Officer – Lt L.S. Adlington
Bn Liaison Officer – Lt G.E. Langley
Bn Catering Officer – Lt J.E. Rayer
Bn Quartermaster – Lt P. Stratton
Bn Engineer Officer – 2nd Lt J.A. Burton
Bn Signals Officer – 2nd Lt W.H. Cale
Bn Ammunition Officer – 2nd Lt J.C. Walker
Hon Chaplain – Revd O.R. Brandon
Hon Chaplain – Revd J.A. Crofts

HQ Coy
10 officers and 259 other ranks
Coy Cmdr – Maj A.D. Parry
Coy 2nd in Command – Capt N.E. Davies
Coy Medical Officer – Capt M.P. Martin DSO
Coy Quartermaster – Lt W. Child
Coy Intelligence Officer – Lt W.S. Long
Coy Training Officer – Lt W. Warner
No 16 (HQ) Pln Cmdr – Lt W.G. Elmes
No 16 Pln Officer – 2nd Lt F. Nicklin
No 17 (HQ) Pln Cmdr – Lt W. Jeffries
No 17 Pln Officer – Lt D. Rabjohns

A Coy
Coy HQ – St George's Tavern, Gregory's Bank, Worcester
13 officers and 239 other ranks
Coy Cmdr – Maj C.M. Willis
Company 2nd in Command – Capt C. Darke
Coy Medical Officer – Capt C.T. Mills
Coy 2nd in Command – Capt F.H. Roden
Coy Quartermaster – Lt F. Golledge
Coy Intelligence Officer – Lt P. Whitehouse
Coy Training Officer – 2nd Lt P.C. Southam
No 1 Pln (Waterworks & Barbourne) Cmdr –
   Lt G.C. Tysoe
No 1 Pln Officer – 2nd Lt R.A. Weaver
No 2 Pln Cmdr – Lt C.H. Cayhill
No 2 Pln Officer – 2nd Lt J.H. Green
No 3 Pln (Worcester Windshields & Metal Castings)
Cmdr – Lt C.C. Hannay
No 3 Pln Officer – 2nd Lt H. Croft

B Coy
Coy HQ – Vauxhall Inn, Rainbow Hill, Worcester
12 officers and 342 other ranks
Coy Cmdr – Maj H.V. Edge
Coy 2nd in Command – Capt L.A. Atwell
Role not identified – Capt H. Duff MM
Coy Quartermaster – 2nd Lt G.M. Klee
Coy Intelligence Officer – 2nd Lt J. Judd
Coy Training Officer – 2nd Lt C.A. Smith
No 4 Pln (James Archdale Ltd) Cmdr – Lt H. Griffiths
No 4 Pln Officer – 2nd Lt J.E. Walton
No 5 Pln (H.W. Ward) Cmdr – 2nd Lt L.J. Wilde
No 5 Pln Officer – 2nd Lt J. S. Broadhurst
No 6 Pln (ROF Blackpole) Cmdr – Lt E. Court
No 6 Pln Officer – 2nd Lt A.L. Bate

C Coy
Coy HQ – Metal Box Factory, Perry Wood Walk, Worcester
13 officers and 215 other ranks
Coy Cmdr – Maj E.E. Goate
Coy 2nd in Command – Capt H.G. Gillett DCM MM
Coy Medical Officer – Capt T.E. Lawson
Coy Intelligence Officer – Lt E.G. Ross
Coy Training Officer – 2nd Lt H.A. Jones
No 7 Pln (Metal Box) Cmdr – Lt E.G. Ross
No 7 Pln Officer – 2nd Lt C.E. Carleton
No 8 Pln (Porcelain Works) Cmdr – Lt J.E. Brough
No 8 Pln Officer – Lt J.W. Hawkins
No 9 Pln (Williamsons Providence Works) Cmdr –
    Lt F. Colley
No 9 Pln Officer – 2nd Lt H.L. Sinclair

D Coy (Heenan & Froude)
Coy HQ – Heenan & Froude Factory, Shrub Hill Road, Worcester
12 officers and 318 other ranks
Coy Cmdr – Maj R.C. Wareham
Coy 2nd in Command – Capt F. Wedgebury DSO
    MC DCM MM
Coy Intelligence Officer – 2nd Lt R.J. Kilbey
Coy Quartermaster – 2nd Lt C.E. Jarman
Coy Training Officer – Lt A.E. Shutes
No 10 Pln (Heenan & Froude). Cmdr –
    Lt A.W. Avery MSM
No 10 Pln Officer – 2nd Lt N.P. Dingwell
No 11 Pln (Heenan & Froude) Cmdr – Lt A. Grecian
No 11 Pln Officer – Lt C.T. Hayes

No 12 Pln (Air Ministry Whittington) Cmdr –
    Lt H.W. Smithers
No 12 Pln Officer – 2nd Lt J. Palk

E Coy
Coy HQ – The Bell Inn, St John's, Worcester
13 officers and 318 men
Coy Cmdr – Maj H.P. Waterhouse
Coy 2nd in Command – Capt F.W. Taylor
Coy Medical Officer – Capt E.F. Gleadow
Coy Intelligence Officer – 2nd Lt L.W. Haines
Coy Quartermaster – Lt J.A. Chadwick
No 13 Pln (Meco Works) Cmdr – Lt H. Collins
No 13 Pln Officer – Lt A.F. Hudson
No 14 Pln (Alley & McLellan Ltd) Cmdr –
    Lt F.A. Page
No 14 Pln Officer – Lt C.J. Holloway
No 14 Pln Officer – Lt L. Bevington
No 15 Pln (Worcester Sheet Metal Factory) Cmdr –
    Lt R.E. Taylor
No 15 Pln Officer – Lt L.G. Lipscombe

No 18 Railways Coy
Coy HQ – Shrub Hill Station, Worcester
7 officers and 176 other ranks
Coy Cmdr – Capt A.T. Harding
Coy 2nd in Command – Lt D.L. Burton
Coy Intelligence Officer – Lt T.W.J. Hine
Coy Quartermaster – Lt G.V. Freeman
Pln Cmdr – Lt F.E. Wintle MM
Pln Officer – Lt G.S. Stainton

2nd Worcestershire (Bromsgrove) Battalion
Battalion HQ – The Drill Hall, Recreation Road, Bromsgrove
Battalion Roll – 1,234 officers and men

Bn Cmdr – Lt Col J.T. James TD
Bn 2nd in Command – not identified
Bn Adjutant – Capt H.J. North
Assistant Bn Adjutant – Lt J.D. Smythe
Bn Intelligence Officer – Lt F. Potter
Bn Chemical Warfare Officer – Lt C.K. Brampton
Bn Transport Officer – 2nd Lt J. Leeson
Bn Liaison Officer – Lt J.L.G. Atkinson
Bn Ammunition Officer – Lt J.M. Bailey
Bn Honourary Chaplain – Revd S.J. Davey

HQ Coy
84 officers and other ranks
Coy Cmdr – Maj C.L Hawkins
Role not identified – Capt P.H. Jones
Role not identified – Capt T.H. Murray-Watson

Role not identified – Lt J.S. King
Role not identified – Lt F.H. Bullock
Role not identified – Lt C.K. Brampton

A Coy (Barnt Green)
Coy HQ – Blackwell Golf Club
197 officers and other ranks
Coy Cmdr – Maj B.G. Holt
Coy 2nd in Command – Capt R.B. Sugden
Coy Training Officer – Lt W.F. Olley
Coy Quartermaster – 2nd Lt B.J. Sanders
No 1 Pln Cmdr – Lt B. Douglas
No 2 Pln Cmdr – Lt T. Marsh
No 3 Pln Cmdr – Lt D.R. Thomas
No 4 Pln Cmdr – Lt D.K. Reeve
No 4 Pln Officer – Lt W.E.S. Gilmour

B Coy (Bromsgrove)
Coy HQ – Watt Close School, Bromsgrove
277 officers and other ranks
Coy Cmdr – Maj J.T. Bridge
Coy 2nd in Command – Capt G.C. Gadd
Coy Training Officer – Lt E.A. Cox
Coy Intelligence Officer – Lt H.F.T. Wren
Coy Qaurtermaster – 2nd Lt W.H. Rowlands
No 5 Pln Cmdr – Lt G. Staines
No 5 Pln Officer – 2nd Lt R.C. Russell
No 6 Pln Cmdr – Lt J.F. Barnes
No 6 Pln Officer – 2nd Lt H.E. Taylor
No 7 Pln (Dodford) Cmdr – Lt W.M. Willcox
No 7 Pln Officer – 2nd Lt E.O. Woodhouse
No 8 Pln Cmdr – Lt W. Williamson
No 8 Pln Officer – 2nd Lt G. Warman
No 24 Pln Cmdr – 2nd Lt W.R. Littleton

C Coy (Tardebigge and Stoke Prior)
Coy HQ – The Wagon Works, Aston Fields
333 officers and other ranks, including 2 boy messengers
Coy Cmdr – Maj L.M. Ryland
Coy 2nd in Command – Capt A.R.R. Macdonnell
No 9 Pln Cmdr – 2nd Lt I.E. Kimberley
No 10 Pln Cmdr – Lt L.T. Oldaker
No 11 Pln (Stoke Works, Wychbold & part of
    Hanbury) Cmdr – Lt W.H. Bidwell
No 11 Pln Officer – Lt W.C. Allington
No 12 Pln Cmdr – Lt H.E. Wood MM
No 12 Pln Officer – Lt H.J. Prescott
No 13 Pln (BBC Wychbold) Cmdr – Lt F.T. Sellon

D Coy (Droitwich)
Coy HQ – The Drill Hall, Rickett's Lane, Droitwich
233 officers and other ranks, including 1 boy messenger
Coy Cmdr – Maj C.F.D. Perrins TD
Coy 2nd in Command – Capt J.A. Harmen
Coy Medical Officer – Capt Neligan
Coy Intelligence Officer – Lt H.P. Raban
Coy Training Officer – 2nd Lt W.L. Knight
Coy Quartermaster – 2nd Lt W.H. Wilding
No 14 Pln (Salwarpe) Cmdr – Lt W. Gray
No 15 Pln (Droitwich) Cmdr – Lt W. Macdonald
No 15 Pln Officer – 2nd Lt C.E. Davis
No 16 Pln (Hadzor & Oddingley) Cmdr –
    Lt T.G. Fowler
No 17 Pln (Himbleton) Cmdr – Lt F.E. Fowler
No 18 Pln (Cutnall Green) Cmdr – Lt G.F.R. Pinegar
No 19 Pln (War Office) Cmdr – Lt H.W.R. Maddox

E Coy
Coy HQ – The Drill Hall, Bromsgrove
114 officers and other ranks
Coy Cmdr – Maj D.A.P. Shields
Coy 2nd in Command – Capt A. Shanks MC
Coy Intelligence Officer – 2nd Lt C.C. Smith
Coy Training Officer – 2nd Lt G.S. Gillies
No 21 Pln Cmdr – Lt N. Douglas
No 21 Pln Officer – 2nd Lt L.H. Burford
No 22 Pln Cmdr – Lt W.H. Hill
No 23 Pln Cmdr – Lt R.H. Osborne

3rd Worcestershire (Dudley) Battalion
Battalion HQ – No 2, Birmingham Road, Dudley
Battalion Roll – 1,172 officers and other ranks. Seconded to the 3rd Worcestershire Cadet Battalion,
Lt A.W. Dulson. Permanent Staff Instructor: Sgt J.H. Brown

Bn Cmdr – Lt Col C.G. Elkington DSO DL
Bn 2nd in Command – Maj G. Salter MBE
Bn Adjutant – Capt R.J. Jeffries
Assistant Bn Adjutant – Lt S. Lewis
Bn Medical Officer – Maj F.G. Lewis
Bn Intelligence Officer – Capt B.T. Adshead
Bn Motor Transport Officer – Lt H.P. Case
Bn Chemical Warfare Officer – Lt F. Shaw
Bn Ammunition Officer – Capt F.S. Clark
Bn Catering Officer – Lt W.N. Chilton
Bn Quartermaster – Capt A.J. Hennery
Bn Signals Officer – 2nd Lt W.E.S. Smart
Bn Liaison Officer – Capt J.G. Nickson
Hon Chaplain – Revd E.L. Warren AKC

HQ Coy
107 officers and other ranks.
Coy Cmdr – Maj W.G. Davies
Coy 2nd in Command – Capt A.R. Scriven
Coy Pioneer Officer – 2nd Lt G. Westwood
Coy Quartermaster – 2nd Lt R.W.J. Canning
Pln Cmdr – Lt K.C. Harper

A Coy
1944 Coy HQ not identified
129 officers and other ranks
Coy Cmdr – Maj A.C. Coleman
Coy 2nd in Command – Capt E. Macdonald
Coy Intelligence Officer – 2nd Lt R.W.G. Edwards
Coy Quartermaster – 2nd Lt S.T. Nicholls
Pln Cmdr – Lt F. Simmons
Pln Cmdr – Lt F.F. Slack

B Coy
1944 Coy HQ not identified
221 officers and other ranks
Coy Cmdr – Maj H. Edwards
Coy 2nd in Command – Capt F.C. Briggs
Coy Intelligence Officer – Lt S. Crew
Coy Quartermaster – Lt E.W. Harvey
No 9 Pln Cmdr – Lt H.C. Brimmell
No 15 Pln Cmdr – Lt R.A. Parkes
Pln Cmdr – Lt Holden MM
Pln Cmdr – 2nd Lt J.W. Taylor
Pln Cmdr – 2nd Lt A. Berrington

C Coy
1944 Coy HQ not identified
140 officers and other ranks
Coy Cmdr – Maj H.R. Porter
Coy 2nd in Command – Capt D. Scriven
Coy Training Officer – Lt H. James
Coy Training Officer – 2nd Lt A.H.D. Pugh
Pln Cmdr – Lt H.J. White
Pln Cmdr – Lt A. Dean
Pln Cmdr – 2nd Lt E. Wilkes MM
Pln Officer – 2nd Lt A. Grove.
Pln Officer – 2nd Lt J.W. Hughes
There is some evidence that C Coy comprised a total
of eight Plns, numbered No 19 to No 26, which
would imply considerably more officers formed this
Coy than are listed here.

D Coy
1944 Coy HQ not identified
220 officers and other ranks
Coy Cmdr – Maj R G.W. Little
Coy 2nd in Command – Capt E. Hill
Coy Training Officer – Lt J.M. Holloway
Coy Intelligence Officer – Lt R.H. Smith
Pln Cmdr – Lt A. Ford

Pln Cmdr – Lt A M. Pearson
Pln Cmdr – Lt A.M. Rorison
Pln Cmdr – Lt K.W. Wootton
Pln Cmdr – Lt W.N. Varlow
Pln Cmdr – Lt H. Greenwood
Pln Officer – Lt C. Case

15th Counter-attack Coy
Coy HQ – The Empire, Hall Street, Dudley
112 officers and other ranks
Coy Cmdr – Maj E. Dean Davies
Coy 2nd in Command – Capt E.H. Pearson
Coy Quartermaster – Lt G.H. Smith
Pln Cmdr – 2nd Lt C.F. Barton
Pln Cmdr – 2nd Lt A.E. Westley
Pln Cmdr – 2nd Lt T. Westley
Pln Officer – 2nd Lt G.W.A. Griffiths

16th Counter-attack Coy
1944 Coy HQ not identified
106 officers and other ranks
Coy Cmdr – Maj B. Bratt
Coy Intelligence Officer – Lt W.L. Partridge
Pln Cmdr – Lt F.K. Lees
Pln Cmdr – Lt H. Bonser
Pln Cmdr – Lt H. Parry
Pln Officer – Lt J. Bridgeford
Pln Officer – 2nd Lt A. Robinson

R Coy
1944 Coy HQ not identified
142 officers and other ranks
Coy Cmdr – Capt C.E. Reeves
Pln Cmdr – Lt T. Homer
Pln Cmdr – Lt S. Round
Pln Cmdr – Lt D. Grainger
Pln Cmdr – 2nd Lt E.L. Rowley

4th Worcestershire (Evesham) Battalion
Battalion HQ – W ick House, Wick, near Pershore
Permanent Staff Instructors: Sgts Fernhead, Parriss & Taylor

Bn Cmdr – Lt Col W.H. Taylor
Bn 2nd in Command – Maj H.C.M. Porter DSO
Bn Adjutant – Capt J.L. Woods
Bn Quartermaster – Capt G.K. Stephens
Assistant Adjutant – Lt R.A. Arkwright
Bn Medical Officer – Maj J.C. Wilson
Bn Intelligence Officer – Lt A.W. Westover

HQ Coy
145 officers and other ranks
Coy Cmdr – Maj S.B. Carter MBE
Coy 2nd in Command – Capt T.H. Collett
Coy Training Officer – Capt J.C. Eeuens
Coy Transport Officer – Lt J.E. Liley
Coy Intelligence Officer – Lt A.W. Wilkerson
Coy Chemical Warfare Officer – Lt M.J. Hodges
Coy Liaiason Officer – Capt T.H. Robinson
Coy Catering Officer – Lt L.C. Potter
Coy Quartermaster – Lt G.W. Edwards
Coy Pioneer Officer – Lt W.A. Cox

Coy Signals Officer – Lt F.M. Warren
Coy Ammunition Officer – Capt C. Renfrew
Pln Cmdr – Lt A.K. Patterson DCM
Joint Liaison Officer for N Sector – Lt W.A. Russell

A Coy (Evesham)
Coy HQ – The police station, Abbey Road, Evesham
584 officers and other ranks
Coy Cmdr – Maj H. Davenport-Price MC
Coy 2nd in Command – Capt J. Byrd
Coy Medical Officer – Capt J.M. Robertson
Coy Transport Officer – Lt N. Rees
Coy Intelligence Officer – Lt R.K. Munro
Coy Quartermaster – Lt J.F. Collins
No 1 Pln (Greenhill) Cmdr – Lt H.R. Smith
No 1 Pln Officer – Lt J.A. Tate
No 2 Pln (Hampton) Cmdr – Lt T.V. Wheeler
No 3 Pln (Norton) Cmdr – Lt A.J. Harthan
No 4 Pln (Evesham) Cmdr – Lt V.A. Morrall
No 4 Pln Officer – Lt P.K. Miles
Pln Cmdr – Lt R. Randall
Pln Officer – Lt W.L. Carter
The Pln number for the last two officers has not been
identified.

B Coy (Broadway)
Coy HQ – Wickhamford Manor
526 officers and other ranks
Coy Cmdr – Maj G.C. Lees-Milne
Coy 2nd in Command – Capt W. Ogilvy MBE
Coy Medical Officer – Capt E. Wharton
Coy Training Officer – Lt S.G. Russell
Coy Intelligence Officer – Lt T.F. Newberry MC
Coy Ammunition Officer – 2nd Lt A.J. Wheatley
Coy Quartermaster – Lt V. Schofield
No 5 Pln (Broadway) Cmdr – Lt Poulter
No 6 Pln (Badsey & Wickhamford) Officer –
    2nd Lt F.B. Cole
No 7 Pln (Honeybourne) Cmdr – Lt E.W. Cotton
No 8 Pln (Middle Littleton) Cmdr –
    Lt McKillop-Clark
No 24 Pln (Cleeve Prior) Cmdr – Lt E.E. Clarke
No 26 Pln Cmdr – Lt S.O. Berry
Pln Officer – 2nd Lt E.A. Darley
Pln Officer – 2nd Lt H.E. Rose
Pln Officer – Lt L.T. Stafford

C Coy (Pershore)
Coy HQ – The Drill Hall, Defford Road, Pershore
320 officers and other ranks
Coy Cmdr – Maj R.C. Lees MC
Coy 2nd in Command – Capt P.H. West
Coy Medical Officer – Capt A.R.R. Le Fleming

Coy Quartermaster – Lt A.T. Winter
Coy Training Officer – Lt C.N.C. Herridge
Coy Intelligence Officer – Lt C. Clemens
No 9 Pln (Pershore) Cmdr – Lt G.F. Hemming
No 10 Pln (Besford, Pirton, Wadborough, Defford,
    Birlingham & Eckington) Cmdr – Lt F.D. O'Neil
No 10 Pln Officers – Lt W. Mathews
    & 2nd Lt P.R.A. Haynes
No 11 Pln Cmdr – Lt J.H. Goodson
No 12 Pln (Bredon) Cmdr – Lt W.G. Humphries
Pln Officer – Lt C.R. Hands
Pln Officer – 2nd Lt W.F.L. Davies

D Coy (Pinvin)
Coy HQ – Throckmorton Court
214 officers and other ranks
Coy Cmdr – Maj R.H. Stallard MC
Coy 2nd in Command – Capt E.J.C. Vint
Coy Medical Officer – Maj J.C. Wilson
Coy Training Officer – Lt C.E. Smith
Coy Intelligence Officer – 2nd Lt F.J.B. Rundle
Coy Quartermaster – Lt Revd J. Cathcart-Davies
Nos 13 & 15 Plns Cmdr – Lt G.H.E. Evans
Nos 13 & 15 Plns Officer – Lt W.F. Upstone
No 14 Pln (Fladbury) Cmdr – Lt W.F. Swift
No 14 Pln Officer – Lt A.J. Ballard
No 16 Pln (Bishampton) Cmdr – Lt S.J. Harris MM
No 16 Pln Officer – Lt S.B. Stallard-Penoyre

E Coy (BBC Wood Norton)
Coy HQ – BBC Wood Norton
Numbers of officers and men not known
Coy Cmdr – Capt W.J. Titshall
Coy Medical Officer – Capt J.M. Robertson
Coy Quartermaster – Lt H.J. Harrington
Pln Cmdr – Lt L.R. Hill
Pln Cmdr – Lt A.E. Church

F Coy (Evesham)
1944 Coy HQ not identified
Numbers of officers and men not known
Coy Cmdr – Maj H.J. Cotton DCM
Coy 2nd in Command – Capt R.J.W. Monnington
Coy Quartermaster – Lt J.E. Humberstone
Coy Intelligence Officer – Lt L. Bettridge
Coy Transport Officer – Lt W.H. Denbigh
No 19 Pln Cmdr – Lt J.D. Wilson
No 20 (Beckford) Pln Cmdr – Lt E.W. Cotton
No 21 Pln Officer – Lt J.S. Rowland
Pln Officer – 2nd Lt W. Ashwin
A Pln Cmdr for No 21 Pln is missing from this list.

5th Worcestershire (Halesowen) Battalion
Headquarters, The Drill Hall, Grammar School Lane, Halesowen
Battalion Roll – 1,006 officers and other ranks. In addition there were 16 cadets employed as boy messengers.
The Permanent Staff Instructors: Sgts G. Berry (RA), R.E. Hopkins (South Staffs Regt,
& F. Longhurst (KSLI). Seconded to the Army Cadet Force was 2nd Lt G.V. Martin.

Bn Cmdr – Lt Col B.J. Keene
Bn 2nd in Command – Maj D.H. Brindley
Bn Adjutant – Capt J.H. Groves
Assistant Adjutant – Lt F. Summers OBE
Bn Quartermaster – Capt H.C.S. Dukes
Bn Medical Officer – Maj H.W. Bland
Additional Bn Medical Officer – Capt J. Donnelly
Bn Weapons Training Officer – Lt F.G. Ketelbey
Bn Ammunition Officer – Lt G.A. Emms
Bn Training Officer – Capt G.W. Langford
Bn Intelligence Officer – Lt E. Lewis
Bn Chemical Warfare Officer – Lt J.G. Mountford
Bn Liaison Officer – Capt W.P. Marsh
Bn Catering Officer – Lt J.L. Downs
Hon Chaplain – Revd J.T. Davies

HQ Coy
162 officers and other ranks
Coy Cmdr – Maj H.B. Hodson
Coy 2nd in Command – Capt F.E. Parkes
Coy Quartermaster – Lt C.K. Lewis
Coy Signals Officer & No 1 Pln Cmdr –
　　Lt L. Phipson
No 1 Pln Officer – 2nd Lt H. Hackett MSM
No 2 Pln Cmdr – Lt J. B. Willetts
No 3 Pln Cmdr – 2nd Lt E. Webster
Coy Transport Officer & No 4 Pln Cmdr –
　　Lt J.B. Pickerell
Coy Pioneer Officer & No 5 Pln Cmdr –
　　Lt H.C. Raybould

A Coy
**Coy HQ – Stewarts and Lloyds Works Canteen,
Coombs Wood, Halesowen**
146 officers and other ranks
Coy Cmdr – Maj T.W. Barber
Coy 2nd in Command – Capt H. Smith
Coy Quartermaster – Lt L. Whyley
No 6 Pln Cmdr – Lt H.L. Little
No 7 Pln Cmdr – 2nd Lt J.A. Shaw
No 8 Pln Cmdr – Lt F. Clarke
No 9 Pln Cmdr – Lt B.A. Searancke

B Coy
**Coy HQ – SW & S Electric Power Coy,
Mucklow Hill, Halesowen**
149 officers and other ranks
Coy Cmdr – Maj A. Stephens
Coy 2nd in Command – Capt T. Hodgetts
Coy Quartermaster – Lt P.W. Wardle
Coy Intelligence Officer – Lt A.T. Bowater
No 10 Pln Cmdr – Sgt T. Bradney
No 11 Pln Cmdr – Lt W.L. Brooks
No 12 Pln Cmdr – 2nd Lt G.G. Thompson
No 13 Pln Cmdr – Lt J.C. Grainger

C Coy
**Coy HQ – Latterly, the Searchlight Site huts,
Beecher Road, Cradley**
135 officers and other ranks
Coy Cmdr – Maj T. Holden
Coy 2nd in Command – Capt A.G. Barton
Coy Medical Officer – Capt J.N. McCarthy
Coy Training Officer – Lt F. Coombs
Coy Quartermaster – Lt H.H. Elcock
No 14 Pln (Harper & Moores) Cmdr – Lt A. Bowen
No 15 Pln Cmdr – Lt J.D. Cobourne
No 16 Pln (Beech Tree Colliery) Cmdr &
　　Bn Bandmaster – Lt A. Cornock
No 17 Pln (Beech Tree Colliery) Cmdr – Lt C.F. Smith

D Coy
1944 Coy HQ not identified
124 officers and other ranks.
Coy Cmdr – Maj J.B.L. Stevenson
Coy 2nd in Command – Capt D.S. Clemence
Coy Quartermaster – Lt E.H. Penn
No 18 Pln Cmdr – Lt R.H. Green
No 19 Pln Cmdr – Lt G. Hodgetts
No 20 Pln Cmdr – 2nd Lt C. Pettican

E Coy
1944 Coy HQ not identified
106 officers and other ranks
Coy Cmdr – Maj S.H. Hammersley
Coy 2nd in Command – Capt W.R. Cartwright
Coy Quartermaster – Lt T.E. Scamp
No 21 Pln Cmdr – 2nd Lt C.V.F. Rich
No 22 Pln Cmdr – Lt J. Kendrick
No 23 Pln Cmdr – Lt W.C.L. Martin

F Coy (Cradley)
Coy HQ –The Searchlight Site huts, Cradley.
(Whether the same huts as C Coy has not been established)
113 officers and other ranks
Coy Cmdr – Maj J.H. Vernon

Coy 2nd in Command – Capt W.H. Oliver
Coy Quartermaster – Lt F.R. Young
No 24 Pln Cmdr – Lt W.T. Partridge
No 25 Pln Cmdr – Lt R. Hipkiss
No 25 Pln Officer – 2nd Lt J. Silcox
No 26 Pln Cmdr – Sgt H. Saunders

6th Worcestershire (Kidderminster) Battalion
Battalion HQ – Castle Motor Works, New Road, Kidderminster (from February 1944).
Prior to that it was at Kingsley Buildings, Vicar Street
Battalion Roll – 950 officers and other ranks

Bn Cmdr – Lt Col C. Thatcher
Bn 2nd in Command – Maj W.H.X. Smith
Bn Adjutant – Capt C. W. Lester
Assistant Adjutant – 2nd Lt H. Pessol
Bn Medical Officer – Maj D.G. Dykes
Bn Training Officer – Capt J.L. Robey
Bn Transport Officer – 2nd Lt R. Loynes
Bn Intelligence Officer – Capt W.A. Greenway
Bn Chemical Warfare Officer – 2nd Lt F.G. Nicholls
Bn Liaison Officer – Capt H. Houghton-Brown
Bn Catering Officer – Lt H. Nicholls
Bn Signals Officer – Lt H.W. French
Bn Ammunition Officer – Capt N.F. Duffield

HQ Coy
169 officers and other ranks
Coy Cmdr – Maj F.C. Perrett
Coy Medical Officer – Capt M.L. Nairac
Coy Quartermaster – Lt R.D. Mason
Coy Pioneer Officer – 2nd Lt G.H. Thomas
No 1 Pln Cmdr – Lt A.L. Smith

A Coy
1944 Coy HQ not identified
119 officers and other ranks
Coy Cmdr – Maj J. Parkes MC DCM
Coy 2nd in Command – Capt E. Marks
Coy Intelligence Officer – 2nd Lt E. Marks
No 2 Pln Cmdr – Lt J.D. Parkes
No 3 Pln Cmdr – Lt A. James MM
No 4 Pln Cmdr – 2nd Lt A.E. Price
No 5 Pln Cmdr – 2nd Lt H.G. Green

B Coy
1944 Coy HQ not identified
227 officers and other ranks, including a Midland Red
    Section and a Factory Section
Coy Cmdr – Maj G.H. Head DCM
Coy 2nd in Command – Capt R.H. Lewis
Coy Quartermaster – Lt F.A. Jones
Coy Intelligence Officer – 2nd Lt W.B. Holden
No 6 Pln Cmdr – Lt W.J. Brockway

No 7 Pln Cmdr – Lt S.F. Legge
No 8 Pln Cmdr – 2nd Lt F.W. Dansern
No 9 Pln Cmdr – not identified
No 10 Pln Cmdr – Lt A.L. Whitehouse
No 11 Pln Cmdr – 2nd Lt W.H. Common

C Coy
1944 Coy HQ not identified
202 officers and other ranks, including a GWR
    Section of 53 commanded by Jock Fergusson
Coy Cmdr – Maj J.G. Anton
Coy 2nd in Command – Capt E.A.K. Forrest
Coy Quartermaster – Lt L.R. Carter
Coy Training Officer – 2nd Lt E.C. Watson
No 12 Pln Cmdr – Lt R.A. Owens
No 13 Pln Cmdr – Lt L.A. Dudley
No 14 Pln Cmdr – Lt H.V.L. Ellis
No 15 Pln Cmdr – 2nd Lt E.C. Watson
No 16 Pln Cmdr – Lt H.J. Gibson

D Coy
1944 Coy HQ not identified
101 officers and other ranks
Coy Cmdr – Maj R.E. Grove
Coy 2nd in Command – Capt G.E. Lloyd
Coy Intelligence Officer – Lt H. Pratt
Coy Training Officer – 2nd Lt A. Payne
Coy Quartermaster – Lt H.A. Watkins
No 18 Pln Cmdr – Lt E.W. Weatherhead
No 19 Pln Cmdr – Lt Whatmore
No 20 Pln Cmdr – Lt A.C. Robinson

E Coy
1944 Coy HQ not identified
89 officers and other ranks
Coy Cmdr – Maj H.G. Mantle
Coy 2nd in Command – Capt H.W. Gregory
Coy Quartermaster – Lt H. Earnshaw
Coy Training Officer – 2nd Lt R.C. Jellyman
Coy Intelligence Officer – 2nd Lt L.E. Wakelin
No 21 Pln Cmdr – Lt W. W. Mallard
No 22 Pln Cmdr – 2nd Lt A. Wyer
No 23 Pln Cmdr – 2nd Lt H. Williams

7th Worcestershire (Malvern) Battalion
Battalion HQ, St Andrews Golf Clubhouse then Clarence Road Drill Hall from October 1944
Battalion Roll – 2,124 officers and other ranks

Bn Cmdr – Lt Col J. Johnstone
Bn 2nd in Command – Maj (Col retired)
    J.B. Wheeler MC
Bn Adjutant – Capt H.L. Nell
Assistant Adjutant – Lt J.W. Bowen
Bn Administrative Officer – Capt H.A. Hammond
Bn Medical Officer – Maj R.A. Fuller MC
Bn Transport Officer – Lt R.G. Malby
Bn Training Officer – Capt H.M. De Salis La
    Terriere MC
Bn Intelligence Officer – Capt D. Wood AMG
Bn Liaison Officer – Capt A.R. Marsh
Bn Catering Officer – Lt H.L. Morris
Bn Quartermaster – 2nd Lt H.E. Doughty
Bn Signals Officer – Lt E.J. Bowen

HQ Coy
110 officers and other ranks
Coy Cmdr – Maj H.E. Day DSO MVO
Coy 2nd in Command – Capt J.S. Canning
Coy Training Officer – 2nd Lt R. Trevor-Jones CIE MC
Coy Quartermaster – Lt J.H. Powles
Pln Cmdr – Lt E. Rose
Pln Cmdr – Lt E.H. Humphries
Pln Officer – Lt E.H. Berrow
Pln Officer – 2nd Lt A.E. Hill

M (Malvern) Coy
Coy HQ – Lyttelton House, Great Malvern
273 officers and other ranks
Coy Cmdr – Maj W.J.C. Kendall MC MBE
Coy 2nd in Command – Capt G.T. Baldwin
Coy Medical Officer – Capt W.G. Shakespeare
Coy Training Officer – Lt B.I. Wilson MSM
Coy Quartermaster – Lt A.E. Thomas
Coy Intelligence Officer – Lt S.G. Campion
Coy Bomb Disposal Officer – 2nd Lt M.J. Hayes
Pln Cmdr – Lt A.F Cotterell
Pln Cmdr – Lt J.F. Frederick
No 12 Pln (ADRDE) Cmdr – Lt J.B. Walker
Pln Officer – Lt H.G. Davies
Pln Officer – Lt W.R. Evans
Pln Officer – Lt J.G. Huddleston
Pln Officer – Lt L.G. Recordon
Pln Officer – 2nd Lt D.M Loudon
Pln Officer – 2nd Lt G.R. Newberry
Pln Officer – 2nd Lt A.A. Hamilton

U (Upton) Coy
Coy HQ – The police station, School Lane, Upton upon Severn
459 officers and other ranks, & 11 nominated women
Coy Cmdr – Maj M.F.S. Jewell
Coy 2nd in Command & No 18 (Upton & Hanley
    Castle) Pln Cmdr – Capt Sir Ronald Lechmere
    Bt DL
Coy Medical Officer – Capt H.J. Couchman
Coy Quartermaster – Lt C. N. Norman
Coy Intelligence Officer – Lt E.C.S. Howard
No 13 Pln (Berrow) Cmdr – Lt J. Roxburgh
No 13 Pln Officer – Lt E. Butler
No 14 Pln (Bushley & Longdon) Cmdr –
    Lt D.P. Morgan MC Croix de Guerre
No 14 Pln Officer – Lt W.G. Woodward
No 15 Pln (Hanley Swan) Cmdr –
    Lt W.E.C. Watkinson
No 15 Pln Officer – Lt M.J. Quirke
No 16 Pln (Ripple) Cmdr – Lt G.J. Hunter
No 17 Pln (Severn Stoke) Cmdr – Lt C. Nixon
No 17 Pln Officer – Lt E. Rimell
No 18 Pln Officer – Lt J. Pumphrey
No 19 Pln (Welland) Cmdr – Lt (Col retired)
    C.B. Grice-Hutchinson DSO

O (Ombersley) Coy
Coy HQ – Nissen Huts, immediately north of Holt Fleet bridge
2790 officers and other ranks
Coy Cmdr – Maj J.L. Wood
Coy 2nd in Command – Capt V.F. Newman
Coy Medical Officer – Capt E.B. Pawson
Coy Intelligence Officer – Lt C.A. Perkins
Coy Quartermaster – Lt R.L. Bradley
Coy Training Officer – Lt H.E.J. Fussell
Pln (Ombersley) Cmdr – Lt W.E. Ford TD
Pln (Grimley) Cmdr – Lt E.O. Hartwright
Pln Cmdr – Lt K.I. Humphries
Pln Officer – Lt C.E.S. Seymour
Pln Officer – Lt C.A. Arnold MC
Pln Officer – 2nd Lt J. Standen
Pln (Claines) Officer – 2nd Lt N.T.A. Griffin
Pln Officer – 2nd Lt J.T. Higgins
This Coy included No 21 (Sinton Green) Pln, No
22 (Claines) Pln, & No 23 (Fernhill Heath) Pln, but
which officers belong to which Plns has not been
identified.

C (Crowle) Coy
Coy HQ at 'The Oak House', Crowle,
or Spetchley Stables
256 officers and other ranks
Coy Cmdr – Maj J.F.C. Keep
Coy 2nd in Command – Capt J.W.V. Haskins
Coy Intelligence Officer – Lt A.E. Turner
Coy Quartermaster – 2nd Lt S.J.C. Cumming
Pln Cmdr – Lt L.R. Hyde
Pln Cmdr – Lt H.M. Morgan
Pln Cmdr – Lt G.A. Cooper
Pln Cmdr – Lt G.H. Derrington
Pln Officer – Lt M.Y. Townsend
Pln Officer – 2nd Lt O.J. Turner
Pln Officer – 2nd Lt T.A. Comely
Pln Officer – 2nd Lt B.A. Doorbar
Pln Officer – 2nd Lt J.A. Appleton
This Coy included No 25 Pln at Spetchley Stables,
No 26 Pln at Norton, & No 27 Pln at Kempsey, but
which officers belong to which Plns has not been
identified.

P (Powick) Coy
Coy HQ – Crown East Court (Aymestrey School)
239 officers and other ranks
Coy Cmdr – Maj D.A.N. Asterley
Coy 2nd in Command – Capt E. Mingay
Coy Medical Officer – Capt J.B. Cavanagh MC
Coy Training Officer – Lt W.M. Aldersley
Coy Quartermaster – Lt C.G. Fowler
Coy Intelligence Officer – Lt M.W. Jones
Pln Cmdr – Lt G.R. Gabb
Pln Cmdr – Lt P.B. Rigden
No 30 (Hallow) Pln Cmdr – Lt A.N. Garratt
No 30 (Hallow) Pln Officer – Lt E. Munslow
Pln Officer – Lt F.B. Richardson
Pln Officer – 2nd Lt H.D. Pennington
Pln Officer – 2nd Lt W.A. Goodall
This Coy included No 28 Pln (Manor Farm, Powick)
& No 29 (Crown East), but which officers belong to
which platoon has not been identified.

K (Knightwick) Coy
Coy HQ – Woodford House, Knightwick
187 officers and other ranks
Coy Cmdr – Maj R.H. Clarke
Coy 2nd in Command – Capt L.C. Schiller MC
Coy Intelligence Officer – 2nd Lt F. Woodyatt
Pln Cmdr – Lt D.W. Walker
Pln Cmdr – Lt J.F.P. Clift
Pln Cmdr – Lt J. Field
Pln Officer – Lt (Col retired) H. Sheppard DCM
Pln Officer – Lt J.F. Gimson
Pln Officer – Lt R.L. Gibbons
Pln Officer – Lt J.S. Twinberrow

62nd Mobile Coy
Coy HQ – The Morgan Works, Pickersleigh Road,
Malvern
133 officers and men
Coy Cmdr – Maj G.L. Stone
Coy 2nd in Command – Capt E.C.B. Dale
Coy Training Officer – Lt J. Lloyd
Coy Intelligence Officer – 2nd Lt E. Coppack
Coy Quartermaster – 2nd Lt W.N. Percival
Pln Cmdr – Lt E. Chapman
Pln Cmdr – 2nd Lt F.D. Arkinstall
Pln Cmdr – 2nd Lt F.B. Smith
Pln Officer – 2nd Lt G.E.L. Walker
Pln Officer – 2nd Lt C.T. Jay

T Battle Group (TRE)
Coy HQ – Malvern College, College Road,
Great Malvern
Group Cmdr – Capt H.G. Scott
Pln Cmdr – Lt A.G. Ward
Pln Cmdr – Lt L.A. Moncrieff MSM OBE
Pln Cmdr – Lt J. Dain
Pln Officer – Lt R.L. Elliot
Pln Officer – 2nd Lt R.C.M. Barnes
Pln Officer – 2nd Lt H.K. Sutcliffe
Pln Officer – 2nd Lt F.D. Boardman
Pln Officer – 2nd Lt D.R. Howard
Pln Officer – 2nd Lt A.F. Woolner
Pln Officer – 2nd Lt S. Ratcliffe
Pln Officer – 2nd Lt J.E. Lockyer

8th Worcestershire (Oldbury) Battalion
Battalion HQ – The Grange, Halesowen
Battalion Roll – 1,558 officers and other ranks. Permanent Staff Instructor:
Colour Sgt W.E. Evans (Royal Warks Regiment)

HQ Coy
Formed on 1 January 1944, the Coy had 544 officers
and other ranks as follows
Bn Cmdr – Lt Col T.C. Fillery
Bn 2nd in Command – Maj F. Bryan
Bn Adjutant – Capt A.V. Rogers
Bn Medical Officer – Maj A.M. Stevens
Bn Training Officer – Lt S.T.C. Anthony
Bn Intelligence Officer – Lt S.C. Gray
Bn Chemical Warfare Officer – Lt H.D. Hughes
Bn Catering Officer – Lt A.H.C. Colley
Bn Pioneer Officer – Lt W.E.K. Piercy
Bn Signals Officer – Lt D.M.C. Bloomer
Bn Ammunition Officer – Lt C.W. Tod
Bn Guide – Lt D.W. Wybourn
The roles of the following officers have not been
identified: Capt F.G.S. White, Lt W.F. Knight, 2nd
Lt S. Williams, 2nd Lt W.S. Payne, 2nd Lt H.O.
Bradshaw, 2nd Lt R. Turby, 2nd Lt E.G. Skidmore,
2nd Lt A. Durrens, & 2nd Lt R. Merther.

A Coy
1944 Coy HQ not identified
121 officers and other ranks
Coy Cmdr – Capt J.P. Barlow
Coy 2nd in Command – Capt C.D. Mitchell
Coy Intelligence Officer – 2nd Lt G. Limrick
No 3 Pln Officer – 2nd Lt C.E. Rowberry
No 4 Pln Officer – 2nd Lt J.W. Harrington
No ? Pln Officer – 2nd Lt B. Law

B Coy
1944 Coy HQ not identified
153 officers and other ranks
Coy Cmdr – Capt J.P. Barlow
Coy Quartermaster – 2nd Lt E. James
Pln Cmdr – Lt F. James
Pln Cmdr – Lt A.E. Chatwin
Pln Cmdr – Lt G.G. Smith
Pln Officer – 2nd Lt K. Lester
Pln Officer – 2nd Lt G. Steventon
Pln Officer – 2nd Lt R. Bailey

C Coy
1944 Coy HQ not identified
154 officers and other ranks
Coy Cmdr – Maj A.A. Powell MM
Coy 2nd in Command – Capt H. Roberts
Coy Intelligence Officer – 2nd Lt S.W. Clark

Pln Cmdr – 2nd Lt J. Parkes
Pln Cmdr – Lt J.W. Edwards
Pln Cmdr – Lt H. Bradley MM
Pln Cmdr – Lt F.L. Archer
No 9 Pln Officer – 2nd Lt F.J. Powell
No ? Pln Officer – 2nd Lt C. Willot
No 11 Pln Officer – 2nd Lt S. Lloyd
No ? Pln Officer – 2nd Lt F. Moss

The following factory units appear to have formed C
Coy: Messrs Edwin Danks (Oldbury), William Hunt,
R. Simpson, & Messrs Brooks.

D Coy
1944 Coy HQ not identified
254 officers and other ranks
Coy Cmdr – Maj W.H. Reynolds
Coy 2nd in Command – Capt C.W. Loveday
Coy Intelligence Officer – 2nd Lt E. Hill
Coy Training Officer – 2nd Lt C.A. Hopcraft
Coy Quartermaster – 2nd Lt C.H. Kilvert
Light Anti-Aircraft Troop – Capt J. Partington
Light Anti-Aircraft Troop – 2nd Lt N.F. Raggett
Light Anti-Aircraft Troop – 2nd Lt A.H. Gould
Light Anti-Aircraft Troop – 2nd Lt R.W. Kenny
Bomb Disposal Unit – Lt C. Teague
Pln Cmdr – 2nd Lt A.D. Edwards
Pln Officer – 2nd Lt K.C. Field
No 13 Pln Officer – 2nd Lt J.C. Kyte
No 14 Pln Officer – 2nd Lt E. Jones
Pln Officer – 2nd Lt F. Hickman
Pln Officer – 2nd Lt W.E. Westwood
Role not identified – 2nd Lt J. Haden

E Coy
1944 Coy HQ not identified
158 officers and other ranks
Coy Cmdr – Maj J.C. Christopherson
Coy 2nd in Command – Capt R. Dorey
Coy Quartermaster – 2nd Lt A. Heaton
Coy Intelligence Officer – 2nd Lt S. Williams
No 18 Pln Cmdr – 2nd Lt G. Cumming
No ? Pln Cmdr – Lt R.G. Stilton
No 20 Pln Cmdr – 2nd Lt E.K. Parkinson

The following factory units appear to have formed E
Coy: SW&S, Chance & Hunt, & Albright & Wilson

F Coy
1944 Coy HQ not identified
161 officers and other ranks
Coy Cmdr – Capt J.E. Meggeson
Coy Intelligence Officer – 2nd Lt W.S. Payne
Coy Quartermaster – 2nd Lt W.H. Griffiths
Pln Cmdr – Lt F.E. Daniel
Pln Officer – 2nd Lt A.J. Leon
No 21 Pln Officer – 2nd Lt H. Lowery
No 22 Pln Officer – 2nd Lt P. Aston
No 23 Pln Officer – 2nd Lt P.G. Jackson
No 24 Pln Cmdr – 2nd Lt F.J. Hooper

G Coy
1944 Coy HQ not identified
166 officers and other ranks
Coy Cmdr – Maj W.J. Ward
Coy 2nd in Command – Capt R.C. Cropper
Coy Quartermaster – 2nd Lt W.H. Preston
Coy Training Officer – Lt G.V. Benn
Coy Intelligence Officer – 2nd Lt H.O. Bradshaw
Pln Cmdr – Lt B.J. Gill
No 27 Pln Officer – 2nd Lt E.S. Cotley
No 28 Pln Cmdr – 2nd Lt H.E. Richards

9th Worcestershire (Redditch) Battalion
Battalion HQ – The Drill Hall, Church Road, Redditch
Battalion Roll – 1,627 officers and other ranks, 6 nominated women and 4 boy messengers. Seconded to the Redditch Cadets, 2nd Lt N.A. Taylor. Supernumerary to establishment, Lt D.M. Young.

Bn Cmdr – Lt Col E.A. Grace
Bn 2nd in Command – Maj R.C. Morom
Bn Adjutant – Capt F.J. Hartley
Bn Medical Officer – Maj N.C. Burns
Bn Training Officer – Capt J.K. Seal
Bn Transport Officer – Lt F.J. Allwood
Bn Intelligence Officer – Lt J.C. Moys
Bn Chemical Warfare Officer – Lt W.W. Holder
Bn Liaison Officer – Capt K.H. Pattison
Joint Liaison Officer with N Sector – 2nd Lt J.J. Booker
Bn Catering Officer – Lt R.V.W. Ellis
Bn Quartermaster – Lt L.W. Askew
Bn Signals Officer – Lt H. Johnson
Bn Ammunition Officer – Capt A.E. Newby

HQ Coy
200 officers and other ranks
Coy Cmdr – Maj J. Morrall
Coy Quartermaster – 2nd Lt W. Mack
Coy Training Officer – Lt T.F. Womack
Coy Intelligence Officer – Lt R.D. Reid
Pln Cmdr – Lt H.G. Dagger
Pln Officer – 2nd Lt C.V. Howe
Role not identified – Lt C.H. Hamilton

A Coy (Alvechurch)
Coy HQ at Walkers Store, Alvechurch
153 0fficers and other ranks, 4 nominated women and
    2 boy messengers
Coy Cmdr – Maj W.M. Mullins
Coy 2nd in Command – Capt F. Jephcott
Coy Medical Officer – Capt M.J. Dick
Coy Intelligence Officer – 2nd Lt A.C. Evans
Coy Quartermaster – 2nd Lt E.J. Hare
No 1 Pln Cmdr – Lt H.P. Burman
No 2 Pln Cmdr – Lt F.H.M. Jephcott

No 3 Pln Cmdr – 2nd Lt W.A. Kedwards
Pln Officer – 2nd Lt F. Tuffin
Delingpole's factory unit was part of No 3 Pln

B Coy
Coy HQ at the Drill Hall, Church Road, Redditch
196 officers and other ranks, and 8 nominated women
Coy Cmdr – Maj F.H. Jones
Coy 2nd in Command – Capt G.G. Wilkins
Coy Quartermaster – Lt S. Guise
Pln Cmdr – Lt F. Bowen
Pln Cmdr – Lt R.E. Fox
Pln Cmdr – Lt P. Kenyon
Pln Cmdr – Lt L.J. Plumb
Pln Officer – 2nd Lt K.L. Blakeman
Pln Officer – 2nd Lt H.W. James
Pln Officer – 2nd Lt J. Smith
Pln Officer – 2nd Lt A.E. Vale

C Coy
Coy HQ at the Coop Society Hall, Headless Cross
273 officers and other ranks, 2 nominated women and
2 boy messengers
Coy Cmdr – Maj E. Young MC
Coy 2nd in Command – Capt J.T. Phillips
Coy Medical Officer – Capt G.F. Henderson
Coy Quartermaster – Lt H.R. Bird
Coy Training Officer – 2nd Lt A.E. Jackson
Pln Cmdr – Lt R.H. Hodge
Pln Cmdr – Lt A.B. Maries
No 8 Pln (Crabbs Cross) Cmdr – Lt J. Price
Pln Officer – 2nd Lt S.E. Prescott
Pln Officer – 2nd Lt G.E. Bryant
Pln Officer – 2nd Lt W.K. Atack
The other platoons were No 9 (Headless Cross), No
10 (Webheath), and No 11 (Hewell) although the pln
cmdrs have not been identified.

D Coy

Coy HQ at the Perkins Factory Astwood Bank

166 officers and other ranks, 7 nominated women
and 5 boy messengers
Coy Cmdr – Maj W.M. Yeomans
Coy 2nd in Command – Capt P. Neale
Coy Medical Officer – Capt E.P. Walsh
Coy Quartermaster – 2nd Lt C.C. Clough
No 12 Pln Cmdr – Lt E. Ames
No 12 Pln Officer – 2nd Lt A. Stanton
No 13 Pln Cmdr – Lt F.J. Huxley
No 14 Pln Cmdr – Lt J.E. Farmer
No 15 Pln Cmdr – 2nd Lt E.N. Byrd
Role not identified – 2nd Lt R.B. Broady

E Coy (Enfield Unit)

HQ at the Enfield factory, Hewell Road, Redditch

89 officers and other ranks, 7 nominated women
and 2 boy messengers
Coy Cmdr – Maj F.W. Smith
Coy 2nd in Command – Lt G.H. Smith
Coy Intelligence Officer – 2nd Lt H.R. Mole
Pln Cmdr – Lt S.H. Smith
Pln Cmdr – Lt O. Wythes
Pln Cmdr – 2nd Lt G.H. Fairgrieve

E Coy (HDA Unit)

HQ at the HDA Factory, Windsor Road, Redditch

159 officers and other ranks
Coy Cmdr – Capt G. Payne MC
Coy 2nd in Command – Lt G.C.G. Chrippes
Coy Quartermaster – 2nd Lt G.F. Mutton
Coy Training Officer – 2nd Lt W. Darby
Coy Intelligence Officer – 2nd Lt R. Bruce
Bomb Disposal Unit – Capt C.I. Irving
Bomb Disposal Unit – Lt C.T. Farley
Pln Cmdr – Lt J.E. Moran
Pln Cmdr – Lt H. Croft
Pln Cmdr – 2nd Lt E.C. Turnhill
Pln Cmdr – 2nd Lt S. Wilson
Pln Officer – 2nd Lt C.H. Chillingworth

F Coy (BSA Unit)

HQ at the BSA Factory, Ipsley, Redditch

112 officers and other ranks, 5 nominated women
and 2 boy messengers
Coy Cmdr Lt H. Croft
Coy 2nd in Command – Lt F.H. Daffern
Coy Intelligence Officer – Lt H.W. Hirons
Pln Cmdr – Lt E.L. King
Pln Officer – 2nd Lt A.F. Martin
Pln Officer – 2nd Lt P. Pennells
Pln Officer – 2nd Lt D.A. Stormont

F Coy (Terry's Unit)

HQ at the Terry's Factory, Lodge Road, Redditch

109 officers and other ranks, and 18 nominated
women
Coy Cmdr – Capt J.V. Sara
Coy 2nd in Command – Lt H.E. Burton
Pln Cmdr – Lt G. B.Kearsley
Pln Cmdr – Lt P.A. Spencer
Pln Cmdr – 2nd Lt E.F. Smith

F Coy (Britannia Batteries)

**HQ at the Britannia Batteries Factory, Union
Street, Redditch**

46 officers and other ranks, and 2 nominated women
Coy Cmdr – Maj R.M. Broomfield
Coy 2nd in Command – Lt J.A. Mitchell
Coy Quartermaster – 2nd Lt L.H. Hodges
Pln Cmdr – Lt J.A. Hunt

F Coy (Reynolds Unit)

HQ at the Reynolds Factory, Ipsley Road, Redditch

58 officers and other ranks, and 1 boy messenger
Coy Cmdr – Capt R.H. George
Coy 2nd in Command – 2nd Lt E.A. Mason
Light Anti-Aircraft Troop Leader –
    2nd Lt R.S. Goostry
Light Anti-Aircraft Relief Cmdr – 2nd Lt J.H. Sanders

The Monochrome Unit details have not been found
for the Stand Down period.

10th Worcestershire (Stourbridge) Battalion
Battalion HQ – George Street, Kidderminster
Battalion Roll – 1,514 officers and other ranks. Permanent Staff Instructor: Sgt J.H.T. Bradley.
The information below may not be complete but represents what has been found from Part 2 orders.

Bn HQ Coy
93 officers and other ranks, and 2 boy messengers
Bn Cmdr – Lt Col L.C. Goodwin
Bn 2nd in Command – Maj J.E. Grosvenor MBE TD
Bn Adjutant – Capt J.B. Chance MC DCM
Bn Medical Officer – Maj R.E. Smith OBE
Bn Medical Officer – Capt E.W. Evans
Bn Medical Officer – Capt E.R. Swinton
Bn Medical Officer – Capt J.S. Price
Bn Weapons Training Officer – Lt D.H. Ferguson
Bn Training Officer – Capt W. Boddington
Bn Transport Officer – Lt L.C.C. Brinton
Bn Intelligence Officer – Lt A. Johnson MC
Bn Liaison Officer – Capt H.S. Williams-Thomas
Bn Catering Officer – Lt A.A. Moore
Bn Quartermaster – Lt W.C. Edwards
Bn Pioneer Officer – Lt H. Palethorpe
Bn Signals Officer – Lt C.F.N. Boulton
Bn Assistant Signals Officer – Lt R.B. Robinson
Bn Ammunition Officer – Capt N.E. Woodward
Bn Assistant Ammunition Officer – Lt S.T. Haynes
Role not identified – Capt H. Osborne
Role not identified – Capt A. Knight
Role not identified – Lt C.A. Horton
Coy Training Officer – Lt A.A. Harper MM
Hon Chaplain – Revd S.R. Waring
Hon Chaplain – Revd N. Panter

A Coy
Coy HQ – The Oaks, West Hagley
227 officers and other ranks
Coy Cmdr – Maj W.H. Cooper
Coy 2nd in Command – Capt A.C. Cope
Coy Intelligence Officer – Lt J.C. Holcroft
Pln Cmdr – Lt A.L. Parkes
No 4 Pln Cmdr – Lt J.E. Phesey MC
Pln Cmdr – Lt J.H. King
Pln Cmdr – Lt H. Lench
Pln Officer – 2nd Lt D.E. Price
Role not identified – Lt R.P.S. Bache

B Coy
Coy HQ – Stone Manor, Stone
159 officers and other ranks
Coy Cmdr – Maj G.G. Watson
Coy 2nd in Command – Capt H.G. Hill
Blakedown Pln Cmdr – Lt F.J. Coates MM
Pln Cmdr – Lt J.C. Marriot

Churchill Pln Cmdr – Lt J. Palethorpe MC AFC
Pln Officer – 2nd Lt A.L. Levi
Pln Officer – 2nd Lt A.F. Hobson
Pln Officer – Lt C.F.K. Bamford

C Coy
Coy HQ – Caswall's Shop, Cookley
189 officers and other ranks
Coy Cmdr – Maj R.C. Walls MC
Coy 2nd in Command – Capt R.A.H. Gofley
Pln Officer – Lt R.A.A. Knight
Role not identified – 2nd Lt R. Tolley
It is likely that there were more officers than are listed
here to make up the Coy command.

D Coy (Wollaston)
Coy HQ – Eggington Barn, Wollaston
359 officers and other ranks, and 1 boy messenger
Coy Cmdr – Maj F.A.J. Hejl
Coy 2nd in Command – Capt H.J.N. Skinner
Coy Quartermaster – Lt J. Wooley
Coy Intelligence Officer – 2nd Lt C.C. Davies
Pln Cmdr – Lt N.T. Rabey
Pln Cmdr – Lt O.T. Russell
Pln Cmdr – Lt S. Tooby
Pln Cmdr – Lt F. Simpson
Pln Officer – 2nd Lt W.F.R. Claxton
Pln Officer – 2nd Lt H.L. Edwards
Pln Officer – 2nd Lt L. White
Bandmaster – L. Handy
This Coy incorporated Numbers 16 to 20 Plns, which
implies that there were more officers than are listed
here. It has not been possible to identify which Pln
was commanded by which officers from this list.

E Coy
Coy HQ – The Grove, Norton
148 officers and other ranks
Coy Cmdr – Maj A.B. Clibbery
Coy 2nd in Command – Capt H.J. Stringer
Coy Quartermaster – Lt H.D. Croft
Pln Cmdr – 2nd Lt G.N. Crook
Pln Cmdr – Lt R.E.W. Gascoigne
Pln Cmdr – Lt R.L. Griffin
Pln Cmdr – 2nd Lt H.M. Perrin
Pln Cmdr – Lt T.A. Mobberley
Lt Mobberley died on 10th December 1944.

F Coy
Coy HQ – The Post, Pedmore
156 officers and other ranks
Coy Cmdr – Maj W.C. Boulton
Coy 2nd in Command – Capt J.H. Yardley
Coy Intelligence Officer – 2nd Lt G. Drewry
Coy Quartermaster – Lt G.H. Eveson
Coy Training Officer – Lt W.R. Warrington
Pln Cmdr – Lt W.R. Fulleylove
Pln Cmdr – Lt C. Hildick
Pln Cmdr – Lt R. Scott

G Coy
1944 Coy HQ not identified
Coy Cmdr – Capt H.B. Hunt
Coy 2nd in Command – Lt H. Sollars

The position in the Bn of the following officers serving at the time has not been identified: Lt E.P. Davies (Pln Cmdr), 2nd Lt R. Tolley, Capt H. Osborne, Capt A. Knight, & 2nd Lt C.A. Horton.

11th Worcestershire (Stourport) Battalion
Battalion HQ – The Drill Hall, Lion Hill, Stourport
Battalion Roll – 1,419 officers and other ranks. Permanent Staff Instructors:
Sgt Maj J.W. Harrison, Sgt J.I. Davies, & Sgt Maj M.O.T. Jones

HQ Coy
Bn Cmdr – Lt Col J.A. Dyson Perrins
Bn 2nd in Command – Maj C.S. Newton
Bn Adjutant – Capt P.G. Eccles
Bn Medical Officer – Maj C. Mackie
Bn Weapons Training Officer – Lt J.S. Barker
Bn Transport Officer – Lt W.H. Owen
Bn Training Officer – Capt R.V. Price
Bn Intelligence Officer – Capt R.S. Searle
Bn Chemical Warfare Officer – Lt E.H. Kuestner
Bn Liaison Officer – Capt H.P. Long
Bn Catering Officer – Lt H. Prescott
Bn Pioneer Officer – Lt A.G. Nicholls
Bn Signals Officer – Lt W.J. Tew
Bn Ammunition Officer – Capt C.H. Hodgson

A Coy.
Coy HQ – The Drill Hall, Lion Hill, Stourport
Combined with the HQ officers the roll for A Coy
    was 253 officers and other ranks
Coy Cmdr – Maj A.L. Thomas
Coy 2nd in Command – Capt N.H. Capel-Loft
Coy Quartermaster – Lt H. Hill
Coy Training Officer – Lt L.J. Long
Coy Intelligence Officer – Lt J.A. Price
No1 Pln Cmdr – Lt E. Downes
No1 Pln Officer – 2nd Lt F.E. Madden
No2 Pln Cmdr – Lt V.W.R. Crane
No2 Pln Officer – Lt T.A. Bush
No3 Pln Cmdr – Lt H.C. Perrins
No 3 Pln Officer – Lt J. Pratt
A Coy included a Gun Section of 13 NCOs & men under the command of Sgt Burton. This will have been for the 6 pounder Hotchkiss gun initially mounted in the emplacement which used to stand opposite what is now the Civic Centre in Stourport.

B Coy
Coy HQ – The Drill Hall, Lion Hill, Stourport
259 officers and other ranks.
Coy Cmdr – Maj W.E. Richardson MC
Coy 2nd in Command – Capt T.C. Prince
Coy Quartermaster – Lt C. Hartland
Coy Intelligence Officer – 2nd Lt C. Hartland
No 4 Pln Cmdr – Lt Lown
No 5 Pln Cmdr – Lt H. Pope
No 7 Pln (SW&S) Cmdr – Lt W.S. Harper
No 8 Pln Cmdr – Lt R.B. Comber
Pln Officer – Lt G.T. Chuter
Pln Officer – Lt N. Martin
Pln Officer – Lt C.V. Hill
Pln Officer – Lt G.H. Halton MBE
Pln Officer – 2nd Lt H.S. McCullock
In addition to the Power Station staff (SW&S), the other Plns were formed by Baldwins Wilden Works, Parsons Chain Coy & the Steatite & Porcelain Works, but which of the above Plns has not been identified.

C Coy (Abberley)
Coy HQ – Abberley School
262 officers and other ranks, 11 nominated women
    and 3 boy messengers
Coy Cmdr – Maj G. Ashton MC
Coy 2nd in Command – Capt N.C. Wood
Coy Medical Officer – Capt W.J. Johnson
Coy Intelligence Officer – Lt J.G. Richardson
No 9 (Abberley) Pln Cmdr – Lt A. Astley-Jones
No 10 (Great Witley) Pln Cmdr – Lt J.F.C. Brinton
No 10 Pln Officer – 2nd Lt T.H.F. Banks
Nos 11 (Stanford Bridge) & 13 (Clifton on Teme)
Plns Cmdr – Lt H.R. Winn
No 11 Pln Officer – Lt A.L. Moore
No 12 (Martley) Pln Cmdr – Lt F.N. Bond
No 12 Pln Officer – Lt C.W. Hodgetts

No 14 (Clows Top) Pln Cmdr – Lt E. Evans
No 14 Pln Officer – Lt G. Kay
No 15 (Bayton Collieries) Pln Cmdr – Lt G. Bramall

D Coy (Tenbury)
Coy HQ – The Drill Hall, Berrington Road, Tenbury
160 officers and other ranks
Coy Cmdr – Maj H. Bentham
Coy 2nd in Command – Capt J. Nott
Coy Medical Officer – Capt J.E.B. Williams
Coy Quartermaster – Lt R.C. Guinness
Coy Intelligence Officer – Lt J.E. Jenner
No 17 Pln Cmdr – Lt I.C. Riley
No 18 Pln Cmdr – Lt J.F. Higginson
No 19 Pln Cmdr – Lt R.K.R. Baker
No 34 Pln Cmdr – Lt H.C. Morgan
Pln Officer – Lt G.W. Selby
Pln Officer – 2nd Lt W.C. Vilas

E Coy (Bewdley)
Coy HQ – St George's Hall, Bewdley
196 officers and other ranks
Coy Cmdr – Maj H. Goodwin MC
Coy 2nd in Command – Capt C.R.F. Threllfall
Coy Medical Officer – Capt H.N. Miles
Coy Quartermaster – Lt E.W. Moule

Coy Training Officer – Lt D.F. Lawson
No 20 (Wribbenhall) Pln Cmdr – 2nd Lt F.E. Page
No 21 (Bewdley) Pln Cmdr – Lt W. Bishop
No 22 (Rock) Pln Cmdr – Lt A.O. Betts
No 33 (HQ) Pln Cmdr – Lt A.E. Crossman

F Coy (25 MU Hartlebury)
Coy HQ – 25 MU Hartlebury
299 officers and other ranks
Coy Cmdr – Maj G. Holmes
Coy 2nd in Command – Capt F.C. Westacott
Coy Quartermaster – Lt R. Strathan
Coy Training Officer – Lt L.L. Hind
Coy Intelligence Officer – 2nd Lt W.V. Morris
No 23 Pln Cmdr – Lt A.J. Warner
No 24 Pln Cmdr – Lt C.E.G. Beech
No 25 Pln Cmdr – Lt S.B. Denbert
No 26 Pln Cmdr – Lt A.H. Booth
No 27 Pln Cmdr – Lt J. Franklyn
No 28 Pln Cmdr – Lt R.D. Connop
No 29 Pln Cmdr – Lt J.R. Bailey
No 30 Pln Cmdr – Lt H.J.S. Bridges
No 31 Pln Cmdr – Lt C.C.A. Richards
No 32 Pln Cmdr – Lt A.E. Crossman

12th Worcestershire (Warley) Battalion

Battalion HQ – 'High Tor', Perry Hill Road, Quinton, until 11th December 1944.
Afterwards at the Drill Hall, Langley.

Battalion Roll – 804 officers and other ranks, with 16 boy messengers shared between E & F Companies.
Permanent Staff Instructor: Sgt Maj J.T. Adams (KSLI & Staffordshire Regiments).

HQ (E) Coy

226 officers and other ranks
Bn Cmdr – Lt Col W.J. Balderstone
Bn 2nd in Command – Maj A.E. Church, who died on
    2nd December 1944
Bn Adjutant – Capt H.S. Kemshead
Assistant Adjutant – Lt W.J. Twiss
Bn Medical Officer – Maj W.H. Shilvock
    (Cmdr of Medical Section of No 4 Pln)
Bn Transport Officer – Lt H.J. Hall
Bn Training Officer – Capt T. Wright
    (Cmdr of Training Section of No 4 Pln)
Bn Intelligence Officer – Lt R.J. Wickes
    (Cmdr of No 3 Intelligence Pln)
Bn Chemical Warfare Officer – Lt F.A. Billington
    (Cmdr of the Gas Section of No 4 Pln)
Bn Liaison Officer – Lt S.H. Rowe
Bn Catering Officer – Lt W.G. Tyler
    (Cmdr of the Cooks Section of No 4 Pln)
Bn Quartermaster – Lt W.J. Black
    (Cmdr of the Stores Section of No 4 Pln)
Bn Pioneer Officer – Lt T. Poole
    (Cmdr of No 2 Pioneer Pln)
Bn Signals Officer – Lt J. Inman
    (Cmdr of No 1 Signals Pln)
E Coy Cmdr – Maj R.B. Greatorex
Coy 2nd in Command – Capt L. Slade
Coy Intelligence Officer – 2nd Lt K.M. Bloomer
No 5 Pln (Firth Vickers) Pln Cmdr –
    Lt W.H.T. Turner
Supernumery – Lt J.R.M. Partridge (but Cmdr of the
    Arms & Ammunition Section of No 4 Pln)

A Coy
1944 Coy HQ not identified

163 officers and other ranks
Coy Cmdr – Maj J.T. Hobday
Coy 2nd in Command – Capt H. Coleyshaw
Coy Intelligence Officer – 2nd Lt W.G. Bade
Coy Quartermaster – 2nd Lt S.C. Adams
Pln Cmdr – Lt N.L. Penn
Pln Cmdr – Lt R.P.L. Bird
Pln Officer – 2nd Lt R.H. Drives
Pln Officer – 2nd Lt A.P. Grant

B Coy
Coy HQ – George Road School, Warley

149 officers and other ranks
Coy Cmdr – Maj A.H. Taylor
Coy 2nd in Command – Capt P. Hutchinson
Coy Qaurtermaster – Lt S. Bell MM
Coy Intelligence Officer – 2nd Lt J.W. Partington
Pln Cmdr – Lt J.C. Taylor
Pln Cmdr – Lt H. Phillips
Pln Officer – 2nd Lt J. Babbington
Pln Officer – 2nd Lt J.L. Phillpot

C Coy
Coy HQ – Broomfield Cricket Club, Smethwick

129 officers and men
Coy Cmdr – Maj R.E.H. Humphries
Coy 2nd in Command – Capt W.A. Scott
Coy Intelligence Officer – 2nd Lt J.W. Payne
Coy Quartermaster – Lt W. Salisbury
Pln Cmdr – Lt A.P. Willetts
Pln Cmdr – Lt H. Robinson
Pln Officer – 2nd Lt L.S. Rhodes
Pln Officer – 2nd Lt C. Rowley

D Coy
1944 Coy HQ not identified

137 officers and other ranks
Coy Cmdr – Maj H. Prince
Coy 2nd in Command – Capt P. O'Neill
Coy Intelligence Officer – 2nd Lt C.B. Yates
Coy Qaurtermaster – 2nd Lt N.J. Roberts
Pln Cmdr – Lt W. Linton
Pln Cmdr – Lt A.D. Sulley
Pln Officer – 2nd Lt E. Lewis
Pln Officer – 2nd Lt W. Williams

Appendix 5

Worcestershire men known to have participated in the London Stand Down Parade on 3rd December 1944

Private C. Bayliss, Malvern Battalion
Private S. Bastin, B Company, Bromsgrove Battalion
Sergeant T.G. Bennett, Kidderminster Battalion
Private G. Bishop, E Company, Stourport Battalion
Sergeant D.S. Britain, B Company, Bromsgrove Battalion
Private W.G. Davies, A Company, Evesham Battalion
Private J. Foster, Kidderminster Battalion
Private D.M. Howell, Stourbridge Battalion
Lance Corporal A.G. Hussey, B Company, Evesham Battalion
Private L.F. Jones, C Company, Bromsgrove Battalion
Private D.J. Jordon, Stourport Battalion
Private N.C. Kemp, Stourport Battalion
Private E.F. Lewis, F Company, Evesham Battalion
Lance Corporal F.A. Mason, D Company, Stourport Battalion
Private J.H. Powell, O Sector HQ
Private P.H. Rowley, C Company, Stourport Battalion
Private ? Smith, Kidderminster Battalion
Company Sergeant Major F.J. Smith, D Company, Evesham Battalion
Private C.F. Walker, Kidderminster Battalion
Sergeant J. Wilmshurst MM, Stourbridge Battalion

It is recorded that 87 other ranks and three officers from Worcestershire participated in the London parade. The above list represents less than 25% of this number and any information to extend or complete this list would be welcome.

Appendix 6

Recipients of awards and Certificates of Good Service

Civil Awards
Commander of the Order of the Bath (CB)
Lt Colonel (Brevett Colonel) William Henry Wiggin CB DSO TD DL, Worcestershire
    Home Guard Zone Commander (January 1944)

Military Awards
Order of the British Empire (OBE)
Lieutenant Colonel (Acting Colonel) George Mackie DSO MD MB, of the Worcester City
    Battalion (June 1944)
Colonel E.F. du Sautoy (December 1944)

Member of the British Empire (MBE)
Major S.B. Carter of the Evesham Battalion
Major W.J.C. Kendall of the Malvern Battalion (1945)
Major G. Salter, of Dudley Battalion. He had joined in 1940 without any previous military
    experience (December 1944)
Captain J.K. Seal of Redditch Battalion (December 1944)
Major D.A.P. Shields, Training Officer Bromsgrove Battalion for valuable service to the
    Home Guard (January 1944)

Certificate for Gallantry or Good Service
These certificates were awarded by the General Officer Commanding Western Command and
were normally accompanied by congratulations from him, the Area Commander and Battalion
Commander. Most of the following awards were made at Stand Down for good service. Where
an award is known to have been made for gallantry this is marked with an asterisk.[1]

Sergeant P. Abbot of A Company, Bromsgrove Battalion
Sergeant G.Ball of the Oldbury Battalion
Sergeant A. Baker of A Company, Evesham Battalion
Sergeant L. Banner of C Company, Bromsgrove Battalion
Sergeant K. Barnard of the Warley Battalion
Sergeant F. Barnett of the Evesham Battalion
Sergeant W.F.R. Bate of the Warley Battalion
Private L. Belcher of the Halesowen Battalion
Corporal F.H. Birbeck of the Worcester City Battalion
Lieutenant W. Black of the Warley Battalion
Sergeant C.L. Bloomer of the Kidderminster Battalion

Sergeant W.B. Bourne of the Malvern Battalion
Sergeant G.H. Bowkett of the Stourport Battalion
Private F. Brooks of A Company, Bromsgrove Battalion
Sergeant W.E. Brown of the Warley Battalion
Major F. Bryan of the Oldbury Battalion
Sergeant G.F. Bushell of the Evesham Battalion
Sergeant R.J. Carty of the Malvern Battalion
Corporal W.C. Childs of the Dudley Battalion.
Sergeant P.W. Clewlow DCM of Battalion HQ, Bromsgrove Battalion
Sergeant F.B. Cole (later 2nd Lieutenant), B Company, Evesham Battalion.
Colour Sergeant C.H. Cook of E Company, Warley Battalion
Sergeant W.H. Cookson of the Kidderminster Battalion
Regimental Sergeant Major H. Currell of the Stourport Battalion
Company Sergeant Major H.J. Cuttriss of the Bromsgrove Battalion
Captain W.J. Denton of the Worcester City Battalion
Sergeant F.A. Derry of the Worcester City Battalion
Sergeant J. Detheridge of HQ Company, Halesowen Battalion
Platoon Sergeant F.S. Devereux of F Company, Evesham Battalion
Sergeant ? Dew of C Company, Stourport Battalion.
Major P.W. Dickson of the Halesowen Battalion
Sergeant A. Dolton of the Redditch Battalion
Regimental QM Sergeant H.E. Doughty of the Malvern Battalion
Sergeant R. Drew of the Stourport Battalion
Company Sergeant Major B. Dudley, Halesowen Battalion
Private H. Dutton of the Oldbury Battalion
Company QM Sergeant H. Earnshaw of the Kidderminster Battalion
Sergeant A.T. Edkins of the Evesham Battalion
Corporal W. Exall of the Oldbury Battalion
Colour Sergeant W.E. Evans, PSI (Royal Warwicks) of the Oldbury Battalion
Sergeant W.C. Fell of the Stourport Battalion
Company Sergeant Major F. Field DCM MM, of the BSA Unit, Redditch Battalion
Sergeant L. Field of A Company, Warley Battalion
Company Sergeant Major J.T. Flack of B Company, Bromsgrove Battalion
Private E. Foster of the Kidderminster Battalion
Sergeant F. Fourt of the Malvern Battalion
Sergeant C.P. Fowler of B Company, Evesham Battalion
Private G. Fox of the Dudley Battalion
Lance Corporal C.J.W. French of the Stourport Battalion
Sergeant G.R. Gilley of C Company, Stourbridge Battalion
Sergeant A. Glaze of the Stourport Battalion
Sergeant J.R. Gledhill of the Kidderminster Battalion
Sergeant A.E. Goodall of the Evesham Battalion
Company QM Sergeant G.H. Goodrich of the Worcester City Battalion
Sergeant J.W. Greenhow of the Stourport Battalion

Sergeant A. George of C Company, Warley Battalion
Sergeant J.E. Gunn of the Halesowen Battalion
Sergeant G. Hadley of E Company, Warley Battalion
Sergeant J. Halford of B Company, Evesham Battalion
Sergeant R.E. Hand of D Company, Stourbridge Battalion
Sergeant T.E. Harcombe of the Malvern Battalion
Sergeant F.J. Harper of the Malvern Battalion
Sergeant R. Harris of the Redditch Battalion
Lieutenant C.H. Harrison of the Redditch Battalion
Lance Corporal L. Heally of the Warley Battalion
Regimental Sergeant Major A.J. Hennery of the Dudley Battalion
Sergeant W. Hill of the Malvern Battalion
Company Quartermaster Sergeant H. Hobbs of the Bromsgrove Battalion
Captain R.W. Holder of the Worcester City Battalion and Warwick M T Column
Lance Sergeant E.S. Holland of the Dudley Battalion
Sergeant K.L. Hollis of the Redditch Battalion
Company QM Sergeant L. Howles of the Kidderminster Battalion
Company QM Sergeant F.A. Jones of the Kidderminster Battalion
Sergeant J.V. Jones of B Company, Warley Battalion
Corporal W.R. Jones of the Dudley Battalion
Sergeant S. John of the Dudley Battalion
Volunteer E.T.G. Kingsworth of B Company, Warley Battalion
Company Sergeant Major W.F. Knight of D Company, Bromsgrove Battalion
Sergeant J.H. List of the Stourport Battalion
Captain H.P. Long of the Stourport Battalion
Sergeant W.F. Lott of C Company, Stourbridge Battalion
Sergeant T.M. Mathews of E Company, Halesowen Battalion
Sergeant C.J. McCann of the Malvern Battalion
Captain C.R. Millett of the Kidderminster Battalion
Sergeant R.J. Newey of the Dudley Battalion
Company QM Sergeant F.W. Overton of the Dudley Battalion
Lieutenant H. Palethorpe of the Stourbridge Battalion
Sergeant J. Parker of Halesowen Battalion
Sergeant A. Peake of A Company, Bromsgrove Battalion
Sergeant S.A. Percival of the Worcester City Battalion
Captain F.C. Perrett of the Kidderminster Battalion*
Private J. Phillips of B Company, Bromsgrove Battalion
Sergeant W.B. Powell of F Company, Stourbridge Battalion
Private J.W. Preece of the Kidderminster Battalion
Sergeant J.F. Price of C Company, Warley Battalion
Lance Corporal S.J. Raybould of the Dudley Battalion
Sergeant G.C. Rees of A Company, Evesham Battalion
Corporal T. Rees of the Kidderminster Battalion
Captain C.E. Reeves of the Dudley Battalion

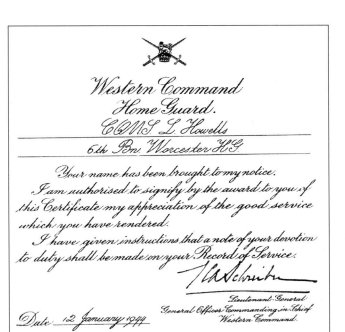

Company Quartermaster Sergeant Lionel Howles, of C Company, Kidderminster Battalion was one of the recipients of the Certificate of Good Service from Western Command, although his name was misspelt on the certificate. CQMS Howles can be seen in the group photograph taken at the King Charles Grammar School in December 1944. He is standing at the right-hand end of the second row. (Both the photograph and the copy of the certificate are courtesy of Judith Ashcroft, daughter of CQMS Howles)

Sergeant W.J. Reynolds, of U Company of Malvern Battalion
Sergeant G.W. Robinson of the Redditch Battalion
Sergeant W.J. Sandals of F Company, Evesham Battalion
Company Sergeant Major H.A. Salisbury of the Evesham Battalion
Sergeant A.V. Savery of the Stourport Battalion
Private R. Savage of the Worcester City Battalion
Private G.P. Sealey of Battalion HQ, Redditch Battalion
Corporal J. Simmons of the Terry's Unit, Redditch Battalion
Private R.M. Simpson of the Kidderminster Battalion
Sergeant S. Smallwood of the Oldbury Battalion
Sergeant A.S. Smith of the Kidderminster Battalion
Sergeant G.F. Smith of the Halesowen Battalion
Staff Sergeant R.V. Smith of the Dudley Battalion
Sergeant A.P. Stephens of the Worcester City Battalion
Major A.N. Stevens, Medical Officer of the Oldbury Battalion
Regimental Sergeant Major G.C. Stevens of the Kidderminster Battalion
Sergeant D.C. Storey of the Stourport Battalion
Sergeant A. Stott of the Halesowen Battalion
Sergeant E.H. Taylor of Malvern Battalion
Sergeant H. Taylor of E Company, Bromsgrove Battalion
Sergeant A.R. Teague of HQ Company, Evesham Battalion
Lance Corporal C. Tilley of the Warley Battalion
2nd Lieutenant R. Tolley of the Stourbridge Battalion
Private E. Vale of the Evesham Battalion
Sergeant J.H. Vobes of the Stourport Battalion
Sergeant H.G. Warner of the Evesham Battalion
Sergeant G.H. Webb of the Evesham Battalion
Sergeant (later 2nd Lieutenant) L.W. Wilkerson of HQ Company, Evesham Battalion
Sergeant J.T. Williams of the Halesowen Battalion
Sergeant P. Wiltshire of the Malvern Battalion*
Sergeant T. Worrall of the Halesowen Battalion
Sergeant C.A. Wright of the Worcester City Battalion
Sergeant P.H. Wright of the Kidderminster Battalion
Sergeant F. Yeomans of the Warley Battalion

In the case of Captain Perrett, the gallantry in question was that when a number of Home Guard were on bombing practice in Kidderminster, one member accidentally dropped a live bomb and with great presence of mind Captain Perrett immediately ordered the men to evacuate the bomb pit and personally seized the dangerous missile which he threw into a place of safety at great risk to himself.[2] This was just one example of gallantry during a number of such instances which occurred during live grenade practice by Home Guards in Worcestershire. Not all were rewarded in this way.

Appendix 7

Rifle Clubs formed after Stand Down in 1944

Normally the number of the battalion was used in the title of rifle clubs but, as elsewhere in this account, the town name is given to clarify the location of the club. In general, the open ranges were used for full-bore (.300 and .303 calibre) shooting and the miniature ranges for .22 calibre shooting. The clubs and their home ranges are:[1]

Worcester City Battalion, HQ Unit, Rifle Club. Brickyard Open Range, and the Drill Hall Miniature Range at 16 Silver Street, Worcester.

Worcester City Battalion, West Unit, Rifle Club. Brickyard Open Range and the Drill Hall Miniature Range at 16 Silver Street, Worcester.

A Company, Worcester City Battalion Rifle Club. Perry Wood Open Range and the Drill Hall Miniature Range at 16 Silver Street, Worcester.

Worcester City Battalion, Railways Rifle Club. No open range, but used the Indoor (Miniature) Range at Shrub Hill Station, Worcester.

Worcester City Battalion, Post Office Rifle Club. Perry Wood Open Range and the Drill Hall Miniature Range at 16 Silver Street, Worcester.

A Company, Bromsgrove Battalion Rifle Club. Hampton Lovett and Whitford Mill Open Ranges and the National Rifle Association Miniature Range at Shepley Sand Pits, near Fairfield.

Bromsgrove Battalion, Wychbold Rifle Club. Hampton Lovett Open Range and the Drill Hall Miniature Range, Droitwich.

B and E Companies, Bromsgrove Battalion Rifle Club. Whitford Range, Bromsgrove, and the Bromsgrove Drill Hall Miniature Range.

Dudley Battalion Rifle Club. Saltwells Open Rifle Range and the Drill Hall Miniature Range, Trindle Road, Dudley.

Dudley Battalion, Goodyear Rifle Club. Saltwells Open Range and the Drill Hall Miniature Range, Trindle Road, Dudley.

No 16 Platoon, D Company, Evesham Battalion Rifle Club. No open range but the Radford Brickyard Miniature Range.

No 11 Platoon (Bredon), Evesham Battalion Rifle Club. No open range but the Bredon Rectory Miniature Range.

Kidderminster Battalion Rifle Club. Hampton Lovett and Tyddesley Wood Open Ranges, but no miniature range.

Crowle Company, Malvern Battalion Rifle Club. Perry Wood, Oddingley and Upton Snodsbury Open Ranges, and the Drill Hall Miniature Range, 16 Silver Street, Worcester.

62nd Mobile Company, Malvern Battalion Rifle Club. West Malvern Range and the Royal Oak Miniature Range, Malvern.

Alvechurch, Redditch Battalion, Home Guard Association Rifle Club, Hampton Lovett Open Range and the Church Road and Easemore Road Drill Halls Miniature Ranges.

Ridgeway and Inkberrow Rifle Club (late D Company 63rd Mobile, Redditch Battalion). Hampton Lovett Open Range but no miniature range.

BSA, Redditch Battalion, Rifle Club. No open range but used the Drill Hall Miniature Range, Church Road, Redditch.

Enfield, Redditch Battalion, Rifle Club. Hampton Lovett Open Range and the Church Road and Easemore Road Drill Halls Miniature Ranges.

Terry's, Redditch Battalion, Rifle Club. Hampton Lovett Open Range and Terry's Miniature Range.

C Company, Redditch Battalion, Rifle Club. Hampton Lovett Open Range and Church Road and Easemore Road Drill Halls Miniature Ranges.

Redditch Battalion HQ Rifle Club. Hampton Lovett Open Range and Church Street and Easemore Road Drill Halls Miniature Ranges.

C Company, Stourport Battalion Rifle Club. No ranges listed.

Warley District Rifle Club (Warley Battalion). Webbs Green Open Range at Witley, and the Drill Hall Miniature Range at Langley.

Quinton District Rifle Club (Warley Battalion). Webbs Green Open Range at Witley, and the Drill Hall Miniature Range at Langley.

Appendix 8

Personnel known to have served in the Worcestershire Auxiliary Units[1]

Captain Lewis Edward Van Moppes (of Ombersley) – Group I (Worcestershire) Leader – Code name 'Castor'. Formerly with Malvern Home Guard Battalion. Date of transfer not recorded, but listed in Part 2 Orders of 8th September 1941 as being already in the Auxiliaries. Still serving in the Auxiliaries at Stand Down. Commissioned Lieutenant in September 1941 and promoted to Captain in April 1944.

Sergeant Thomas Copeland Dawe – Quartermaster Sergeant (of Wolverton Hall, near Peopleton). Enrolled in the Auxiliaries in September 1942 and still serving at Stand Down. Promoted to Corporal in September 1942 and to Sergeant by 1944. He had previously served elsewhere in the LDV/Home Guard, but had resigned in September 1940.

Group 1(a) Patrols

Lieutenant Edmund ('Gug') Van Moppes (of Ombersley) – Group I (a) Leader – Code name 'Pollux'. Formerly with Malvern Battalion Home Guard. Date of transfer not recorded, but listed in Part 2 Orders of 8th September 1941 as already being in the Auxiliaries. Still serving in the Auxiliaries at Stand Down. Commissioned Lieutenant September 1941 and responsible for the following patrols:

David Patrol (Radford/Lenches Area)

Sergeant Algy Herbert 'Alec' Fernihough (of Radford). Formerly with Evesham Battalion Home Guard. Date of transfer not recorded, but listed in Part 2 Orders of 31st January 1942 as already serving in the Auxiliaries. Still serving in the Auxiliaries at Stand Down. Appointed Lance Corporal in June 1941 and promoted to Sergeant by August 1942.

Corporal Harry Theodore Curnock (of Inkberrow). Formerly with Evesham Battalion Home Guard. Date of transfer not recorded, but listed in Part 2 Orders of 31st January 1942 as already serving in the Auxiliaries. Still serving in the Auxiliaries at Stand Down. Appointed Corporal in February 1943.

Private Colin Curnock (of Rous Lench). Formerly with Evesham Battalion Home Guard. Date of transfer not recorded, but listed in Part 2 Orders of 31st January 1942 as already being in the Auxiliaries. Still serving in the Auxiliaries at Stand Down.

Private Arthur Peace 'Tom' Harwood (of Abbots Morton). Formerly with Evesham Battalion Home Guard. Date of transfer not recorded, but listed in Part 2 Orders of 31st January 1942 as already serving in the Auxiliaries. Still serving in the Auxiliaries at Stand Down.

Private Harold Plain (of Radford). Formerly with Evesham Battalion Home Guard, date of transfer not recorded, but listed in Part 2 Orders of 31st January 1942 as already serving in the Auxiliaries. Still serving in the Auxiliaries at Stand Down.

Private Ernest Raymond Shervington (of Rous Lench). Formerly with Evesham Battalion Home Guard. Date of transfer not recorded, but listed in Part 2 Orders of 31st January 1942 as already serving in the Auxiliaries. Still serving in the Auxiliaries at Stand Down.

Private Harold Wilkins (of Rous Lench). Formerly with Evesham Battalion Home Guard. Date of transfer not recorded, but listed in Part 2 Orders of 31st January 1942 as already serving in the Auxiliaries. Still serving with the Auxiliaries at Stand Down.

Jehu Patrol (Alfrick/Lulsley Area)

Sergeant Anthony Seymour Barling (of Alfrick). Formerly with Malvern Battalion Home Guard. Date of transfer not recorded, but listed in Part 2 Orders of 22nd October 1941 as already serving in the Auxiliaries. Discharged from the Auxiliaries to the Parachute Regiment in December 1942. Appointed Sergeant in March 1941.

Sergeant George Dalley (of Suckley). Formerly with Malvern Battalion Home Guard. Date of transfer not recorded, but listed in Part 2 Orders of 22nd October as already serving in the Auxiliaries. Still serving with the Auxiliaries at Stand Down. Appointed Section Commander in the Home Guard in August 1940. Appointed Corporal in the Auxiliaries in February 1943 and Sergeant in April 1943.

Corporal Arthur Leighton Allen (of Dines Green). Formerly with Worcester City Battalion Home Guard. Date of transfer not recorded, but still already serving in the Auxiliaries at Stand Down. Appointed Corporal in April 1943.

Private Christopher Bullock (of Alfrick). Formerly with Malvern Battalion Home Guard. Date of transfer not recorded, but discharged from the Auxiliaries to the RAF in July 1941.

Private Peter Bussey (of Ladywood, Droitwich). Enrolled in the Worcester City Battalion Home Guard in March 1942. Date of transfer not recorded, but serving with the Auxiliaries at Stand Down.

Private William James Griffin (of Suckley). Enrolled in the Malvern Home Guard in August 1942 and transferred to the Auxiliaries in September 1942. Still serving with the Auxiliaries at Stand Down.

Private William Fergus Jauncey (of Storridge). Formerly with Malvern Battalion Home Guard. Transfer not recorded, but listed in Part 2 Orders of 22nd October 1941 as being in the Auxiliaries. Transferred from the Auxiliaries back to that battalion in July 1942.

Private Albert George Jeynes (of Suckley). Formerly with Malvern Battalion Home Guard. Transfer not recorded, but listed in Part 2 Orders of 22nd October 1941 as already being in the Auxiliaries. Transferred from the Auxiliaries back to that battalion in December 1942. Appointed Corporal in May 1941.

Private Reginald Francis Mason (of Lulsley). Formerly with Malvern Battalion Home Guard. Transfer not recorded, but listed as in Part 2 Orders of 22nd October 1941 as already being in the Auxiliaries. Transferred from the Auxiliaries back to that battalion in November 1941. Appointed Lance Corporal in October 1942.

Private William James Plaskett (of Longley Green). Formerly with Malvern Battalion Home Guard. Transfer not recorded, but listed in Part 2 Orders of 22nd October 1941 as already being in the Auxiliaries. Still serving in the Auxiliaries at Stand Down.

Private Horace Kitchener Phillips (of Suckley). Formerly with Malvern Battalion Home Guard. Transferred to Jehu Patrol in November 1941 and transferred back to the Home Guard in September 1942.

Private Joseph Poole (of Upper Broadheath). Enrolled in the Auxiliaries in August 1943 and still serving at Stand Down. No reference to him being in a local Home Guard battalion is recorded.

Overbury Patrol (the biblical name has not been identified)

Sergeant Thurston Holland-Martin (of Overbury). Formerly with Evesham Battalion Home Guard. Transfer not recorded, but listed in Part 2 Orders of 31st January 1942 as already a Sergeant in the Auxiliaries. Discharged in February 1943 as a result of ill health. Appointed Section Commander in December 1940 and promoted to Sergeant in March 1941.

Sergeant Basil Kenneth Tadman (of Overbury). Formerly with Evesham Battalion Home Guard. Transfer not recorded, but listed in Part 2 Orders of 31st January 1942 as already being in the Auxiliaries. Still serving with the Auxiliaries at Stand Down. Appointed Squad Commander in October 1940, but relinquished this position in March 1941. Appointed Sergeant in August 1942.

Corporal Wilfrid Jack Hall (of Overbury). Formerly with Evesham Battalion Home Guard. Transfer not recorded, but listed in Part 2 Orders of 31st January 1942 as already being in the Auxiliaries. Still serving in the Auxiliaries at Stand Down. Appointed Corporal in February 1943.

Private Edmund Atkins (of Overbury). Enrolled in Auxiliaries in January 1943 and still serving in the Auxiliaries at Stand Down. No reference to him previously being in a local Home Guard battalion is recorded.

Private Charles Henry Morris (of Dumbleton). Formerly with the Evesham Battalion Home Guard. Transfer not recorded, but listed in Part 2 Orders of 31st January 1942 as already being in the Auxiliaries. Discharged from the Auxiliaries in November 1943 as disabled following a road accident.

Private Alfred Henry 'Packy' Packwood (of Overbury). Formerly with Evesham Battalion Home Guard. Transfer not recorded, but listed in Part 2 Orders of 31st January 1942 as already being in the Auxiliaries. Still serving with the Auxiliaries at Stand Down.

Private Reg Wilkinson (of Overbury). Formerly with Evesham Battalion Home Guard. Transfer not recorded, but listed in Part 2 Orders of 31st January 1942 as already being in the Auxiliaries. Still serving with the Auxiliaries at Stand Down.

Group 1(b) Patrols

2nd Lieutenant Roger Smith (of Lower Crowle). Formerly with Malvern Battalion Home Guard. Transfer not recorded, but listed in Part 2 Orders of 1st October 1941 as already being a Volunteer in the Auxiliaries. Still serving in the Auxiliaries at Stand Down. Promoted to Sergeant in Joshua Patrol in March 1941. Commissioned 2nd Lieutenant in May 1944 and appointed Group I (b) Leader (code name not known), responsible for the following patrols:

Claines Patrol (the biblical name has not been identified)

Sergeant Richard Hugh Philips (of Claines). Formerly with Worcester City Battalion Home Guard. Transfer not recorded, but still serving with the Auxiliaries at Stand Down. Appointed Sergeant in July 1942.

Corporal Vincent Poland (of Ombersley). Formerly with Malvern Battalion Home Guard. Transfer not recorded, but listed in Part 2 Orders of 1st October 1941 as already being in the Auxiliaries. Still serving in the Auxiliaries at Stand Down. Appointed Corporal in February 1943.

Private Henry Roy Dorrell (of Spetchley). Appears to have joined the Auxiliaries directly in August 1943 and it is assumed, because the Dorrell family had connections with the Claines Patrol, this was the patrol he joined. His discharge date is not recorded but it was before Stand Down. No record of him previously serving in a local Home Guard battalion has been found.

Private George Fowler Graham (of Ombersley). Formerly with Worcester City Battalion Home Guard, but date of transfer not recorded. Discharged from the Auxiliaries in April 1943 to HM Forces.

Private Andrew George Green (of Ombersley). Formerly with Malvern Battalion Home Guard, date of transfer not recorded, but still serving in the Auxiliaries at Stand Down.

Private Hubert Samuel Jackson (of Acton, near Ombersley). Formerly with Malvern Battalion Home Guard and transferred to the Auxiliary Patrol in October 1941. Still serving in the Auxiliaries at Stand Down.

Private Horace Cuthbert Roberts (of Dunhampton, near Ombersley). Formerly with Malvern Battalion Home Guard and transferred to the Auxiliary Patrol in August 1942. Still serving in the Auxiliaries at Stand Down.

Private Frederick Gerald Rowe (of Worcester). Formerly with Worcester City Battalion Home Guard, but date of transfer not recorded. Discharged from the Auxiliaries in December 1942 as medically unfit.

Joshua Patrol (Crowle Area)

Sergeant John Wythes (of Crowle). Formerly with Malvern Battalion Home Guard. Date of transfer not recorded, but listed in Part 2 Orders of 22nd October 1941 as already being in the Auxiliaries. Still serving in the Auxiliaries at Stand Down. Promoted to Corporal in the Auxiliaries in February 1942 and to Sergeant in May 1944 in place of Roger Smith.

Corporal John Ivor Thomas (of Crowle). Formerly with Malvern Battalion Home Guard. Date of transfer not recorded, but listed in Part 2 Orders of 22nd October 1941 as already being in the Auxiliaries. Still serving in the Auxiliaries at Stand Down. Promoted to Corporal in June 1944.

Private Jack Burnley Badger (of Broughton Hackett). Formerly with Malvern Battalion Home Guard. Date of transfer not recorded, but listed in Part 2 Orders of 22nd October 1941 as already being in the Auxiliaries. Still serving in the Auxiliaries at Stand Down.

Private John Edward Hartwright (of Worcester). Enrolled in the Auxiliary Patrol in May 1944 and was still serving in the Auxiliaries at Stand Down. No reference to him being in a local Home Guard battalion is recorded.

Private Albert James Holt (of Crowle). Formerly with Malvern Battalion Home Guard. Date of transfer not recorded, but listed in Part 2 Orders of 22nd October 1942 as already being in the Auxiliaries. Still serving in the Auxiliaries at Stand Down.

Private Noel Herbert Huband (of Crowle). Formerly with Malvern Battalion Home Guard. Date of transfer not recorded, but listed in Part 2 Orders of 22nd October 1942 as already being in the Auxiliaries. Still serving in the Auxiliaries at Stand Down.

Samson Patrol (Broadheath Area)

Sergeant Geoffrey Alfred Devereux (of Lower Broadheath). Formerly with Malvern Battalion Home Guard. Formed the Auxiliary Patrol in July/August 1940. Discharged from the

Auxiliaries to the Grenadier Guards in August 1941. Date of appointment to Sergeant not found.

Sergeant Rupert Valentine Clines (of Upper Broadheath). Formerly with Malvern Battalion Home Guard, transferred in July/August 1940 and still serving in the Auxiliaries at Stand Down. Appointed Sergeant to replace Geoff Devereux in September 1941.

Private Archibald Victor Clines (of Upper Broadheath). Formerly with Malvern Battalion Home Guard, transferred in July/August 1940, and discharged from the Auxiliaries to the Merchant Navy in February 1944. Appointed Corporal in February 1943.

Private Robert Henry Boaz (of Cotheridge). Formerly with Malvern Battalion Home Guard transferred in July/August 1940, and discharged from the Auxiliaries to the RAF in January 1942.

Private John Frederick Boaz (of Cotheridge). Formerly with Malvern Battalion Home Guard, transferred in November 1941 and still serving in the Auxiliaries at Stand Down.

Private Joseph King (of Lower Broadheath). Formerly with Worcester City Battalion Home Guard, transferred in July/August 1940, and discharged from the Auxiliaries to an Anti-Tank Regiment. Date not found.

Private Peter Robert King (of Lower Broadheath). Formerly with Worcester City Battalion Home Guard, date of transfer not recorded, but still serving in the Auxiliaries at Stand Down.

Private Ronald Percival Frank Seymour (of Worcester) Formerly with Worcester City Battalion Home Guard and transferred in July/August 1940. Transferred from the Auxiliaries to a Heavy Anti-Aircraft unit of the Gloucestershire Home Guard in January 1942.

Private Peter Pryce Wright (of Lower Broadheath). Formerly with Worcester City Battalion Home Guard, date of transfer not recorded, but still serving in the Auxiliaries at Stand Down.

Patrols which pre-dated the group system

BBC Wood Norton Patrol (the biblical name has not been identified)

Volunteer William Bruce Purslow, Patrol Leader (of Wood Norton). Served with Evesham Battalion Home Guard. Date of transfer not recorded, but listed in Part 2 Orders of 31st January 1942 as already a Volunteer in the Auxiliaries. Discharged from the Auxiliaries between February and September 1942.

Volunteer William Hudson Birrell Harley (of Stratford on Avon). Served with Evesham Battalion Home Guard. Date of transfer not recorded, but listed in Part 2 Orders of 31st January 1942 as already a Volunteer in the Auxiliaries. Discharged from the Auxiliaries between February and September 1942. Appointed Section Commander in May 1940.

Malvern Patrol (the biblical name has not been identified)

Volunteer Acres. Formerly of Malvern Battalion Home Guard, date of transfer not recorded but discharged from both the Home Guard and Auxiliaries as surplus to establishment in July 1941.

Volunteer Burton. As above.

Volunteer Vincent. As above.

Volunteer Vines. As above.

Volunteer Whitely. As above.   (Unfortunately, no first names have been found)

Appendix 9

Training Facilities[1]

Out of county Home Guard training schools

In addition to the Home Guard training schools at Osterley, Dorking, Moncrieff House and Onibury, a number of other schools outside the Midlands and attended by Worcestershire Home Guards have been identified as:

Blacon Camp, near Chester, where week-long courses on Field Defences were given from 1941.

Burwash, in Kent, where from 1942, the South East Command Army Field Craft School was being run by Major J Langton Davies. He also had had experience of the Spanish Civil War and was to write and broadcast on the BBC on the subject of battle craft.

Burscough REME Central Armourers Workshops, north of Liverpool. Here week-long courses were available from 1941 for Home Guard NCOs wishing to qualify as armourers and be able to carry out minor repairs and adjustments to weapons issued to the force.

Cambridge, presumably one of the university colleges, where training was given to Home Guard Medical Officers.

Doddington Hall, near Nantwich where, from 1942, a Western Command School provided two-week courses for Senior Home Guard officers, including battalion and company commanders. Umpires courses were also provided.

Glenridding, near Ullswater in the Lake District, the Army Gas School, where week-long courses on the subject were available.

Knutsford had the Northern Junior Leaders School from 1941, where week-long courses on tactics were provided.

Prestatyn, north Wales, where the 12th Pioneer Corps Training Centre provided signals training for Home Guards during 1944.

Ripon, where a two-week course for Bomb Disposal Auxiliaries was provided.

Winterbourne Gunner, near Salisbury, the Army Chemical Warfare School, where five day courses were available from 1942.

Local Home Guard schools

Local Home Guard schools were established in the following locations:

Barnt Green, Worcestershire. The location of the Birmingham Zone Weapons Training School here has yet to be identified, where six-day courses were provided in 1941 and '42. Men from battalions from outside the Birmingham Zone attended this school, including Worcestershire. In January 1943, this school moved to Umberslade Park in Warwickshire.

Birmingham, Bristol Road, where the GHQ School of Street Fighting was located. Two-day courses were also available at Birmingham University for Home Guard Intelligence Officers, and six-day courses at the Central Midlands District School of Tactics in Sutton Park.

Burnhill Green, to the west of Wolverhampton. The Birmingham Zone Weapons Training School was located here and was attended by at least some of the Dudley Home Guards.

Bromsgrove. Properties in St Johns Street were used to provide Street Fighting courses.

Chateau Impney, Droitwich. The Civil Defence Training School here provided Rescue Squad training.

Highdown Camp at Bishops Tachbrook, to the south of Warwick, provided a variety of courses including anti-sabotage, as well as five days of wireless training for those Home Guards already classified as signallers and capable of reading ten words a minute.

Ludlow, Castle Lodge Junior Leaders School, where courses covered leadership, fire control, fieldcraft, reconnaissance, day and night fighting and patrols, plans, orders, messages and reports, map reading, wood, village and street fighting, TEWTs, quick decision making, preparation of training schemes and administration in the field.

Malvern. The West of England Quarry was utilised for gas decontamination demonstrations to Home Guards and Civil Defence personnel from elsewhere in the county.

Neechells, in the Black Country. Demonstrations were given in the public swimming baths there of swimming in uniform and with equipment.

Norton Barracks, Worcester. No 23 Infantry Training Centre made their training staff available to the Home Guard battalions in the county. The staff would either visit and provide instruction at Battalion or Company Headquarters, or would provide training at the Barracks. The latter included such diverse instruction as junior leaders courses, live grenade training, including the qualification of Home Guard instructors, as at Altcar, battle innoculation and cooking courses.

Redditch. Intelligence courses, in the form of evening lectures, were provided in the County High School from 1943. The courses covered: Organisation of Intelligence – how to get information and how to distribute it; Organisation of a Battle Room and duties of Intelligence personnel during operations; Organisation of an OP; Message and report writing and keeping an intelligence diary. An unarmed combat demonstration was also held at the Drill Hall in Church Road.

Umberslade Park, between Tanworth in Arden and Hockley Heath, was the location of Central Midland District Weapons Training School from 1943, and provided five-day courses on subjects as diverse as Demolitions and the 2 Pounder Anti-Tank Gun.

Wickhamford. The Evesham Battalion organised a battalion training school at Wickhamford Manor under the direction of Major Sydney Carter.

Whittington Barracks, Lichfield, provided shooting camps.

Worcester. The District Home Guard School at Silver Street Drill Hall, provided Intelligence Courses over a week of evenings. Street fighting was taught in the housing areas in Sidbury.

Home Guard camp sites

The following Home Guard camp venues for each battalion or sector have been identified:

Worcester City Battalion. The hutments at Tyddesley Wood Rifle Range (SO921 449).

Bromsgrove Battalion. Hewell Grange (SP 009 6890 and Hagley Park (SO 920 808).

Evesham Battalion. The Dingle, Elmley Castle (SO 980 405) and the Tyddesley Wood Rifle Range hutments.

Halesowen Battalion. Walton. (Presumed to be Walton Hill, Clent, at SO 940 796).

Kidderminster Battalion. Sutton Park, Kidderminster, adjoining the rifle range (SO 812 748).

Malvern Battalion. The Hill, Berrow, at SO 805 351, for battalion weekend camps, with M (Malvern) Company also using Fairoaks Farm, Malvern Wells, O (Ombersley) Company using Hadley Farm barn, Tyddesley Wood and Horsham, and U (Upton) Company using the searchlight site hutments at Severn Stoke.

Oldbury Battalion. Lapal (exact site not identified).

Redditch Battalion. Weatheroak Park at SP 063 745, Berrow Hill near Feckenham, at SO 997 622, and the searchlight hutments at Holberrow Green, at SP 023 594.

Stourbridge Battalion. Whittington, near Kinver, at SO 850 829.

Stourport Battalion. The area immediately around Witley Court, at SO 769 649. Also the field opposite the church at Shelsley Beauchamp used by D Company (Tenbury) and the Abberley Platoon.

Warley Battalion. Lapal (site not identified).

O Sector. Palmers Hill, Hagley.

19th Century and Territorial Army Rifle Ranges

A number of rifle ranges established by the 19th Century Rifle Volunteers and kept in use by the Territorial Force (later Territorial Army) until the Second World War, were used by the Home Guard. These were:

Hampton Lovett. A 600 yard range at SO 895 656. No longer used and only the location of the butts can now be seen. Land adjoining this range was also used by the Home Guard for sub-artillery firing. Both the Bromsgrove and Redditch Battalions used the rifle range regularly.

Hanbury. A 600 yard range near Summerhill Farm at SO 833 633. No longer used but the butts and some of the firing points can still be seen. This range appears to have been used only by the Hanbury Home Guard

Kidderminster, Sutton Park, off Rifle Range Road. A 700 yard range at SO 812 747. This range was used by the Home Guard for both rifle and machinegun practice and the area around for fieldcraft training. The range was used by the Kidderminster, Stourport and Halesowen Battalions, until it was prematurely closed during the war as a result of development within the danger zone. The butts and some of the firing points still exist.

Malvern. Two ranges were used at Malvern: a 600 yard range in West Malvern, at SO 760 467. This range is no longer in use but the butts location can be clearly seen from the North Hill as a notch in the woodlands parallel to the Malvern Hills and one or two of the longer range firing platforms can be found in the farmland. The other range was that established by Malvern College for their OTC and located to the south of the college, near the Firs Close.

Tenbury. A 600 yard range at SO 589 680. No longer used and nothing remains to be seen. This range was interesting in so far as the firing points were in the meadow on the north side of the River Teme and the butts on the south side with shots carrying over the river at an oblique angle. Used by D Company (Tenbury) of the Stourport Battalion.

Tyddesley Wood, near Pershore. A 600 yard range at SO 924 448. Used by both the Worcester and Evesham Battalions during the Second World War. It is still in use.

Upton upon Severn. Located on Upper Ham, to the south-east of the town, at SO 859 385, this was a 1,000 yard range. It is no longer used but the substantial brick-built butts can still be seen at the southern end of the Ham, together with a few of the firing points. Used by U (Upton) Company of the Malvern Battalion.

Whitford Mill, Bromsgrove. A 600 yard range at SO 946 706. This was removed when the M5 was built and nothing remains. Used by both Redditch and Bromsgrove Battalions.

Worcester. A 600 yard range below Perry Wood, at SO 863 547. The area has been developed with housing and nothing of the range remains. Used by many Home Guard companies during sector and inter-zonal competitions. A second pre-war short range, located in the Merriman's Hill brickyard at SO 851 564, was also used by Worcester City Battalion for full-bore (.300 calibre) rifle shooting and automatic weapons firing.

A number of these older established ranges continued to be used by the Territorial Army in the post-war years, and were available for use by the 1950s Home Guard, notably the Tyddesley Wood, Whitford Mill and Hampton Lovett ranges. The Territorial Drill Hall in each town also had a built-in small bore 25 yard range, which was made available to the Home Guard.

Temporary Home Guard ranges

Temporary Ranges were established by the Home Guard at the following locations:

Abberley. A short automatic firing range was established in the quarry at Apostle's Oak by C Company of the Stourport Battalion at SO 747 675.

Alvechurch. The former brickyard, now the marina, to the west of the village was used by the Alvechurch Company for rifle and automatic firing at SP 021 721.

Churchill. A full-bore 200 yard range was established by the Stourbridge Battalion, near Brake Lane, at SO 889 803. It is strange that the former, but long abandoned, 19th-century 600 yard range, located only a short distance to the west, was not reactivated.

Cookhill. A short, full-bore range was established by the Cookhill Home Guard, just to the east of The Ridgeway at SP 057 586.

Cookley. A full-bore range was established on the north-east side of the village by the Stourbridge Battalion at SO 836 804.

Eastham. A temporary range was constructed by the Tenbury Home Guard, in a quarry on the north side of the main Worcester to Tenbury road, at approximately SO 661 695.

Fladbury. A full-bore range was established at Machine Farm by the Evesham Battalion Home Guard at approximately SO 998 476.

Great Witley. A 200 yard full-bore range was established by C Company of the Stourport Battalion near Hill House Farm, firing from near the main road, across a small valley into the bank opposite, at SO 763 662.

Hallow. A full-bore 200 yard range was established by P Company of the Malvern Battalion to the east of Hallow Park, firing from the riverside into the bank below the big house at SO 831 583. A second small-bore (.22 calibre) range was also established to the south of Peachley Lane firing into the bank of Laugherne Brook at SO 824 578.

Hartlebury Common. A small bore .22 range was established by the Stourport Battalion in a small quarry at SO 825 710. It is surprising that one or other of the several 19th-century ranges on the Common, abandoned at the turn of the 20th century, was not re-commissioned by the Home Guard!

Hartlebury 25 MU. A sophisticated indoor small bore range was constructed here in 1944, which included a model landscape and simulated parachute landings.

Holt Fleet. A full bore 200 yard range was established in the large field to the east of The Wharf Inn, at SO 828 634, by O Company of the Malvern Battalion, firing from near the river and diagonally across the field, into the bank. This range was also used for sub-artillery firing.

Inkberrow. A short, full-bore range was established on the opposite side of the lane to the church by D Company of the Redditch Battalion at SP 017 574.

Kidderminster. A short automatic firing range was established by the Kidderminster Battalion in the quarry within Oldington Wood, on the Stourport Road. This was located at SO 824 745.

Knightwick. A full-bore 200 yard range was established here by K Company of the Malvern Battalion to the south of the A44 road, firing from near the road into Osebury Rock, on the south side of the River Teme, at SO 737 557. This range was also used for automatic weapon (BAR) firing. A second short range for Sten practice was established nearby at Black's Well, at SO 736 554, firing into the end of the hill here.

Malvern Link. The clay pit at Belmont Brickworks, Cowleigh Bank, provided a short range for automatic weapons practice for the Malvern Battalion. The pit has now been filled and covered with new houses but was located at SO 771 476.

Marsh Common, Baughton. A temporary full-bore 200 yard range was established here by M Company of the 7th Malvern Battalion firing from where the M5 Motorway is now into the bank below the wood to the east at SO 888 421.

Redditch. A full-bore 200 yard range was established behind the HDA Company works in Windsor Road by the 9th Worcestershire (Redditch) Battalion firing from south to north into Lowan's Hill at SP 037 688. A second full-bore 200 yard range was established by the Terry family firing from behind their house alongside The Slough into the hill of Rough Hill Wood at SP 050 639. A third full-bore range, used by the BSA Company, utilised their weapons testing range and butts behind the works at SP 055 668.

A number of small-bore ranges were established, including at Terry's Spring Works and at HDA.

Ribbesford House. A 200 yard full-bore range, established by the Free French at the House, was regularly used by the Stourport and Kidderminster Battalions for firing practice. The location of the firing points was to the south of the House at SO 786 738, and that of the butts on the edge of Ribbesford Woods, near the present mobile home park.

Saltwells, at Brierley Hill. Used by the Dudley Battalion, this range was established in the former quarry, at SO 937 871, in what is now Saltwells Park, to the east of the present day Merry Hill Shopping Centre.

Severn Stoke. A full-bore 200 yard range was established here by the Malvern Battalion, firing from near the church into Severn Bank Wood. Nothing remains to be seen of the range that was located at SO 856 435.

Welland. A short, small bore range was established by the Welland Platoon to the north-east of the village, in a small valley at SO 803 400.

Wildmoor. A short full-bore range was established by the Bromsgrove Battalion in the large sandpit to the south of the A491 at SO 952 759. This range was also used for automatic weapons practice.

Witley Bank, Stourbridge Road, Halesowen. A short full-bore range established by the Halesowen Battalion.

Wollaston. A full and small-bore 25 yard range, was established by the Stourbridge Battalion in the former quarry behind the Foresters Arms on the Bridgnorth road out of Wollaston, at SO 882 848.

A number of small bore ranges are mentioned above but there were many others used by the Home Guards, including those at every drill hall in the county, and those at the Post Offices in Great Malvern and Worcester.

Grenade ranges

The following Home Guard grenade ranges in the county have been recorded:

Alvechurch. The brickyard was used for grenade training, as well as for rifle firing, by the Alvechurch Company.

Berrow Hill, near Martley. This range was established by K Company of the Malvern Battalion in the ramparts on the west side of this former Iron Age Fort at SO 744 585. This range was also used for Blacker Bombard and Northover Projector firing.

Bushley. Established in a former quarry, alongside the drive to Pull Court by U Company of Malvern Battalion, at SO 862 351.

Elmley Lovett. This range was established by the Bromsgrove Battalion in the open field beyond the wooded area, to the east of the railway, at SO 892 655, where the land form provides a natural amphitheatre. Bill Allington, who was an authorised instructor on grenades for the Bromsgrove Battalion, described the facility as a three-bay sandbagged breastwork, each bay of 'U' shape. The first bay was used for fusing grenades, the second bay for throwing and a third so that, if a grenade was accidentally dropped, it was possible to quickly duck around to the adjoining bay for protection from the blast. A 100 yard protection zone around the throwing bay meant that the facility was placed near the centre of the field. The Americans also used this range and Bill recalls that they were not too careful where they left their grenades. On one occasion he trod on a grenade left by them in the grass of the throwing bay! This range was also used for Blacker Bombard and Northover Projector practice.

Great Witley. Walsgrove Quarry, at SO 744 660, was utilised for throwing practice with Molotov Cocktails by C Company of the Stourport Battalion.

Hanbury Brick Works. This was in the former clay pit, now a waste disposal site between the canal and railway at SO 926 630.

Hartlebury Common. The location of this range has yet to be positively identified but is said to be somewhere on the ridgeline at approximately SO 828 708. A Flame Fougasse demonstration was also given on Hartlebury Common and was likely to have been in the same location.

Hinton on the Green. A purpose-built grenade range was constructed on the side of the wooded Furze Hill by the Evesham Battalion at approximately SP 005 405.

Holt Heath. The small quarry at SO 816 626, alongside the drive to Bentley Farm, was used by the Ombersley Company.

Norton. In addition to the grenade range at the Barracks, the clay pit at the brickworks, to the south of the Barracks, at SO 874 513, was also used by Home Guards, including the Ombersley Company, who trained with the sticky bomb here.

Redditch. This range was established by the Redditch Battalion in the butts of the former 19th-century rifle range in Pitcher Oak Wood. This is located in the disused quarry at SP 032 672.

Romsley. The Halesowen Battalion established a range at Shutt Mill Quarry. The location of this facility has yet to be identified.

Rowney Green. A sand pit here (not identified) was used by the Alvechurch Company for throwing practice with Molotov Cocktails.

Tyddesley Wood. Throwing bays adjoining the rifle range were used for grenade training.

Artillery and sub-artillery ranges

The following artillery and sub-artillery ranges have been recorded:

Berrow Hill, near Martley. This grenade range was also used by the Malvern Battalion for both Northover Projector and Spigot Mortar firing. Some of the Home Guard battalions from the Birmingham area also used this range.

Bredon's Norton. Evesham Battalion established a sub-artillery range in Norton Park behind the big house and firing towards Bredon Hill, at SO 938 391.

Bushley. Both Northover Projectors and Spigot Mortars were fired here, firing from the bottom of the hill, near Pull Court, at SO 864 355, into the quarry referred to above as a grenade range. Small artillery pieces were also observed by a local witness to be fired on this range but the type was not identified. These may have been Hotchkiss 6pdrs.

British Camp, Malvern. Instruction on the 6 Pounder Hotchkiss guns was given initially here by Royal Artillery staff and later the range was used for live firing practice by various Home Guard battalions from both Worcestershire and Warwickshire. The firing point was from close by the Wardens House, on the north side of the reservoir, and the targets were placed on the opposite side of the reservoir, where the shot would be absorbed by the butt of Broad Down Hill. This site, at SO 764 399, appears to have been the only practice range in the county for this weapon.

Castlemorton Common. The common was used by the Malvern Battalion for Spigot Mortar practice. Firing was from near the junction of the main road and the road to the Gullet quarry towards a target on the common to the west at approximately SO 786 391.

Elmley Lovett. As noted above, the open field to the east of the railway at SO 892 655 was used for Northover Projector practice and competitions; the surrounding slopes would contain any wayward bombs. This range is separate from, and some way to the south of, the rifle range.

High Habberley. Spigot Mortar Range used by the Stourport Battalion. Precise site not identified.

Holt Fleet. The rifle range established by the Ombersley Company, to the east of the Wharfe Inn, was also used for Spigot Mortar firing. A separate range for the Northover Projector involved firing from in front of the Holt Fleet Hotel, across the river into the triangular field opposite, at SO 824 634.

Hinton on the Green. The grenade range at Furze Hill was also used by the Evesham Battalion for Spigot Mortar practice.

Knightwick. Both Northover Projectors and Spigot Mortars were fired at a moving target, towed behind Major Clarke's car to simulate a moving tank. The firing point was from the rear of the Knightwick Company headquarters, i.e. Dr Clarke's back garden, across the River Teme into the Ham behind the Talbot Inn at SO 730 561.

Malvern Common. The Malvern Company used this venue for firing the Spigot Mortar, firing from the western extremity, parallel to Longridge Road towards Poolbrook at SO 784 442. Apparently one wayward inert practice round was fired into the pool on the common and remains there to this day. The Wells Common, further up Peachfield Road, was also used by the TRE Home Guard for Northover practice.

Tyddesley Wood. The rifle range here was also used for Spigot Mortar practice.

Field or battle training

Areas of countryside used for this purpose are:

Berrow. Apparently organised by Colonel Johnson of the Malvern Battalion, this facility at The Hill, near Birtsmorton Court, (SO 807 350) allowed for fieldcraft training and battle training with live firing. The men staying for a weekend course would be accommodated in the farm buildings.

Berrow Hill, near Feckenham. Located at SO 997 621, Redditch Battalion used this for battle training.

Combe Green Common. Malvern Battalion used the area of common opposite Birt Street, at SO 775 365, for fieldcraft training.

The Dingle, Elmley Castle. The Evesham Battalion established a Battle Innoculation facility at SO 980 405 in 1943.

Elmley Lovett. Bromsgrove Battalion established a similar facility in the wooded area, to the east of the church, at SO 891 656.

Madresfield Park and Upper Woodsfield Farm. Used particularly by the Malvern Company for battle training, the farm at SO 816 486, apparently being the scene of a memorable 'battle' in October 1941.

Stambermill, Lye. Located at SO 918 848, this wooded valley was used by the Stourbridge Battalion for fieldcraft and battle training. An old building on the site provided the opportunity to practise street fighting, with grenades being hurled through windows and so on.

Sources of Information

Published Sources

Alanbrooke, Field Marshal Lord *War Diaries 1939-1945* (Weidenfeld and Nicholson, 2001)

Anonymous, *Local Defence Volunteers Instruction 1940 - Tanks and Tank Destruction* (GS Publications, 1940)

Anonymous, *Local Defence Volunteers Instruction 1940 - Notes on Field Defences* (GS Publications, 1940)

Anonymous, *Manual of Small Arms and Special Weapons,* (Barnards Publishers Ltd, undated wartime)

Anonymous, *Small Arms Training Pamphlet - Anti-Tank Rifle 1942* (GS Publications, 1942)

Anonymous, *Home Guard Instruction - Introduction and Battlecraft 1942* (GHQ Home Forces 1942)

Anonymous, *Home Guard Instruction - Patrolling 1943* (GHQ Home Forces 1943)

Anonymous, *Field Engineering (All Arms) - Military Training Pamphlet No. 30 - Part III : Obstacles - 1943* (The War Office, 1943).

Anonymous, *Battlecraft and Battle drill for the Home Guard* (GHQ Home Forces, 1943)

Armour, Major M.D.S. *Total War Training for Home Guard Officers and NCO s* (Thorsons Publishers Ltd, London, undated wartime)

Barlow, Lt Col J.A. SAC. *Small Arms Manual* (John Murran, London 1942)

Battalion Board of the 2nd and 7th Warwickshire Battalions Home Guard, *The Story of A Sector Warwickshire Home Guard* (George Over [Rugby] Ltd 1946)

Bekker, Cajus *The Luftwaffe War Diaries* (Macdonald & Co Ltd, 1967)

Birt, David *The Battle of Bewdley* (Peter Huxtable Designs Ltd, 1988)

Bodman, Sergeant H.W. *Sten Machine Carbine 9 mm Mk II and Mk III* (Bravon Ledger Co, 1942)

Bright-Astley, Joan *Gubbins and SOE* (Leo Cooper, 1997)

Brophy, John *A Home Guard Drill Book and Field Service Manual* (Hodder & Stoughton, 1941)

Brophy, John. H*ome Guard Proficiency* (Hodder & Stoughton, 1942)

Brophy, John *Britain's Home Guard - A Character Study* (Harrap & Co, 1945)

Churchill, Winston S. *The Second World War. Volume II. Their Finest Hour* (Cassell, 1949)

Crocker. Lt Col H.E. CMG DSO *The Imaginary Battles of Handley Cross* (Keliher, Hudson & Kearns Ltd, undated wartime)

Cullen, Stephen *Home Guard Socialism – A Vision of a People's Army* (Allotment Hut Books, 2006)

Cullen, Stephen *In Search of the Real Dad's Army. The Home Guard and the Defence of the United Kingdom, 1940-1944* (Pen and Sword Books Ltd, 2011)

Cuthbert, Captain S.J. *We Shall Fight in the Streets - Guide to Street Fighting.* (Gale & Polden, 1941)

Douglas, Alton *The Black Country at War* (Beacon Radio, 1984)

Elliot, Andrew G. and others *The Home Guard Encyclopedia* (Thorsons Publishers, undated wartime)

Fairbairn, Captain W.E. and Wallbridge, Captain P.N. *All-In Fighting* (Faber & Faber, 1942)

Gander, Terry *Allied Infantry Weapons of World War Two* (The Crowood Press, 2000)

Gaunt, H.C.A. *Two Exiles – A School in Wartime* (Samson Lowe, Marston Co Ltd, 1946)

Graves, Charles *The Home Guard of Britain.* (Hutchinson, 1943)

Gilbert, Martin *Finest Hour - Winston S Churchill 1939-41* (William Heineman Ltd, 1983)

Green, Brig General A.F.U. *Home Guard Pocket Book* (Worthington Gazette, undated wartime)

Haycraft, Major J.M. *The Company Commanders Training and Administrative Handbook* (Gale & Polden, 1941)

Hipkiss, James *Your Answer to Invasion - Unarmed Combat* (F.W. Bridges Ltd, undated wartime)

Hogg, Ian *The Encyclopedia of Infantry Weapons of World War II* (Bison Books, 1977)

Holloway, B.G. and Banks, H. *The Northamptonshire Home Guard.* (Northamptonshire Home Guard, 1949)

Jones, Colin; Lowry, Bernard and Wilks, Mick. *20th Century Defences in Britain – The West Midlands Area* (Logaston Press, 2008)

Jong, Louis de *The German Fifth Column in the Second World War* (Routledge and Keegan Paul, 1956)

Kirkland, K.D. *America's Premier Gunmakers* (Magna Books, 1990)

Kissel, Hans *Hitler's Last Levy – The Volksturm 1944-45.* (Helion & Co, 2005)

Knowles, David J. *With Resolve - With Valour. Volunteers of WWII on the Home Shores* (Knowles Publishing, 2002)

Land, Neville *The History of Redditch* (? 1984)

Langton-Davies, Major John *The Home Guard Field Craft Manual.* (John Murray & Pilot Press, 1942)

Langton-Davies, Major John *The Home Guard Training Manual* (no details but a wartime publication)

Levy, 'Yank' *Guerrilla Warfare* (Penguin Books, 1941)

Lousada. Major W.P. MC. *A Guide for the Preparation of Candidates for Home Guard Proficiency Test and Certificate A.* (Gale & Polden, 1944)

Lowry, Bernard *British Home Defences 1940-45* (Osprey Publishing Ltd, 2004)

Lowry, Bernard *The Shropshire Home Guard.* (Logaston Press, 2010)

Lowry, Bernard and Wilks, Mick. *The Mercian Maquis* (Logaston Press, 2002, 2007 and 2012)

Mackay, Major G.S. *General Knowledge for Home Guards* (Arthur Pearson Ltd, 1941).

Mackenzie. S P. *The Home Guard. A Military and Political History* (Oxford University Press, 1995)

Macleod and Kelly (eds) *The Ironside Diaries 1937-1940* (Constable, 1962)

Miller, Howard *Tenbury and District in Wartime* (Howard Miller, undated but 1990s)

Myatt, Major Frederick M. MC *Modern Small Arms* (Salamander Books Ltd, 1978)

Penrose, Roland *Home Guard Manual of Camouflage* (Routledge & Sons, 1941)

RASC, Institution of *The Story of the RASC* (G. Bell & Sons Ltd, 1955)

Sainsbury, Lt Col J.D. *Hazardous Work* (Hart Books, 1985)

Saville-Sneath, R.A. *Aircraft Recognition* (Penguin Books, 1941)

Shore, Captain C. W*ith British Snipers to the Reich* (Greenhill Books, 1948)

Spence, Lt J.C. *They Aslo Serve – The 39th Cheshire Battalion Home Guard* (Nicholls & Co Ltd, 1945)

Street, A.G. *From Dusk to Dawn* (Harrap & Co Ltd, 1942)

Summerfield, P. and Peniston-Bird, C. *Contesting Home Defence – Men, Women and the Home Guard in the Second World War* (Manchester University Press, 2007)

Territorial Army Association, Cambridge *We Also Serve – The Story of the Home Guard in Cambridgeshire and Isle of Ely 1940-1943* (Heffer and Sons Ltd, 1944)

Wade, Col G.A. MC *The Defence of Bloodford Village* (War Office, 1940)

Walker, A.T. *Fieldcraft for the Home Guard* (John Menzies & Co Ltd, 1940)

Warren, G. *Worcestershire at War* (Privately published by the author 1991)

Warwicker, John *With Britain in Mortal Danger* (Cerberus Publishing Ltd, 2002)

Warwicker, John. *Churchill's Underground Army.* (Frontline Books, 2008)

Whittaker, L.B. *Stand Down. Orders of Battle for the units of the Home Guard of the United Kingdom. November 1944* (Ray Westlake Military Books, 1990).

Wintringham, Tom *New Ways of War* (Penguin Books, 1940)

Wintringham, Tom *People's War* (Penguin Books, 1942)

Yelton, David K. *Hitler's Home Guard – Volksturmann – Western Front 1944-45* (Osprey Publishing, 2006)

Other Sources of Information

Worcestershire Home Guard Personnel Records, Worcestershire Home Guard Part I and II Orders, and Home Guards Officers Lists, formerly held by the Army Medal Office, Droitwich, until its closure in 2005

Home Guard papers and photographs held by Evesham Almonry Museum

Home Guard files held by Tenbury Museum

Home Guard files held by the Trustees of the Regimental Museum, Army Reserve Centre, Pheasant Street, Worcester

Home Guard files held by Worcester City Museum

Article by Major A Shelley-Peake in the Worcestershire Regimental magazine, *Firm* of January 1949

The National Archive Files

CAB 123/204 - Home Guard and Civil Defence. (Also deals with Womens Home Guard)

HO 45/25113 - Arrangements for the Demobilisation of the Home Guard

WO 163/414 – Home Guard Sub-Committee of the Army Council

WO 166/1224 - War Diary of the South Midland Area HQ 1939-41

WO 166/1226 - War Diary of the Central Midland Area HQ 1940-41

WO 166/1332 - War Diary of the Birmingham Garrison
WO 166/1634 - War Diary of the 62nd Anti-Tank Regiment 1939-40
WO 166/6786 - War Diary of the Worcestershire Sub Area HQ 1942
WO 166/6787 - War Diary of the Worcestershire Sub Area HQ 1941-42
WO 166/6822 - War Diary of the Central Midland District HQ 1942
WO 166/11016 - War Diary of the Worcester Sub District HQ 1943
WO 166/11027 - War Diary for the Birmingham Garrison 1943
WO 166/16589 - War Diary of the Worcester Sub District HQ 1945
CAB 106/1189 - Summary Report to the Massachusetts Committee on Public Safety, about the Home Guard 1941
CAB 106/1190 - Supplementary Report to the Massachusetts Committee on Public Safety
CAB 123/204 - Home Guard and Civil Defence
PREM 3/223/2 - PM's Correspondence re Home Guard
WO 32/17724 - Disposal of Home Guard Records
WO 199/342 - Railway Home Guard Units
WO 199/344 - Home Guard Sector and Battalion Organisation 1944
WO 199/345 - Home Guard Operational Layouts
WO 199/346 - Home Guard Mounted Patrols
WO 199/350 - Home Guard Stand Down Parades
WO 199/356A - Home Guard LAA Units
WO 199/363 - The Role of the Home Guard
WO 199/365 - The Role of the Home Guard
WO 199/381 - Home Guard LAA Units
WO 199/383 - Home Guard LAA Orders of Battle 1944
WO 199/385 - Home Guard and the RAF Regiment 1942-44
WO 199/387 - Home Guard Training 1942-44
WO 199/388 - Home Guard - Issue of Weapons
WO 199/395 - Home Guard Mobile Units
WO 199/397 - Home Guard Transport Companies 1941-44
WO 199/398 - Enrolment of Boys into the Home Guard and Cadet Force 1942-44
WO 199/399 - Enrolment of boys in the Home Guard and Cadet Force
WO 199/400 - Home Guard Auxiliary Bomb Disposal Units 1942-44
WO 199/401 - Women in the Home Guard
WO 199/414 - Report of Sub-Committee of the Army Council on the HG Oct 1940
WO 199/544 - Keeps, Fortified Villages, Nodal Points and A/T Islands
WO 199/545 - Cooperation with Civil Authorities in Nodal Points
WO 199/589 - Correspondence between the PM and C in C Home Forces
WO 199/605 - Armoured Trains
WO 199/657 - Guards on Vulnerable Points 1942
WO 199/872B - LDV/Home Guard Instruction Pamphlets May 1940 to July 1944
WO 199/1800 - Southern Command memoranda to, inter alia, Central Midland Area
WO 199/1801 - Construction of GHQ Defence Lines
WO 199/3243 - The History of the Formation and Organisation of the HG 1940-44
WO 199/3375 - A History of the Birmingham City Transport Home Guard
WO 199/3376 - A History of the 45th Warwickshire (Birmingham) Bn Home Guard

County Record Office Files
Ref: 004.6 (BA 5204 Parcels 2 and 6) - Territorial Army Association records

References

Introduction

1. From the Foreword to *Halesowen Home Guard 1940 to 1944* compiled by Lieutenant J.G. Mountford, Halesowen August 1944
2. *Finest Hour – Winston S. Churchill 1939 to 1941* by Martin Gilbert
3. *The Home Guard of Britain* by Charles Graves
4. *Halesowen Home Guard*
5. Graves, p.11
6. *Stand Down* by L.B. Whittaker, p.19
7. Graves, p.16
8. TNA File No WO 199/3237 – Emergency Powers (Defence)
9. TNA File Ref No CAB 120/237 – Cabinet Papers
10. These defence arrangements, and particularly those for Worcestershire, are looked at in some detail in my book *The Defence of Worcestershire and the Southern Approaches to Birmingham* (Logaston Press 2007)
11. See *Contesting Home Defence* by Penny Summerfield and Corinna Peniston-Bird

Chapter 1

1. The *Worcester Evening News and Times*, 15th May 1940
2. From a study of enrolment forms formerly held by the Army Medal Office, Droitwich
3. The *Kidderminster Shuttle*, 18th & 25th May 1940
4. The *Redditch Indicator*, 18th May 1940
5. The *Dudley Herald*, 25th May 1940
6. *The History of the 12th (Warley) Battalion Home Guard*
7. The *Malvern Gazette*, 18th May 1940, and pers. comm. Stuart Hill, 22nd November 2000
8. *The Evesham Journal and Four Shires Advertiser*, 18th May 1940
9. *The History of U Company* by Major Jewell
10. *The Battle of Bewdley* by David Birt
11. A report of the Worcestershire TAA meeting of 18th October 1940 on CRO File Ref 004.6, BA 520, Parcel 6
12. *The Alcester Chronicle*, 25th May 1940, *Kidderminster Times*, 14th February 1942, as well as *The Redditch Indicator* and *Berrows Worcester Journal* of 8th January 1944, and Worcester City Battalion Part 2 Orders of 1st May 1944
13. A report of the TAA meeting of 18th October 1940, and the *History of the 12th (Warley) Battalion Home Guard*

14. *The History of the Evesham Battalion Home Guard*
15. *The History of U Company Home Guard*
16. Graves
17. *Britain's Home Guard* by John Brophy, p.19
18. Graves, p.168
19. From an analysis of Worcestershire Home Guard enrolment forms formerly held by the Army Medal Office at Droitwich until it was closed in 2005
20. From the Worcestershire Regiment Museum Archive
21. From the Kemerton Section Roll, courtesy of Dave Devereux
22. *The Tenbury Wells Advertiser*, 1st June 1940
23. *The History of Northamptonshire Home Guard*
24. *The Last English Revolutionary – Tom Wintringham 1898-1949* by Hugh Purcell
25. *The Worcester Evening News and Times*, 20th May 1940
26. *The Kidderminster Shuttle*, 25th May 1940
27. *The Malvern Gazette*, 25th May 1940
28. A retrospective report in *The Malvern Gazette*, 11th November 1944
29. *The Kidderminster Times*, 14th February 1942 and *A Memoir – Wars and Rumours of Wars* by General Sir James Marshall-Cornwall, who described General Weir as a 'charming cavalryman of the old school'
30. pers.comm. Albert Tolley, 7th May 2005
31. pers.comm. a number of ex-Home Guards
32. *The West Suffolk Sub District Home Guard Company Battle Book of 1944*
33. See *The Defence of Worcestershire* for more details
34. TNA File WO 199/872B – War Office instructions to the LDV/Home Guard
35. TNA File WO 199/872B
36. *The History of Evesham Battalion*
37. pers.comm. from the late Jack Leighton at an unrecorded interview
38. *The Tenbury Wells Advertiser* and *Dudley Herald*, 8th June 1940
39. ACI 653
40. From the report of the TAA meeting of 14th October 1940
41. Graves, p.91
42. *The Malvern Gazette*, 10th July 1943
43. pers.comm. Bill Allington, 24th September 2001

44. *The Battle of Bewdley* by Birt
45. *The History of C Company, Stourport Battalion*
46. From Birt and pers.comm. the late Sam Beard who was part of the marching column
47. Birt
48. *The Kidderminster Times*, 30th September 1944
49. TNA File WO 166/94 – Western Command War Diary for 1940
50. *The Kidderminster Times*, 4th June 1940
51. See *The Defence of Worcestershire and the Southern Approaches to Birmingham* for a list of known VPs in the county
52. Uncatalogued Home Guard files held in the Worcestershire Regimental Museum Archive
53. TNA File WO 199/363 – The Home Guard Role February to May 1942
54. TNA File 199/1869 – GOC instructions to Corps Commanders – Operational Role of the Home Guard June 1942
55. *The History of C Company of the Stourport Battalion*
56. TNA File WO 199/872B
57. *A History of Shropshire Home Guard* by Bernard Lowry (Logaston Press, 2010)
58. From uncatalogued Home Guard files held in the Worcestershire Regiment Museum Archive
59. *War Illustrated* magazine, 26th July 1940

Chapter 2
1. TNA File PREM 3 – Cabinet Papers
2. TNA File PREM 3
3. *The County Express and Shropshire Star*, 3rd August 1940
4. *Northampton Home Guard*
5. See also *The Defence of Worcestershire*
6. From correspondence between the Harold Goodwin Company Secretary and the Warley Battalion Home Guard, 14th September 1942, on Home Guard files formerly held by the Army Medal Office at Droitwich
7. ADRDE Home Guard files of August 1941
8. *The History of Northamptonshire Home Guard*
9. Part 2 Orders of the Midland Red Carrying Company Home Guard by Major LA. Youngs of 19th October, 27th March 1943, & 1st May 1943
10. *The Messenger*, July 2000
11. Home Guard personnel records formerly held by the Army Medal Office at Droitwich
12. Uncatalogued Home Guard files held in the Worcestershire Regiment Museum Archive

13. *The Kidderminster Times*, 13th July 1940 and pers.comm. former Company Sergeant Major Tom Healey of Kidderminster, March 2002
14. pers.comm. Wilf Mound former Malvern Home Guard
15. *War Diaries 1939-1945* by Field Marshal Lord Alanbrooke
16. *The Kidderminster Shuttle*, 10th August 1940
17. *Britain at War* magazine of August 2010
18. TNA File WO 166/1226 – The War Diary of Central Midland Command for 1940-41, and TNA File WO 166/4617 – The War Diary of the 11th Battalion, Royal Warwickshire Regiment for 1940
19. *The Kidderminster Times*; *The Bromsgrove, Droitwich and Redditch Weekly Messenger*, and *The Evening Standard*, 24th August 1940
20. pers.comm. Bill Allington, 24th September 2001
21. pers.comm. the late Egbert Ganderton of the Redditch Battalion, 16th December 2002
22. Western Command Operation Instruction No 17 of 22nd August 1940
23. TNA File WO 166/4617 – The War Diary for the 11th Battalion, Royal Warwickshire Regiment
24. From the War Diary of the Central Midland District for 1940-41
25. pers.comm. Bill Hay, 29th December 2002
26. pers.comm. Geoff Devereux
27. From an HDA Defence Scheme sourced by Mike Johnson, author of *The Redditch Home Guard 1940-1945*
28. Western Command Operation Order No 21 of 31st August 1940
29. pers.comm. Egbert Ganderton, 16th December 2002
30. Instruction leaflet issued to the Home Guard in August 1940
31. War Office instruction issued to all Home Guard Zone Commanders, 4th September 1940
32. From the TAA report of the meeting on 17th October 1941
33. TNA Files WO 166/1226 and WO 166/4617
34. Gilbert
35. TNA File WO 166/1226
36. Western Command Order No 1537 issued in September 1940
37. To convert this and other 1940s costs to approximate present day values multiply by 50
38. *The Redditch Indicator*, 19th October 1940
39. *The Bromsgrove, Redditch and Droitwich Weekly Messenger*, 23rd December 1944

40. From a number of interviews with former Redditch Home Guards
41. *Halesowen Home Guard*
42. *The Dudley Herald*, 16th November 1940
43. Whittaker
44. Warley Battalion Part 2 Orders, 29th December 1941
45. Uncatalogued Home Guard files held by the Worcestershire Regiment Museum Archive
46. TNA File WO 166/1226 – War Diary of the Central Midland Area for 1940-41. See also *The Defence of Worcestershire* for more detail of typical defences

Chapter 3
1. A Special Order of the Day from the king on the first birthday of the Home Guard on 14th May 1941
2. Reported at the TAA meeting of 17th October 1941
3. From the report of the TAA meeting of 17th October 1941
4. Copy of a War Office letter of 13th March found in Part 2 Orders of 17th Battalion Warwickshire Home Guard
5. Part 1 Orders of the Redditch Battalion of 20th June 1941
6. The history of *Halesowen Battalion*
7. Part 2 Orders of several Home Guard battalions
8. *We Also Served – The Story of the Home Guard in Cambridgeshire and the Isle of Ely 1940-1943*
9. *The Dudley Herald*, 15th February 1941
10. pers.comm. George Pitman, 23rd May 2003
11. Home Guard Instruction No 27 of 1941 – Defence of Urban Areas. Some aspects of this instruction reflect the lessons about street fighting that Tom Wintringham, and his comrade Hugh Slater, had been teaching since 1940 and seemed to reflect his ideas for a 'web defence'. Hugh Slater's book, *Home Guard for Victory* was also a best selling textbook, proposing 'defended areas' as a basis for counter-attack
12. A War Office letter, 24th March 1941, referred to in the TAA report of 17th October 1941
13. *Ibid*
14. Halesowen Battalion Part 1 Orders of 3rd September 1942
15. *The Malvern Gazette*, 10th June & 3rd August 1946
16. TNA File WO 166/1332 – The War Diary for the Birmingham Garrison of 1940-41
17. TNA File WO 166/1226 – Central Midland Area War Diary entry of 14th November 1941
18. The sector arrangements were gleaned from various Battalion Part 1 and 2 Orders, the report to the October 1942 meeting of the TAA, *The Kidderminster Times* of 24th April 1943 and *Redditch Indicator* of the following week
19. TNA file WO 166/1332 – The War Diary for the Birmingham Garrison
20. TNA File WO 166/3054 – 37th Searchlight Battery War Diary for 1941
21. The Vale of Evesham Historical Society Home Guard archive
22. *The History of U Company*
23. *The Bromsgrove, Droitwich and Redditch Weekly Messenger*, 31st May 1941
24. *The Evesham Standard*, 11th October 1941
25. Uncatalogued Home Guard files held in the Worcestershire Regiment Museum Archive
26. pers.comm. Bill Allington, 24th September 2001 and from *Worcestershire at War* by Glynn Warren
27. TNA File WO 166/6786 – Worcestershire Sub District War Diary for 1942
28. Warren
29. pers.comm. Dennis Burrows, 2nd June 2005
30. Warren
31. *The Malvern and Newland Parish Magazine*, 1989
32. From Part 1 Orders of Halesowen Battalion of 16th April 1942
33. From a War Office letter of 13th March 1941 to the Central Midland Area HQ, found in Part 1 Orders for the 17th Battalion, Warwickshire Home Guard
34. Bromsgrove Battalion Part 1 Orders of 2nd August 1941
35. Redditch Battalion Part 1 Orders of 8th October 1941
36. Bromsgrove Battalion Part 1 Orders of 11th October 1941
37. Home Guard Instruction No 35 issued on 10th July 1941
38. Gilbert
39. Evesham Battalion Part 1 Orders, date not noted
40. *The Evesham Standard*, 16th August 1941 and *The Kidderminster Times*, 30th August 1941
41. Warley Battalion Part I Orders of 15th December 1941
42. Gilbert
43. Warley Battalion Part 1 Orders of 15th December 1941

44. Bromsgrove Battalion Part 1 orders of 6th December 1941

Chapter 4

1. Bromsgrove Battalion Part 1 Orders of 14th February 1942
2. *The Evesham Journal and Four Shires Advertiser*, 20th December 1941
3. *The History of U Company*
4. Redditch Battalion Part 1 Orders of 25th February 1942. It is significant that the Part 2 Orders of the same day indicated that 109 men had resigned!
5. *The Kidderminster Times*, 30th September 1944
6. Report of the TAA meeting of 10th April 1942
7. Gleaned from Part 2 Orders of the various battalions in Worcestershire and the report of the TAA meeting of 2nd October 1942
8. pers.comm. Bill Allington, September 2001
9. *The Worcester Evening News and Times* and Part 2 Orders of the Oldbury and Redditch Battalions
10. Redditch Battalion Part 2 Orders of 24th November 1942
11. Warley Battalion Part 1 Orders of 9th March 1942
12. pers.comm. Malcolm Atkin
13. TNA file WO 166/6822 – Central Midland Area War Diary of 1942, and both *The Evesham Standard* and *The Malvern Gazette* of 14th February 1942
14. pers.comm. Dr Dennis Williams
15. TNA Files WO 166/6786 – Worcestershire Sub District War Diary for 1942, and WO 166/6822 – Central Midland Area War Diary of 1942, and both *The Malvern Gazette* and *The Evesham Standard* of 21st February 1942
16. TNA Files WO 166/6786 – Worcestershire Sub Area and WO 166/6822 Central Midland Area War Diaries for 1942
17. From Worcestershire Sub Area instruction to Home Guard battalions in the Worcester Zone, dated 7th April 1942
18. pers.comm. Egbert Ganderton, 16th December 2006
19. From the report of the TAA meeting of 10th April 1942
20. Bromsgrove Battalion Part 1 Orders of 20th November 1943
21. The history of *Halesowen Battalion*
22. pers.comm. Morris Jephcott, 23rd April 2009
23. Worcestershire Zone Home Guard Instruction No 122 dated 22nd July 1942
24. *The Story of the RASC 1939-45*
25. Whittaker
26. TNA file WO 199/387 – Home Guard Transport Companies May 1941 to September 1944
27. Shropshire Home Guard Fighting Books Operational Instruction No 1 – North Wales District Home Guard Motor Transport Column – undated
28. *The Worcester Evening News and Times*, 18th November 1944
29. Graves
30. TNA File WO 199/398 – Enrolment of Boys in the Home Guard and Cadet Force from July 1942 to December 1944
31. From Part 2 Orders of various battalions
32. *The County Express and Dudley Mercury*, 9th & 16th May 1942
33. *The County Express and Dudley Mercury*, 16th May 1942
34. From Part 1 Orders of the Warley Battalion of 1st June 1942
35. *Ack Ack* by Sir Frederick Pile
36. Gleaned from various Battalion Part 2 Orders
37. pers.comm. Harry Workman, 27th January 2011
38. TNA File WO 199/383 – Home Guard LAA Orders of Battle 1944
39. See *Two Exiles – A School in Wartime* by H.C.A. Gaunt for a very graphic description of the move of TRE into Malvern
40. From various Malvern Battalion Part 2 Orders and pers.comm. ex Home Guard Lt of the TRE Home Guard, Stan Ratcliffe
41. From ADRDE Home Guard correspondence files formerly held by Qinetiq
42. TNA File WO 166/6786 Worcestershire Sub District War Diary for 1942
43. *Ibid*
44. *Ibid*
45. *The Bromsgrove, Droitwich and Redditch Weekly Messenger,* 27th June 1942
46. *The Kidderminster Times*, 30th May 1942
47. Halesowen Battalion Part 2 Orders of 9th July 1942
48. 12th Warley Battalion Part 2 Orders – dates not noted
49. The history of *Halesowen Home Guard*
50. A Worcestershire Sub District Operation Instruction of 22nd August 1943
51. Birmingham VITGUARD Operation Instruction of 8th December 1944
52. Worcestershire Sub District Operation Instruction of 22nd August 1943

53. Bromsgrove Battalion Part 1 Orders of 26th September 1942
54. pers.comm. Bill Harper, 19th April 2012
55. TNA File WO 166/6822 – Central Midland Area War Diary for 1942
56. *The Story of A Sector, Warwickshire Home Guard*
57. *The Evesham Standard*, 3rd October 1942
58. *The Worcester Evening News and Times*, 16th April 1942 and 1st January 1943
59. TNA File No WO 166/6786 – Central Midland District War Diary 1942
60. *The County Express*, 31st October 1942
61. *In the Space of a Single Day* by Jon Mills and Terry Carney
62. TNA File WO 199/40 – Home Guard Auxiliary Bomb Disposal Units. August 1942 to November 1944
63. pers.comm. Clifford Lord, 16th April 2012

Chapter 5
1. Home Guard Information Circular No 26 issued to all Home Guard commanders dated 28th December 1942
2. A Worcestershire Sub District Instruction dated 1st November 1943
3. Malvern Battalion Part 2 Orders of 30th October and 24th November 1943
4. Bromsgrove Battalion Part 1 Orders of 24th April 1943
5. Operational Orders of 39th Warwickshire Home Guard of 30th November 1943
6. TNA File WO 166/1107 – Birmingham Garrison War Diary 1943
7. pers.comm. John Ralphs, 15th February 2003
8. Oldbury Battalion Part 1 Orders 1st March 1943
9. TNA File WO 166/11027 – Birmingham Garrison War Diary for 1943
10. Oldbury Battalion Part 1 Orders 27th March 1943
11. Halesowen Battalion Part 1 Orders and the history of *Halesowen Home Guard*; Bromsgrove Battalion Part 1 Orders; *The Redditch Indicator*, 24th April 1943; and pers. comm. Bill Allington & Charles Stallard
12. Redditch Battalion Part 2 Orders of 21st December 1943

Chapter 6
1. Worcester Sub District Orders of 10th April 1944
2. ADRDE Home Guard files formerly held by DERA

3. Home Guard files held the Worcester Regiment Museum archive
4. Operational Instruction from M Sector dated 18th February 1944
5. Bromsgrove Battalion part 1 Orders of 11th March 1944
6. Operational Instructions dated 11th February 1944 on Home Guard files held by the Worcestershire Regiment Museum Archive
7. Worcester Sub District Orders for the Protection of Communications 10th April 1944
8. Redditch Battalion Part 1 Orders of 18th January 1944
9. Home Guard files held by the Worcestershire Regiment Museum Archive
10. Warley Battalion Part 2 Orders of 15th April 1944
11. *The Redditch Indicator*, 19th February 1944
12. Bromsgrove Battalion Part 1 orders 6th May 1944
13. A Worcestershire Sub District letter of 14th June 1944
14. TNA File WO 166/14558 – Worcestershire Sub District War Diary for 1944
15. TNA File WO 166/14558 – Worcestershire Sub District War Diary for 1944
16. pers.comm. Charles Stallard, 13th January 2003
17. *The History of the Evesham Battalion*
18. From Warley Battalion Part 2 Orders of 31st July 1944
19. Dudley Battalion Part 1 Orders of 25th July 1944
20. Mackenzie
21. Oldbury Battalion Part 2 Orders of 22nd August 1944
22. Tenbury Museum Home Guard files
23. Redditch Battalion Part 1 Orders of 5th September 1944
24. TNA File WO 166/14558 – Worcester Sub District War Diary for 1944
25. Stourport Battalion Part 1 Orders of 5th October 1944
26. TNA File WO 166/14558
27. Stourport Battalion Part I Orders of 9th September 1944
28. TNA File WO 166/14558
29. Dudley Battalion Part 1 Orders of 19th September 1944
30. pers.comm. Charles Stallard, 13th January 2003
31. Bromsgrove Battalion Part 1 Orders of 4th November 1944

32. TNA File WO 166/14558 – Worcester Sub District War Diary
33. *Ibid*
34. *The Kidderminster Times*, 30th September 1944
35. *The Redditch Indicator*, 30th September 1944
35. *The Evesham Standard*, 25th November 1944
36. Memorandum dated 12th December 1944 from the Commander of D Company of the Stourport Battalion to members of the Company
37. *The Evesham Journal and Four Shires Advertiser*, 30th December 1944 & 6th January 1945

Chapter 7
1. *The Malvern Gazette*, 27th January, 10th February 1945 & 12th January 1946
2. A letter by Lt Colonel Gaskell, Secretary of the TAA Association, on Home Guard files held in the Worcestershire Regiment Association archive
3. *The Malvern Gazette*, 16th May 1952
4. Army Order from the War Office 27th March 1945
5. Home Office Aliens Circular No 339/1945
6. Gilbert
7. TNA File WO 199/3301 – Home Guard and Civil Defence – 1948 to 1950
8. TNA File WO 199/3303 – Home Guard April 1951 to September 1952. Minutes of an MOD Working Party of 11th September 1951
9. MacKenzie
10. Gilbert
11. *The Malvern Gazette*, 25th January 1952
12. *The Malvern Gazette*, 22nd February 1952
13. From CRO File Ref 004.6. BA 5204. Parcel 31 – TAAFA Records
14. Gilbert
15. CRO File Reference 004.6, BA 5204, Parcel 2 – Worcestershire TAAFA meeetings
16. Collection of papers of the late 2nd Lt Faulkner, deposited with the County Record Office, but not yet catalogued. Local Home Guard papers surviving from the 1950s are more difficult to source than those of the war years, and so this small collection of papers is most useful, and give a partial insight to the organisation and training of the Kidderminster Battalion. It has to be assumed that similar arrangements were being made by the remaining battalions in the county.
17. Mackenzie
18. Gilbert
19. CRO File 004.6
20. *Ibid*
21. Mackenzie
22. CRO File 004.6
23. Mackenzie

Chapter 8
1. Memorandum by Captain Duncan Sandys to Winston Churchill, 8th August 1940, quoted in *Churchill's Underground Army* by John Warwicker
2. *With Britain in Mortal Danger* by John Warwicker
3. pers.comm. Geoff Devereux and John Wythes from October 1998
4. pers.comm. Colin Curnock & 'Tom' Harwood
5. Graves, *The Mercian Maquis*, *The Defence of Worcestershire*, Part 2 Orders of the Evesham and Malvern Battalions, and interviews with former members of the patrols
6. pers.comm. Geoff Devereux, Tony Barling & John Boaz
7. pers.comms. a number of Auxiliers including John Thornton of Herefordshire's Bromyard Patrol
8. Malvern Battalion Part 2 Orders of 3rd December 1941
9. From Part 2 Orders of the Malvern Battalion Home Guard, 22nd October 1941
10. Evesham Battalion Part 2 Orders of 31st January 1942
11. From Malvern Battalion Part 2 Orders of 20th November 1942
12. pers.comm. Malcolm Atkin
13. pers.comm. the late John Boaz of Sampson Patrol

Chapter 9
1. Summerfield and Peniston-Bird
2. *The History of 'U Company*
3. TNA File CAB 123/204 – Home Guard and Civil Defence
4. Summerfield and Peniston-Bird
5. TNA File WO 199/401 – Women and the Home Guard
6. TNA File CAB 123/204 – Home Guard and Civil Defence
7. *The History of 'C Company, 11th Worcestershire Battalion Home Guard*
8. pers.comm. Joan Warren in June 2005 and group photograph
9. *The history of U Company*

10. TNA File WO 199/401 – Women and the Home Guard
11. CRO File Ref 004.6
12. Redditch Battalion Part 2 Orders of 7th March 1944
13. *The Worcester Evening News and Times*, 4th December 1944
14. *The history of C Company, Stourport Home Guard*

Chapter 10
1. pers.comm. Bill Allington, 24th September 2001
2. Gleaned from various early war issues of the *Picture Post* magazine and pers.comm. Malcolm Atkin
3. *The Last English Revolutionary* by Hugh Purcell
4. Home Guard Information Circular No 45, 5th April 1944
5. From various Part 2 Orders issued by Worcestershire Home Guard battalions
6. TNA File WO 166/4617 – The War Diary of the 11th RWR for 1941
7. Warley Battalion Part 1 Orders,12th January 1942. Similar orders were issued by the Oldbury and Redditch Battalions
8. pers.comm. Robin Morom, 30th June 2003
9. pers.comm. Derrick Pearson, 19th November 2005
10. Home Guard Circular No 45, 29th March 1944
11. *The History of Evesham Home Guard*
12. Part 1 Orders to the Oldbury Battalion for June 1941
13. Worcester City Battalion Part 2 Orders of 18th September 1944
14. *The Malvern Gazette*, 23rd August 1941
15. *The Kidderminster Times*, 27th June 1942
16. *The Kidderminster Times*, 3rd October 1942
17. Warley Battalion Part 1 Orders, 13th July 1942
18. Warley Battalion Part 1 Orders, 19th August 1942
19. *The Kidderminster Times*, 2nd January 1943
20. *The Kidderminster Times*, 26th August 1944
21. *The Kidderminster Times*, 14th October 1944
22. Report of TAA meeting, 17th October 1941
23. Evesham Battalion papers held by the The Vale of Evesham Historical Society
24. Bromsgrove Battalion Part 1 orders of 12th August 1944
25. Warley Battalion Part 1 Orders of 26th January 1942
26. TNA File WO 166/6786 – Worcestershire Sub District War Diary for 1942
27. Warley Battalion Part 1 Orders of 12th January 1942
28. A history of the 45th Warwickshire (Birmingham) Battalion Home Guard dated July 1945
29. Part I of Home Guard Instruction No 51
30. Home Guard Instruction No 61 – Battle Innoculation GHQ Home Forces – January 1944
31. *The History of Evesham Battalion*
32. pers.comm. Bill Allington, 24th September 2001
33. *The history of Halesowen Home Guard*
34. TNA File WO 166/4558 – Worcestershire Sub District War Diary for 1944
35. Worcester City Battalion Part 2 Orders of 8th August 1944
36. Warley Battalion Part 2 Orders
37. pers.comm. the late Chris Bayliss, 27th June 2005
38. Instruction from Worcester City Battalion Commanding Officer, 25th August 1943 in Home Guard files held by the Worcestershire Regiment Museum archive
39. TNA File WO 199/872B – LDV/ Home Guard Instructions
40. *The Redditch Indicator*, 13th March 1943
41. *The Bromsgrove, Droitwich and Redditch Weekly Messenger*, & *The Evesham Standard*, 10th May 1941
42. *The Redditch Indicator*, 13th March 1943
43. Information on films was gleaned from Part 1 Orders of various battalions and from Home Guard Information Circular No 45, 29th March 1944
44. Warley Battalion Part 1 Orders of 23rd March 1942
45. *The Kidderminster Times*, 31st July 1943
46. Stourport Battalion Part 1 Orders, 25th November 1943
47. *The County Express*, 8th May 1942
48. *The Story of A Sector Warwickshire Home Guard*
49. Halesowen Battalion Part 2 Orders of 11th February 1943
50. *They Also Serve – The 39th Cheshire Battalion Home Guard* by Lt Spence
51. pers.comm. various of the Worcestershire Auxiliers
52. pers.comm. Ron Seymour, May 2000

Chapter 11
1. *The Bromsgrove, Droitwich, and Redditch Weekly Messenger*, 11th November 1944

2. Birmingham Garrison Operation Instruction, 8th December 1944
3. pers.comm. a number of Home Guards and eyewitnesses
4. Report of the TAA meeting, 18th October 1940
5. Redditch Battalion Part 1 Orders, 26th May 1941
6. Report of the TAA meeting, 17th October 1941
7. pers.comm. Malcolm Atkin
8. pers comm Bill Aliband of the Redditch Battalion
9. pers.comm. Malcolm Atkin
10. *Britain at War* magazine, December 2007
11. pers.comm. Malcolm Atkin. Also Purcell
12. TAA meeting, 10th April 1943
13. *The history of the Halesowen Home Guard*
14. Much of the basic information on weapons in this chapter has been gleaned from the writings of Ian V. Hogg and Terry Gander, supplemented with information from Home Guard Part 1 Orders, together with privately published and War Office instruction pamphlets and manuals, as well as pers comms by Home Guards and Malcolm Atkin
15. Bromsgrove Battalion Part 1 Orders of 11th September 1942
16. TNA File WO 199/1891 – Letter from Southern Command to, inter alia, Central Midland Area, 24th June 1940
17. Malvern Battalion Home Guard Part 1 Orders of 3rd June 1941
18. Part 1 Orders to the 17th Warwickshire Battalion Home Guard of 24th June 1941
19. Bromsgrove Battalion Part 1 Orders of 25th October 1941
20. Uncatalogued Home Guard files held in the Worcestershire Regiment Museum Archive
21. *Britain at War* magazine, August 2007 and Worcestershire TAA report of October 1941
22. An undated instruction issued to the Dudley Battalion
23. Bromsgrove Battalion Part 1 Orders of 3rd January 1942
24. pers.comm. Bill Allington, September 2001
25. Warley Battalion Part 1 Orders of 12th January 1942 and 'Small Arms Training – Grenade' Instruction issued by the War Office in July 1942
26. Instructions issued to the 5th Cambridge Battalion Home Guard, September 1942
27. See also 'Small Arms Training – Grenade' issued by the War Office in July 1942
28. Bromsgrove Battalion Part I Orders of 9th September 1944
29. *America's Premier Gunmakers* by K.D. Kirkland
30. Undated notes issued to the Evesham Battalion
31. Kidderminster Battalion Part 2 Orders, date not noted
32. Bromsgrove Battalion Part 1 Orders of 26th September 1942
33. pers.comm. Albert Toon of the BSA Home Guard
34. pers.comm. John Leighton, ex-Worcestershire Regiment shooting competitor and qualified sniper
35. *The Malvern Gazette*, 24th April 1943
36. Oldbury Battalion Part 1 Orders of 14th July 1943
37. pers.comm. Derrick Pearson
38. pers.comm the late Sam Beard, ex-Norton Barracks permanent staff
39. pers.comm. Egbert Ganderton
40. A female tank was armed with with a combination of Vickers and Hotchkiss machine guns, while the male tank was armed with the 6 Pounder Hotchkiss Quick Firing Gun. See Chapter 11 for more details
41. Uncatalogued Home Guard files held by the Worcestershire Regiment Museum archive and the DEMS Pocket Book 1942 issued by the Admiralty
42. See The Handbook of the Thompson Submachine Gun issued by the Auto-Ordnance Corporation, USA in 1941
43. Oldbury Battalion Part 1 Orders of 27th August 1941
44. TNA File WO 166/6786 – Worcester Sub District War Diary of 1942
45. TNA file WO 166/6786 Worcester Sub District War Diary of 1942
46. *The Small Arms Training Manual – Sten Machine Carbine* issued by the War Office
47. See also *The Browning Machine Gun Mechanism Made Easy* published by Gale and Polden in 1942
48. See also 'Handbook for Projectors 2½ inch Mks 1 and 2' issued by the Chief Inspector of Armaments in September 1941
49. Bromsgrove Battalion Part I Orders of 16th August 1941
50. *The History of Northampton Home Guard*
51. Redditch Battalion Part 1 Orders of 12th January 1943
52. TNA File 166/6786 – Worcester Sub District War Diary for 1942
53. pers.comm. Bill Hay, October 2002

54. *The RAF Regiment at War 1942-46* by Kingsley M. Oliver
55. TNA File WO 199/388 – 'Notes on Tactical Handling of the Smith Gun' dated December 1942
56. TNA File WO 166/6786 – Worcestershire Sub District War Diary for 1942
57. See note 40 above
58. See *The Defence of Worcestershire and the Southern Approaches to Birmingham* for more details of these defence posts
59. An article by Major A. Shelley-Creake in the Worcestershire Regiment magazine, *Firm*, January 1949
60. TNA File WO 166/6786 – The Worcestershire Sub District War Diary for 1942
61. *The History of U Company* by Major Jewell
62. pers.comm. Jack Miles and Wilf Mound, both of the Malvern Battalion
63. pers.comm. Eric Doughty & Bill Hay in 2002

Chapter 12
1. Graves, p.92
2. *The Halesowen Home Guard 1940-1944*
3. Collection of Home Guard papers held by Kidderminster Library
4. TAA report of meeting, 8th October 1940
5. *The Bromsgrove, Droitwich and Redditch Weekly Messenger*, 24th August 1940
6. *The Malvern Gazette*, 3rd August 1940
7. Oldbury Battalion Part 1 Orders of 1st February 1941
8. Worcestershire Regiment Museum Archive
9. *The Story of A Sector Warwickshire Home Guard*
10. Redditch Battalion Part 1 Orders of 13th April 1943
11. Part I Orders of the Redditch Battalion Home Guard of 30th June 1941
12. Part I Orders 8th Oldbury Battalion Home Guard of 6th August 1941
13. *The County Express and Dudley Mercury*, 16th August 1941
14. Oldbury Battalion Part I Orders of 27th August 1941
15. Warley Battalion Part 1 Orders of 15th December 1941
16. Western Command Order No 64 of 8th July 1942
17. TNA File WO 199/40. Home Guard Auxiliary Bomb Disposal Units. August 1942 to November 1944
18. Bromsgrove Battalion Part 1 Orders of 28th August 1943
19. Bromsgrove Battalion Part 1 Orders of 11th March 1944
20. Home Guard Instruction Circular No 47 of 26th April 1944
21. Bromsgrove Battalion Part 1 Orders of 29th July 1944
22. County Record Office File Ref 004.6 BA 5204 Parcel 31

Conclusions
1. These were largely the men of the Territorial Battalions, mobilised at the beginning of the war and who had formed a significant proportion of the British Expeditionary Force. After Dunkirk they were quickly released from military service if they had special skills, for example as toolmakers and machinists, now urgently needed for the production of armaments
2. *The Ironside Diaries 1937-1940*, Constable and Co Ltd, London, 1963
3. TNA File WO 163/414 – Home Guard Sub-Committee of the Army Council
4. TNA File CAB 106/1189 – Report of the Massachusits Committee on Public Safety
5. *The Worcester Evening News and Times,* 15th January 1944
6. *Hitler's Last Levy – The Volkssturm 1944-45* by Hans Kissel and *The Last Nazis* by Perry Biddlescombe
7. TNA File CAB 106/1189
8. *Invasion 1940* by Peter Fleming
9. *Gubbins and SOE* by Joan Bright-Astley
10. See *The Defence of Worcestershire* for more details of these

Appendix 1
1. 'The Home Guard' by Major Shelley Creak in the Worcestershire Regimental Magazine, *Firm*, of January 1949
2. Commonwealth War Graves Commission and *Evesham Standard*, 30th January 1943
3. Commonwealth War Graves Commission and *Evesham Journal and Four Shires Advertiser*, 25th September 1941
4. Commonwealth War Graves Commission and Whittaker
5. Commonwealth War Graves Commission, the *Bromsgrove, Droitwich and Redditch Weekly Messenger*, 27th May 1944, and an interview of former Home Guard Lieutenant, Bill Allington, on 1st October 2001
6. Commonwealth War Graves Commission and *Malvern Gazette*, 6th June 1942

7. Commonwealth War Graves Commission and *Evesham Standard*, 21st June 1941
8. Commonwealth War Graves Commission and *Worcester Evening News and Times*, 8th March 1943
9. Commonwealth War Graves Commission and *Evesham Standard*, 21st June 1941
10. Commonwealth War Graves Commission
11. *The Dudley Herald*, 30th August 1941
12. *The County Express and Dudley Mercury*, 9th & 16th May 1942
13. *The County Express and Dudley Mercury*, 27th June 1942
14. *The Evesham Standard*, 3rd May 1941
15. This letter was reported in the Part 1 Orders of the 33rd Warwickshire Battalion Home Guard

Appendix 2

1. From various reports to the Worcestershire TAA found on CRO file ref. 004.6. BA 5204. Parcel 2

Appendix 3

1. From an instruction from the Worcestershire Sub Area Headquarters at Droitwich to the Home Guard in the Worcestershire Zone dated 7th April 1942, with additions from the Sub District War Diary for 1942

Appendix 6

1. Primarily from Western Command Orders of 16th March 1945, supplemented with entries from Part II Orders of the various battalions
2. *The Kidderminster Shuttle*, 19th June 1943

Appendix 7

1. County Record Office File Ref 004.6. BA 5204. Parcel 32, undated

Appendix 8

1. Based upon the personnel list of Auxiliary Units in Worcestershire produced on handover of administration to the TAA York in September 1942, and the final personnel rolls produced by the TAA York on TNA file WO 199/3389, supplemented from an anlysis of Part 2 Orders of the parent Home Guard battalions and Home Guard/LDV enrolment forms formerly held by the Army Medal Office at Droitwich and now inaccessible, as well as oral evidence from former Auxiliers and their families. Unfortunately the date of transfer of most men to the Auxiliary Patrols is generally not recorded, however the date of promotion, where it occurs, is a clue!

Appendix 9

1. Information on most of the training venues was gleaned from various Part 1 and 2 Orders issued to Worcestershire units and interviews with former Home Guards

Index of Personal Names

Cale, Lt W.H. *115*, 277
Campion, Lt S.G. 284
Canning, 2nd Lt R.J.W. 279
Canning, Capt J.S. 284
Capel-Loft, Capt N.H. 290
Carder, Capt W.C. 65
Carleton, 2nd Lt. C.E. 278
Carter, Capt G.H. *142*
Carter, Fred *199*
Carter, Lt L.R. 283
Carter, Maj Sydney B. 116, *116*, 183-4, 191, 195,
    280, 294, 307
Carter, Lt W.L. 281
Cartwright, Capt W.R. 282
Carty, Sgt R.J. 295
Case, Lt C.
Case, Lt H.P. 279
Castles, Thomas William George 267
Cathcart-Davies, Lt Revd J. 281
Cavanagh, Capt J.B. 285
Cayhill, Lt C.H. 277
Chadwick, Maj G.S. 275
Chadwick, Lt J.A. 278
Chance, Dennis
Chance, Capt J.B. 65, 289
Chance, Thomas *151*
Chaplin, Frank 267
Chapman, Lt E. 285
Chatwin, Lt A.E. 286
Cheese, Bert *244*
Cheese, Walter *45*
Child, Lt W. 277
Childs, Cpl W.C. 295
Chillingworth, 2nd Lt C.H. 288
Chilton, Lt W.N. 279
Chrippes, Lt G.C.G. 288
Christopherson, Maj J.C. 286
Church, Lt A.E. 281
Church, Maj A.E. 292
Churchill, Len *68*
Churchill, Winston 1, 3, 36, 88, 138, 147, 148, 150,
    155, 233, 264
Chuter, Lt G.T. 290
Clark, Capt F.S. 279
Clark, 2nd Lt S.W. 286
Clarke, Dr *90*
Clarke, Lt E.E. 281
Clarke, Maj E.H. 273
Clarke, Lt F. 282
Clarke, Capt G.C. 271
Clarke, Maj R.H. 285
Claxton, 2nd Lt W.F.R. 289
Clemence, Capt D.S. 282

Clemens, Lt C. 281
Clewlow, Sgt P.W. 295
Clibbery, Maj A.B. 275, 289
Clift, Lt J.F.P. 285
Clines, Archibald Victor ('Arch') 160, *160*, 305
Clines, Sgt Rupert Valentine ('Val') 160, 166, *170*,
    305
Clough, 2nd Lt C.C. 288
Coates, Lt F.J. 289
Cobham, Lord 13, 105
Cobourne, Lt J.D. 282
Cole, Mr *101*
Cole, 2nd Lt F.B. 281, 295
Coleman, Maj A.C. 279
Coleyshaw, Capt H. 292
Collett, Capt T.H. *190*, 200, 280
Colley, Lt A.H.C. 286
Colley, Lt F. 278
Collins, Lt H. 278
Collins, Lt J.F. 281
Comber, Lt R.B. 290
Comely, 2nd Lt T.A. 285
Common, 2nd Lt W.H. 283
Connop, Lt R.D. 291
Cook, Lt C.A. 84
Cook, Sgt C.H. 295
Cooke, Stan *48*
Cookson, Sgt W.H. 295
Coombs, Lt F. 282
Cooper, Lt G.A. 285
Cooper, Maj W.H. 289
Cope, Capt A.C. 289
Coppack, 2nd Lt E. 285
Cornock, Lt A. 282
Cosier, F. *202*
Cotley, 2nd Lt E.S. 287
Cotterell, Lt A.F. 284
Cotton, Lt E.W. 281
Cotton, Maj H.J. 272, 281
Cotton, Colonel W.E.L. 14
Couchman, Capt H.J. 284
Court, Lt E. 277
Court, John *115*
Cox, Frank *86*
Cox, Lt E.A. 279
Cox, Lt W.A. 280
Crane, Lt V.W.R. 290
Crew, Lt S. 280
Croft, 2nd Lt H. 277
Croft, Lt H. 288
Croft, Lt H.D. 289
Crofts, Revd J.A. 277
Crook, Pt *255*

Crook, 2nd Lt G.N. 289
Cropper, Capt R.C. 287
Crossman, Lt A.E. 291
Cumming, 2nd Lt G. 286
Cumming, 2nd Lt S.J.C. 285
Curnock, Colin *170*, 231, 301
Curnock, Cpl Harry Theodore *170*, 301
Currell, Sgt Maj H. 295
Cuttriss, Sgt Maj H.J. 295

Daffern, Lt F.H. 288
Dagger, Lt H.G. 287
Dain, Lt J. 285
Dale, Capt E.C.B. 285
Dalley, Sgt George 169, *170*, 302
Daniel, Lt F.E. 287
Daniels, Cpl R. *202*
Dansern, 2nd Lt F.W. 283
Darby, 2nd Lt W. 288
Dare, Alec *199*
Dare, R. *68*
Darke, Capt C. 277
Darley, 2nd Lt E.A. 281
Darlington, P.A. 118
Davenport-Price, Maj H. 272, 281
Davey, Revd S.J. 278
Davies, Betty *177*
Davies, 2nd Lt C.C. 289
Davies, Dot *177*
Davies, Maj E.
Davies, Lt E.P. 290
Davies, Gen Sir Francis 200
Davies, Lt H.G. 284
Davies, Sgt J.I. 290
Davies, Revd J.T. 282
Davies, Langton 203
Davies, Capt N.E. 277
Davies, Maj O. 273
Davies, 2nd Lt W.F.L. 281
Davies, Maj W.G. 279
Davies, W.G. 293
Davis, 2nd Lt C.E. 279
Davis, Harry *84*
Davis, Pop *84*
Dawe, Sgt Thomas Copeland *170*, 301
Day, George 108
Day, Maj H.E. 273, 284
De Salis La Terriere, Capt H.M. 284
De Sautoy, Colonel E.F. 14, 105, 294
Dean, Lt A. 280
Dean, Fred 51
Denbert, Lt S.B. 291
Denbigh, Lt W.H. 281

Denton, Capt W.J. 277, 295
Derrington, Lt G.H. 285
Derry, Sgt F.A. 295
Detheridge, Sgt J. 295
Devereux, Sgt Frank S. 253, 295
Devereux, Geoffrey Alfred 51, 160, *160*, 161, 166, 169, 216, 232, 263-4, 304
Dew, Sgt 295
Dick, Capt M.J. 287
Dickson, Maj P.W. 295
Dingwell, 2nd Lt N.P. 278
Disney, Maj 272
Dolton, Sgt A. 295
Donnelly, Capt J. 74, 282
Doorbar, 2nd Lt B.A. 285
Dorey, Capt R. 286
Dorrell, Henry Roy 304
Doughty, A.E. *248*
Doughty, 2nd Lt H.E. 284
Doughty, Sgt H.E. 295
Douglas, Lt B. 278
Douglas, Col F.W.R. 171
Douglas, Lt N. 279
Dovey, G. *68*
Dovey, Jim *68, 199*
Dovey, Joe *68*
Downes, Lt E. 290
Downs, Lt J.L. 282
Drew, Sgt R. 295
Drewry, 2nd Lt G. 290
Drives, 2nd Lt R.H. 292
Dudley, Sgt Maj B. 295
Dudley, Lt L.A. 283
Duff, Capt H. 277
Duffield, Capt N.F. 283
Dukes, Capt H.C.S. 282
Dulson, Lt A.W. 279
Durrens, 2nd Lt A. 286
Dutton, H. 295
Dykes, Maj D.G. 74, 283

Earnshaw, Lt H. 283
Earnshaw, Sgt H. 295
Eastwood, Lt General 24
Eccles, Capt P.G. 290
Eden, Sir Anthony 155, 173
Edge, Maj H.V. 271, 277
Edkins, Sgt A.T. 295
Edwards, 2nd Lt A.D. 286
Edwards, Lt G.W. 280
Edwards, Maj H. 280
Edwards, 2nd Lt H.L. 289
Edwards, Lt J.W. 286

Edwards, Mr *255*
Edwards, 2nd Lt R.W.G. 279
Edwards, S. *68*
Edwards, Lt W.C. 289
Eeuens, Capt J.C. 280
Elcock, Lt H.H. 282
Elkington, Lt Col C.G. 279
Elliott, Lt R.L. 285
Elliott, Mr 40
Ellis, Lt H.V.L. 283
Ellis, Lt R.V.W. *59*, 287
Elmes, Lt W.G. 277
Emms, Lt G.A. 282
Evans, 2nd Lt A.C. 287
Evans, Capt A.H. 277
Evans, L/Cpl Bill *90*
Evans, Cumming Benyon 268
Evans, Lt E. 291
Evans, Capt E.W. 289
Evans, Lt G.H.E. 281
Evans, Sgt W.E. 295
Evans, Lt W.R. *45*, 284
Everall, Sgt 201
Eveson, Lt G.H. 290
Exall, Cpl W. 295

Fairgrieve, 2nd Lt G.H. 288
Farley, Lt C.T. 288
Farmer, Lt J.E. 288
Fearnside, Capt W. 65
Fell, Sgt W.C. 295
Ferguson, Lt D.H. 289
Fergusson, Jock
Fernhead, Sgt 280
Fernihough, Sgt Algy Herbert 'Alec' 165, *170*, 301
Field, Sgt Maj F. 295
Field, Lt J. 285
Field, 2nd Lt K.C. 286
Field, Sgt L. 295
Fillery, Lt Col T.C. 148, 150, 286
Flack, Sgt Maj J.T. 295
Fleming, Peter 264, 266
Fletcher, George 97
Fletcher, Harold *48*
Ford, Lt A. 280
Ford, Lt W.E. 284
Forrest, Capt E.A.K. 283
Foster, E. 295
Foster, J. 293
Fourt, Sgt F. 295
Fowler, Lt C.G. 285
Fowler, Sgt C.P. 295
Fowler, Lt F.E. 279

Fowler, Jack *202*
Fowler, Mr *202*
Fowler, Lt T.G.
Fox, G. 295
Fox, Lt R.E. 287
Fox, Capt V.J. 65
Franklyn, Gen H.E. 171
Franklyn, Lt J. 291
Frederick, Lt J.F. 284
Freeman, Lt. G.V. 278
French, L/Cpl C.J.W. 295
French, Lt H.W. 283
Fuller, Maj R.A. 74, 284
Fulleylove, Lt W.R. 290
Fussell, Lt H.E.J. 284

Gabb, Col 99
Gabb, Lt G.R. 285
Gadd, Capt G.C. 279
Gale, Cpl Jack *90*
Ganderton, Egbert *48*, 49, 53, 102, 214
Ganderton, Len *48*
Garbutt, Mr *101*
Garratt, Lt A.N. 285
Gascoigne, Lt R.E.W. 289
Gengl, Lt Herbert 84
George, Sgt A. 296
George, Fred 85
George, Capt R.H. 288
Gibbons, Lt R.L. 285
Gibson, Lt H.J. 283
Gilbert, Maj F. 275
Gill, Lt B.J. 287
Gillespie, Bob *90*
Gillett, Capt H.G. 278
Gilley, Sgt G.R. 295
Gillies, 2nd Lt G.S. 279
Gilmour, Lt W.E.S. 278
Gimson, Lt J.F. 285
Glaze, Sgt A. 295
Gleadow, Capt E.F. 278
Gledhill, Sgt J.R. 295
Gleichen, Lady Helena 2
Goate, Maj E.E. 271, 278
Godfrey, Maj A.F.R. *142*
Gofley, Capt R.A.H. 289
Golledge, Lt F. 277
Goodall, Sgt A.E. 295
Goodall, 2nd Lt W.A. 285
Goodrich, E.V. 42
Goodrich, Sgt G.H. 295
Goodson, Lt J.H. 281
Goodwin, Capt 29

Haynes, Lt P.R.A. 281
Haynes, Lt S.T. 289
Head, Maj G.H. 283
Healing, Mr *202*
Heally, L/Cpl L. 296
Heath, Major H. 14
Heaton, 2nd Lt A. 286
Hebden, June *178*
Hejl, Maj F.A.J. 275, 289
Hemming, Lt G.F. 281
Henderson, Capt G.F. 287
Hennery, Capt A.J. 279
Hennery, Sgt Maj A.J. 296
Herridge, Lt C.N.C. 281
Hickman, 2nd Lt F. 286
Higgins, 2nd Lt J.T. 284
Higginson, Lt J.F. 291
Higginson, Cpl Tommy *90*
Hildick, Lt C. 290
Hill, 2nd Lt A.E. 284
Hill, Bert *84*
Hill, Lt C.V. 290
Hill, Capt E. 280
Hill, 2nd Lt E. 286
Hill, Frank
Hill, Lt H. 290
Hill, Capt H.G. 289
Hill, Lt L.R. 281
Hill, Stuart 12
Hill, Sgt W. *107*, 296
Hill, Lt W.H. 279
Hind, Lt L.L. 291
Hine, Lt T.W.J. 278
Hipkiss, James 188, 189
Hipkiss, Lt R. 283
Hirons, Lt H.W. 288
Hobbs, Sgt H. 296
Hobday, Maj J.T. 292
Hobson, 2nd Lt A.F. 289
Hodge, Lt R.H. 287
Hodges, Arthur *45*
Hodges, 2nd Lt L.H. 288
Hodges, Lt M.J. 280
Hodgetts, Lt C.W. 290
Hodgetts, Maj E. 274
Hodgetts, Lt G. 282
Hodgetts, Capt T. 282
Hodgson, Capt C.H. 290
Hodson, Maj H.B. 282
Holcroft, Lt J.C. 289
Holden, Lt 280
Holden, Maj T. 282
Holden, 2nd Lt W.B. 283

Holder, Capt R.W. 105, 296
Holder, Lt W.W. 287
Holland, John
Holland, L/Sgt E.S. 296
Holland-Martin, Sgt Thurston 165, 166, 303
Hollis, Sgt K.L. 296
Holloway, Lt C.J. *153*, 278
Holloway, Major Eric 2, 37
Holloway, Lt J.M. 280
Holmes, Maj G. 291
Holt, Albert James 304
Holt, Maj B.J. 271, 278
Holt, Cpl *101*
Holt, Jim *170*
Homer, Lt T.
Hooper, 2nd Lt F.J. 287
Hopcraft, 2nd Lt C.A. 286
Hopkins, Sgt R.E. 282
Horton, 2nd Lt C.A. 290
Horton, Lt C.A. 289
Houghton, Frank *48*
Houghton, Norman *48*
Houghton-Brown, Capt H. 283
Howard, 2nd Lt D.R. 285
Howard, Lt E.C.S. 284
Howe, 2nd Lt C.V. 287
Howell, D.M. 293
Howell, Sidney Vincent 231
Howles, Sgt L. 296, *297*
Huband, Noel Herbert *170*, 304
Huddleston, Lt J.G. 284
Hudson, Lt A.F. 278
Hughes, Lt H.D. 286
Hughes, 2nd Lt J.W. 280
Hulton, Edward 32, 213
Hulton, Lord 184
Humberstone, Lt J.E. 281
Humphries, Lt E.H. 284
Humphries, Lt K.I. 284
Humphries, Maj R.E.H. 292
Humphries, Lt W.G. 281
Hunt, Capt H.B. 290
Hunt, Lt J.A. 288
Hunter, Lt G.J. 284
Hussey, L/Cpl A.G. 293
Hutchinson, Lt Grice *199*
Hutchinson, Capt P. 292
Huxley, Lt F.J. 288
Hyde, Lt L.R. 285

Inman, Lt J. 292
Ironside, General 5, 24, 46, 216, 260
Irving, Capt C.I. 288

338

339

Radburn, Mr 40
Radley, F. *202*
Radley, Fred *202*
Raggett, 2nd Lt N.F. 286
Ralphs, John 124
Randall, Lt R. 281
Ratcliffe, 2nd Lt S. 285
Raybould, Lt H.C. 282
Raybould, L/Cpl S.J. 296
Rayer, Fred *202*
Rayer, Lt. J.E. 277
Rayer, Norman *202*
Reading, 2nd Lt G.R. 206
Recordon, Lt L.G. 284
Redfern, Lt Col E.A. 152
Reece-Pinchin, Vernon
Rees, Sgt G.C.
Rees, Lt N. 281
Rees, Cpl T. 296
Reeve, Lt D.K. 278
Reeves, Capt C.E. 296
Reeves, Capt C.F.
Reid, Lt R.D. 287
Renfrew, Capt C. 281
Reynolds, Norman *48*
Reynolds, Maj W.H. 286
Reynolds, Sgt W.J. 298
Reynolds, Sgt Walter *68, 199*
Rhodes, 2nd Lt L.S. 292
Rich, 2nd Lt C.V.F. 282
Richards, Lt C.C.A. 291
Richards, 2nd Lt H.E. 287
Richards, Howard Walter 268
Richardson, Lt F.B. 285
Richardson, Maj H. 275
Richardson, Lt J.G. 290
Richardson, Maj W.E. 290
Rigden, Lt P.B. 285
Riley, Lt I.C. 291
Rimell, Lt E. 284
Roberts, Capt H. 286
Roberts, Horace Cuthbert *170*, 304
Roberts, 2nd Lt N.J. 292
Robertson, Capt J.M. 281
Robey, Capt J.L. 283
Robins, Cpl Arthur *82*
Robinson, 2nd Lt A.
Robinson, Lt A.C. 283
Robinson, Lt Col F.W. 15
Robinson, Sgt G.W. 298
Robinson, Lt H. 292
Robinson, Lt R.B. 289
Robinson, Capt T.H. 280

Roden, Capt F.H. 277
Rodway, Sgt Bert *45*
Rogers, Capt A.V. 65, 286
Romney, Mr F.W. 12
Rorison, Lt A.M.
Rose, Lt E. 284
Rose, 2nd Lt H.E. 281
Ross, Lt E.G. 278
Round, Lt S.
Rouse, Ernie *199*
Rouse, W. *68*
Rowberry, 2nd Lt C.E. 286
Rowberry, H. *101*
Rowberry, Sgt John A. *101*, *153*, 206
Rowberry, Peter *101, 244*
Rowe, A.P. 111
Rowe, Frederick Gerald 304
Rowe, Lt S.H. 292
Rowland, Lt J.S. 281
Rowlands, 2nd Lt W.H. 279
Rowley, 2nd Lt C. 292
Rowley, 2nd Lt E.L.
Rowley, P.H. 293
Roxburgh, Lt J. 284
Rundle, 2nd Lt F.J.B. 281
Rushton, Maj H.P. 274
Russell, Lt O.T. 289
Russell, 2nd Lt R.C. 279
Russell, Lt S.G. 213, 281
Russell, Lt W.A. 281
Ryland, Maj L.M. *47*, 271, 279

Salisbury, Sgt Maj H.A. 298
Salisbury, Lt W. 292
Salter, Maj G. 279, 294
Sandals, Sgt W.J. 298
Sanders, 2nd Lt B.J. 278
Sanders, 2nd Lt J.H. 288
Sanders, Pt W.C. 176
Sandford, Cpt 208
Sara, Capt. J.V. 288
Savage, R.
Saunders, Sgt H. 283
Saunders, Cpl Jack *90*
Saunders, Nora *176*
Savery, Sgt A.V. 298
Scamp, Lt T.E. 282
Schiller, Capt L.C. 285
Schofield, Lt V. 281
Scothern, Lt Col A.E. 15, 77, 274
Scott, Capt H.G. 285
Scott, Lt R. 290
Scott, Capt W.A. 292

Stormont, 2nd Lt D.A. 288
Stott, Sgt A. 298
Stranks, Mabel 161
Strathan, Lt R. 291
Stratton, Lt P. 277
Stringer, Capt H.J. 289
Sugden, Capt R.B. 278
Sulley, Lt A.D. 292
Summers, Lt F. 282
Summerskill, Dame Edith 8, 173
Sutcliffe, 2nd Lt H.K. 285
Swift, Lt W.F. 281
Swinton, Capt E.R. 289
Sykes, Brig J.H. 149, 150, 152
Symes, Capt J.D. *142*
Symonds, George *90*

Tadman, Sgt Basil 166, *170*, 303
Tanfield, Lt Col A.R. 14, 272
Tanker, Sgt G. 277
Tanser, Capt W.W. *142*
Tate, Lt J.A. 281
Taylor, Maj A.H. 292
Taylor, Sgt E.H. 298
Taylor, Capt F.W. 271, 278
Taylor, Sgt H. 298
Taylor, 2nd Lt H.E. 279
Taylor, Lt J.C. 292
Taylor, 2nd Lt J.W. 280
Taylor, 2nd Lt N.A. 287
Taylor, Lt R.E. 278
Taylor, Reg *111*
Taylor, Sgt 280
Taylor, Lt Col. W.H. 14, 15, 99, 272
Taylor, Maj W.F. *153*
Teague, Sgt A.R. 298
Teague, Lt C. 118, 286
Teague, Mr *255*
Terry, Phillip 214
Tew, Lt W.J. 290
Thatcher, Lt Col Clifford 77, 151, 283
Thomas, Lt A.E. 284
Thomas, Maj A.L. 275, 290
Thomas, Lt D.R. 278
Thomas, 2nd Lt G.H. 283
Thomas, Cpl Ivor *170*
Thomas, Cpl John Ivor 304
Thompson, 2nd Lt G.G. 282
Thompson, Josie *176*
Thompson, Mrs 176, *176*
Thompson, Sgt *101*
Thorne, Gen Andrew 264
Threllfall, Capt C.R.F. 291

Tilley, L/Cpl C. 298
Tinkler, Mr E.W. 11
Titshall, Capt W.J. 281
Tod, Lt C.W. 286
Todd, Capt John 160, 161, *162*, 166, 207, 208, 216
Tolley, Albert 23
Tolley, 2nd Lt R. 289, 290, 298
Tooby, Lt S. 289
Toon, Albert 233
Townsend, Lt M.Y. 285
Trevor-Jones, 2nd Lt R. 284
Tuffin, 2nd Lt F. 287
Turbutt, Cpl Ray *90*
Turby, 2nd Lt R. 286
Turner, Lt A.E. 285
Turner (née Millward), Mrs Mabel *176*
Turner, 2nd Lt O.J. 285
Turner, Lt W.H.T. 292
Turnhill, 2nd Lt E.C. 288
Twinberrow, Lt *90*
Twinberrow, Lt J.S. 285
Twiss, Lt W.J. 292
Twist, Maj F.M. 274
Tyler, Des *48*
Tyler, Lt W.G. 292
Tyrwhitt, Col F.St J. 15
Tyrwhitt, Col P. 273
Tysoe, Lt. G.C. 277

Upstone, Lt W.F. 281

Vale, 2nd Lt A.E. 287
Vale, E. 298
van Moppes, Lt Edmund 'Gug' 167, *170,* 172, 301
van Moppes, Capt Lewis Edward 167, *170*, 172, 301
Varlow, Lt W.N.
Vernon, Maj J.H. 283
Vernon, Wilfred 182
Vilas, 2nd Lt W.C. 291
Vincent, Mr 305
Vines, Mr 305
Viney, Maj H.T. 273
Vint, Capt E.J.C. 281
Vobes, Sgt J.H. 298

Wakelin, 2nd Lt L.E. 283
Walk, Maj G.E. 33
Walker, C.F. 293
Walker, Lt D.W. 285
Walker, 2nd Lt G.E.L. 285
Walker, Geoffrey *48*
Walker, Lt J.B. *111*, 129, 284

General Index